Lecture Notes in Computer Scie

T0238625

Commenced Publication in 1973
Founding and Former Series Editors:
Gerhard Goos, Juris Hartmanis, and Jan van Leeuwen

Editorial Board

Bruno Müller-Clostermann
Klaus Echtle   Erwin P. Rathgeb (Eds.)

Measurement, Modelling, and Evaluation of Computing Systems and Dependability and Fault Tolerance

15th International GI/ITG Conference, MMB&DFT 2010
Essen, Germany, March 15-17, 2010
Proceedings

 Springer

Volume Editors

Bruno Müller-Clostermann
University of Duisburg-Essen
Institute for Computer Science
and Business Information Systems
Systems Modelling Group
Schützenbahn 70, 45127 Essen, Germany
E-mail: bmc@icb.uni-due.de

Klaus Echtle
University of Duisburg-Essen
Institute for Computer Science
and Business Information Systems
Dependability of Computing Systems Group
Schützenbahn 70, 45127 Essen, Germany
E-mail: echtle@dc.uni-due.de

Erwin P. Rathgeb
University of Duisburg-Essen
Institute for Experimental Mathematics
Computer Networking Technology Group
Ellernstr. 29, 45326 Essen, Germany
E-mail: erwin.rathgeb@iem.uni-due.de

Library of Congress Control Number: 2010922318

CR Subject Classification (1998): C.2, C.4, C.1, D.2.8, D.2, D.4.8, D.4

LNCS Sublibrary: SL 2 – Programming and Software Engineering

ISSN   0302-9743
ISBN-10   3-642-12103-9 Springer Berlin Heidelberg New York
ISBN-13   978-3-642-12103-6 Springer Berlin Heidelberg New York

Typesetting: Camera-ready by author, data conversion by Scientific Publishing Services, Chennai, India
Printed on acid-free paper   06/3180

Preface

This volume contains the papers presented at the International GI/ITG Conference on "Measurement, Modelling and Evaluation of Computing Systems" and "Dependability and Fault Tolerance," held during March 15–17, 2010 in Essen, Germany, hosted by the University of Duisburg-Essen. The Technical Committees of MMB and DFT cover all aspects of performance and dependability evaluation of systems including networks, computer architectures, distributed systems, software, fault-tolerant and secure systems. In 2010, both committees joined forces in a common conference MMB & DFT 2010. This current conference was the 15th in a series of biannual conferences, initially started in 1981, with previous editions in Aachen, Dresden, Nuremberg and Dortmund.

MMB & DFT 2010 received 42 submissions (37 regular papers and 5 tool descriptions) by authors from 15 different countries. Each regular paper was reviewed by at least three (and up to five) Program Committee members and external reviewers; tool papers were reviewed by two reviewers. In total we received 158 reviews and the Program Committee decided to accept 19 full papers and 5 tool papers.

The program was completed by two invited talks and we were happy that Phil Koopman from Carnegie Mellon University and Paul Kühn from the University of Stuttgart accepted to give an invited talk at the conference.

We are grateful to all those involved in organizing the conference, to the speakers and the attendees of MMB & DFT 2010. Our deepest thanks go to the many Program Committee members and the external reviewers for their very thorough and diligent opinions contributing to the high scientific standard of the MMB conference series. We also appreciate the support of EasyChair for managing the processes of submission, reviewing and preparing the production of the proceedings.

January 2010

Bruno Müller-Clostermann
Klaus Echtle
Erwin Rathgeb

Organization

MMB & DFT 2010 was organized by the Institute of Computer Science and Business Information Systems, University of Duisburg-Essen, Germany.

Organizing Committee

Program Chairs	Bruno Müller-Clostermann
	Klaus Echtle
	Erwin Rathgeb
Tools Chair	Andreas Pillekeit

Program Committee

Falko Bause	Technical University of Dortmund
Lothar Breuer	University of Kent
Peter Buchholz	Technical University of Dortmund
Georg Carle	Technical University of Munich
Joachim Charzinski	Nokia Siemens Networks
Hans Daduna	University of Hamburg
Hermann de Meer	University of Passau
Thomas Dreibholz	University of Duisburg-Essen
Reinhard German	University of Erlangen
Kurt Geihs	University of Kassel
Carmelita Görg	University of Bremen
Karl-Erwin Großpietsch	Fraunhofer-Gesellschaft, IAIS
Franz Hartleb	T-Systems, Darmstadt
Gerhard Haßlinger	T-Systems, Darmstadt
Boudewijn Haverkort	ESI Eindhoven and University of Twente
Armin Heindl	University of Erlangen-Nuremberg
Holger Hermanns	University of Saarbrücken
Joost-Pieter Katoen	RWTH Aachen University
Jörg Keller	FernUniversität in Hagen
Udo Krieger	University of Bamberg
Matthias Kuntz	University of Konstanz
Wolfram Lautenschläger	Alcatel-Lucent
Axel Lehmann	University of the Armed Forces, Munich
Ralf Lehnert	Technical University of Dresden
Philipp Limbourg	University of Duisburg-Essen
Christoph Lindemann	University of Leipzig
Erik Maehle	University of Lübeck
Michael Menth	University of Würzburg
Andreas Mitschele-Thiel	Technical University of Ilmenau

Martin Paterok	Deutsche Bahn AG
Peter Reichl	Research Center Telecommunication, Vienna
Johannes Riedl	Siemens AG
Oliver Rose	Technical University of Dresden
Francesca Saglietti	University of Erlangen-Nuremberg
Werner Sandmann	Technical University of Clausthal
Andreas Schmietendorf	Berlin School of Economics and Law
Jens Schmitt	Technical University of Kaiserslautern
Markus Siegle	University of the Armed Forces, Munich
Helena Szczerbicka	University of Hannover
Aad van Moorsel	University of Newcastle
Max Walter	Technical University of Munich
Bernd Wolfinger	University of Hamburg
Katinka Wolter	Humboldt-University Berlin
Armin Zimmermann	Technical University of Ilmenau

Additional Reviewers

Esam Alnasouri	Technical University of Ilmenau
Sebastian Bohlmann	University of Hannover
Henrik Bohnenkamp	RWTH Aachen University
Christian Brosch	Technical University of Ilmenau
Le Phu Do	Technical University of Dresden
Martin Drozda	University of Hannover
Martin Franzke	T-Systems, Darmstadt
Dirk Haage	Technical University of Munich
Ernst Moritz Hahn	University of Saarbrücken
Arnd Hartmanns	University of Saarbrücken
Stephan Heckmüller	University of Hamburg
Robert Henjes	University of Würzburg
Mohamed Kalil	Technical University of Ilmenau
Dominik Klein	University of Würzburg
Andreas Klenk	Technical University of Munich
Andrey Kolesnikov	University of Hamburg
Xi Li	University of Bremen
Gerhard Münz	Technical University of Munich
David Parker	RWTH Aachen University
Volker Richter	Technical University of Dresden
Martin Riedl	University of the Armed Forces, Munich
Markus Schmid	University of Kassel
Johann Schuster	University of the Armed Forces, Munich
Hendrik Skubch	Technical University of Kassel
Samer Sulaiman	Technical University of Dresden
Abutaleb Turky	Technical University of Ilmenau
Patrick Wuechner	University of Passau
Thomas Zinner	University of Würzburg

Table of Contents

Tool Papers

Invited Talk
Mitigating the Effects of Internet Timing Faults Across Embedded Network Gateways

Philip Koopman and Justin Ray

Carnegie Mellon University, ECE Department, 5000 Forbes Ave.
Pittsburgh, PA 15213, USA
koopman@cmu.edu, justinr2@cmu.edu

Extended Abstract. Traditional embedded systems such as automobiles and industrial controls are increasingly being connected to enterprise computing facilities and the Internet. The usual approach to making such a connection is to install a *gateway* node which translates from Internet protocols to embedded field bus network protocols. Such connections raise obvious security concerns, because the gateway must guard against attacks on the embedded devices it serves. For our purposes, we'll assume that typical enterprise and Internet vulnerabilities, such as buffer overflows, have already been taken care of. (Securing devices against traditional attacks is no small matter, but we are interested in uniquely embedded issues.)

Beyond normal gateway functions, an Internet to embedded gateway must also prevent timing faults and timing attacks from crossing over the gateway to affect the operation of attached embedded systems. An example of timing fault propagation would be severe clumping of messages on the Internet side so that many messages arrive at the gateway all at once, disrupting embedded system operation. While a queue can reduce the loss of incoming data and mitigate network overload, it cannot necessarily protect against timing-related faults on the embedded side of the gateway.

We report simulation results for several mechanisms to mitigate the effects of Internet message timing variations (whether due to faults or malicious attacks) on the performance of networked embedded systems using real-time data. Problems are caused primarily by excessive data delivery delay rather than messages being dropped from arriving clumps. This means that putting a queue in the gateway to manage arriving data clumps is typically worse than using no mitigation mechanism at all. Using a predictive filter seems intuitively better than using a queue, but finding a good generalized predictive filter is also quite difficult.

We believe that managing data streams from the Internet to embedded systems will require careful attention to the nature and time constants of data flowing through the gateway. Moreover, it seems likely that each distinct data stream will need a different set of data management mechanisms and policies at the gateway. In this case, one size *does not* fit all, making the design of a robust gateway a difficult problem that will require careful modeling of data value behavior for every gateway built.

Keywords: Embedded network, gateway, embedded security, timing fault, simulation, predictive filter.

B. Müller-Clostermann et al. (Eds.): MMB & DFT 2010, LNCS 5987, p. 1, 2010.

Invited Talk
Green IT - The Power Saving Challenge and ICT Solutions

Paul J. Kühn

Institute of Communication Networks and Computer Engineering (IKR)
University of Stuttgart
Pfaffenwaldring 47, 70569 Stuttgart, Germany
paul.j.kuehn@ikr.uni-stuttgart.de, www.ikr.uni-stuttgart.de

Extended Abstract. Energy consumption, the finite horizon of conventional fossil energy resources and maintaining sustainable environmental conditions form the biggest challenges in the near future. Renewable energy sources like wind, water, solar energy or biomass are limited and unsteady substitutes and require a radical rethinking of the energy problem. There are two main solution approaches: power saving and intelligent management of the use of energy. Both require advanced technologies and a close adaption between energy production and energy usage. Information Technologies (IT) themselves account for a major energy consumer by contribution of about 10 % to the global CO_2 production and will be a target for power saving but Information and Communication Technology (ICT) are the key for the intelligent power management.

The first part of the contribution addresses in a systematic way power consumption in ICT on different levels from hardware and device technologies up to application processes, as well as possible approaches and solutions such as new technologies (such as nanotubes), control of power consumption on the chip level, system level and application level by methods of dynamic power supply, adaptive sleep modes, disabling of temporarily unnecessary functionalities, and network virtualization.

In the second part, the purpose and the architectures of energy information networks will be discussed, a comparatively new approach to monitor and to control the consumption of energy depending on the currently available energy sources (such as wind, solar energy or batteries of automotive vehicles), costs for the energy itself and for its transport to the customer. Such energy information networks can be based on existing communication infrastructures (access networks, sensor networks, core networks) which have to be enhanced by other technologies (such as power line communications) and upgraded with respect to security, privacy protection and reliability.

In the final part, the contribution addresses the specific aspect of performance modelling. From this point of view, the issue can be considered as a resource sharing problem. Examples will be given how queuing theory can be used to optimize the use of resources (such as processors, communication links, storage areas, etc.) under stochastic conditions and dynamic scheduling schemes.

Keywords: Green IT, power saving, adaptive power control, energy information networks, performance modelling, resource sharing.

B. Müller-Clostermann et al. (Eds.): MMB & DFT 2010, LNCS 5987, p. 2, 2010.

In Memory of Dr. Gunter Bolch

Martin Paterok[1], Hermann de Meer[2], and Patrick Wüchner[2]

[1] Deutsche Bahn, DB Systel GmbH,
Kleyerstraße 27, 60326 Frankfurt am Main, Germany
`martin.paterok@deutschebahn.com`
[2] Faculty of Informatics and Mathematics, University of Passau,
Innstraße 43, 94032 Passau, Germany
`hermann.demeer@uni-passau.de`

⋆ December 26, 1940 − † May 29, 2008

The *MMB Special Interest Group* mourns for a highly valued member. Gunter Bolch died on May 29, 2008 in Erlangen, after a serious illness. He was very open minded, a beautifully moderate person, and a friend in its truest meaning. With *MMB*, he shared his academic passion of performance modelling, in general, and queueing networks, in particular.

Gunter was born in 1940 in Reichenbach, a small town near Aalen. He studied communications engineering in Karlsruhe and Berlin. In 1973, he finished his PhD on the "Identifikation linearer Systeme durch Anwendung von Momentenmethoden" in Karlsruhe. In the same year, he took a position as *Akademischer*

B. Müller-Clostermann et al. (Eds.): MMB & DFT 2010, LNCS 5987, pp. 3–7, 2010.

Rat at the Friedrich-Alexander University in Erlangen. From 1982, he led the newly-founded *Research Group on Analytical Modelling* (ANA Group) which achieved international reputation in the following years.

He has co-authored seven scholarly written books that have widely been cited and have gained world-wide acknowledgment. One of his latest achievements was the second edition of "Queueing Networks and Markov Chains" (2006) and the corresponding Solution Manual (2008) published by John Wiley & Sons. The book has been cited several hundred times. For the German performance modeling community, also his older book "Leistungsbewertung von Rechensystemen" (1989) is a well-known classic.

In 2007, Gunter became the Honorary Chair of the "International Conference on Analytical and Stochastic Modelling Techniques and Applications (ASMTA)", a conference series he started in 1995.

Gunter supervised more than 100 semester and M.Sc. theses (Studien- and Diplomarbeiten). Thirteen doctorates have been conferred under his guidance and four former members of the ANA Group are now professors: Ian Akyildiz, Hermann de Meer, Helmut Herold, and Georg Trogemann. Likewise, many of his students were motivated by his academic and personal spirit and followed up contributing in similar research areas.

Many more colleagues from different continents have also taken pride in cooperation and joint publications with him during his overly productive life. Gunter published more than fifty conference papers and more than thirty journal articles. These publications were supplemented by several contributions to books, co-edited proceedings, and many technical reports.

Gunter's algorithmic work was complemented by his initiatives to provide corresponding software tool support. Here, we only mention the most prominent ones PEPSY-QNS (performance evaluation of queueing networks using various methods; 1990), MOSES (Markovian performance and reliability analysis of discrete-event systems; 1994), MOSEL (modeling language and evaluation environment for discrete-event systems; 1995, revised 2003), and WinPEPSY-QNS (PEPSY-QNS for Windows, 2004).

But Gunter Bolch was not only a very productive professional. He was also a pleasant person. His personality was calm and friendly, always trying to help, in particular in difficult times. During the ups and downs of scientific work, he always maintained an optimistic and positive view, thus helping us to find our ways through the woods as we were students, assistant researchers, and even later on. There was always time to talk about other topics, be it politics and society, or his hobbies like jazz music or the family.

Traveling and research stays in foreign countries were opportunities that Gunter enjoyed very much. He preferred countries like Brazil, Hungary, and the former USSR, i.e., countries that were challenging but not en vogue for researchers at that time. This behaviour is very typical for Gunter's way of life as well as his forward-looking way of thinking. His attitude of giving more than taking is also reflected in his long-standing engagement for the *Brasilieninitiative Erlangen-Nürnberg e.V.*

In early 2006, Gunter retired as an *Akademischer Direktor*. Unfortunately, his illness kept him from enjoying his retirement in an adequate way. Fortunately, he did not wait until his retirement to find a balance between his profession and his social life.

We will aways remember him as a remarkable person who was not only a colleague but also a companion and friend to us.

Finally, we want to thank Ian Akyildiz and Udo Krieger for their contributions to this memorial and the editors for giving us this opportunity to pay our respects to Gunter in the name of many friends and colleagues.

Martin Paterok, Prof. Hermann de Meer, Patrick Wüchner
(Frankfurt am Main & Passau, November 30, 2009)

Eulogy for Gunter Bolch

On Thursday, May 29, 2008 when I was in Tashkent in Uzbekistan, I received the sad news that Gunter Bolch had lost the long battle with his illness at a relatively young age. This tragic news immediately triggered fond memories of our association spanning the last 30 years.

I first met Gunter Bolch in May 1979, though it seems like yesterday to me. At that time, I was writing a pre-master degree thesis under his guidance. He had just come back from Rio de Janeiro, where he had spent his sabbatical for more than two years.

In our first meeting, he introduced me to his beloved subject on queuing networks, which was then to become an important part of my professional research for the next decade. Apart from academic discussions, he also shared his cultural and social views with me. Our talks often ran into several hours, and ranged from topics of research interest to general experiences in life. He taught me how to conduct research and produce high quality results. My interaction with him spurred me on to take his classes on queuing theory and process automation. It was great fun and a rewarding experience to write a textbook together, which was published in 1982. He was very dedicated to his teaching, research and overall to his profession. He advised numerous students who saw him as a father, mentor and advisor.

Gunter, his spouse Monika and his children Jessica and Tobias were always like a family to me. Gunter was the best man in my wedding in 1982. Gunter and Monika were at the Nuremberg airport very early morning at 6 a.m. on February 1, 1985 when I was immigrating to United States. Though we pursued our careers in different continents, Gunter was always there for me when I needed him. We visited each other often, and every time I visited Erlangen, I always received a very warm welcome from them.

The last time I saw Gunter was during his retirement party in March 2006. He was very happy that all of his former students and colleagues celebrated this event with him. His stories and the collection of photos that he shared with us during his party vividly portrayed his love and enthusiasm for Brazil. In fact, the theme of the party was totally based on the culture of Brazil, including the food, music, and decorations. He looked forward to this retirement so that he would have more opportunity to enjoy his hobbies, spend time with his grandchildren and also continue his research. Unfortunately, his plans could not be realized in their entirety due to his unexpected illness.

I have personally never met anybody like Gunter, who had a saint-like approach to life: he was not only always positive about himself but always had positive thoughts about the events in his life, and for the people around him. He had a very calm personality and looked forward to life with interest and enthusiasm.

Gunter Bolch will be dearly missed and will be remembered forever by all of us. He left a mark in our lives with his lovely wife Monika, his wonderful children, beautiful grandchildren, successful students, excellent textbooks, several research contributions, and above all, with his outstanding positive personality.

Prof. Ian F. Akyildiz
(Atlanta, March 18, 2009)

In Memoriam

Gunter Bolch has been one of the pioneers of *performance analysis by numerical methods* in Germany. His interest in this topic stems from the analytic performance investigations of multiprocessor architectures and process automation, in particular by product-form networks, in the late seventies. The activity has originated in the first instructive German textbook "Analyse von Rechensystemen - Analytische Methoden zur Leistungsbewertung und Leistungsvorhersage", by I. Akyildiz and G. Bolch, 1982. It has been an absolutely essential tool for the German performance analysis community MMB and all young students of this field of applied stochastic in the 80s.

However, powerful numerical solution methods for finite Markov chains that are not limited to BCMP networks were not treated in this book. To overcome this issue, a fruitful information exchange of Gunter Bolch with Deutsche Telekom Research Laboratories has been initiated after the MMB Conference 1987 in Erlangen and, in particular, after a talk in Erlangen on the memorable November 9, 1989. The latter exchange was fed by Telekom's MACOM project carried out by Prof. Beilner's team at University of Dortmund which tried to model networks by Markovian arrival processes. Gunter Bolch has always been open-minded to respond to new development and immediately realized the potential of such concepts. Thus, together with his students he started to create new public tools to extend these ideas and to apply them to relevant performance engineering issues. MOSEL and the related publications of his group on MAP modeling are a well known outcome in this respect.

These efforts reflect in an excellent manner the unique altruistic personality of Gunter Bolch. We have recognized him as a generous colleague who has never claimed results by himself in a selfish manner. He has treated both his distinguished scientific collaborators and an unknown young student in the same polite manner. His objective has been to serve the community at national and global levels by his talents and efforts together with his co-workers. For those contributing to numerical solution methods for finite Markov chains it has been a great honor to collaborate with Gunter Bolch. In the scientific world his achievements in this field will be visible permanently due to the excellent book "Queueing Networks and Markov Chains" written in cooperation with H. de Meer, S. Greiner, and K.S. Trivedi.

However, Gunter Bolch's humanitarian activities reach far beyond all scientific investigations. For this reason we will always remember Gunter as a distinguished member of our community. His life has shown us that in a competitive environment science can grow by an altruistic behavior and its development can be dedicated to the good of humanity in **ONE world** if a humanist acts as its convincing advocate.

Prof. Udo Krieger
(Bamberg, November 23, 2009)

Verification of a Control System Built Using Remote Redundancy by Means of Timed Automata and State Space Exploration

Klaus Echtle and Thorsten Kimmeskamp

ICB / Dependability of Computing Systems,
Universität Duisburg-Essen, Schützenbahn 70, 45117 Essen, Germany
echtle@dc.uni-due.de, kimmeskamp@dc.uni-due.de

Abstract. Remote redundancy is a novel efficient TMR (triple modular redundancy) structure for real-time control systems. It allows for 2-out-of-3 voting by using only two redundant computing nodes (called local nodes) with access to sensor and actuator peripherals. The third node of the TMR structure is replaced just by a remote process on any node in the network, where some computing capacity is available. This approach significantly reduces the amount of hardware redundancy at the cost of both an increased communication overhead (which is not problematic in modern real-time networks) and an increased complexity. To nevertheless assess the correctness of the approach, this paper presents a functional model using a network of timed automata, allowing to prove the accurate behavior of a fault-tolerant example system under the influence of different fault scenarios. By state space exploration, that verification has successfully been achieved, confirming the results of prior fault tree analysis conducted by the authors and thus providing a well-founded basis for further experimental research on the subject.

Keywords: Fault-tolerant real-time control system, dedicated redundancy, remote redundancy, fault modeling, state space exploration, verification.

1 Introduction

High safety requirements of controlled systems cannot be satisfied without appropriate countermeasures against technical faults [BFM03]. The intuitive approach for fail-operational behaviour is the provision of a spare computing node. However, many control systems do not allow for such simple dynamic redundancy for two reasons: Switching to the spare node and recovery of the data may be so time- consuming that real-time constraints are violated. Furthermore, faults of the primary node can only be detected by absolute tests checking for consistency, plausibility, range violations etc. Even if numerous absolute tests are applied, the overall coverage is limited. Depending on the system, it may be closer to 99% than to 100%.

For these reasons, static redundancy has been developed, where three nodes work concurrently as their outputs are voted 2-out-of-3. For other degrees of redundancy, according e.g. to the respective SIL-level [IEC09], this TMR concept has been extended to NMR (n-modular redundancy). Static redundancy works with relative tests.

B. Müller-Clostermann et al. (Eds.): MMB & DFT 2010, LNCS 5987, pp. 8–23, 2010.

As long as the processes are deterministic, the set of faulty nodes is the minority of the nodes and the set of faulty voters is the minority of voters, fault coverage reaches 100% perfectly.

At first sight, the overhead seems to amount to a factor of 3. However, communication between n redundant nodes and n redundant voters [EJT04] requires $O(n^2)$ messages (a special solution is the m-protocol [Echt86]). In addition, statically redundant sensors and actuators are required. Some actuators cause further problems. Three connected motors, for example, would induce destructive high currents when driven in opposite directions. Hence, special (and often costly) solutions must be found. An additional problem is the wiring between nodes and peripherals, typically realized by a lot of direct wires and connectors, which tend to be unreliable anyway.

In this paper we present a model and formal verification results of a control system built using a new approach called "remote reduncy" (introduced in [EKJM09], [EcKi09]) in order to prove that it is possible to reduce such overhead significantly without compromising fault tolerance characteristics. We start by describing the traditional approach mentioned above (here called "dedicated redundancy", referring to the direct wiring between components) in two variants of a control system in chapter 2. The following chapter 3 contains both variants of the very same control system built using the concept of remote redundancy. In chapter 4, one of these systems is modeled as a network of timed automata using the UPPAAL model checker-tool [UPPA09]. The design and results of according verification experiments are shown in chapter 5. In chapter 6, we finally summarize our results and present an outlook on our future work.

2 Dedicated Redundancy

The abovementioned reasons lead to a TMR structure of real-time control systems which is more complex than pure TMR. We call the structure exemplified in Fig. 1 *dedicated redundancy*. The system implements a control loop with reference value v_r (transmitted via the busses B_1 and B_2). The actual value is read from position sensors P_1, P_2 and P_3, respectively. The nodes N_1, N_2 and N_3 calculate the control value and send it to the bridge driver Q_1 for motor M_1, or bridge driver Q_2 for motor M_2, respectively (in Fig. 1 black arrows represent cables and the direction of information flow).

The motors are duplicated whereas control nodes are triplicated. A wrongly driven motor is passivated after a short delay, which is not critical due to inertia of motors. The motor driven by node N_1 can only be passivated by joint passivation by both nodes N_2 and N_3. This is a special approach to 2-out-of-3 voting – requiring cables and potentially fault-prone connectors from each node to each motor.

The bridges Q_1 and Q_2 obtain electrical energy from output stages O_{31} and O_{21}, or O_{12} and O_{32}, respectively (in Fig. 1 fat black arrows represent switched power lines). As soon as the nodes controlling the output stages detect wrong motion of the motor by reading the rotation sensors R_1 or R_2, respectively, they trigger their local output stages to withdraw energy. Thus, joint passivation decisions of N_2 and N_3 passivate motor M_1. Accordingly, joint passivation decisions of N_1 and N_3 passivate motor M_2. However, unjustified passivation decisions of a single faulty node or energy withdrawal of a single faulty output stage does not cause passivation. In the critical situation when node N_3 is faulty it may stop providing energy towards both M_1 and M_2. But both motors are still supplied via O_{21} and O_{12}. A faulty rotation sensor may pretend wrong motor movement and thus cause unjustified passivation, but does not affect correct operation of the respective other motor.

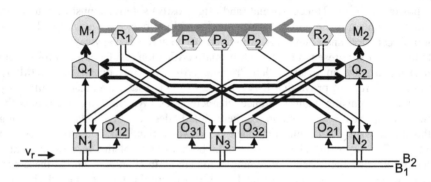

Fig. 1. Control system with dedicated redundancy. The fat grey arrows are mechanical shafts from the motors to the differential gear in the middle (grey box).

In all, the system is equivalent to a TMR system covering a single fault in any of its components whether computing node, bus, sensor, electronic output peripheral, electro-mechanic motor, wire or connector. However, the system has its cost because of the redundant components. Approaches to cost reduction by fully preserving single fault tolerance are not obvious, as the following consideration shows.

Replacement of the direct communication between nodes and peripherals by bus communication does not really help solving the wiring problem. When bus-connected a peripheral device must act as a communication node – which must not disturb bus communication. Consequently each node must exhibit at least a duplex structure, where each of the two subnodes is wired somehow to the peripheral device. When wires are saved, critical single points of failure are likely to be inserted.

When safety-critical real-time control tasks have to be performed, TMR systems cause an overhead beyond triplication. If one had an "ideal decision component" always correctly informed about the fault state of the whole system, one would just need duplication. Such an ideal component can never be built, of course, but it motivates the search for improved solutions. Ideally, the redundancy overhead would be cut down while the fault tolerance capability is fully preserved. Since most redundant systems tolerate only single faults (due to cost reasons) the fault hypothesis is simple: All malfunctions of any single component must be tolerated. Special care is necessary to guarantee the absence of any "hole" in the countermeasures against faults. Even unexpected very rare malfunctions must not lead to system failure. Violations of real-time constraints must be avoided as well.

There are many variations of dedicated redundancy depending on the properties of the controlled process as well as the peripherals, mostly the actuators. Typically, the torques of the motors are added by a differential gear. If a motor is passivated, its shaft must be blocked by a holding brake – requiring fault-tolerant control of the brake in addition (by driver S_{21} and grounding driver G_{31} for holding brake H_1, for example, as shown in Fig. 2). Whereas the energy flow from the output stages to the bridge drivers of the motors is or-connected (motor is only passivated if both output stages withdraw energy), the energy flow to the brake drivers is and-connected (close the brake only if required by both output stages). This way, the brakes' behaviour is always the complement of the energy provision to the bridge drivers. Depending on the implementation of the brakes, further variants can be recommended (brakes may be driven by an electrical motor or just by a magnetic coil, for example).

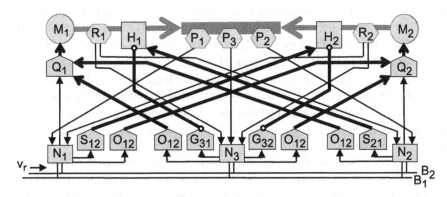

Fig. 2. Variant of dedicated redundancy with motors and brakes H_1 and H_2

The brakes together with their fault-tolerant control can be omitted, if the motors own a worm gear or the differential gear owns worm screws itself, as we have developed for our experimental system (see Fig. 3). Worm screw W_1 is driven by motor M_1, worm screw W_2 is driven by M_2. The electronic system implementing the control loop may exhibit either dedicated redundancy or remote redundancy (see section 3). If both W_1 and W_2 rotate correctly, the cog-wheel C between then is moved linearly without being rotated. In case of passivating, say, M_1 and W_1, cog-wheel C is moved by W_2 on one side only. Consequently, it rotates and rolls along W_1, causing linear movement as well – with half the speed as before, which is an inevitable natural property of any differential gear. In any case the linear movement of the cog-wheel can be taken as final "output" of the fault-tolerant system. Its only non-fault-tolerant elements are the cog-wheel itself, the space where it moves (must be free of obstacles), and the sprockets of the two worm screws (must not tear off).

The question of more efficient solutions arises for all variants of dedicated redundancy. By removing redundant elements, one must not limit the tolerance of any single fault. In the next section, a significantly more efficient approach is presented which works for all variants of dedicated redundancy.

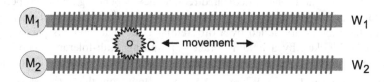

Fig. 3. Gear with two worm screws and cog-wheel C

3   Remote Redundancy

In an ideal approach, cross-wise links from nodes to peripherals are avoided. Moreover, in case of single fault tolerance, triplication is replaced by duplication. These challenging goals are almost achieved by the new concept of *remote redundancy* [EcKi09]. It comprises only two nodes (N_1 and N_2 in Fig. 4) to control actuators M_1 and M_2. The third node is replaced just by a software process running on any node in the network (on N_3 in Fig. 4, for example). This node – called "remote redundancy" – may serve for any other application as well. We only need sufficient free computing capacity for the process. In addition, the network must be redundant (busses B_1 and B_2), exhibit sufficient communication capacity, and guarantee real-time operation. All these points are satisfied well with nowadays real-time networks (like FlexRay [Raus07], for example).

The remotely redundant node N_3 is not connected to the peripherals of the considered control loop. Furthermore, node N_2 does not own a line to bridge driver Q_1 it should passivate if necessary. Likewise, bridge driver Q_2 is missing incoming power lines from N_1 and N_3. Instead, local output stages O_1 and O_2 control the power of bridge drivers Q_1 and Q_2, respectively. A bridge driver is passivated by withdrawing energy, as was the case with dedicated redundancy. However, according to the concept of remote redundancy, the output stages are controlled remotely via the network by N_3 and the respective other node (N_1 for N_2 and N_2 for N_1).

The problem of remote control is its sensitivity to faults in any unit which forwards control information. A faulty node N_1, for example, could generate any control information for O_1 regardless of the correct information it receives from N_3. For this reason three countermeasures are taken when remote redundancy is realized:

— Control signals are always activation signals rather than passivation signals. If a faulty forwarding node drops an activation signal, the final receiver (O_1 in the previous example) detects the missing signal by timeout and interprets this situation as a passivation command.
— Control signals are signed by the sender (N_3). The receiver (O_1 in the example) checks the signature for correctness. If it is wrong, the receiver interprets it as passivation command. By a digital signature we mean an individual check word, which length s is in the range of 8 to 32 bits. Compared to cryptographically strong signatures, remote redundancy may use simple signatures because they should reveal just technical faults in forwarding nodes, not intelligent attacks of

humans. In [EcKi09] we have presented a signature scheme consisting of CRC generation and multiplication by a secret factor. The corresponding signature check consists of CRC generation followed by two multiplications. All multiplications are modulo 2^S, not modulo a prime number. The whole signature scheme keeps the computation requirements very low, such that it can be performed even by components with very few resources.
— Sequence numbers are associated to messages to prevent faulty forwarding nodes from forwarding past signed information undetectably – see [EcKi09] for an efficient solution to the problem of re-sending a very old message with the correct sequence number from the previous cycle of sequence numbers.

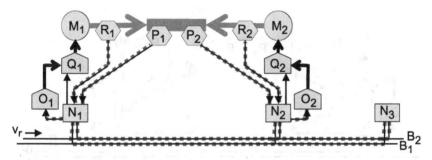

Fig. 4. Control system with remote redundancy. The arrows have the same meaning as in Fig. 1. Dotted lines indicate flow of signed information.

Signatures are also used to protect the information flow from sensors to other nodes via the busses. If the forwarding nodes corrupt a signature, the receiver can conclude fault occurrence, but is unable to locate the fault either in the signing sensor or the forwarding node. Consequently, it stops sending activation signals in the direction of the forwarding node. In section 5 we will verify that nevertheless remote redundancy works correctly in all single fault cases.

In all, remote redundancy requires a flow of signed information between the following components (dotted lines in Fig. 4).

— from position sensor P_i via node N_i to the two remaining nodes
— from rotation sensor R_i via node N_i to the two remaining nodes
— from the remaining nodes via N_i to output stage O_i (where $i \in \{1, 2\}$). As is the case in dedicated redundancy, an output stage passivates itself if it does not receive a signed activation command from any of the remaining nodes in time.

Remote redundancy allows for a solution with only two position sensors, if the rotation sensors are accurate enough to reconstruct missing position information. Since the rotation information can be easily distributed to all nodes via the busses, they can integrate rotation over time. This information is not used directly in the control loop, but in case of significant deviation between P_1 and P_2, it may be used to decide for the value from either P_1 or P_2. The decision is taken consistently in the whole system, because all position and rotation values are signed (under the assumption that signatures cannot be corrupted undetectably). The consistency will also be verified in section 5.

Remote redundancy also contributes to a reduction in the necessary amount of redundancy when holding brakes have to be controlled in addition (see Fig. 2 for the solution with dedicated redundancy). In remote redundancy, cross-wise wiring can be avoided by adding two drivers for each brake – S_{1a} and S_{1b} for brake H_1, for example (see Fig. 5). The brake is closed if at least one driver forces it to do so. A driver decides for closing the brake, if the activation signals are missing from both remaining nodes. In other words: The complements of the activation signals are and-connected at the input side of the drivers. The drivers' outputs are or-connected by the brake.

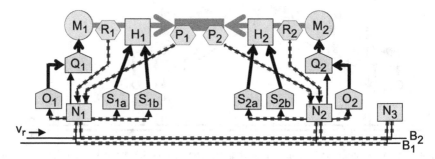

Fig. 5. Control system with motors and brakes, all implemented by remote redundancy

The main properties of remote redundancy are a very simple system structure consisting of only few elements. A complete node (replaced by just a process), a position sensor, and – in particular – a lot of the wiring can be saved.

4 Model

4.1 Overall Structure

In order to prove the fault-tolerance characteristics of remote redundancy, a model based on the system presented in Fig. 4 has been created using the UPPAAL model checker [UPPA09], [BDL04]. The tool allows for modeling real-time systems as networks of timed automata. The processes comprising such a model may communicate via a mechanism called "channel synchronization" while exchanging data by means of shared global variables. Starting from a well-defined initial state, any valid sequence of actions through the state space can be simulated interactively. Furthermore it is possible to verify properties formulated in a formal query language, thus e. g. checking if a certain state is reachable.

The overall structure of this model is depicted in Fig. 6. For the sake of legibility, data transmission over bus systems or wires is not modeled explicitly. Arrows thus only represent the control flow; information is passed by means of shared global memory. A verification of the bus system itself may be conducted separately and is not subject of this paper, as thoroughly tested bus systems are commercially available. A timed `Ticker`-process cyclically triggers the computation and passes control flow to the three control processes `CompCtrl`. Two output stages `OutpStg`, which may be disabled by passivation processes `CompPass`, read the control information and trigger the `Motor`-processes. The resulting rotation is translated by a `Carriage`-process into the movement of the controlled object. Both rotation of the motors and position of the carriage are measured by sensor processes R and, respectively, P. The third position sensor is, as illustrated in chapter 3, replaced by a remote software process `CompSens` which may be located anywhere in the system. Finally, a timed `Target`-process induces a control difference into the system, thus making it possible to verify that the system correctly responds to that disturbance.

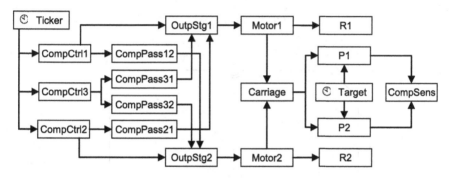

Fig. 6. Model structure

4.2 Control Process (CompCtrlT)

In each of the three instances of `CompCtrlT` (cf. Fig. 7), when synchronizing with the Ticker, the difference `diff` between actual value of the carriage (based on the information `PosV[i]` provided by the respective position sensor) and the target or reference value `RefV` is calculated. After a time of `CtrlD`, the local control command `CtrlV[i]` is calculated accordingly (with the values of -1, 0 and 1 being used for the commands left, still or right. The availability of this command is signaled via `CompCtrlCh[i]` to subsequent processes.

4.3 Passivation Process (CompPassT)

The template (as described in Fig. 8) is parameterized in such a way that the passivation process of node i observes the motor-rotation of node j (with i<>j). Passivation processes synchronize storing the control command in variable `own`. Not until time `CheckD`, however, the actual rotation `RotV[j]` of the observed motor is available and may be stored locally in variable `ext`. If those two values eventually deviate or if the signature of the external value (`RotS[j]`) is corrupt, passivation in variable `PassV[i][j]` is set accordingly and signed (`PassS[i][j]`) while the process itself returns to `idle`.

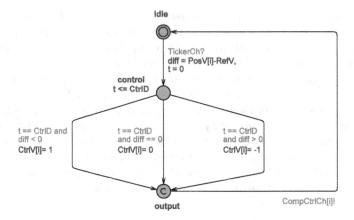

Fig. 7. Control process

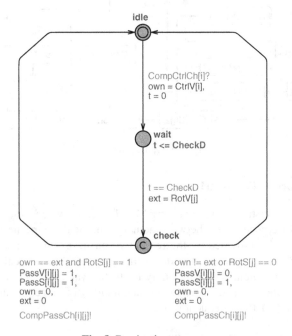

Fig. 8. Passivation process

4.4 Output Stage (OutputStageT)

The two output stages (see Fig. 9) are parameterized with i, j and k, indicating that motor i is jointly en-/disabled by passivation processes j and k. As a node may not passivate its own motor, these parameters are set to (1, 2, 3) and (2, 1, 3), respectively. Each output stage updates its state according to the control value delivered by the control processes. At a later point in the control cycle, synchronization with the

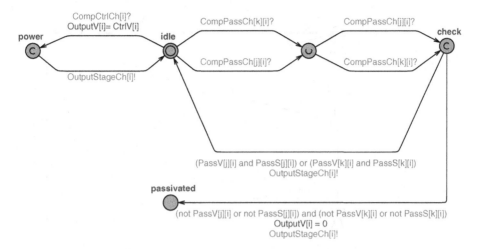

Fig. 9. Output stage process

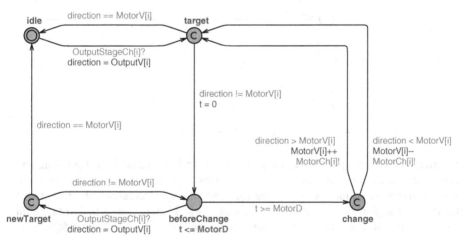

Fig. 10. Motor process

two passivation processes occurs (the sequence is non-deterministic). If at least one of these processes provides a correctly signed signal for continuation, the respective motor is powered on. Otherwise, it is permanently shut off.

4.5 Motor (MotorT)

Starting from its `idle` state, a motor process (cf. Fig. 10) locally stores the value delivered by the associated output stage in a local variable `direction`. In the case that no change of direction occurs (`direction == MotorV[i]`), it returns to the initial state. Otherwise, the process waits in state `beforeChange` until the time

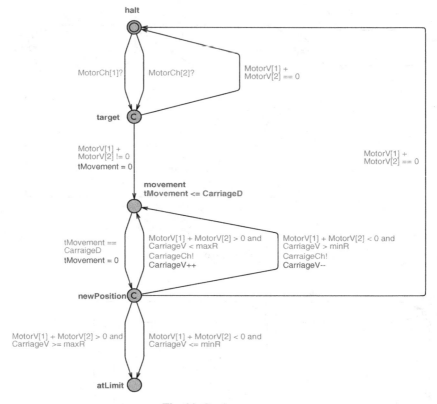

Fig. 11. Carriage process

specified by MotorD passes. A change of the control command is still possible and leads to a transition to state newTarget. At time MotorD, the process moves into state change, subsequently increasing (or, respectively, decreasing) the rotation of the motor and triggering the rotation sensors, which store the actual rotation in RotV[i] and, if faultless, sign that value by setting RotS[i] = 1 (not depicted).

4.6 Carriage (CarriageT)

Synchronizing via channel MotorCh[1] or MotorCh[2], the carriage process (depicted in Fig. 11) changes to state target. If neither of the two motors rotates, the process returns into state halt. Otherwise, it waits in state movement until a time of CarriageD passes. At exactly that time, the transition into state newPosition takes place. In the case that a change into the positive or negative direction takes place, the process returns into state movement, increasing or decreasing the variable CarriageV and thus indicating its new position according to that movement. The two position sensors synchronize and set PosV[i] accordingly (not depicted). Otherwise, the process returns to state idle. On exceeding a boundary of minR or maxR, respectively, the process changes to state atLimit, thus signaling that the carriage – as a result of a malfunction – has been moved too far.

4.7 Virtual Position Sensor (CompSensT)

The process `CompSens` (see Fig. 12) models the virtual (third) position sensor. It uses both rotation values to obtain a reference for the case that the two physical position sensors diverge. The computation of the corresponding value is triggered each time the two position sensors are updated. If one signature is corrupt, the respective other sensor is evaluated as `PosV[3]` (valid under one fault assumption). If both `P1` and `P2` deliver the same position value, arbitrarily `P1` is taken. Only in case that the two values deviate, the function `correctP()` is called, which is computing an approximation for P3 based on the rotation of the two motors and chooses the position sensor which deviates least to that reference value.

```
int[-1,1] dir(int v) { // direction as 1, -1, 0
    if (v > 0)
        return 1;
    else if (v < 0 )
        return -1;
    else
        return 0;
}

int[1,2] correctP() { // index of correct P-Sensor
    int[minR-2,maxR+2] p3appr = PosW[3] +
                      dir(RotW[1]+RotW[2]);
    if (abs(p3appr-PosW[1]) > abs(p3appr-PosW[2]))
        return 2;
    else
        return 1;
}
```

Fig. 12. Virtual position sensor (program code)

5 Analysis

In order to verify the fault-tolerance characteristics of the example system described above, the model has been modified so that faults of specific processes may be observed.

In the modified model, several components, namely position and rotation sensors as well as passivation processes (i. e. all units operating remotely) may exhibit arbitrarily wrong values and corrupt signatures. Components that do not interact with other nodes but act only locally (control processes and the virtual position sensor) may behave faulty with regard to the value domain only, as no remote communication is involved at all. Faulty motors always halt, as they cannot generate energy on their own. They may be controlled into a wrong direction by a faulty control process but this fault is not attributed to the affected motor. Selection of faulty values is modeled as by transitions in additional processes (cf. Fig. 13); components are actually made behave faulty by replacing regular update-statements like e. g. `RotW[i] = MotorW[i]` by `RotW[i] = (i!=fiRotW?MotorW[i]:fidir)` in the process template, where a global integer constant `fiRotW = 2` would e. g. mark the second rotation sensor as faulty.

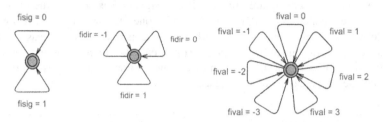

Fig. 13. Fault model

Due to space restrictions, only component variants without the fault model are depicted in this paper. Please note that delay, loss and corruption of messages are modeled as corrupt signatures; faults of the output stage are modeled as a wrong direction of the associated control process.

An adequate property to test the fault-tolerance capabilities of a system has to assure that the system under test exhibits its specified behavior in the presence of all faults contained in the fault model. For our example, such a property may be formulated as: "at most n cycles after a control difference has been induced, that difference has been regulated down by the system with a certain tolerance" (property P1, cf. following table 1). It is thus sufficient to verify this single property, as it models the very definition of fault-tolerance for the system under test.

Additional properties P2-P5 allow observing whether or not a passivation always (or ever) occurs (for each motor separately). Those properties are, however, only "sanity-checks" as they do not imply the correct regulation of the control difference but only the detection of a fault by observing the expected counteraction. Properties P6-P7 are further plausibility-tests regarding the carriage position, while properties P8-P9 jointly guarantee that control differences are actually induced. Finally, property P10 requires the system not to create any deadlock-situations.

The verification results presented in table 2 yield that property P1 always holds, i.e. the system does indeed regulate the induced control difference in the presence of all single faults (and also in the fault-free case).

The results of properties P2-P5 indicate that any faults concerning Rot1, Pos1, CompCtrl1 or Motor1 always lead to the passivation of the affected motor, while Motor2 continues its operation correctly (i. e. it is not wrongly passivated) and vice versa. Faults in CompCtrl3, the virtual position sensor CompSens3 or any of the processes CompPass12, CompPass31, CompPass32 and CompPass21 do never lead to passivation, as a second vote would be necessary for that action. The plausibility tests in properties P6-P10 hold for all fault modes, thus confirming the correct operation of the overall system and the test case itself.

Table 1. Complete list of examined properties

Nr.	Property	Explanation
P1	`A[] (cycle >= 6 imply (CarriageV-RefV>= -2 and CarriageV-RefV <= 2))`	Six cycles after induced control difference, that difference is at most two.
P2	`A<> OutpStg1.passivated`	Output stage one will in any case be passivated.
P3	`A[] not OutpStg2.passivated`	Output stage two is never passivated.
P4	`A<> OutpStg2.passivated`	Output stage two will in any case be passivated.
P5	`A[] not OutpStg1.passivated`	Output stage one is never passivated.
P6	`A[] not Carriage.atLimit`	Carriage position will never be out of bounds.
P7	`A[] (CarriageV >= -2 and CarriageV-diffR <= 2)`	Overshoot/undershoot of carriage will never be more than I 2 I.
P8	`CarriageV >= diffR --> CarriageV >= diffR`	Each induced control difference is followed by another one.
P9	`A<> CarriageV >= diffR`	There is a first control difference induced in any case.
P10	`A[] not deadlock`	System is free of deadlocks.

Table 2. Verification results

Faulty unit	Fault mode	P1	P2	P3	P4	P5	P6	P7	P8	P9	P10
-	-	✓	✗	✓	✗	✓	✓	✓	✓	✓	✓
Rot1/2	wrong value	✓	✓/✗	✓/✗	✗/✓	✗/✓	✓	✓	✓	✓	✓
Rot1/2	corr. sign.	✓	✓/✗	✓/✗	✗/✓	✗/✓	✓	✓	✓	✓	✓
Pos1/2	wrong value	✓	✓/✗	✓/✗	✗/✓	✗/✓	✓	✓	✓	✓	✓
Pos1/2	corr. sign.	✓	✓/✗	✓/✗	✗/✓	✗/✓	✓	✓	✓	✓	✓
CompSens3	wrong value	✓	✗	✗	✗	✗	✓	✓	✓	✓	✓
CompCtrl1/2/3	wrong value	✓	✓/✗/✗	✓/✗/✗	✗/✓/✗	✗/✓/✗	✓	✓	✓	✓	✓
CompPass 12/31/32/21	wrong value	✓	✗	✗	✗	✗	✓	✓	✓	✓	✓
CompPass 12/31/32/21	corr. sign.	✓	✗	✗	✗	✗	✓	✓	✓	✓	✓
Motor1/2	halt	✓	✓/✗	✓/✗	✗/✓	✗/✓	✓	✓	✓	✓	✓

These results support the findings of an earlier fault-tree analysis presented in [EKJM09] insofar that all single faults in the fault model are tolerated also in the functional UPPAAL-model. Some double faults are tolerated as well, but this was not subject of the current investigations and depends on certain design decisions to be discussed separately. Please note that the criticality of common mode failures applies to any system not featuring diversity. The decision of whether using dedicated or remote redundancy thus has no influence on this issue whatsoever.

6 Conclusion and Outlook

In this paper, we presented dedicated redundancy and the new concept of remote redundancy and pinpointed the possible advantage of the new scheme with regard to system design and hardware costs. Possible fields of application such as automotive and avionics provide examples for both fail-safe and fault-tolerant systems.

As remote redundancy introduces in part radically new system variants, thorough analysis is necessary to prove that fault tolerance characteristics are not compromised. While previous investigations [EASI09], [EKJM09] concentrated on fundamental principles and a rather coarse model mainly based on fault trees, the present study displays a first functional demonstration. By using formal verification in UPPAAL, we were able to prove that an example system built using remote redundancy tolerates all single faults and thus exhibits the claimed behaviour. A similar system could be created for the example with brakes (Fig. 5).

Having thus elaborated a first prove of concept, planned further work includes a more detailed model in MATLAB/Simulink featuring simulated bus communication. A prototypical implementation of the signature scheme in VHDL using FPGA- and FlexRay-Boards will follow in order to demonstrate the technical feasibility of remote redundancy.

References

[BDL04]   Behrmann, G., David, A., Larsen, K.: A Tutorial on Uppaal. In: Bernardo, M., Corradini, F. (eds.) SFM-RT 2004. LNCS, vol. 3185, pp. 200–236. Springer, Heidelberg (2004)

[BFM03]   Baleani, M., Ferrari, A., Mangeruca, L., Sangiovanni-Vincentelli, L., Peri, M., Pezzini, S.: Fault-Tolerant Platforms for Automotive Safety-Critical Applications. In: Proc. of CASES, pp. 170–177. ACM, New York (2003)

[EASI09] Electronic Architecture and Systems Engineering for Integrated Safety Systems (EASIS): Discussions and findings on fault tolerance, http://www.easis-online.org/wEnglish/download/Deliverables/EASIS_Deliverable_D1.2-5_V1.0.pdf (2009-10-09)

[Echt86] Echtle, K.: Fault-Masking with Reduced Redundant Communication. Fault-Tolerant Computing Symposium FTCS-16, Digest of Papers. IEEE Press, Los Alamitos (1986)

[EcKi09] Echtle, K., Kimmeskamp, T.: Fault-Tolerant and Fail-Safe Control Systems Using Remote Redundancy. In: Proc. of ARCS (2009)

[EJT04]   Echtle, K., Jochim, M., Tappe, D.: Sicherheit und Fehlertoleranz – Zusammenspiel sicherheitsrelevanter Software und fehlertoleranter Datenbusse. Automotive Elektronik 3, 44–48 (2004)

[EKJM09] Echtle, K., Kimmeskamp, T., Jacquet, S., Malassé, O., Pock, M., Walter, M.: Reliability Analysis of a Control System Built Using Remote Redundancy. In: Advances in Risk and Reliability Technology Symposium (AR2TS), Conf. Proc., Loughborough (2009)

[IEC09]   Int. Electrotechnical Commission (IEC): Functional safety and IEC 61508, `http://www.iec.ch/zone/fsafety/pdf_safe/hld.pdf` (date of retrieval: 2009-10-09)

[Raus07]   Rausch, M.: FlexRay. Hanser Publishing House, Munich (2007)

[UPPA09] Uppaal – an integrated tool environment for modeling, validation and verification of real-time systems,
`http://www.it.uu.se/research/group/darts/uppaal/about.sh tml#introduction` (date of retrieval: 2009-12-08)

Software Reliability Assessment
Based on the Evaluation of Operational Experience

Sven Söhnlein[1], Francesca Saglietti[1], Frank Bitzer[2],
Matthias Meitner[1], and Siegfried Baryschew

[1] Chair of Software Engineering, University of Erlangen-Nuremberg
91058 Erlangen, Germany
{soehnlein,saglietti,meitner}@informatik.uni-erlangen.de
[2] LPE2-FB/Functions Basic Development, ZF Friedrichshafen AG
88038 Friedrichshafen, Germany
franz.bitzer@zf.com

Abstract. This paper illustrates a practicable approach to reliability evaluation for highly reliable software systems based on the analysis of their operational experience and demonstrates its applicability to the control software of a gearbox system. The investigations were carried out within a cooperation of academia and automotive industry. The article also elaborates on the possibility of assessing software reliability at system level by combination of component-specific software reliability estimates.

Keywords: Highly reliable software, operational experience, statistical testing, component-based systems.

1 Introduction

The application of software systems in environments demanding ultrahigh dependability (e.g. safety-critical applications) requires extremely rigorous verification and validation procedures aimed at demonstrating prescribed reliability targets. Such applications often rely on re-usable components for manifold reasons: in addition to obvious economical benefits, the positive operating experience gained during past usage provides valuable evidence of 'proven-in-use'-quality. For the purpose of a quantitative assessment of such evidence and of its impact on software reliability, sound and effective techniques are required.

A well-founded and rigorous approach to the quantitative assessment of software reliability during testing makes use of statistical sampling theory [5, 6, 10, 12, 13, 14] and permits - at least in principle - to derive for any given confidence level a corresponding conservative reliability estimate. While the effort required to apply this technique during testing may reveal as prohibitively expensive [3, 9, 11] the exploitation of past operational experience actually helps to enhance its practical applicability.

This potential is arousing the interest of developers in different industrial domains, especially concerning application variants based on reconfigurable pre-developed components. Among them, the automotive industry certainly plays a major role [8].

B. Müller-Clostermann et al. (Eds.): MMB & DFT 2010, LNCS 5987, pp. 24–38, 2010.

Tailored on its specific needs, a feasibility study on software reliability assessment by evaluation of the operational experience is being conducted within an industrial research cooperation between academia and automotive industry.

The practicality of the approach developed is first demonstrated by means of its application to the control software of a gearbox system developed by the automotive supplier ZF Friedrichshafen AG. Successively, the article presents novel techniques for assessing software reliability at system level by combining component-specific reliability estimates, thus allowing for a substantial effort reduction.

The paper is organized as follows: in section 2 the basics of statistical sampling theory are summarized. Section 3 proposes a systematic procedure for the extraction of statistically relevant operational data, successively applied to the gearbox control software (section 4). In section 5, compositional reliability techniques are derived both for the case of parallel and serial architectures. Finally, chapter 6 illustrates potential benefits by means of examples.

2 Reliability Estimation by Statistical Sampling Theory

The basic concepts of statistical sampling theory applied to testing resp. operational evidence are briefly summarized in the following; for a more detailed description the reader is referred to [5, 10, 12]. This theory allows to derive - to any given confidence level β and any number $n > 100$ of correct runs - an upper bound $\tilde{p}$ of the unknown probability p of observing failures during operation, i.e.

$$P(p \le \tilde{p}) = \beta \tag{1}$$

assuming the following assumptions being fulfilled:

Assumption 1 - Independent selection of test cases resp. operational runs: the selection of a test case resp. operational run does not affect the selection of others.

Assumption 2 - Independent execution of test cases resp. operational runs: the execution of a test case resp. operational run does not affect the outcome of others.

Assumption 3 - Operationally representative profile: test cases resp. operational runs are selected according to the frequency of occurrence expected during operation.

Assumption 4 – Positive test resp. operating experience: no failure occurs during the execution of any of the test cases resp. operational runs selected. A more general theory allows for a number of failure observations (s. [19, 21]) at the cost, however, of deriving correspondingly lower reliability estimates. For high software reliability demands (as in case of safety-critical applications), therefore, the strict assumption excluding failures during test is considered as more appropriate.

The upper bound $\tilde{p}$ that statistical sampling theory allows to derive under these assumptions reads [5, 10, 12]:

$$(1 - \tilde{p})^n = 1 - \beta \tag{2}$$

Conversely, in order to claim this inequality (for $\tilde{p} \ll 1$) at a given confidence β it is required to observe n correct and independent runs with

$$n \cong -\frac{\ln(1-\beta)}{\tilde{p}} \tag{3}$$

For example, in order to bound the failure probability by $\tilde{p} = 10^{-4}$ at a confidence level of 99% this technique requires 46 052 correct and independent runs.

3 Extraction of Statistically Relevant Operational Data

In order to apply statistical sampling theory to operational data collected during usage, the data recorded has to be analyzed in terms of the validity of assumptions 1 – 5, as introduced in section 2 and, where required, accordingly filtered. For this purpose, the following practical procedure supporting the extraction of statistically relevant operational data was developed:

Step 1 - Identification of component functionality to be assessed: define the application, functionality or control flow path for which to assess reliability, in particular by delimitating the software component(s) to be considered.

Step 2 - Identification of operationally independent runs: in order to ensure assumption 2, characterize and determine memoryless execution sequences, i.e. sequences of operations whose behaviour does not depend on execution history.

Step 3 - Definition of the structure of an operational run: identify all relevant input parameters and exclude from the test case structure all information without impact on the functionality to be assessed.

Step 4 - Determination of the operational profile: determine the frequency of occurrence of each software-implemented functional demand during operation.

Step 5 - Filtering of the operational data: extract from the operational data a representative, independent subset, i.e. a subset fulfilling assumption 1 and reflecting the operational profile determined in step 4.

4 Application to a Software-Controlled Gearbox System

This section illustrates how the guideline described in section 3 is practically applied to the reliability assessment of a software-controlled gearbox system for trucks. This project is being carried out within an industrial research cooperation of the University of Erlangen-Nuremberg and the automotive provider ZF Friedrichshafen AG. For reasons of confidentiality the data presented was previously rendered anonymous.

The software controls twelve forward gears, two reverse gears and one neutral gear, which can be controlled manually by the driver, or automatically by a software component implementing a strategy-based driving assistant. In addition to the "current gear" (in the following abbreviated by CG) and to the "desired gear" (in the following abbreviated by DG) the functionality of the software controller also depends on further environmental parameters ρ_i, like the current speed or the position of the accelerator pedal.

A substantial amount of operational experience was collected during extensive road testing based on typical functional demands. The value of all relevant parameters was recorded at each point in time. Table 1 visualizes the data, where for reasons of confidentiality the individual gears are symbolized by characters a, b, c, ..., m, while the environmental parameters ρ_i are provided on a percentage scale.

Based on the available operational data, the guideline proposed in section 3 is applied as follows.

Step 1 - Identification of component functionality to be assessed: The underlying system architecture sketched in Figure 1 was first analyzed for the purpose of delimitating the software functionality for which to assess reliability.

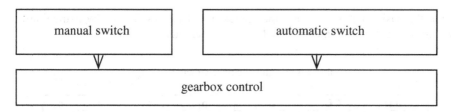

Fig. 1. Software Architecture

In accordance with the software developers the scope of the assessment was focused on the software component implementing the gearbox control functions. This component receives manual switching commands from the driver or automatic switching commands from an intelligent driving assistant, whose functionality is outside the scope of the reliability assessment.

Step 2 - Identification of operationally independent runs: The operational data collection was preceded by an initialization phase devoted to parameter calibration after which the switching of gears performs in a memoryless way (s. assumption 2). In other words, switching from gear c to gear d does not depend on previous switching operations, i.e. it is not relevant for the functionality whether gear a or gear b was engaged before gear c.

Step 3 - Definition of the structure of an operational run: Operational runs obviously depend on the current gear CG and on the desired gear DG, as well as on four further parameters ρ_1, ρ_2, ρ_3 and ρ_4, which are relevant for the switching functionality, like the speed and the accelerator pedal position.

With respect to the data collected, relevant operational cases can be identified whenever a new switching command was risen (be it by a driver or by a driving assistant) by the values of the corresponding parameters. Table 1 shows an excerpt of the data collected and highlights the structure of a relevant operational case at time 926.8, where a new switching command was given, which was successfully completed at time 927.5.

Table 1. Relevant operational case at time 926.8

Time	DG	CG	ρ_1	ρ_2	ρ_3	ρ_4
926.5	g	g	3.00 %	0.4 %	21.6 %	0 %
926.6	g	g	3.00 %	0.4 %	21.6 %	0 %
926.7	g	g	2.50 %	0.4 %	21.6 %	0 %
926.8	**f**	**g**	**2.39 %**	**0.4 %**	**21.6 %**	**0 %**
926.9	f	g	2.00 %	0.0 %	21.6 %	0 %
927.0	f	g	2.00 %	0.0 %	21.6 %	0 %
927.1	f	g	2.00 %	0.4 %	21.6 %	0 %
927.2	f	g	1.09 %	0.4 %	21.2 %	0 %
927.3	f	g	1.09 %	0.4 %	21.2 %	0 %
927.4	f	g	1.09 %	0.4 %	21.2 %	0 %
927.5	f	f	1.09 %	0.0 %	21.2 %	0 %

On the basis of this structure, the operational data was filtered by extracting all switching commands with corresponding parameter values (s. Table 2).

Table 2. Operational cases extracted (excerpt)

Time	CG	DG	ρ_1	ρ_2	ρ_3	ρ_4
...	...	...	...	...	...	...
5940.6	k	l	64.35	88.8	0.0	0
6012.3	l	j	57.55	0.4	0.0	0
6016.2	j	h	42.23	0.4	16.0	0
...	...	...	...	...	...	...

Step 4 - Determination of the operational profile: According to the operational case structure identified in step 3, the operational profile was determined in two phases. First, the frequencies of switching commands, i.e. of combinations (CG, DG) were determined on the basis of the operational data (s. Table 3 and Fig. 2).

Table 3. Frequencies of switching commands (matrix, excerpt)

	d	e	f	g	h	i	...
...	...	...	...	...	...	...	...
d	--	06.06 %	16.13 %	00.00 %	01.35 %	00.00 %	...
e	...	--	16.13 %	13.33 %	00.00 %	00.00 %	...
f	...	06.06 %	--	18.33 %	17.57 %	01.10 %	...
g	...	63.64 %	19.35 %	--	25.68 %	15.38 %	...
h	...	00.00 %	45.16 %	33.33 %	--	25.27 %	...
i	...	00.00 %	00.00 %	33.33 %	43.24 %	--	...
j	...	00.00 %	00.00 %	00.00 %	08.11 %	52.75 %	...
...	...	...	...	...	...	...	...

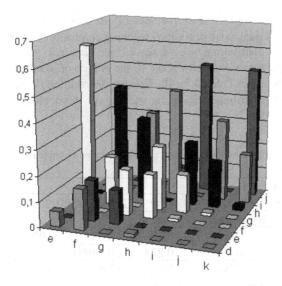

Fig. 2. Frequencies of switching commands (histogram, excerpt)

Successively, for each switching command (CG,DG) the profile of each parameter ρ_i, $i \in \{1 \ldots 4\}$ was estimated by distribution fitting techniques [7] based on hypotheses on distribution classes, parameter estimation and goodness-of-fit assessment. This task was supported by a software tool helping in identifying the most suitable

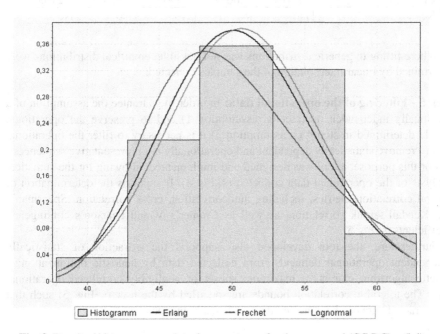

Fig. 3. Density / histogram overplot of parameter ρ_1 for the command (CG,DG) = (k,j)

distribution classes as well as their parameters, as shown in Fig. 3 by a density histogram overplot of parameter ρ_1 for the switching command (CG,DG) = (k,j).

The fit of each distribution was assessed by classical goodness-of-fit tests including the Kolmogorow-Smirnow test [7], the Anderson-Darling test [7] and the χ^2 test [7], as illustrated in Table 4 for the Fréchet distribution (which was estimated as the most suitable distribution for parameter ρ_1 for the combination (CG,DG) = (k,j)).

Table 4. Goodness-of-fit tests for parameter ρ_1 and switching command (CG,DG) = (k,j)

Distribution: Fréchet					
Distribution Parameters: $0.17241 \cdot 10^{-9}$; $0.90725 \cdot 10^{-9}$; $-0.90725 \cdot 10^{-9}$					
Kolmogorow-Smirnow test					
α	0.2	0.1	0.05	0.02	0.01
Critical value	0.1968	0.22497	0.24993	0.27942	0.29971
Reject?	No	No	No	No	No
Anderson-Darling test					
α	0.2	0.1	0.05	0.02	0.01
Critical value	1.3749	1.9286	2.5018	3.2892	3.9074
Reject?	No	No	No	No	No
χ^2 test					
α	0.2	0.1	0.05	0.02	0.01
Critical value	3.2189	4.6052	5.9915	7.824	9.2103
Reject?	No	No	No	No	No

Where fitting to generic distributions was not possible, empirical distributions were determined by linear interpolation of the samples collected.

Step 5 - Filtering of the operational data: In order to guarantee the assumption of a statistically independent test set (s. assumption 1) and to preserve the operational profile determined in step 4 (s. assumption 3) it is necessary to filter the operational data to remove statistically dependent and operationally not representative sequences.

For this purpose, a tool was designed and implemented, allowing for the statistical analysis of the operational data collected (s. Fig 4). It supports the determination of several correlation metrics, including autocorrelation, cross correlation, Spearman's and Kendall's rank correlation, as well as Cramer's V and Pearson's contingency coefficients (s. Fig 5).

Furthermore, the tool developed also supports the extraction of statistically independent operational demands from collected data by heuristic optimization: a genetic algorithm extracts a maximum subset of negligibly correlated operational data. The tolerable correlation bounds are specified by the user (s. Fig. 5) such that the extracted data can be considered as statistically independent.

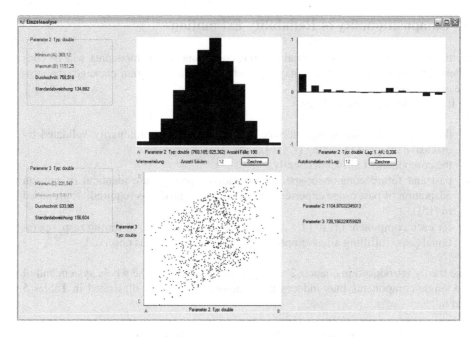

Fig. 4. Statistical analysis of the collected operational data

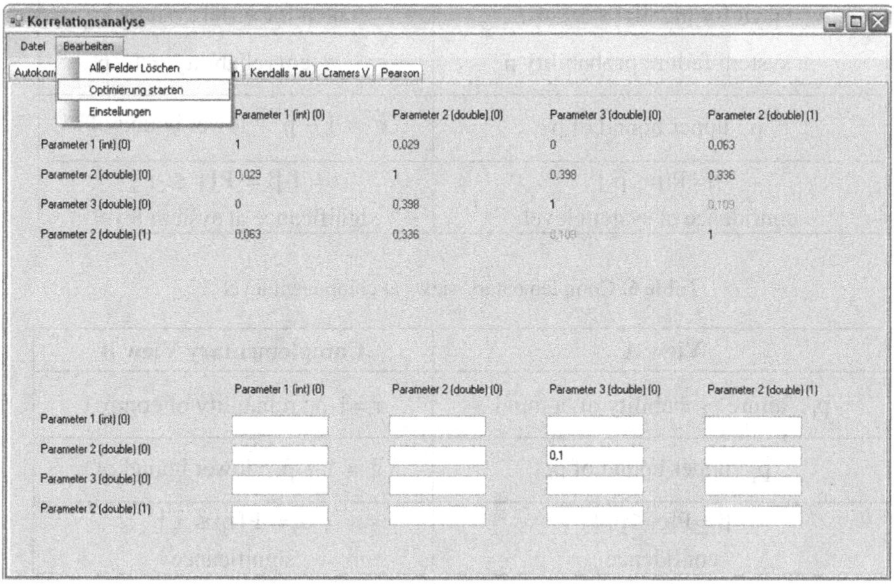

Fig. 5. Input of correlation limits

5 Compositionality of Reliability Estimation

In the following, parallel and serial systems consisting of k components will be considered, where each component may represent a complex program package or a simple execution path.

It is additionally assumed that

- the architecture (including interface consistency) was preliminarily validated by extensive integration testing (s. [16]),
- the components fail independently,
- past and future component-specific operational profiles are identical (if not, an adaptation of past usage experience to future usage profile is required, as proposed in [15]),
- for each component i (i ∈ {1,...,k}) a certain amount $n_i > 0$ of testing resp. operational runs (fulfilling all assumptions stated in section 2) was observed.

The theory introduced in chapter 2 and applied at the level of the whole system and of the single components thus induces the complementary view illustrated in Tables 5 and 6.

Table 5. Complementary views at system level

View A (taken for parallel systems)	Complementary View B (taken for serial systems)
p: system failure probability p	r: system reliability = 1 - p
$\tilde{p}$: upper bound of p	$\tilde{r} = 1 - \tilde{p}$: lower bound of r
$\beta = P[p \le \tilde{p}]$ confidence at system level	$\alpha = 1 - \beta = P[r \le \tilde{r}]$ significance at system level

Table 6. Complementary views at component level

View A	Complementary View B
p_i : failure probability of comp. i	$r_i = 1 - p_i$: reliability of comp. i
$\tilde{p}_i$: upper bound of p_i	$\tilde{r}_i = 1 - \tilde{p}_i$: lower bound of r_i
$\beta_i = P[p_i \le \tilde{p}_i]$ confidence	$\alpha_i = P[r_i \le \tilde{r}_i]$ significance
$\beta_i = 1 - \exp(-n_i \cdot \tilde{p}_i)$ (s. equation 3)	$\alpha_i = \tilde{r}_i^{n_i}$ (s. equation 2)

5.1 Compositional Reliability Assessment for Parallel Systems

Let's consider first the parallel system consisting of k mutually exclusive components shown in Fig. 6.

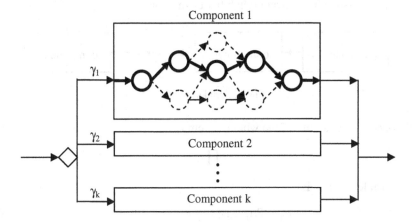

Fig. 6. System consisting of mutually exclusive components

If each component $i \in \{1,\ldots,k\}$ is selected at probability γ_i during operation, then the failure probability of the whole system is

$$p = \sum_{i=1}^{k} \gamma_i p_i \qquad (4)$$

Due to

$$P(\gamma_i \cdot p_i \leq \tilde{p}_i) = P\left(p_i \leq \frac{\tilde{p}_i}{\gamma_i}\right) = 1 - \exp(-\frac{n_i}{\gamma_i} \cdot \tilde{p}_i) \qquad (5)$$

for any $i \in \{1,\ldots,k\}$ and any γ_i with $0 \leq \gamma_i \leq 1$, each p_i (s. Table 6, View A) can be taken as exponentially distributed with rates

$$\lambda_i = \frac{n_i}{\gamma_i} \qquad (6)$$

Being p a **linear combination of independent, exponentially distributed random variables**, its distribution can be derived by convolution, yielding a **hypoexponential distribution** (for details, s. [17, 18, 4, 20, 1]), which allows the sharp determination of the confidence level β:

$$\beta = P\left(\sum_{i=1}^{k} \gamma_i p_i \leq \tilde{p}\right) = 1 - \sum_{i=1}^{k} \prod_{\substack{j=1 \\ j \neq i}}^{k} \frac{\frac{n_j}{\gamma_j}}{\frac{n_j}{\gamma_j} - \frac{n_i}{\gamma_i}} \cdot \exp(-\frac{n_i}{\gamma_i} \cdot \tilde{p}) \quad \text{for} \quad \frac{n_i}{\gamma_i} \neq \frac{n_j}{\gamma_j} \quad \forall i \neq j \qquad (7)$$

Summarizing, the operating experience gained at component level can be successfully merged to obtain a sharp reliability estimation at system level.

5.2 Compositional Reliability Assessment for Serial Systems

Similarly to the approach developed above for mutually exclusive components, also serial architectures as shown in Fig. 7 are investigated in terms of the compositionality of component-specific software reliability estimations.

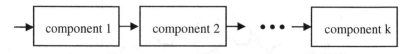

Fig. 7. Serial system

In this case the reliability of the whole system is

$$r = \prod_{i=1}^{k} r_i$$

Due to (s. Table 6, View B)

$$\alpha_i = P[r_i \leq \tilde{r}_i] = \tilde{r}_i^{n_i} \tag{8}$$

each r_i can be taken as Beta-distributed with parameters n_i and 1. Being the system reliability r the product of the individual component reliabilities

$$r = \prod_{i=1}^{k} r_i \tag{9}$$

and therefore a **product of k independent, Beta-distributed random variables** (with parameters n_i and 1, $i \in \{1,...,k\}$), its distribution can be analytically derived as done in [2] and used to identify a quantitative relationship between a lower reliability bound and its confidence level:

$$1 - \beta = P[r \leq \tilde{r}] = P\left[\prod_{i=1}^{k} r_i \leq \tilde{r}\right] = \prod_{i=1}^{k} n_i \cdot \sum_{i=1}^{k} \frac{\tilde{r}^{-n_i}}{n_i \cdot \prod_{\substack{j=1 \\ j \neq i}}^{k} (n_j - n_i)} \quad \text{for } n_i \neq n_j \ \forall \ i \neq j \tag{10}$$

Summarizing, also for serial systems (and therefore also for arbitrary architectures combining parallel and serial component configurations) compositionality of reliability estimations based on component-specific operating experiences could be ensured.

6 Examples

6.1 Examples for Parallel Systems

In the following, a system is assumed to consist of two functionally independent components selected by mutual exclusion (as considered in section 5.1). For each of the components, operating experience amounting to $n_1 = 30000$ runs resp. $n_2 = 60000$ runs was collected. Table 7 shows the upper bound $\tilde{p}$ at a confidence level of 99%.

Table 7. System reliability estimation in case of 2 components with n_1=30000, n_2=60000

$\beta = 0.99$	$\tilde{p}$
$\gamma_1 = 0.7$, $\gamma_2 = 0.3$	0.000114
$\gamma_1 = 0.5$, $\gamma_2 = 0.5$	0.000088
$\gamma_1 = 0.2$, $\gamma_2 = 0.8$	0.000071

For the reliability target $\tilde{p} = 0.0001$ and different usage profiles Table 8 shows the corresponding confidence levels.

Table 8. Confidence levels in case of 2 components with n_1=30000, n_2=60000

$\tilde{p} = 0.0001$	β
$\gamma_1 = 0.7$, $\gamma_2 = 0.3$	0.982
$\gamma_1 = 0.5$, $\gamma_2 = 0.5$	0.995
$\gamma_1 = 0.2$, $\gamma_2 = 0.8$	0.998

Finally, Table 9 shows the optimal amount (estimated by the gradient approach described in [17]) of operational experience required in order to validate an upper bound of $\tilde{p} = 0.0001$ at confidence level 99% for a system consisting of 5 uniformly used components (i.e. $\gamma_i = 1/5$, $1 \leq i \leq k$).

Table 9. Amount of testing effort required for k=5

n_1	23 213
n_2	23 214
n_3	23 215
n_4	23 216
n_5	23 217
$\Sigma\, n_i$	116 075

6.2 Examples for Serial Systems

Table 10 shows the upper bound $\tilde{p}$ which can be determined for a serial system with k=2, 3 resp. 4 components at confidence 99%.

Table 10. Upper bound for serial system

k	n_i	$\tilde{p}$
2	$n_1 = 46000$ $n_2 = 46001$	0.000144
3	$n_1 = 46000$ $n_2 = 46001$ $n_3 = 46002$	0.000183
4	$n_1 = 46000$ $n_2 = 46001$ $n_3 = 46002$ $n_4 = 46003$	0.000219

Table 11 shows the confidence level β at which $\tilde{p} = 10^{-4}$ can be validated for a serial system with k = 2, 3 resp. 4 components.

Table 11. Confidence level for serial system

k	n_i	β
2	$n_1 = 46000$ $n_2 = 46001$	0.943723
3	$n_1 = 46000$ $n_2 = 46001$ $n_3 = 46002$	0.837396
4	$n_1 = 46000$ $n_2 = 46001$ $n_3 = 46002$ $n_4 = 46003$	0.674356

Finally, Table 12 shows the number of test cases required at component level in order to validate an upper bound of $\tilde{p} = 10^{-4}$ at confidence 99% for a serial system with 4 components.

Table 12. Operating experience for a serial system

n_1	100445
n_2	100446
n_3	100447
n_4	100448
$\Sigma\, n_i$	401786

7 Conclusion

In this article a guideline for the estimation of software reliability based on operational experience was developed and illustrated by practical application to a software-controlled gearbox system. In addition, new methods supporting system reliability assessment on the basis of component-specific reliability estimates were derived. The benefits they offer were illustrated by means of several examples.

References

1. Amari, S., Misra, R.: Closed-form Expressions for Distribution of Sum of Exponential Random Variables. IEEE Transactions on Reliability 46(4) (1997)
2. Bhargava, R.P., Khatri, C.G.: The Distribution of Product of Independent Beta Random Variables with Application to Multivariate Analysis. Annals of the Institute of Statistical Mathematics 33, 287–296 (1981)
3. Butler, R., Finelli, G.: The Infeasibility of Quantifying the Reliability of Life-critical Real-time Software. Software Engineering 19(1) (1993)
4. Cox, D.: Renewal Theory. Methuen & Co. (1962)
5. Ehrenberger, W.: Software-Verifikation. Hanser (2002)
6. Heinhold, J., Gaede, K.: Ingenieur-Statistik. Oldenbourg (1972)
7. Law, A.M., Kelton, W.D.: Simulation, Modeling and Analysis. McGraw-Hill, New York (2000)
8. Limbourg, P., Savic, R., Petersen, J., Kochs, H.D.: Modelling Uncertainty in Fault Tree Analyses Using Evidence Theory. Journal of Risk and Reliability 222, 291–302 (2008)
9. Littlewood, B., Strigini, L.: Validation of Ultra-high Dependability for Software-based Systems. Communications of the ACM 36(11) (1993)
10. Littlewood, B., Wright, D.: Stopping Rules for Operational Testing of Safety Critical Software. In: Proc. 25th International Symposium Fault Tolerant Computing (FTCS 25). IEEE, Los Alamitos (1995)
11. Littlewood, B., Strigini, L.: Software Reliability and Dependability: A Roadmap. In: The Future of Software Engineering. ACM, New York (2000)
12. Miller, K.W., Morell, L.J., Noonan, R.E., Park, S.K., Nicol, D.M., Murrill, B.W., Voas, J.F.: Estimating the Probability of Failure When Testing Reveals No Failures. IEEE Transactions on Software Engineering 18(1) (January 1992)
13. Parnas, D., van Schouwen, J., Kwan, S.: Evaluation of Safety-critical Software. Communications of the ACM 33(6) (1990)
14. Quirk, W.J. (ed.): Verification and Validation of Real-time Software. Springer, Heidelberg (1985)
15. Saglietti, F.: Evaluation of Pre-developed Software for Usage in Safety Critical Systems. In: Proc. 26th EUROMICRO Conference (EUROMICRO 2000). IEEE, Los Alamitos (2000)
16. Saglietti, F., Pinte, F., Söhnlein, S.: Integration and Reliability Testing for Component-based Software Systems. In: Proc. 35th EUROMICRO Conference on Software Engineering and Advanced Applications (SEAA 2009). IEEE, Los Alamitos (2009)
17. Söhnlein, S., Saglietti, F.: Auswertung der Betriebserfahrung zum Zuverlässigkeitsnachweis sicherheitskritischer Softwaresysteme. In: Proc. Automotive 2008 - Safety & Security, Sicherheit und Zuverlässigkeit für automobile Informationstechnik, Stuttgart (2008)

18. Söhnlein, S., Saglietti, F., Bitzer, F., Baryschew, S.: Zuverlässigkeitsbewertung einer Getriebesteuerungs-Software durch Auswertung der Betriebserfahrung. Softwaretechnik-Trends, GI 29(3) (2009)
19. Störmer, H.: Mathematische Theorie der Zuverlässigkeit. Oldenbourg (1970)
20. Trivedi, K.: Probability & Statistics with Reliability, Queuing, and Computer Science Applications. Prentice-Hall, Englewood Cliffs (1982)
21. Wilks, S.: Determination of Sample Sizes for Setting Tolerance Limits. Annals of Mathematical Statistics 12, 91–96 (1941)

Clock Synchronization Issues
in Multi-Cluster Time-Triggered Networks

Klaus Echtle and Soubhi Mohamed

University of Duisburg-Essen,
Institute for Computer Science and Business Information Systems,
45141 Essen, Germany
{echtle,msoubhi}@dc.uni-due.de

Abstract. We address the issue of establishing and maintaining a system-wide common time base in fault-tolerant multi-cluster time-triggered systems.

We propose an approach how to synchronize system nodes among several clusters using the fault-tolerant mid-point algorithm. Before executing clock synchronization each node measures the clock deviation values and stores them in a convenient data structure. From these values the clock synchronization algorithm calculates a correction term which should be added or subtracted from the local clock. For distributed real-time systems that are structured in a set of clusters the set of clock deviations can be subdivided into a set of local clock deviations and a set of global clock deviations. Local clock deviation values (respectively global clock deviation values) of a specific node are captured by building the time difference between the observed and expected arrival time of synchronization messages sent by a node belonging to the same cluster (respectively to another cluster).

In order to receive messages from other clusters the clock deviation between the sender and the receivers should be bounded. We derive the lower bound of the network precision of a multi-cluster system that executes the FlexRay protocol and will show that it depends mainly on the transmission delays and measurement errors. Further, we inquire about the amount of the minimum time gap between two successive messages that could be exchanged via the FlexRay System. This time gap is an important parameter for developing a correct configuration of multi-cluster systems.

1 Introduction

Distributed fault-tolerant real-time systems are deployed in a huge set of safety-critical applications i.e. in automotive, aerospace, railways, automation and process control. They meet their service requirements related to the timeliness and correctness of its reaction and resilience to faults. Time-triggered systems are often preferred due to their deterministic behaviour. They enable predictable transmission of messages and fault-tolerant global notion of time among all nodes. Keeping the local times of these nodes synchronized even in the presence of arbitrary faults is a challenging task due, on the one hand to physical characteristics of the clock oscillators, on the other hand to varying message transmission delays (jitter). Thus, continuous clock synchronization is

B. Müller-Clostermann et al. (Eds.): MMB & DFT 2010, LNCS 5987, pp. 39–61, 2010.

an indispensable primitive function of time-triggered systems. Many of such systems consist of a single cluster i.e. a set of nodes that share a reliable communication medium and communicate over it in dedicated time intervals (see section 5). In order to ease the complexity in system design, to reduce the development effort and to overwhelm bandwidth limitations large real-time systems should be organized in clusters. The interconnection between clusters is realized by a well-defined interface called gateway. This structure demands additional effort regarding the inter-cluster communication and clock synchronization.

Synchronization often relies on the precision of the clock oscillators which is an important quality attribute to be guaranteed by the manufacturer. Another not less important oscillator characteristic is the long-term stability which means that even though the clock is subject to massive transient disturbance the synchrony can be maintained. A good clock synchronization of a cluster strive to maintain the clock skew within the cluster precision which may facilitate the design of fault-tolerant services that can be built on it. The cluster precision is the upper limit for the time difference between the fastest and the slowest node within the cluster. In multi-cluster systems we distinguish between local and global synchronization. Two nodes are locally synchronized if they belong to the same cluster and if at any point in real-time the distance between their clock values is bounded by their cluster precision. A node is globally synchronized if at any point in real-time the distance between its clock value and the clock value of any node that belongs to a different cluster is bounded by a priori given constant called the global precision. The network precision is the time difference between any two node clocks in the whole system.

The objective of this work is to discuss clock synchronization issues in multi-cluster time-triggered systems and to provide the lower bound of the network precision as well as the calculation of the minimum time gap between two messages, by means of an example where at most two faulty nodes exist (see section 5). The obtained results are not intended to be generalized, but rather to provide basis for the configuration of a functional multi-cluster system and to understand the added amount in comparison with single-cluster systems. A generalization of the results requires a formal verification that is still under work.

2 Time-Triggered Communication Network

Time-triggered networks are becoming the technology of choice for the design of safety-critical distributed systems because of their deterministic behaviour that can be incorporated with fault-tolerance mechanisms such as CRC and redundancy. Many time-triggered systems have been established over the last years. Examples are FlexRay[1], Time Triggered Protocol[2], Time triggered Controller area Network TTCAN[3], DACAPO[4]. Understanding the principle of operation of such protocols is an interesting topic.

In this paper we to limit the multi-cluster clock synchronization analysis of FlexRay as a representative time-triggered protocol (see section 4) and by means of an example.

2.1 Basics of Clocks

Hardware clock: In a time-triggered system each node possesses a timer control unit that generates an event to increase the time counter[5]. The periodic event is called tick of the clock. The duration between two consecutive ticks is called the granularity of the clock, denoted by g .

A hardware clock of a given node i can be defined as: $H_i : R\Gamma \rightarrow C_{lk}\Gamma$, where $R\Gamma$ denotes the set of the real-time values, and $C_{lk}\Gamma$ the set of clock values.

H_i is said correct at a given time t if for all times t_0 and t_1 such that $t_0 \leq t \leq t_1$, H_i measures the passage of time during real-time interval $[t_0, t_1]$ with an error of at most $\rho(t_1 - t_0) + g$, where ρ refers to the maximum hardware drift rate specified by the manufacturer[13]:

$$(1 - \rho)(t_1 - t_0) - g \leq H_i(t_1) - H_i(t_0) \leq (1 + \rho)(t_1 - t_0) + g \qquad (1)$$

Hardware Drift: The hardware drift of a clock k between two consecutive ticks i and $i+1$ is the frequency ratio between this clock and the real-time at the instant of tick i. The drift is determined by measuring the duration of a granular of clock k with real-time t and dividing it by the nominal number n^k of real-time's ticks in a granular:

$$drift_i^k = \frac{t(tick_{i+1}^k) - t(tick_i^k)}{n^k} \qquad (2)$$

$t(tick_i^k)$ denotes the point in real-time when the tick i of clock k occurs.

The drift of a hardware clock comprises a systematic drift and a stochastic drift. The systematic part of the hardware drift is a constant deviation of the frequency from the specified nominal value. This part is mostly affected by numerous factors such as temperature variation and aging. The stochastic part of the drift appears randomly within a certain range. In practice this part is about 100 times smaller than the systematic part[6].

Drift rate: The drift rate of a clock k (ρ_k) represents its deviation from real-time, measured in second per real second. Because a good clock has a drift close to 1, ρ_k can be defined as follows:

$$\rho_k = |drift_i^k - 1| \qquad (3)$$

Local time: The hardware clock of a node i is adjusted by a term that is calculated by the clock synchronization algorithm. Applying the calculated adjustment term Adj_i the local clock may be faster or slower than other local clocks. The local clock of a node i can be defined as follows:

$$Clk_i : R\Gamma \rightarrow C_{lk}\Gamma \text{ and } Clk_i(t) = H_i(t) + Adj_i \tag{4}$$

2.2 Communication in Time-Triggered Systems

In a distributed time-triggered system, communication is performed using the time division multiple access (TDMA) arbitration scheme. Thereby, the time is divided into slots. Slots are fixed time intervals within a communication round in which a transmission of a message (called frame) can be carried out. In an a priori given planning called schedule it is defined which slot is assigned to which node and which node should receive a message (see also section 4).

2.3 Clock Synchronization in Time-Triggered Network

Synchronization is necessary to bring all participating nodes of a network into timely agreement so that they communicate in correct order. It reduces the causal implications between events in the nodes[10]. The clock synchronization in time-triggered systems is a cyclic activity performed by each node. Two nodes i and j are clock-synchronized with precision π if the following property holds:

$$\forall t \in R\Gamma : |Clk_i(t) - Clk_j(t)| \leq \pi \tag{5}$$

Over a given period of time R the time difference between two clocks may increase up to $2\rho R$ due to the clock drift rate ρ. Assuming that the initial deviation between two correct clocks is π_{in}, then the skew grows up to $\pi_{in} + 2\rho R$ during R. Therefore, the correction must be performed periodically to guarantee the tightness of synchronization. The time interval R is termed the re-synchronization interval where each node proceeds in the following steps:

- **Remote clock reading:** Each node derives clock values of a specific set of nodes using the messages received from them. The obtained values represent only an estimation of the remote clocks because of jitters and clock drifts[11].
- **Execute the clock synchronization algorithm:** As previously mentioned the clock synchronization algorithm calculates the correction term relying on the remote clock values.
- **Clock adjustment:** The calculated correction value should be applied to the local clock in a discrete or continuous manner (known as clock amortization[11]) or a combination of the two.

2.3.1 Clock Synchronization Algorithms

The theory of clock synchronization algorithms has been exhaustively described in the literature. The most popular algorithms are:

- **Fault-tolerant midpoint algorithm (FTM):** The fault tolerant midpoint algorithm[12] has been established in many protocols over the last years. The algorithm sorts the remote clock values $x_1, \ldots, x_n$ and returns the midpoint $\dfrac{x_{F+1} + x_{n-F}}{2}$ of the range after discarding the F highest and F lowest values where F is the number of faulty clocks. The algorithm takes into account that faulty clocks may run either too slow or too fast and that correct clocks are in-between.

- **Egocentric average algorithm:** The egocentric average[14] returns the average of the remote clock values of all x_j $(1 \le j \le n)$ where $\left| x_j - x_p \right| \le \omega$ whre x_p denotes the clock value of the node executing the algorithm and ω the achievable precision. By building the average, x_j is replaced by x_p if they deviate from each other by more than ω.

- **Fast convergence algorithm:** The fast convergence algorithm is described in [16]. The algorithm returns the average of all remote clock values that are within ω of at least $n - F$ remote clock readings. It has been proven that this technique provides better precision. However, it is costly as for each clock x_j a comparison with $n - 1$ remaining clocks is necessary to determine the deviation [16].

3 The Time Triggered Protocol FlexRay

FlexRay is a state-of-the-art communication system that provides flexibility and determinism. Flexibility is achieved by combining a scalable static and dynamic message transmission and capturing the merits of synchronous and asynchronous protocols.

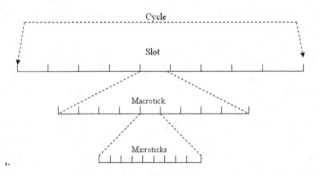

Fig. 1. Timing levels in FlexRay

3.1 Time Representation in FlexRay

The time domain inside FlexRay nodes is organized in four timing levels as depicted in figure1:

Microtick level: Microticks (μTs) correspond to the ticks of the node's oscillator and represent the time granularity in FlexRay.

Macrotick: A macrotick is an integral number of microticks. It represents the global notion of time. Every action inside FlexRay nodes is triggered based on its local view of the global time (cluster time in macroticks).

Slot: A time window where a message could be transmitted. In the static segment of FlexRay all slots exhibit the same slot-length (expressed in macroticks).

Cycle: corresponds to the common round in a time-triggered protocol. It consists of a predefined set of slots. All nodes of a given cluster have the same nominal cycle length. A cycle in FlexRay is subdivided into a static segment, a dynamic segment, a symbol window and a network idle time where clock synchronization is executed[1].

3.2 Sync Frames in FlexRay

Sync frames are special messages used to derive the clock value (estimation) of the sending nodes by measuring the time difference between the observed and the expected arrival time (expressed in μTs). The transmission of a frame takes place after an offset called action point offset. The action point offset should be configured greater than the assumed worst-case precision so that even when the sender runs faster (respectively slower) than the receiver the frame could be received. However, unnecessary large values of action point offset result in lost bandwidth (large gap between messages).

3.3 Calculation and Application of the Clock Correction Terms

FlexRay uses the FTM algorithm to calculate the correction terms for the offset (phase differences) and rate (frequency differences) correction. As described before the FTM sorts the deviation values in ascending order and discards the k smallest and the k largest values. It builds then the average on the resulting range bounds. The average indicates the number of μTs the node's communication cycle should be increased or decreased[1].

FlexRay uses a combination of discrete clock adjustment (offset correction) and continuous clock adjustment (rate correction). The calculated offset correction value is applied in the same cycle while rate correction is spread over the consecutive two cycles. It has been proven that continuous clock adjustment (clock amortization) has no impact on the clock skew[17].

In contrast to the common use of the FTM algorithm the value of k is determined dynamically and depends on the number of valid deviation values (including the own value if the node sends sync frames). For the rate calculation the time difference from two consecutive cycles is used. The calculations for both offset correction and rate correction are performed in the network idle time of the communication cycle, i.e. in the absence of bus activities.

The main motivation for the use of the FTM algorithm, in comparison with other algorithms that simply average the values, is attributed to the fact that faulty nodes are running either too fast or too slow and thus are automatically discarded, and consequently have no impact on the calculated value.

4 Multi-Clusters

Partitioning the system in multiple clusters is an enabling approach for the design of distributed critical applications. Moreover, multi-cluster structures permit the integration and the re-use of already known and best experienced single clusters. The interconnection between clusters is realized by an interface called gateway. In time-triggered networks the interconnected clusters may operate in terms of executing different protocols and running at different baud rates (heterogeneous multi-cluster systems). In that case more effort should be placed on the design of the gateway which should execute numerous services such as conversion routines. The load caused by these services is significant in terms of the time spent by the execution. In this work we deal with multi-cluster systems that operate with identical protocols, in particular FlexRay (see figure 2).

The example shown below consists of two clusters C_1 (with nodes A, B, C and D) and C_2 (with nodes E, F and G) that operate with the same communication rate. Each node in the multi-cluster system adopts the same configuration of the parameters so that the nominal cycle, slot and even the macrotick durations are identical.

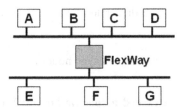

Fig. 2. Example of a Multi-Cluster System

4.1 FlexWay

To name the gateway according to the used protocol we introduce the term of Flex-Way. FlexWay is a device that connects two or more clusters with each other, thus enabling the inter-routing between them. Depending on the schedule FlexWay should forward frames from one cluster towards all (broadcast) or a subset thereof (multicast). These frames are called global frames. FlexWay forwards global frames immediately rather than buffering them. Frames that do not pass through the FlexWay are called local frames. The main objective is to enable local communication as well as global communication. For this purpose FlexWay should provide switching services and should have access to the global time.

4.2 Schedule in Multi-Cluster Systems

To achieve an efficient utilization of the system a good piece of work in forming a suitable schedule is required. In the meanwhile, many algorithms that provide a good or even an optimal schedule have been established. However, they cannot be applied directly in our case due to the general conditions. Thus, it is essential to develop scheduling solutions that suit best to the individual needs of the application. A promising approach is the planning of global frames first, and local frames then. Figure3 shows a simple schedule example for two FlexWay-connected clusters (The letters in the boxes show the sender of the respective frame).

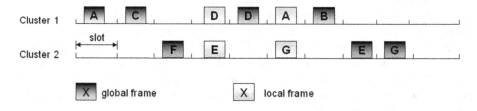

Fig. 3. Example of a communication Schedule in the Multi-Cluster System in one cycle

4.3   Timing Analysis of Multi-Clusters

For a correct execution of local and global synchronization the following requirements are needed:

Bounded clock drift rate: The drift rate of all nodes is bounded by a small constant ρ.

Minimum Redundancy: At least $3F + 1$ sync nodes are required to mask up to F arbitrary failures[13].

Transmission delays do not exceed a specific bound: We distinguish between the following delays:

- Transmission delay caused by the bus driver of the transmitter: τ
- Bus delay: β
- Receiving delay caused by the bus driver of the receiver: Ω
- Activity detection delay to detect the beginning of an incoming frame: α
- Delay caused within the FlexWay due to the switching services: σ

In what follows we define for each variable x the minimum value x_{min} and the maximum value x_{max}. Henceforth, x^* denotes the non-compensated portion of variable x which should be then compensated by the clock synchronisation algorithm. The amount $\alpha + \sigma$ will be replaced by a variable φ which expresses the delay within the FlexWay.

4.3.1   Network Delay
In the case that the used topology consists of only a passive bus the network delay δ can be calculated as follows (see figure 4 and figure 5):

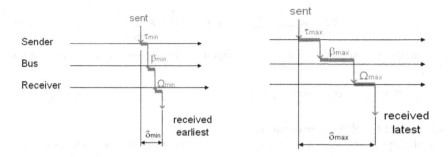

Fig. 4. Minimum Delay   **Fig. 5.** Maximum Delay

$$\delta_{min} = \tau_{min} + \beta_{min} + \Omega_{min} \tag{6}$$

$$\delta_{max} = \tau_{max} + \beta_{max} + \Omega_{max} \tag{7}$$

The network delay for a multi-cluster system where two clusters C_1 and C_2 are connected via the FlexWay can be calculated as follows (see figure 5 and figure 6):

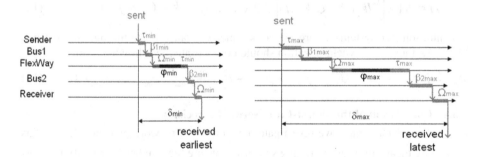

Fig. 6. Minimum Delay   **Fig. 7.** Maximum Delay

$$\delta_{min} = 2\tau_{min} + \beta_{1min} + \beta_{2min} + \varphi_{min} + 2\Omega_{min} \tag{8}$$

$$\delta_{max} = 2\tau_{max} + \beta_{1max} + \beta_{2max} + \varphi_{max} + 2\Omega_{max} \tag{9}$$

β_1 refers to the incoming bus line and β_2 refers to the outgoing bus line.

4.3.2 Local Clock Synchronization

The local synchronization aims at bringing all nodes inside a cluster C_x into agreement.

For each, at time t, correct node i and node j in C_x it holds:

$$\forall t \in R\Gamma : \left| Clk_i(t) - Clk_j(t) \right| \leq \pi_{C_x} \tag{10}$$

The local clock synchronization should compensate the following term (see figure 4 and 5):

$$\delta^*_{max} = \delta_{max} - \delta_{min} = \tau_{max} - \tau_{min} + \beta_{max} - \beta_{min} + \Omega_{max} - \Omega_{min} \tag{11}$$

4.3.3 Global Clock Synchronization

The global synchronization aims at bringing all nodes of the multi-cluster system into agreement with respect to time. For each correct node i in C_x (cluster x) and each correct node j in C_y (cluster y), where $x \neq y$, the following holds:

$$\forall t \in R\Gamma : \left| Clk_i(t) - Clk_j(t) \right| \leq \Delta \tag{12}$$

A set of nodes are globally synchronized with precision Δ (do not confuse with network precision defined in section 2), and are locally synchronized with precision 2Δ :

$$\forall t \in R\Gamma : \left| Clk_i(t) - Clk_j(t) \right| \leq \Delta \quad \text{and} \quad \forall t \in R\Gamma : \left| Clk_k(t) - Clk_j(t) \right| \leq \Delta \tag{13}$$

$$\Rightarrow \forall t \in R\Gamma : \left| Clk_i(t) - Clk_k(t) \right| \leq 2\Delta \text{ , where } i,k \in C_x \wedge j \in C_y \tag{14}$$

For multi-cluster systems where the communication takes place through at most one FlexWay, the global synchronization should compensate the following term:

$$\delta^*_{max} = 2(\tau_{max} - \tau_{min}) + \beta_{1max} - \beta_{1min} + \beta_{2max} - \beta_{2min} + \varphi_{max} - \varphi_{min} + 2(\Omega_{max} - \Omega_{min}) \tag{15}$$

4.3.4 Calculation of the Worst-Case Network Precision

As previously mentioned we investigate the worst case network precision Δ_{max}. This is done by means of a set of "timing scenarios" where the number F of faulty nodes is assumed to be 2 at most (F=2 holds for the remaining of this document). For our calculation we introduce the following variables:

μ : Measurement deviation when measuring the point in time when a frame has been received (caused by asynchrony between the receiver and the incoming message and by any further delay in the receiver affecting the accuracy of the measurement.

λ : Local influence in clock synchronization. This influence λ moves the local clock from the value calculated by the (fault-tolerant) clock correction algorithm towards the local oscillator. In FlexRay this effect is achieved by "cluster drift damping" applied in the rate correction algorithm.

The worst case scenario is characterized as shown in figure 8. The first x-axis shows the arrival points in time as viewed by the *slowest* node in the whole network (multi-cluster system) during one communication cycle. The first two bars represent the point in time when two synchronization frames from two faulty nodes are observed.

The other bars represent the points in time when synchronization frames from fault-free nodes arrive. From the value calculated by the FTM algorithm using only the correct values (marked by the triangle) the amount λ should be subtracted. The received correct synchronization frames may come from any cluster, the network precision is then the difference between the first and last observed correct synchronization frames.

The same holds for the second x-axis where the arrivals of synchronization frames are depicted as viewed by the *fastest* node. The synchronization frames of faulty nodes have collided with other frames and could not be received in this scenario. Δ_{diff} is then the clock deviation between the slowest and the fastest node just after the application of the correction term calculated by the FTM algorithm.

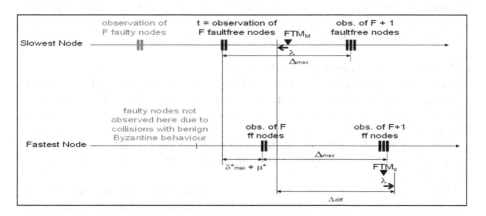

Fig. 8. All sync frames are exchanged via the FlexWay

As shown in figure 8 the F slowest and the F fastest values are ignored. The midpoint of the remaining ranges is then the result of the algorithm.

The slowest node corrects its clock to:

$$t_s = FTM_s - \lambda = t + \frac{\Delta_{\max}}{2} - \lambda \tag{16}$$

The fastest node corrects its clock to:

$$t_f = FTM_f + \lambda = t + \delta_{\max}^* + \mu^* + \Delta_{\max} + \lambda \tag{17}$$

The maximum clock deviation after correction:

$$\Delta_{diff} = t_f - t_s = \frac{\Delta_{\max}}{2} + \delta_{\max}^* + \mu^* + 2\lambda \tag{18}$$

The clock deviation Δ_{diff} should remain smaller than the worse case network precision $\Delta_{\max}$ to guarantee the convergence of the clock synchronization algorithm.

Convergence is achieved when:

$$\Delta_{diff} < \Delta_{max} \Rightarrow \frac{\Delta_{max}}{2} + \delta^*_{max} + \mu^* + 2\lambda < \Delta_{max} \qquad (19)$$

Which is equivalent to: $2(\delta^*_{max} + \mu^* + 2\lambda) < \Delta_{max}$ and

$$\Delta_{max} = 2\delta^*_{max} + 2\mu^* + 4\lambda + \varepsilon \qquad (20)$$

Because the clock synchronization is a periodic process in FlexRay and the period is very short (every two cycles) the amount of ε is very small ($2\rho R +$ some ticks that build at most one macrotick. R refers to the duration of one cycle, see section 3.3). The maximum worst case precision is twice the sum of the non-compensated part of the network delay, the maximum measurement error and twice the maximum local influence, plus some epsilon.

4.3.5 The Cost of Switching Inside FlexWay
Depending on the physical characteristics of the device used to build up FlexWay and depending on the schedule the propagation delay within FlexWay can be significant high. For example, when a frame should be conveyed over FlexWay, it must detect the signal activity from the incoming link and decide (according to the schedule) whether this frame should be transmitted to all outgoing links (in case of global communication) or not (local communication), and then execute the transmission routines which can by costly.

The principle of its operation can be compared with a valve: When a global frame should be transmitted the valve is open (switch on) and closed otherwise (switch off). In case of three and more clusters we need a crossbar-switch (out of the scope of this work). If communication is not orchestrated well, an overexerting of the device may be caused, as depicted in figure 9. In this example switching must be executed six times with the cumulative delay of 6σ (section 5.3).

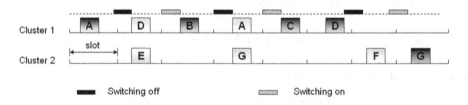

Fig. 9. Switching behaviour of the FlexWay

Figure 9 shows an example of a schedule for cluster 1 and cluster 2. Nodes A, B, C, D and G send global frames in slots 1, 3, 5, 6 and 8, respectively. In slots 2, 4 and 7 local communication takes place. For example, node D sends a frame in slot 2 that can not be visible in cluster 2 and vice versa. In the same slot node E sends a frame that can not be visible in cluster 1.

The amount of the switching delays within a cluster can be heavily reduced when the static window is divided into two parts (global and local part). In the global part only global frames are transferred. At the end of this part the FlexWay switches off and local communication becomes feasible.

4.3.6 Master/Slave Multi-Cluster Synchronization

Another possibility to reduce the complexity of transmitting all sync frames over Flex-Way is the master/slave clock synchronization technique. A cluster is called master cluster if it represents the only source of sync frames. A cluster plays the role of a slave cluster, if all its nodes rely on the sync frames that come from the master cluster to synchronize their clocks. In many implementations the nodes of the master cluster send at least $3F+1$ global sync frames towards the slave cluster. In other words, if the master cluster is the only source of the sync frames it must send at least $3F+1$ sync frames via the FlexWay. Nodes of the master cluster perform the local clock synchronization as stated in the previous sections. Based only on the received global sync frames nodes of the slave cluster perform clock synchronization. However, in the case when FlexWay crashes, nodes of the slave cluster cannot remain synchronized. Another possible implementation allows slave nodes to transmit local sync frames and to obtain a subset of global sync frames from the master cluster. The benefit is that even if the FlexWay experiences a crash failure or a blackout local synchronization can be maintained as long as the slave nodes remain correct. In the subsequent section, we calculate the worst case network precision in umpteen scenarios where only $2F+1$ global sync frames are transmitted from the master cluster and F additional sync frames (termed local sync frames) come from the slave cluster itself.

4.3.6.1   Determining the Worst-Case Network Precision for Master/Slave Multi-Cluster. In this section we devote the amount of the network precision by means of various worst-case scenarios. We assume that the master cluster nodes submit $2F+1$ global sync frames towards the slave cluster which consists of F sync nodes and any number of non-sync nodes in addition. The master nodes perform clock synchronization independently from the slave cluster since each master node receives $3F+1$ local sync frames in total.

For analysis purposes we introduce the following variables:

π_M : The assumed precision within the master cluster.

π_S : The assumed precision within the slave cluster, we assume that

$$\pi_M \leq \pi_S \leq 2\pi_M \qquad (21)$$

π_x : Auxiliary variable that expresses the deviation between both clusters, where

$$0 \leq \pi_x \leq \pi_M \qquad (22)$$

δ_N : Auxiliary variable so that:

$$\delta_N = \delta^*_{max} + \mu^* + 2\lambda \qquad (23)$$

The assumption made in (21) means that the slave cluster should be at most twice the precision in the master cluster (see also equation (12)). The assumption made in (22) results from the assumption in (21). The auxiliary variable δ_N will be used in many equations; therefore we will substitute the right term with it. δ_N denotes the overall network delay.

In subsequent diagrams we use the following symbols to depict the events of sync frame observations:

| Observation of a correct local sync frame within the master cluster.

| Observation of sync frame sent by a faulty node.

Observation of a correct local sync frame within the slave cluster.

Observation of a correct global sync frame at a slave node.

Case 1: Only correct global sync frames have been sent towards the slave cluster.

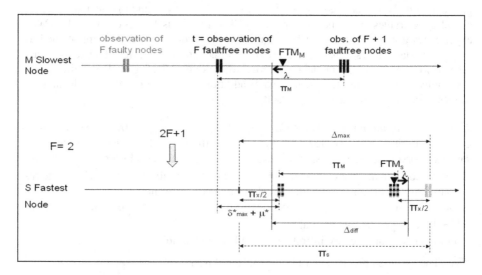

Fig. 10. Possible distribution of global/local sync frame's arrivals (case1)

The slowest node M in the master cluster corrects its clock to:

$$t_M = FTM_M - \lambda = t + \frac{\pi_M}{2} - \lambda \qquad (24)$$

The fastest slave node S corrects its clock to:

$$t_S = FTM_S + \lambda = t + \pi_M + \delta^*_{max} + \mu^* + \lambda \qquad (25)$$

After correction the maximum clock deviation is

$$: \Delta_{diff} = t_S - t_M = \frac{\pi_M}{2} + \delta^*_{max} + \mu^* + 2\lambda = \frac{\pi_M}{2} + \delta_N \qquad (26)$$

Clock synchronization achieves convergence if:

$$\Delta_{diff} < \Delta_{max} = \pi_M + \pi_x = \pi_S \quad \Rightarrow \quad \delta_N < \frac{\pi_M}{2} + \pi_x \qquad (27)$$

Considering the assumed bounds of π_x (22), it holds that:

$$\frac{\pi_M}{2} \le \frac{\pi_M}{2} + \pi_x \le \frac{3}{2}\pi_M$$

The inequation (27) should hold for all values of π_x so that if $\pi_x = 0$ (27) becomes:

$$\delta_N < \frac{\pi_M}{2} \qquad (28)$$

In the other case ($\pi_x > 0$) it holds that:

$$\delta_N \le \frac{3}{2}\pi_M \Rightarrow \pi_M \ge \frac{2}{3}\delta_N \qquad (29)$$

Considering the bounds of π_S (21) and (28) and (29) we obtain:

$$\pi_M \le \Delta_{max} \le 2\pi_M \text{ where } \pi_M > 2\delta_N \qquad (30)$$

Case 2: Only three out-of five global sync frames could be received and the local sync frames' arrival times are between their arrival times.

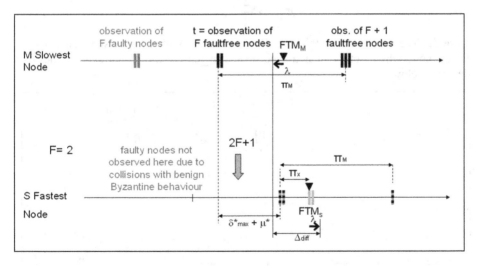

Fig. 11. Possible distribution of global/local sync frame's arrivals (case2)

The slowest node M in the master cluster corrects its clock to:

$$t_M = FTM_M - \lambda = t + \frac{\pi_M}{2} - \lambda \qquad (31)$$

The fastest slave node S corrects its clock to:

$$t_S = FTM_S + \lambda = t + \pi_x + \delta^*_{max} + \mu^* + \lambda \tag{32}$$

After correction the maximum clock deviation is:

$$\Delta_{diff} = t_S - t_M = \pi_x - \frac{\pi_M}{2} + \delta^*_{max} + \mu^* + 2\lambda = \delta_N + \pi_x - \frac{\pi_M}{2} \tag{33}$$

Clock synchronization achieves convergence if:

$$\Delta_{diff} < \Delta_{max} = \pi_M + \pi_S - \pi_x = 2\pi_M \tag{34}$$

(33) und (34) $\Rightarrow$

$$\delta_N < \frac{3}{2}\pi_M + \pi_S - 2\pi_x = \frac{3}{2}\pi_M + \pi_S - 2(\pi_S - \pi_M) = \frac{7}{2}\pi_M - \pi_S \tag{35}$$

This inequation must hold for all π_M and all π_S. Considering the bounds of π_S (21) the necessary condition follows:

$$\delta_N < \frac{7}{2}\pi_M - 2\pi_M = \frac{3}{2}\pi_M \tag{36}$$

This is equivalent to:

$$\pi_M > \frac{2}{3}\delta_N \tag{37}$$

Case 3: The sync nodes within the slave cluster are faulty. In the slave cluster the fastest node which acts as a non-sync node can receive the global sync frames as depicted below:

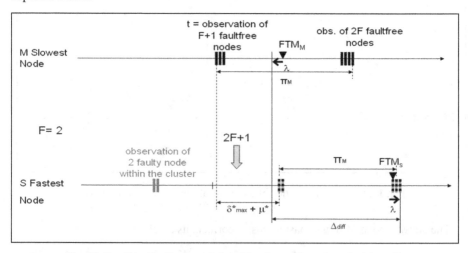

Fig. 12. Possible distribution of global/local sync frame's arrival (case3)

The slowest node M in the master cluster corrects its clock to:

$$t_M = FTM_M - \lambda = t + \frac{\pi_M}{2} - \lambda \tag{38}$$

The fastest slave node S corrects its clock to:

$$t_S = FTM_S + \lambda = t + \pi_M + \delta^*_{max} + \mu^* + \lambda \tag{39}$$

After correction:

$$\Delta_{diff} = t_S - t_M = \frac{\pi_M}{2} + \delta^*_{max} + \mu^* + 2\lambda = \delta_N + \frac{\pi_M}{2} \tag{40}$$

Clock synchronization achieves convergence if:

$$\Delta_{diff} < \Delta_{max} = \pi_M + \pi_x \quad \Rightarrow \quad \delta_N < \frac{1}{2}\pi_M + \pi_x \tag{41}$$

Considering the bounds of π_x (22):

$$\frac{\pi_M}{2} \leq \frac{1}{2}\pi_M + \pi_x \leq \frac{3}{2}\pi_M \tag{42}$$

Similar to case1 and case2:

$$\pi_M \leq \Delta_{max} \leq 2\pi_M \quad \text{where} \quad \pi_M > 2\delta_N \tag{43}$$

Remark: The inequation (43) holds for all values of $\pi_x \geq 0$ regarding the range specified in (22).

We conclude from the analysed worst-case scenarios that the worst-case network precision should be greater than twice the assumed precision within the master cluster to guarantee correct communication among several clusters where the maximum assumed number of faulty node is F = 2 (including case 2 since the right inequation of (43) fulfils also (37)) . The precision of the master cluster should be itself greater than twice δ_N , which represents the sum of the maximum non-compensated propagation delay, the measurement deviation and twice the "cluster drift damping".

It holds. $$\Delta_{max} \leq 2\pi_M \quad \text{and} \quad \pi_M > 2\delta_N \qquad \Delta_{max} = 4\delta_N + \varepsilon \tag{44}$$

Remark: The result stated in (44) cannot be generalized for any number F of faulty nodes unless it is formally verified which is under work and out of the scope of this work. Further, not all worst case scenarios have been discussed in this document and should be analysed in the same manner as done for cases 1, 2 and 3.

The master/slave clock synchronization principle may reduce the transmission complexity since only $2F + 1$ global sync frames should be submitted towards the slave cluster that owns F local sync nodes. However, this kind of clock synchronization leads to inaccuracies in comparison with the approach where all sync frames in the multi-cluster system are exchanged.

4.3.6.2 Blackout Analysis. The system designer must reckon with a blackout of Flex-Way that may hold for a short/long period or permanently (crash). In that case, each node in each cluster rests upon the local sync frames to synchronize its clock. Both clusters may deviate from each other so that after the period of the blackout frame collisions occur and global resynchronization becomes necessary. The effect of Flex-Way blackout can be shown by means of an example (see figure 13). In this example we assume that all nodes remain correct after the blackout and that it occurs after all global sync frames have been received by the nodes of the slave cluster in round x. Furthermore, we assume that all nodes of the master cluster drift with $-\rho$ but still maintain the master cluster precision π_M. Nodes of the slave cluster behave similarly, but move in the opposite with $+\rho$. After clock correction the network precision is Δ_{diff}^0 in round x, Δ_{diff}^1 in round $x+1$, ..., Δ_{diff}^n in round $x+n$, respectively.

Let R be the duration of the synchronization round in μTs (corresponds to the duration of a double cycle in FlexRay). It holds:

$$\Delta_{diff}^1 = \Delta_{diff}^0 + 2\rho R = \Delta_{diff}^0 + 2\rho R \tag{45}$$

$$\Delta_{diff}^2 = \Delta_{diff}^1 + 2\rho R = \Delta_{diff}^0 + 2(2\rho R)$$

$$\cdot \qquad \cdot \qquad \cdot \qquad \cdot \qquad \cdot$$

$$\Delta_{diff}^n = \Delta_{diff}^{n-1} + 2\rho R = \Delta_{diff}^0 + n(2\rho R) \quad \text{(45) (can be eas-}$$

ily proven by induction).

Let n be a round that fulfils the following properties:

$$\Delta_{diff}^{n-1} \le \Delta_{max} \wedge \Delta_{diff}^n > \Delta_{max} \tag{46}$$

$$\Leftrightarrow \quad \Delta_{diff}^0 + (n-1)(2\rho R) \le \Delta_{max} \wedge \Delta_{diff}^0 + n(2\rho R) > \Delta_{max}$$

$$\Leftrightarrow \quad n > \frac{\Delta_{max} - \Delta_{diff}^0}{2\rho R} \wedge n \le \frac{\Delta_{max} - \Delta_{diff}^0}{2\rho R} + 1 \tag{47}$$

If the blackout period is smaller than n that fulfils the inequation (47), and if all nodes remain correct during the blackout, then slave cluster nodes remain globally synchronized. Otherwise, frame collisions are possible and global resynchronization of the slave cluster nodes is required. The FlexRay protocol provides means to establish resynchronization by changing the state of slave cluster nodes from active to passive. In that case, slave nodes do not send any sync frames, but still receive global sync frames on which they synchronize their clock to. However, during this operation the local communication service is not available which is not acceptable for some critical applications. This problem can be overcome by replication. Thereby, two

FlexWays could be used where each is attached to a FlexRay channel. When one of them crashes or suffers a blackout (degradated mode), slave cluster nodes can still receive global sync frames and thus maintain synchronized (see figure14).

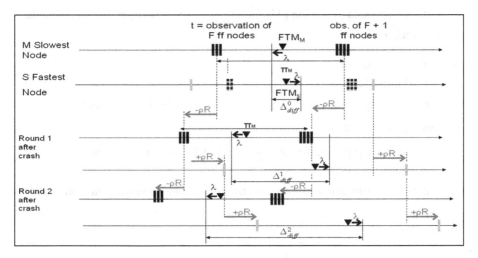

Fig. 13. Clock deviations of both clusters after the crash/blackout of the FlexWay

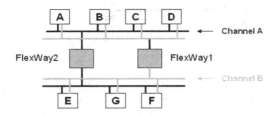

Fig. 14. Multi-Cluster system with two FlexWays

4.4   Slot Utilization

FlexWay is time-controlled by a node which participates in clock synchronization and thus may suffer from inaccuracies. Moreover, global frames can be forwarded towards slave cluster only after execution of the switching service (see section 5.3). Therefore, we distinguish between three transfer phases:

- Phase 1 corresponds to the transfer from the sender to the FlexWay. The respective delay is called δ_1, where $\delta_1 = \tau + \beta_1$.

- Phase 2 corresponds to the transfer within the FlexWay (including frame detection).
  The respective delay is $x = \tau + \alpha + \sigma + \Omega$.

- Phase 3 corresponds to the transfer from the FlexWay to the receiver in the slave cluster. The respective delay is δ_2, where $\delta_2 = \beta_2 + \Omega$.

In this section we calculate the necessary inter-frame gaps (the minimum distance in between two consecutive frames) for the case that all sync frames are exchanged using (21) for Δ_{max}. The same calculation can be done for master/slave clock synchronization mode using equation (44) for Δ_{max}. For this purpose, we introduce the following variables:

- s : Slot duration.
- f : Frame duration.
- g : Gap duration (the difference $g = s - f$, as well as the sum $g = g_s + g_t$).
- g_s : Starting gap duration (from the start of the slot to the beginning of frame transmission).
- g_t : terminating gap duration (from the end of frame transmission to the end of the slot).

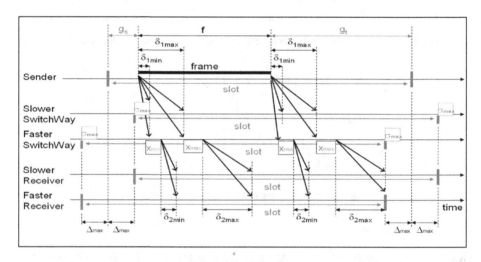

Fig. 15. Slot Utilization

Figure 15 shows the minimum and maximum delays during the transmission of a global frame from the sender to the receiver which is situated in another cluster. It has been distinguished between the cases where this frame passes throughout a *faster* and a *slower* FlexWay. That means that the FlexWay itself may be operating faster (minimum delays) or slower (maximum delays). The same holds for the receiver which is assumed to run faster or slower than the sender.

As it is obvious from figure 16 the time gap can be calculated as follows:

$$g_s = \Delta_{max} + \sigma_{max} - \delta_{1min} \qquad (48)$$

$$g_t = \Delta_{max} + \delta_{max} = \Delta_{max} + (\delta_{1max} + x_{max} + \delta_{2max}) \tag{49}$$

$$g = g_s + g_t = 2\Delta_{max} + \delta_{max} - \delta_{1min} + \sigma_{max} = 2(2\delta_N + \varepsilon) + \delta_{max} - \delta_{1min} + \sigma_{max}$$
$$= 4\delta^*_{max} + 4\mu^* + 8\lambda + 2\varepsilon + \delta_{max} - \delta_{1min} + \sigma_{max} \tag{50}$$

According to the definition of x and δ_x :

$$g = 4(\tau^*_{max} + \beta^*_{1max} + x^*_{max} + \beta^*_{2max} + \Omega^*_{max}) + (\tau_{max} + \beta_{1max} + x_{max} + \beta_{2max} + \Omega_{max} - \delta_{1min}) + 4\mu_{max} + 8\lambda + 2\varepsilon + \sigma_{max}$$
$$= 8\tau^*_{max} + 2\tau_{max} - \tau_{min} + 4\beta^*_{1max} + \beta_{1max} - \beta_{1min} + 4\beta^*_{2max} + \beta_{2max} + 4\alpha^*_{max} + \alpha_{max} + 4\sigma^*_{max} +$$
$$2\sigma_{max} + 8\Omega^*_{max} + 2\Omega_{max} + 4\mu_{max} + 8\lambda + 2\varepsilon \tag{51}$$

4.4.1 Gap Comparison between Multi-Cluster and the Single Cluster

When a single bus is used (without any gateway) the time gap can be calculated as follows:

$$g_{bus} = 4\delta^*_{max} + \delta_{max} - \delta_{min} + 4\mu_{max} + 8\lambda + 2\varepsilon \text{ where } \beta = \beta_1 + \beta_2 \text{ and } \delta = \tau + \beta + \Omega$$
$$= 4\tau^*_{max} + \tau_{max} - \tau_{min} + \beta_{max} - \beta_{min} + \Omega_{max} - \Omega_{min} + 4\beta^*_{max} + 4\Omega^*_{max} + 4\mu_{max} + 8\lambda + 2\varepsilon \tag{52}$$

If we assume the absence of compensation ($x^* = x$) and lack of minimum values ($x_{min} = 0$) we obtain:

$$g_{bus} = 5\tau_{max} + 5\beta_{max} + 5\Omega_{max} + 4\mu_{max} + 8\lambda + 2\varepsilon \tag{53}$$

Using the FlexWay ($g = g_{FW}$):

$$g_{FW} = 10\tau_{max} + 5\beta_{max} + 5\alpha_{max} + 6\sigma_{max} + 10\Omega_{max} + 4\mu_{max} + 8\lambda + 2\varepsilon$$
$$\Leftrightarrow \qquad g_{FW} = 5\tau_{max} + 5\alpha_{max} + 6\sigma_{max} + 5\Omega_{max} + g_{bus} \tag{54}$$

The amount of the minimum time gap in multi-cluster system in comparison with single cluster is:

$$g_{FW} - g_{bus} = 5\tau_{max} + 5\alpha_{max} + 6\sigma_{max} + 5\Omega_{max} \tag{55}$$

The FlexRay protocol specification[1] has defined typical values for the variables in equation(55):

$$\tau_{max} = \Omega_{max} \approx 100 \text{ ns} ; \alpha_{max} = 450 \text{ ns} ; \sigma_{max} \approx 1000 \text{ ns (estimated)}$$

The value of the maximum switching delay σ_{max} is estimated based on the delays caused by the star couplers (at most 700 ns plus 300 ns as a "safety margin"). Quantitatively, the time gap difference in equation (55) is:

$$g_{FW} - g_{bus} \approx 9,25\mu s \tag{56}$$

If the assumptions above are not considered, the previous equation can be generalized to:

$$g_{FW} - g_{bus} = 4\tau_{max}^* + \tau_{max} + 4\alpha_{max}^* + \alpha_{max} + 4\sigma_{max}^* + 2\sigma_{max} + 4\Omega_{max}^* + \Omega_{max} + \Omega_{min} + \beta_{2min}$$

5 Conclusion

In this paper we investigated the clock synchronization in time-triggered multi-cluster systems by means of a FlexRay example. We presented two kinds of clock synchronizations: clock synchronization using several global sync frames in the multi-cluster system, and synchronization called master/slave clock synchronization whereby a subset of global sync frames are submitted towards the slave cluster. In the considered worst case scenarios for F=2 we conclude that the network worst case precision is twice the sum of the non-compensated part of the network delay, the maximum measurement error, and twice the maximum local influence, plus an epsilon in case several sync frames are exchanged.

The clock synchronization relies on the fault-tolerant midpoint algorithm to calculate the correction terms of each clock individually. The algorithm ensures that even in presence of up to F failures, the clock skew of correct nodes is bounded by the network precision.

Clock synchronization that requires the exchanging of all sync frames provides better accuracy compared to master/slave clock synchronization. However, system designers may prefer the master/slave synchronization approach in order to reduce the overall complexity.

We calculated also the amount of the necessary inter-frame gap in multi-clusters in comparison with the single cluster.

References

[1] FlexRay. FlexRay Communications System Protocol specification Version 2.1.Specification, FlexRay Consortium (2005)
[2] Bauer, G.: Implementation and Evaluation of Fault-Tolerant Clock synchronization Algorithm for TTP/C. Master Thesis, Technische Universität wien, Institut für Technische Informatik, Vienna (1999)
[3] Time Triggered Communication on Führer, C.T., Müller, B., Dieterle, W., Hartwich, F., Hugel, R., Walther, M.: Robert Bosch GmbH. In: Proceedings 7th International CAN Conference, Amsterdam (2000)
[4] Rostamzadeh, B., Lönn, H., Snedsbol, R., Torin, J.: A Distributed Computer Architecture for Safety-Critical Control Application (1995)
[5] Kopetz, H.: Real time Systems: Design Principles for Distributed Embedded Applications. Kluwer Academic Publishers, Dordrecht (1997)
[6] Schwabl, W.: Der Einfluss zufällige und systematischer Fehler auf die Uhren Sychronization in verteilten Echtzeitsystemen. PhD Thesis, Technische Universität Wien, Institut für Technische Informatik. Austria (1990)
[7] Christian, F., Fetzer, C.: Probalistic Internal Clock Synchronization. In: Proceedings of the Thirteenth Symposium on Reliable Distributed Systems, Dana Point, Ca (1994)

[8] Barak, B., Halevi, S., Herzberg, A., Naor, D.: Clock Synchronization with faults and recoveries. In: Symposium on Principles of Distributed Computing (2000)

[9] Christian, F., Aghili, H., Strong, R.: Clock Synchronization in the presence of Omission and Performance Failures, and Processor Joins. In: Yang, Z., Anthony Marsland, T. (eds.) Global State and Time in Distributed Systems. IEEE Computer Society Press, Los Alamitos (1994)

[10] Schreiber, F.A.: Is Time a Real Time? An Overview of Time Ontology in Informatics. In: Halang, W.A., Stoyenko, A.D. (eds.) Real Time Computing, pp. 283–307. Springer, Heidelberg (1994)

[11] Anceaume, E., Puaut, I.: Performance Evaluation of Clock Synchronization Algorithms. Technical Report 3526, Institut de Recherche en Informatique et Systèmes Aléatoires (October 1998), http://www.irisa.fr

[12] Lundelius, J., Lynch, N.: A new Fault-Tolerant Algorithm for Clock synchronization. In: Proceedings of the 3rd annual ACM symposium on Principles of Distributed Computing (1984)

[13] Fetzer, C., Christian, F.: Integrating External and Internal Clock Synchronization. Real-Time systems 12(2), 123–171 (1997)

[14] Lamport, L., Milliar-Smith, P.M.: Synchronizing Clock in the presence of Faults. Journal of the ACM 32(1) (1985)

[15] Stephan, R., Mahaney, Schneider, F.B.: Inexact agreement: Accuracy, Precision and graceful Degradation. In: 4th ACM symposium on Principles of Distributed Computing (1985)

[16] Suri, N., Walter, C.J., Hugue, M.M.: Advances in ULTRA-Dependable Distributed Systems. IEEE Computer Society Press, Los Alamitos (1994)

[17] Dolev, D., Halpern, J.: On the possibility and Impossibility of Achieving Clock Synchronization. In: Proceeding of the sixteenth annual ACM Symposium on Theory of Computing (1984)

User-Perceived Performance of the NICE Application Layer Multicast Protocol in Large and Highly Dynamic Groups*

Christian Hübsch, Christoph P. Mayer, and Oliver P. Waldhorst

Institute of Telematics, Karlsruhe Institute of Technology (KIT),
76128 Karlsruhe, Germany
{huebsch,mayer,waldhorst}@kit.edu

Abstract. The presentation of a landmark paper by Chu et al. at SIGMETRICS 2000 introduced application layer multicast (ALM) as completely new area of network research. Many researchers have since proposed ALM protocols, and have shown that these protocols only put a small burden on the network in terms of link-stress and -stretch. However, since the network is typically not a bottleneck, user acceptance remains the limiting factor for the deployment of ALM. In this paper we present an in-depth study of the user-perceived performance of the NICE ALM protocol. We use the OverSim simulation framework to evaluate delay experienced by a user and bandwidth consumption on the user's access link in large multicast groups and under aggressive churn models. Our major results are (1) latencies grow moderate with increasing number of nodes as clusters get optimized, (2) join delays get optimized over time, and (3) despite being a tree-dissemination protocol NICE handles churn surprisingly well when adjusting heartbeat intervals accordingly. We conclude that NICE comes up to the user's expectations even for large groups and under high churn.

1 Introduction

IP multicast is a technology with significant maturity that has been developed for several decades. Nevertheless it lacks global deployment for reasons that are manifold. They include, e. g., that IP multicast was designed without a specific commercial use-case in mind, leading to insufficient support for address allocation, group management, authorization, protection against attacks, and network management [7]. Nevertheless, many applications demand for multicast communication, and the demand is constantly growing in face of current trends towards

---

* This work was partially funded as part of the *Spontaneous Virtual Networks* (*SpoVNet*) project by the Landesstiftung Baden-Württemberg within the BW-FIT program and as part of the Young Investigator Group *Controlling Heterogeneous and Dynamic Mobile Grid and Peer-to-Peer Systems* (*CoMoGriP*) by the *Concept for the Future* of Karlsruhe Institute of Technology (*KIT*) within the framework of the German Excellence Initiative.

B. Müller-Clostermann et al. (Eds.): MMB & DFT 2010, LNCS 5987, pp. 62–77, 2010.

video and TV transmission. A solution to this hassle was presented by [6], which proposed to implement multicast distribution inside the end systems rather than in the network itself, creating an completely new area of research. Many protocols following this paradigm, denoted as end-system or *application layer multicast* (*ALM*), were developed. At the same time, it has been shown that the burden that ALM puts on the network core is small. In particular, *link stress*, i. e., transmitting the same multicast message across a physical link, and *link stretch*, i. e., extending the length of a delivery path compared to a unicast transmission, are bounded and can be easily handled by todays over-provisioned provider networks. Thus, from a provider's point of view ALM is an appealing alternative to IP multicast.

However, pushing multicast away from the network core towards the end systems also shifts the acceptance problem from the providers towards the users. To this end, users must experience a sufficient performance in order to utilize an ALM solution on a large scale. The user-perceived performance is determined by three major factors: First, the user must be able to join an ALM multicast group sufficiently fast, which is important, e. g., when zapping around between multiple TV channels. Second, he should experience only a minimum delay, which is important, e. g., for following a live broadcast or even more for interactive applications like attending a video conference. Third, the bandwidth consumed by the ALM protocol should be low, which is important, e. g., when using a computer for other things than following a multicast transmission. Furthermore, ALM must show the flexibility to be employed in different application scenarios, where two scenarios are of particular interest: The first is broadcasting popular events, which will on the one hand lead to multicast groups of significant size but on the other hand of high stability, since many people will follow the transmission for the entire duration. The second scenario is receiving a multicast transmission along the way, which will lead to fewer, but rather instable users. Examples for the second scenario include, again, zapping between TV stations.

In this paper, we present an in-depth evaluation study of the NICE application layer multicast protocol that significantly extends the results presented in [1,2,3]. In particular, we focus on the *user-perceived* performance of the protocol instead of the performance from the network perspective. The main work on NICE [1,2,3] focused on underlay behavior in terms of stretch and stress. Therewith, the authors have taken a network-view, whereas our work evaluates NICE from the end-user perspective. Similarly to the NICE studies, the work of Tang et al. focused on hop-counts in NICE using different extensions for underlay-awareness [11]. In terms of network dynamics the authors of NICE evaluated the behavior of NICE using a bulk-churn model [3]. Our work uses realistic—but aggressive—churn models to analyze NICE under real-world churn models. We base our churn models on recent work by Stutzbach et al. that analyzed churn-behavior of real-world P2P systems [10]. We do not cover extensions developed to explicitly provide robustness like [5], but rather analyze the robustness of the original NICE towards churn. In summary, we answer questions like: How long does it take until I can view a multicast transmission? What is the transmission delay I have to expect? How much traffic is generated on my dial-up link? How do other people constantly joining and leaving the system affect my transmission quality?

To answer these questions, we conduct experiments using the overlay simulation framework *OverSim* [4] that allows for large-scale simulations and use of different churn models.

Our main findings are: (1) increasing the number of nodes by a factor of 16 increases latencies by only 31%, (2) join delays get optimized over time, and (3) under a heavy churn configuration data success rates of 98.8% can be achieved. From these results, we conclude that NICE is well suited to provide user-perceived performance in large-scale and dynamic environments.

The remainder of this paper is structured as follows: To make the paper self-contained, we give a description of the NICE protocol in Section 2. We also state design decisions in our implementation concerning issues that are not clear in the original proposal [2]. In Section 3 we describe our simulation methodology that is used within the following Sections 4 and 5. In Section 4 we look at NICE's performance in scenarios with higher numbers of nodes. We evaluate the protocol's performance in face of churn in Section 5. Finally, concluding remarks are given in Section 6.

2　NICE

The NICE protocol [1,2,3] is an early ALM approach that implements an unstructured overlay (i. e. a node's position in the overlay is not fixed). It explicitly aims at scalability by establishing a cluster hierarchy among participating member nodes. We first give a general protocol description in Section 2.1 before detailing on specific implementational aspects in Section 2.2.

2.1　Basic Protocol

NICE divides all participating nodes into a set of clusters. In each cluster, a cluster-leader is determined that is responsible for maintenance and refinement in that cluster. Furthermore, all cluster-leaders themselves form a new set of logical clusters in a higher layer, exchanging protocol data. Respective cluster-leaders are determined from one layer for the next higher layer. This process is iteratively repeated until a single cluster-leader in the topmost cluster is left, resulting in a layered hierarchy of clusters (compare Figure 1). Protocol traffic is mainly exchanged between nodes residing in the same cluster, leading to good scalability.

Each cluster holds between k and $(\alpha k - 1)$ nodes, α and k being protocol parameters. In case the number of nodes in a cluster exceeds the upper bound the cluster is split into two clusters of equal size. If the lower bound is undercut, the cluster is merged with a nearby cluster. Clusters are formed on the basis of a 'distance' evaluation between nodes, where distance is basically given by network latency. Cluster-leader election is accomplished by determining the graph-theoretic center of the cluster and choosing the node closest to that point. Nodes in the same cluster periodically exchange heartbeat messages to indicate their liveliness and report measurements of mutual distance to other nodes in that cluster. Cluster-leaders decide on splitting and merging of clusters as they are aware of the current cluster size and all distances between nodes inside their cluster.

The objective of NICE is to scalably maintain the hierarchy as new nodes join and existing nodes depart. Therefore, the following invariants are maintained:

1. At every layer, nodes are partitioned into clusters of size between k and $(\alpha k - 1)$.
2. All nodes belong to a L_0 cluster and each node belongs only to one single cluster at any layer.
3. Cluster-leaders are the center of their respective cluster and form the immediate higher layer.

For bootstrapping, the joining node queries a *Rendezvous Point* (RP) for the set of nodes that reside in the highest cluster. The node then queries the nearest of these nodes for the set of the next lower layer, iteratively repeating this process until the lowest layer L_0 of the hierarchy is reached. As soon as this nearest cluster is determined, the node requests from the L_0 cluster's leader to join and finally becomes part of the cluster. Graceful or ungraceful leaving of nodes is either detected by explicit protocol messages or through missing heartbeat messages.

A node intending to send out multicast data sends its data to all nodes in all clusters it currently resides in. A node receiving data from inside its cluster forwards the packet to clusters it is part of except the cluster it received the data from. This leads to each participant implicitly employing a dissemination tree to all other nodes in the structure.

An exemplary NICE structure, consisting of three hierarchical layers (L_0–L_2) is shown in Figure 1. Here, Layer L_0 holds five clusters containing five member nodes each. The four phases (a) to (d) demonstrate the steps in data dissemination for a given initial sender. Members forwarding the data in each

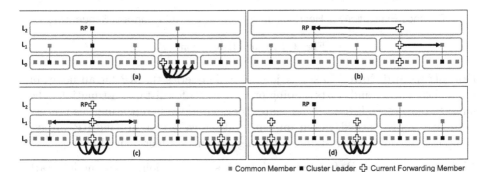

■ Common Member ■ Cluster Leader ✣ Current Forwarding Member

Fig. 1. Layered hierarchical NICE structure

step are symbolized by crosses. Also in this example, the cluster-leader of the highest cluster in the hierarchy constitutes the RP.

2.2 Design Decisions

We implemented NICE in the open-source overlay simulation framework Over-Sim [4] based on the technical descriptions given in [3]. We will now detail on relevant design decisions that are not specified by the protocol itself to ease the understanding of the evaluations given in this paper.

Heartbeats and Distance Evaluation. Heartbeat messages are sent to direct cluster neighbors participating in any cluster the sender resides in. The heartbeat interval HBI triggers periodic heartbeat messages. We use heartbeats for protocol information exchange and simultaneously for the evaluation of mutual distances between nodes (cf. Figure 2a). Distances in NICE are evaluated through round-trip time measurements between heartbeat-exchanging nodes. As those evaluations are prone to variance we use an exponentially weighted moving average to smooth distance measurements over time. Also, to avoid intersecting heartbeats that would tamper with measurements, we use dedicated heartbeat sequencing (cf. Figure 2b), helping to avoid error-prone distance evaluations when out-of-order packet receptions occur.

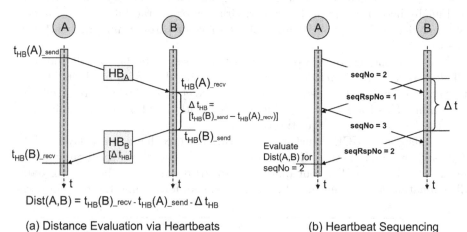

(a) Distance Evaluation via Heartbeats   (b) Heartbeat Sequencing

Fig. 2. Distance Evaluation

Bootstrap and Join Phase. A joining node queries the RP for all nodes of the highest cluster and starts sending probe packets for distance estimation. The joining node descends towards its nearest node, iteratively repeating this process until layer L_0 is reached. In our implementation, we use an in-band RP, always being the cluster-leader residing in the highest current hierarchy cluster.

Maintenance and Refinement. After a successful join phase nodes start maintaining the overlay structure with respect to their point of view. This is realized by periodic heartbeats to all cluster neighbors to validate liveliness and ensure protocol invariants (cf. Section 2.1).

Heartbeat messages are used for propagation of distance measurements. This way nodes are able to make decisions autonomously. A node being cluster-leader in cluster C_i in layer L_i emits a special leader-heartbeat in this cluster, holding contents of a normal heartbeat as well as information about members in the direct super-cluster C_{i+1} in layer L_{i+1}. This information is used by neighbors in C_i to find better cluster-leaders in C_{i+1}. A node in the super-cluster is considered better if the distance to this node is at least min_SC_Dist percent smaller than towards the current cluster-leader (min_SC_Dist being a protocol parameter). Should a closer cluster-leader B in C_{i+1} be found for a querying node A, the latter will change its cluster membership to the cluster in layer L_i that B is leader of. Furthermore, neighbors in C_i use the neighbor information in the leader-heartbeat to update their view of the current cluster memberships, i.e. they add new nodes or delete nodes that are no longer part of the cluster.

If a cluster-leader detects a violation of the cluster size upper bound it determines the resulting two new clusters as follows: Let C_i be the cluster to split, C_j, C_k the resulting sub-clusters. For all possible combinations $\{C_j, C_k | C_j \subseteq C_i \backslash C_k \land C_k \subseteq C_i \backslash C_j\}$ determine the particular resulting cluster-leader and check the maximum distance from each such leader inside the respective cluster. The number of combinations is bounded by the clustersize parameter k. If C_i holds n nodes, $n \leq (\alpha k)$, this leads to $\frac{n!}{2(\frac{n}{2}!)^2}$ combinations to test. As soon as an appropriate cluster-split-set has been determined, the cluster-leader signals the change throughout the specific cluster and all involved higher-layer clusters.

Should a cluster hold less than k nodes, it will be merged with one of its neighboring clusters on the same layer. The leader of the specific cluster C_i in layer L_i is also part of cluster C_{i+1} in layer L_{i+1}, knowing its distances to the nodes residing in the latter. With this information, the leader is able to determine the nearest node of cluster C_{i+1}, being the candidate to merge cluster C_i with, and initiate the merge operation.

As part of the periodic refinement process, cluster nodes decide if the current cluster-leader remains optimal. This is accomplished by finding the node with the smallest maximum distance to all other members in this cluster, based on each nodes local distance knowledge. To avoid fluctuations we use a lower bound min_CL_Dist which has to be exceeded in order to trigger a cluster-leader change.

Protocol Recovery. Changes in the network or the NICE hierarchy can lead to temporary soft-state inconsistencies between nodes. In case of severe hierarchy inconsistencies like partitioning or failure, nodes can decide to reconnect to the structure. It can further occur that more than one cluster-leader becomes responsible for one node. This can happen due to temporary duplicate leaderships in clusters, packet loss during leader transfer, or other inaccurate negotiation procedures. In our implementation duplicate leaderships are detected by heartbeat messages. If a node A after reception of heartbeat H_1 at time t_1 from leader B receives a heartbeat H_2 from leader C at time t_2 with $t_2 - t_1 <$ HBI it checks if the predecessing heartbeat before H_1 was sent from leader B. This will with high probability indicate a child relationship to both B and C. Node A will then resolve the situation with a proactive cluster leave sent to leader C.

In addition to nodes detecting duplicate leaders, cluster-leaders also have to be able to detect mutual duplicate leaderships inside a cluster. Duplicate cluster-leaderships appear if one node decides to be new cluster-leader while the old leader did not take this decision—or in some cases never will due to different distance knowledge. Such situations are detected if a cluster-leader receives a leader-heartbeat message in the same cluster he is leader of.

3   Evaluation Methodology

In this Section, we detail on the simulation environment and the setup of our simulations. Furthermore, we discuss relevant performance measures that are used in the remainder of this paper.

3.1   Simulation Environment

Our experiments are conducted using the peer-to-peer simulation framework *OverSim* [4]. OverSim provides a flexible environment for simulation of structured and unstructured overlay networks with focus on scalability of the simulation models with respect to the number of simulated nodes as well as re-use of modules implementing overlay functionality. The core part of OverSim comprises various network models, that each model the underlying network with a different level of detail, and thus, complexity of the simulation model and simulation runtime. The network model of our choice is OverSim's *Simple Underlay* that is frequently employed for performance evaluation from the end-system perspective. This network model abstracts from network and transport mechanisms and arranges nodes in Euclidean space. The Euclidean distance of two nodes determines the basic network latency between them. A random jitter between 0%–5% is added to this latency for each packet transmission. Note that this network model does not capture packet losses, i. e., every packet that is sent t is received by the destination. This behavior is consistent with the behavior in other ALM simulation studies, e. g. [2]. We provide details on the setup of our OverSim simulations in the next section.

3.2   Simulation Setup

We have implemented the NICE protocol as described in Section 2 as an OverSim application that is executed by OverSim's simulation models. In our simulations we analyze up to 8 000 NICE nodes, where the number of nodes differs with the experiments. Nodes are arranged randomly in a two dimensional field of size [150,150], i. e., the maximum delay experienced for a transmission between two nodes is $\approx 212\,ms$ with addition of the random jitter. Based on the parameter terms introduced in Section 2.2 we use the protocol parameter values given in

Table 1 (unless stated different in the specific experiments). Furthermore, we use a simulation setup that is given by the simulation parameters also shown in Table 1.

Our simulation experiment can be subdivided into two phases. In the *initial phase* after the start of the simulation, the NICE hierarchy is incrementally constructed. That is, one new node joins the network every second, until the anticipated number of nodes is reached. We choose this approach to avoid difficult effects that could appear in the initial phase and that are not subject to our evaluations. After the last node has joined we employ a backoff time of 60 seconds to stabilize the hierarchy. The initial phase is followed by the *data exchange phase*. In this phase, a given node, fixed but chosen uniformly at random from the set of all nodes, sends a multicast packet every 5 seconds for evaluation of scalability in Section 4, and every 1 seconds for evaluation of churn in Section 5. Note that although the resulting data rate is very low, this is sufficient to compute the performance measures of interest as described in Section 3.4. After 10 minutes of data exchange, we again employ a backoff of 60 seconds before finishing the simulation run.

Note that depending on the considered application scenario nodes may be either stable during the data exchange phase or join/leave the NICE hierarchy at arbitrary times due to churn. Since we consider both types of application scenarios, we describe our model of dynamic node behavior in the next section.

Table 1. Protocol and simulation parameters

NICE-specific		Simulation-specific	
Parameter	Value	Parameter	Value
α, k	3	Number of nodes	500–8 000
HBI	$\{1,5,10\}$ s	Offset after last join	60 s
Maintenance Interval	3.3 s	Measurement phase	300 s
Peer Timeout	2 HBI	Joins	∼every 1 s
Query Timeout	2 s	Data Interval	1 s (churn), 5 s (scalability)
Structure Timeout	3 HBI	Field Size	[150,150]
min_CL_Dist	30%	Simulation Time	2 000 s
min_SC_Dist	30%		

3.3 Churn Model

Churn is the process of nodes joining and leaving the overlay structure. As joins and leaves trigger adaptation and therewith restructuring of the overlay, they can cause packet loss due to inconsistencies, or partitioning. Resilience to churn is conventionally achieved through redundant links in the overlay structure, resulting in higher cost [8]. Furthermore, dedicated mechanisms for overlay robustness have been developed to cope with high churn [9].

To study the performance of NICE under heavy churn we have to define appropriate churn models for our simulations. Several churn models have been described in the literature, which use either Poisson, Random, Exponential, or

Weibull distributions to model a node's session length, i. e., its dwell time in the hierarchy. A recent study of Stutzbach et al. [10] analyzed different real-world networks (Gnutella, Kad, BitTorrent) and identified that (1) session length distribution is quite similar over different networks, and (2) that the session length distributed is best modeled through a Weibull distribution. Prior work on NICE evaluated the protocol under bulk churn where groups of nodes collectively join and leave the overlay simultaneously [2]. Opposed to [2], we use individual churn following the Weibull distribution in our simulations according to the Weibull PDF defined as follows:

$$f(x; \lambda, \mu) = \begin{cases} \frac{\mu}{\lambda} \left(\frac{x}{\lambda}\right)^{\mu-1} e^{-(x/\lambda)^\mu} & x \geq 0 \\ 0 & x < 0 \end{cases} \tag{1}$$

We use shape parameter $\mu = 0.5$, as a compromise of shape values identified in the work of Stutzbach. As the scale parameter λ varies greatly depending on the observed system, we perform simulations with different λ values to achieve different mean lifetimes of the nodes, i. e., different degrees of churn. All parameter values of the churn model together with the corresponding mean (in minutes and seconds) and variance of the session length are shown in Table 2. As our goal is to find the limits of robustness for NICE, our scaling values result in much smaller mean lifetimes than the values presented by Stutzbach et al., which are also shown in the table.

For churn simulations we use a mean of 128 nodes and single-source multicast. The simulation time is 3 600 s, subdivided as follows: Again, we have an initial phase where 128 are created in the first 128 s, one node per second. We start the churn model together with the data transmission face at simulation time 200 s and end it at simulation time 3 540 s. The source node of the transmission is selected as described above and is not subject to churn. Finally, the simulation ends at 3600 s. We evaluate different churn rates as detailed in Table 2. Finally we perform one simulation with no churn as reference model.

3.4   Performance Measures

In our simulations, we consider four measures to capture user-perceived performance of the ALM protocol:

Join Delay: This is the delay for integrating a new node into the NICE hierarchy. Since it is the time a user has to wait until he can receive a multicast

Table 2. Weibull parameters and properties used for churn simulation in our work and real-world observations from Stutzbach et al.

								Our Work		Stutzbach et al.		
μ		0.50								0.34	0.38	0.59
λ	0.83	2.50	5.00	7.50	10.00	12.5	15			21.30	42.40	41.90
mean [minutes]	1.66	5	10	15	20	25	30			117.25	163.38	64.46
mean [seconds]	100	300	600	900	1 200	1 500	1 800			7 035	9 802	3 867
variance [minutes]	14	125	500	1 125	2 000	3 125	4 500			241 986	313 390	13 395

transmission, we consider this measure of particular interest from the user's perspective. For a given node, we measure this delay by the time between contacting the rendezvous point and finally integrating the node in a cluster at layer L_0 following the procedure described in Section 2.

Data and Heartbeat Latency: Data latency is the time required to transmit a data packet from the multicast source to a given destination node. This latency is of particular interest for users following a real-time transmission. It can be measured by setting timestamps when sending and receiving a multicast packet, respectively. Furthermore, the *hopcount*, i. e., the number of hops in the NICE hierarchy that must be traversed to deliver a multicast packet, can be computed using a field in the packet header. We will show that data latency depends to some extent on the latency for transmissions inside a cluster. Thus, we will also measure heartbeat latency, which is the delay experienced by heartbeat messages as described in Section 2.2.

Overhead: Maintaining the NICE hierarchy comes at a cost, which is quantified by the overhead for sending control messages. Overhead is relevant from the user's perspective since it must be transmitted over the user's access link. We measure the overhead for a given node by summing up the sizes of all control messages it generates according to the protocol description in Section 2. We assume addresses to be 32 bit and that e. g. heartbeat messages hold all known cluster members together with their related distance evaluations, each stored also in a 32 bit value.

Successfully Delivered Packets: Although OverSim's simple underlay does not consider packet losses, a multicast data packets may be lost due to structural problems in the NICE hierarchy, in particular under heavy churn. Since data packet losses directly affect the transmission quality, we consider them of particular interest from the user's perspective. To compute the fraction of successfully delivered packets is non trivial, since it is not clear how to count a node that is part of the hierarchy when a data packet is send by the source, but leaves the hierarchy before the packet is able to reach it. Thus, we measure successfully delivered packets only for those nodes that are a part of the hierarchy when a packet is sent and do not leave the hierarchy until transmission of the next packet.

In the following sections, we use the performance measures defined here to evaluate the performance of the NICE protocol.

4   Protocol Scalability

This section analyzes user-perceived performance of the NICE protocol from a scalability perspective. Consistent with [2], it focuses on the performance during initial construction and during stable operation of the multicast structure, while the performance under churn is considered in Section 5. Opposed to [2], we analyze large scenarios (i. e., up to 8000 nodes) and focus on user-perceived rather then network-centric performance.

In a first experiment, we analyze the join delay as defined in Section 3.4. We plot join delay as a function of time in Figure 3 for different sizes N of the multicast group. Recall that in the experiment one node per second joins the hierarchy. In the figure, one line is drawn for each node's join delay. Join delay depends on the number of layers in the hierarchy, since a node starts to join at the rendezvous point in the highest layer L_k and descends through the hierarchy. In order to relate join delay and hierarchy depth, the figure also depicts the current number of layers in the structure.

The figure shows that for $N < 1500$ the resulting hierarchy has four layers, while it has five layers for larger group sizes. Indeed, we find that the join latency—as expected—depends on the current number of layers with the most significant increase when raising the hierarchy depth from four to five layers. As an interesting fact, the figure indicates that for a hierarchy with Layers $L_0, \ldots, L_k$ the join delay is highest directly after Layer L_k has been established. Afterwards, it decreases constantly until Layer L_{k+1} is added to the hierarchy. This is due to the fact that a new established layer leads to few nodes in the higher layer clusters, as illustrated in Figure 4. This figure plots the mean number of nodes in clusters of each layer computed once a second. The figure shows that the cluster size in the lower layers stays quite constant over time. In contrast higher layer clusters are incrementally filled with nodes, confirming the claim made above. For understanding the decrease in join latency depicted in Figure 3, recall that a node must perform a distance estimation for one cluster on each layer $L_k, \ldots L_1$ until it reaches the lowest layer L_0. That means basically waiting for a response by the cluster member that is closest in each cluster with respect to latency. Since fewer nodes within a cluster reduces the probability for having a nearby node—as we will illustrate later—this increases join delay due to an higher delay for distance probing in the higher layers. However, the join delays are significantly below two seconds with an average of 0.51 seconds. We conclude from Figures 3 and 4 that even for large multicast groups NICE provides a reasonable join delay for the users.

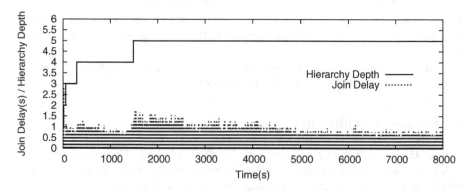

Fig. 3. Per-node delays for hierarchy joins and hierarchy depth, 8000 Nodes

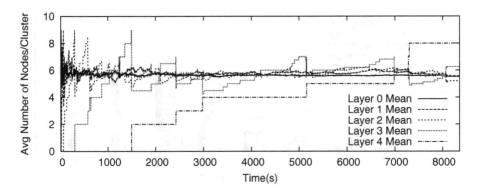

Fig. 4. Average Cluster Sizes per Layer, 8000 Nodes

In the next experiment, we focus on data latency as defined in Section 3.4. We will restrict us to the latency achieved when the structure has stabilized, as results for a structure with nodes entering and leaving are be shown in Section 5. Figure 5 plots the cumulative distribution function (CDF) of the data latency. One would expect data latency to increase with an increasing size N of the multicast group. However, we find that it is quite stable regardless of group size, e. g. a growth in number of nodes from 500 to 8 000 increases mean latencies by 31% from 173.6 ms to 228 ms. To gain deeper insight into this behavior, we plot the CDF of one hop heartbeat latency measured inside each cluster as well as the hopcount distribution for multicast packets in Figures 6 and 7, respectively. Confirming our claim made earlier, Figure 6 indicates that intra cluster latency decreases significantly with an increasing number of nodes, since the probability for clustering nearby nodes increases. Thus, every hop a data packet must traverse for delivery takes less time. This fact compensates the moderate increase in path length that results from increasing the depth of the hierarchy, which is illustrated in Figure 7. We conclude from Figures 6 and 7 that NICE is highly scalable with respect to data latency.

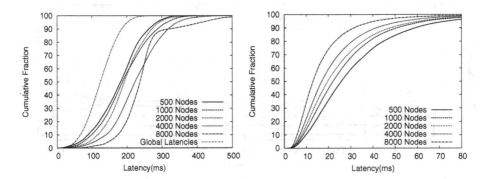

Fig. 5. Latencies for data dissemination   **Fig. 6.** Intra-cluster Latencies

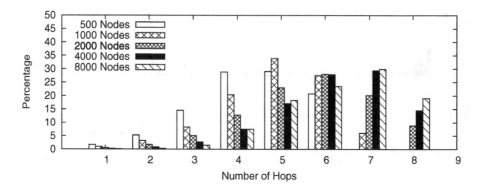

Fig. 7. Distribution of hopcount for delivering multicast packets

The last performance measure we consider is the overhead as defined in Section 3.4. We plot overhead as a function of time in Figure 8. Since control overhead may depend on the position of a node in the cluster hierarchy, we subdivide the overhead by the layers. That is, we plot mean overhead for all nodes that have the highest layer cluster membership on the same layer. The traffic is both aggregated by 1 s and 10 s respectively. As expected, the figure shows that the overhead for nodes in the highest layer cluster and especially for the rendezvous point is significantly higher that for nodes that are only members of lower layer clusters, since heartbeat messages etc. must be send for each cluster. As soon as the depth of the hierarchy is increased from k to $k + 1$, the traffic for the nodes that are member of cluster k but not of cluster $k + 1$ stabilizes. The fact that each additional cluster membership adds a constant overhead for cluster maintenance leads to a linear grow in mean overheads with the number of clusters. For the considered protocol configuration, each additional cluster membership increases overhead by about 1–3 kbit/s. Given a logarithmic growth of hierarchy depth, we conclude from Figure 8 that NICE is scalable with respect to control overhead. Nevertheless, more powerful nodes with high bandwidth connections

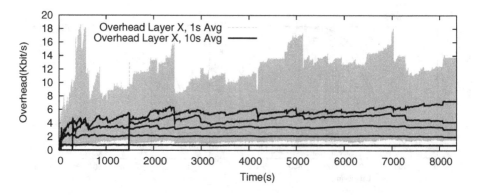

Fig. 8. Average control overhead per node, 8000 nodes

seem more suited for membership in higher layer clusters, leading to the conclusion that the choice of cluster leaders should not only be determined by average latency. While we focus on user-perceived results in this paper, the experiments also pose questions concerning reciprocal effects between the cluster parameters. We are currently investigation issues like efficient parameter selection in specific scenarios in the context of another work.

The experiments shown in this section indicate that the NICE protocol from a user's perspective performs well even for large but stable groups. However, depending on the application scenario, coping with large group sizes might be less important than providing stability of the multicast structure under high node churn. We will enlighten this aspect in the next section.

5   Churn

In this section, we evaluate the user-perceived performance of the NICE protocol under the realistic churn model introduced in Section 3.3. Recall that as our goal is to find the limits of robustness for NICE, our scaling values result in much smaller mean lifetimes than the values presented by Stutzbach. Furthermore, a mean number of 128 nodes is considered in this scenario, being rather instable as a result of churn. We believe this node number is sufficient to get an impression of NICE's abilities to handle fluctuations during multicast transmissions.

In a first experiment, we analyze the impact of churn on the structure of the NICE hierarchy. Similar to Figure 3, we plot both the join delay and the hierarchy depth as a function of time in Figure 9. The figure additionally shows the number of group members. We find that during the data transmission phase the hierarchy depth may alternate between two and three layers due to churn. However, adding or removing layers does only delay the join operation of a few nodes. In fact, the join delay of most nodes is with an average of 470 ms almost unaffected by churn. In an experiment not shown here due to space limitations we find that data latency is not affected by churn, too, although multicast packets may be lost as we show below. We conclude from Figure 9 that NICE performs well under churn from the perspective of user-perceived latencies.

Since packet loss certainly affects user-perceived performance, we analyze the fraction of successfully delivered multicast packets as defined in Section 3.4 in a last experiment. Using variations in heartbeat intervals (HBI) defined in Section 2 and using the churn rates given in Section 3.3 we evaluate the packet loss ratio to find the robustness limits of the NICE structure. Figure 10 plots the probability for successful delivery of a multicast packet as a function of mean node lifetime together with the involved standard deviations. We alternate the heartbeat-interval HBI between values 1s, 5s, and 10s. Note that without churn (not shown in the figure), NICE delivers close almost 100% of the multicast packets successfully, since the NICE hierarchy is stable and packet losses on lower layers are not considered by the underlay model. However, even under moderate churn, a value of HBI larger than 1s implies significant packet loss, such that 10% and more of the packets are not delivered. Only an aggressive HBI value

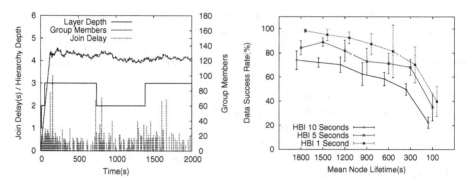

Fig. 9. Structure under churn   **Fig. 10.** Packet success rate under churn

of 1s can compensate the churn up to a certain extend. Nevertheless, for node lifetimes smaller that 900s even such aggressive parametrization of NICE fails to successfully deliver more than 90% of the packets. We conclude from Figure 10 that high churn either requires aggressive efforts to maintain the NICE hierarchy or some resilience mechanisms as introduced, e. g.in [5].

6 Conclusions

In this work we evaluated the NICE application layer multicast protocol from a user perspective. Our focus is on scalability—using large groups of up to 8 000 nodes—and the behavior under churn—using aggressive versions of realistic churn-models. By extensive simulations we achieve the following insights: (1) increasing the number of nodes by a factor of 16 increases latencies by only 31% in the considered scenario, (2) join delays get optimized over time, and (3) under a heavy churn configuration data success rates of 98.8% can be achieved. Despite not being designed for high churn, NICE can cope with such situations by using smaller heartbeat intervals. Furthermore, NICE also achieves good scalability for large groups.

References

1. Banerjee, S., Bhattacharjee, B.: Analysis of the NICE Application Layer Multicast Protocol. Technical Report UMIACS TR 2002-60 and CS-TR 4380, Department of Computer Science, University of Maryland, College Park, MD 20742, USA (June 2002)
2. Banerjee, S., Bhattacharjee, B., Kommareddy, C.: Scalable Application Layer Multicast. In: Proceedings of SIGCOMM, Pittsburgh, Pennsylvania, USA, August 2002, pp. 205–217 (2002)
3. Banerjee, S., Bhattacharjee, B., Kommareddy, C.: Scalable Application Layer Multicast. Technical Report UMIACS TR-2002-53 and CS-TR 4373, Department of Computer Science, University of Maryland, College Park, MD, USA (2002)

4. Baumgart, I., Heep, B., Krause, S.: OverSim: A Flexible Overlay Network Simulation Framework. In: Proceedings of 10th IEEE Global Internet Symposium (GI 2007) in conjunction with IEEE INFOCOM, Anchorage, Alaska, USA, May 2007, pp. 79–84 (2007)
5. Birrer, S., Bustamante, F.E.: Resilience in Overlay Multicast Protocols. In: Proceedings of the IEEE Symposium on Modeling, Analysis, and Simulation of Computer and Telecommunication Systems, Monterey, California, USA, September 2006, pp. 363–372 (2006)
6. Chu, Y., Rao, S., Zhang, H.: A Case For End System Multicast. In: Proceedings of ACM SIGMETRICS, Santa Clara, CA, USA, June 2000, pp. 1–12 (2000)
7. Diot, C., Levine, B.N., Lyles, B., Kassem, H., Balensiefen, D.: Deployment Issues for the IP Multicast Service and Architecture. IEEE Network Magazine Special Issue on Multicasting 14(1), 78–88 (2000)
8. Li, J., Stribling, J., Morris, R., Kaashoek, M.F., Gil, T.M.: A Performance vs. Cost Framework for Evaluating DHT Design Tradeoffs under Churn. In: Proceedings of INFOCOM, Miami, Florida, USA, March 2005, pp. 225–236 (2005)
9. Rhea, S., Geels, D., Roscoe, T., Kubiatowicz, J.: Handling Churn in a DHT. In: Proceedings of the USENIX, Boston, MA, USA, June 2004, pp. 1–14 (2004)
10. Stutzbach, D., Rejaie, R.: Understanding Churn in Peer-to-peer Networks. In: Proceedings of Conference on Internet Measurement, Rio de Janeiro, Brazil, October 2006, pp. 189–202 (2006)
11. Tang, H., Janic, M., Zhou, X.: Hopcount in the NICE Application Layer Multicast Protocol. In: IEEE/SMC Multiconference on Computational Engineering in Systems Applications, Beijing, China, October 2006, pp. 1020–1026 (2006)

Effectiveness of Link Cost Optimization for IP Rerouting and IP Fast Reroute*

David Hock, Matthias Hartmann, Christian Schwartz, and Michael Menth

University of Würzburg, Institute of Computer Science
Am Hubland, D-97074 Würzburg, Germany

Abstract. In this paper, we bring together resilience analysis and routing optimization for IP-based intra-domain networks. When link, node, or multiple failures occur, traffic is rerouted which increases the link load on backup paths and possibly causes congestion. Resilience analysis detects the risk of overload situations a priori based on a large set of most likely failure scenarios. To counteract, the routing can be optimized and configured that such bottlenecks are avoided at least for a smaller set of failure scenarios. In this paper, we demonstrate the effectiveness of this routing optimization in IP networks. We use resilience analysis with suitable aggregate views on relative link loads. Furthermore, we compare conventional IP rerouting with IP fast reroute (IP-FRR) and show that IP-FRR can also significantly profit from routing optimization. This paper reviews major parts of previous publications and presents a new method to visualize and compare the resilience of different routing schemes.

1   Introduction

Outages in communication networks like link and node failures are a matter of fact and cannot be avoided. However, the network can be prepared for such conditions by using self-healing routing mechanisms. When elements on the primary path fail, traffic is rerouted to a backup path. This mechanism alone just assures the connectivity of the network provided that such a backup path exists and can be activated by the protection mechanism. There is another aspect: capacity. Rerouted traffic causes increased load on backup paths so that overload and traffic loss possibly occur. This can be avoided by carefully choosing the layout of primary and backup paths.

In this work, we bring together three issues that have recently attracted attention in the area of fault-tolerant networking. Resilience analysis is an efficient means to quantify the risk of overload in networks due to failures. Optimization of resilient IP routing improves the load conditions in IP networks at least for a small set of likely failure scenarios. Recently developed IP fast reroute (IP-FRR) mechanisms quickly switch traffic to preconfigured backup paths instead of running into transient forwarding loops during the IP rerouting process. We use resilience analysis to demonstrate the effectiveness of routing optimization in IP networks. We compare the likelihood of overload for unoptimized conventional IP rerouting and for IP-FRR. Finally, we illustrate the impact of routing optimization also for IP-FRR.

* This work is funded by Deutsche Forschungsgemeinschaft (DFG) under grant TR257/23-2. The authors alone are responsible for the content of the paper.

B. Müller-Clostermann et al. (Eds.): MMB & DFT 2010, LNCS 5987, pp. 78–90, 2010.

The remainder of this work is structured as follows. In Section 2 we explain the fundamentals of IP routing and introduce IP fast reroute. In Section 3, we give an overview of resilience analysis and link cost optimization. In Section 4 we study the effectiveness of routing optimization for IP rerouting and IP fast reroute. Section 5 concludes this work.

2   Fundamentals of IP Routing

We explain IP routing which follows the principle of least-cost (shortest) paths. We show how ambiguities arising from several least-cost paths can be handled. Finally, we review mechanisms for IP-FRR.

2.1   Conventional IP Routing and Reconvergence

In intra-domain IP networks, routers exchange information about the topology and administrative link costs with each other. Based on these routing messages, each node obtains a full view of the link topology including administrative link costs. It uses this information to set up the routing table whereby it associates any destination in the network with the interface leading towards a least-cost path to the destination. Thus, the routing table helps to look up onto which outgoing interface packets destined to a certain node in the network should be forwarded.

In case of a modification of the topology, e.g., due to a link or router failure, a reconvergence process is invoked. The change is broadcast through the entire local network and routers recalculate the outgoing interface mapping in their routing tables based on the new topology. As long as the network is physically connected, IP routing finds new routes for all source-destination pairs. This makes it very robust against network failures.

2.2   Handling Ambiguities Due to Several Least-Cost Paths

Depending on the link cost settings, possibly several least-cost paths exist between pairs of nodes in a network. In that case the routing is undefined at first step. However, routers use tie-breakers to decide which of the paths to prefer for routing. E.g., the interface towards a least-cost path with the smallest port number may be chosen [1, Sect. 7.2.7]. However, port numbers within routers are not necessarily predictable. Therefore, it is hard or even impossible to predict the route in case of several least-cost paths a priori. In previous work [2], we quantified that optimized routing can lead to significantly larger relative link loads than expected if traffic is forwarded on other least-cost paths than assumed. Hence, predictable load distribution is important for routing optimization, network planning, and traffic engineering in general.

One solution to that problem is equal-cost multipath (ECMP) routing. It splits the traffic equally among all interfaces towards a least-cost path. As packet-by-packet load balancing possibly causes packet reordering, load-balancing is done on the flow level. To that end, hash-based load balancing is used, i.e., typical data of a flow like source and destination IP and port numbers are hashed to some value based on which the packet is forwarded to one of the potential interfaces.

Finally, it is possible to chose link costs such that several least-cost paths do not exist. In [2] we implemented that objective as part of IP routing optimization and showed that so-called unique shortest paths (USP) can be efficiently obtained.

2.3 IP Fast Reroute (IP-FRR)

The reconvergence process in IP networks can take up to several minutes. During this time, forwarding loops can appear when some of the routers have updated their routing tables earlier than others. As a consequence, the affected traffic cannot be delivered to its destination, looping the traffic causes high load on the respective links which causes additional overload. To avoid this phenomenon, IP-FRR has been proposed. Routers detecting a failure immediately switch the affected traffic to preestablished backup paths that are likely to be unaffected by the observed failure. There are multiple proposals for the implementation of IP-FRR [3].

With Loop-Free Alternates (LFAs) [4], routers store alternative next-hops in their routing tables which are used when the primary next-hop fails. However, it is not always possible to find neighbor hops that do not loop back the traffic or create routing loops when more than a single link has failed. Therefore, LFAs cannot always provide 100% failure coverage.

A promising alternative are not-via addresses which are currently being standardized in the IETF [5,6]. For any node N there is a not-via address N_F and packets addressed to N_F are forwarded to N while node F is avoided on the path. Hence, the routing tables in the network require additional entries for these not-via addresses. They are used for IP-FRR as follows. We assume that a node A receives a packet that is normally forwarded over F and the next-next-hop N to its destination, but the next-hop F has failed. Then the node A encapsulates this packet towards the not-via address N_F to tunnel it to N. N decapsulates the packet and forwards it to the destination. If the next-hop F is already the destination, the packet can be delivered if only the link from A to F is down but not F itself. Then, A encapsulates the packet to F_A and forwards it to some of its neighbor nodes so that the packet is carried towards F avoiding the link from A to F. Hence, the not-via mechanism leads the traffic on the shortest path according to administrative link costs around the next-hop to the next-next-hop or around the next-link to the next-hop if the next-hop is the destination node. If due to an additional network failure, traffic encapsulated with a not-via address is tunneled again, this can lead to traffic loops in the network. To avoid this problem, already not-via encapsulated traffic must not be tunneled to not-via addresses again but be dropped instead. In [2], we have argued that IP-FRR needs USP to create a predictable backup path layout. We have also shown that such IP link costs can be efficiently found while optimizing the path layout for IP-FRR.

3 Resilience Analysis and IP Link Cost Optimization

In the following, we review resilience analysis and IP link cost optimization.

3.1 Resilience Analysis

Link and router failures may lead to disconnection of nodes within a network and to rerouted traffic causing increased load on backup paths. The resilience analysis in [7] quantifies the disconnection probability of nodes due to failures and the potential overload caused by backup traffic or abnormal traffic demands.

The resilience analysis requires the network topology, the routing and rerouting model, the link capacities, an availability model for network elements indicating failure probabilities as well as a model of the traffic matrix indicating the probability and the structure of abnormal traffic demands. We define networking scenarios $z = (s, h)$ consisting of a failure scenario s and a traffic matrix h. Failure scenarios and traffic matrices are associated with probabilities $p(s)$ and $p(h)$. We assume independence so that the probability of a networking scenario can be calculated by $p(z) = p(s) \cdot p(h)$. The idea of the analysis is to investigate the disconnection of nodes and relative link loads for individual networking scenarios z and these results contribute with a probability weight of $p(z)$ to the final result. Due to computational limitations, it is not possible to consider all possible failure scenarios and traffic matrices. Therefore, the analysis considers only networking scenarios with a probability of at least p_{min} and this set is denoted by $\mathcal{Z}$. The final results of the analysis are probabilities for the disconnection of a given node pair due to failures and complementary cumulative distribution functions (CCDFs) of the relative load for each link in the network. Both the disconnection probabilities and the CCDF of the relative link load values are conditional in the sense that they refer only to the set of investigated scenarios $\mathcal{Z}$, but upper and lower bounds on the true value are given. In the following we omit this aspect for the sake of simplicity. In this paper, we consider only network element failures as source for increased traffic on links and use only a single standard matrix without anomalies.

Several aggregated views have been developed in [7] to visualize unavailability. CCDFs of relative link loads are displayed per link. However, it is desirable to have a visualization of potential overload in the entire network at a glance. To that end, the information of the CCDF of the relative link loads can be condensed into a single overload value by various mapping functions. These values can be used to color links in a topological representation of the network.

There are several possible applications of resilience analysis. Using this technique, operators can, e.g., check if the network's current state is sufficient to allow additional clients, to sell better Service Level Agreements, or to deal with the traffic increase arising in the next few months. If this is not the case, the resilience analysis can help to decide where to add new links or routers. Furthermore, resilience analysis can be used to study the influence of a new routing or to investigate the effectiveness of routing optimization on potential overload. The latter application is the one addressed in this publication.

Further details to our framework for resilience analysis together with an overview on related work in this area including examples of resilience analysis, can be found in our previous publication [7]. Our framework has been implemented as a software tool. It is presented in [8].

3.2 IP Link Cost Optimization

IP routing follows the least-cost paths according to administrative link costs. Traffic engineering is possible by appropriately choosing those link costs that lead to a good load distribution on the links. An objective function defines what is understood by a good load distribution and is later discussed in more detail. Searching for good IP link costs can be automated which is called link cost optimization, sometimes also referred to as link weight optimization.

The input are a network topology, link capacities, a traffic matrix, and a given set of so-called protected failure scenarios S for which the routing should be optimized. The output of the process are administrative costs for all links in the network. The set S usually comprises all single link and/or node failures (S_L, S_R, S_{RL}). The failure-free state $s = \emptyset$ is always part of this set. For computational reasons, the set of protected failure scenarios S is usually smaller than the set of considered networking scenarios Z that is used as a base for resilience analysis.

Finding optimum IP link costs for a given objective function is usually an NP-hard problem even when only considering the failure-free case $S_\emptyset$. Therefore, heuristic algorithms are used to search good link costs. An overview of related work including different objective functions and heuristic approaches can be found in [2,9]. The heuristic we apply for this work is described in [9,10]. It is similar to the threshold accepting heuristic proposed in [11]. We perform multiple optimization runs with our heuristic and take the result of the best run as final result.

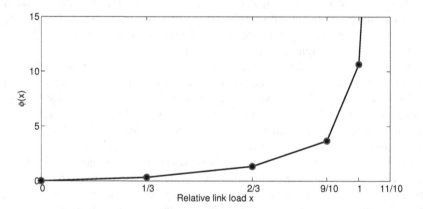

Fig. 1. Fortz's utilization-dependent penalty function ϕ

In [9] we have studied different objective functions for resilient and non-resilient IP routing which can be used for different application scenarios. Two of them are explained in more detail here. Both take the relative link load as a parameter. The relative load $\rho(l)$ of a link l is calculated as the quotient of the total traffic on a link and the link's capacity. To illustrate the severeness of possible overload, relative link loads larger than 100% are allowed in the computation.

- U_S^{max} is the maximum relative link load of all links in all protected failure scenarios S. It is a good choice, if routing optimization is used to guarantee that certain constraints on the relative link load are kept.
- $F_S^{weighted}$ sums up penalties over all links and all protected failure scenarios whereby these penalties increase with increasing relative link load. The penalties are calculated with Fortz's continuous, piecewise linear, monotonically increasing penalty function ϕ [12], which is illustrated in Figure 1. The objective function

$F_S^{weighted}$ is good if the main focus of the optimization lies on the overall link loads and the average path lengths.

Different objective functions lead to significantly different optimization results. To visualize that, we consider routing based on the hop-count metric and optimized routing based on objective function U_S^{max} and $F_S^{weighted}$ whereby S comprises all single link failures.

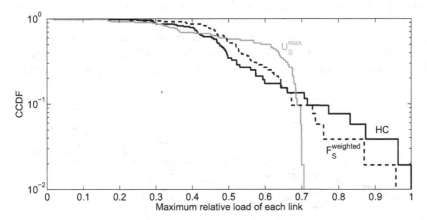

Fig. 2. CCDF of the maximum relative link load over all single link failure scenarios (COST239 network)

Figure 2 shows the maximum relative link load of all links in the COST239 network [9] in all protected failure scenarios S_L. The x-axis indicates the relative link load and the y-axis the fraction of links whose maximum relative link load exceeds the value on the x-axis. Hop-count (HC) routing leads to the highest relative link loads, optimized routing based on U_S^{max} leads to the lowest maximum relative link loads. Objective function $F_S^{weighted}$ achieves a compromise. The drawback of U_S^{max} is that it cannot improve the second-worst link when the worst link cannot be improved further. Therefore, we proposed in [9] to combine both objective functions, i.e., we first minimize U_S^{max} and then $F_S^{weighted}$. This leads to the lowest maximum relative link loads and reduces also the load on other highly loaded links. This is the objective function we use also in this study. Additional constraints can be used, e.g., in [2], we accepted only link cost settings where several least-cost paths are avoided. This is a valuable feature for traffic engineering when ECMP is not used or also for IP-FRR based on not-via addresses. The optimization of IP-FRR has been developed in that work, too.

4 Results

In the following, we study the effectiveness of routing optimization for IP routing and IP-FRR. Therefore, we first analyze unoptimized hop-count routing and then compare it to optimized USP routing. We show that even the link cost optimization with a small set of protected failure scenarios $\mathcal{S}_L$ leads to routings that significantly improve the overall resilience of the network. In a second step, we investigate the difference between unoptimized and optimized routing using not-via IP-FRR techniques.

4.1   Networks under Study

We have run our experiments for different networks including the Rocketfuel topologies [13]. All topologies yield similar results. Here, we show only the results of the Exodus network. The geographical topology of this network is depicted in Figure 3. It is not suitable to add link or node related information, because some nodes are so close to each other that they cannot be differentiated and links overlap. Therefore, we propose another representation of the same topology in Figure 5(a), that will be explained later.

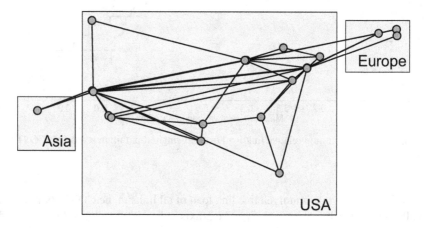

Fig. 3. Exodus network, 22 nodes, 51 links

The used traffic matrix (TM) has been created resembling real-world data according to the method proposed in [14] and enhanced in [15]. All links were expected to have identical capacity and the TM was scaled so that the worst relative load experienced by a link in case of single link failures and hop-count routing is 75%. However, relative link loads larger than 100% can be achieved in single node and multiple failure scenarios.

Based on [7], we chose an unavailability of 10^{-6} for all nodes. Each link is unavailable with the same probability of 10^{-4}. The set of investigated scenarios $\mathcal{Z}$ has been calculated for $p_{min} = 10^{-15}$. This results in a number of $|Z| = 51577$ considered scenarios, about a thousand times more, than the number of single link failures considered for the link cost optimization $|\mathcal{S}_L| = 52$. $\mathcal{Z}$ consists of the failure patterns $\emptyset, L, R, LL, LR, RR, LLL, LLR$, where L denotes a single link and R a single router failure. This way, a resilience analysis with $\mathcal{Z}$ reaches very high precision, while still being computationally feasible. On a "Intel(R) Core(TM)2 Duo CPU E8500 @ 3.16GHz" a resilience analysis of a single routing in the Exodus network with $\mathcal{Z}$ using our software tool [8] took about 300 seconds. The link cost optimization to obtain the best USP routing solution used in this paper took about 66 hours and involved a total number of

18,654,149 routing evaluations with $\mathcal{S}_L$, the best not-via solution was obtained in about 205 hours and 21,816,259 routing evaluations. However good optimization results can already be achieved after some minutes of optimization[1].

4.2 IP Routing and Rerouting Based on the Hop-Count Metric

In the following, we analyze the potential overload in a network when hop-count routing is used. We investigate the relative load for the link from Palo Alto to Santa Clara because its potential overload is especially high in some failure scenarios. Figure 4 shows the CCDF of the relative link load $\rho(l)$ for this link. The CCDF illustration simplifies the observation of the potential overload for a single link. The probability $P(\rho(l) > x)$ that a relative link load $\rho(l)$ exceeds a certain value x is directly displayed in the graph. In this case, e.g., the probability that relative link loads higher than 60% occur from Palo Alto to Santa Clara is about 0.06% $P(\rho(l) > 0.6) \approx 0.06\%$. This value is later referred to as $R_r^{0.6}$. On the other hand, in at least 99.999999% of all scenarios the relative link load is not larger than about 116%, $P(\rho(l) \leq 116\%) > 99.999999\%$. This value is later referred to as $R_q^{0.99999999}$. In particular, this is true for all single and double link failures as well as single node failures.

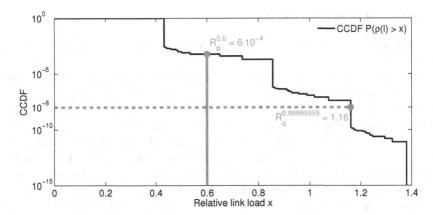

Fig. 4. CCDF of the relative link load $\rho(l)$ for the link between Palo Alto and Santa Clara

If CCDFs are used, a complete figure is necessary to visualize the probabilistic load condition on a link. Monitoring such information for all links in the network becomes more difficult with an increasing network size. Therefore, in [7] we presented various mapping functions to aggregate the information of the per link CCDF into one per link value. Two of those functions are used in this work.

- Mapping function $R_r^x(l) = P(\rho(l) > x)$ is based on overload probabilities. It returns the probability with which the relative load $\rho(l)$ of link l exceeds the relative load value x. Figure 4 illustrates $R_r^{0.6}$.

---

[1] The routing optimization was parallelized on several CPUs so that the effective computation time could be significantly reduced.

- Mapping function $R_q^y(l) = \inf(x : P(\rho(l) \leq x) \geq y)$ is based on relative link load quantiles. This mapping function returns the smallest relative link load value x which is not exceeded by a fraction of at least y of all considered network scenarios. Figure 4 depicts $R_q^{0.99999999}$.

We use the mapping functions to convert the CCDF of each link to a single value. Then, we map those values to a color scale indicating the severeness of the potential overload.

The geographical view in Figure 3 is not suitable to add link or node related information. Some nodes are so close to each other that they cannot be differentiated. Forward and backward directions of links cannot be distinguished, either. Therefore, we propose an adjacency matrix to represent the network topology as in Figure 5. The cell of row i column j in the adjacency matrix corresponds to the link between nodes i and j.

Figure 5 shows the adjacency matrix of the Exodus network colored according to the quantile based mapping function $R_q^{0.99999999}$ for unoptimized hop-count routing and optimized USP routing. This illustration shows the potential overload of the whole network and the link with the risk of highest overload can be directly recognized. The colors in the tiles can be converted to numerical relative load values using the color bar on the right side of the graph.

4.3   Optimized IP Routing and Rerouting

In the following, we show the impact of routing optimization on the potential overload.

Figure 6(a) shows the CCDF of the relative load on the link from Palo Alto to Santa Clara for hop-count routing and optimized USP routing. The curve of the optimized USP routing is at all values smaller than the one for hop-count routing. Thus, the routing optimization indeed reduces the overload risk on this particular link. As a consequence, all mapping functions yield smaller values for optimized USP routing than for hop-count routing. This findings hold only for this particular link which was the worst for hop-count routing. The link, depicted in Figure 6(b), between Santa Clara and Miami presents an interesting counter example. Here, the risk of overload is larger after routing optimization. An optimized path layout does not decrease the total amount of traffic in the network but just distributes it differently over the links. However, Figure 6(b) shows that the resulting load increase on some links does not cause any real problems because the relative link loads still remain relatively low.

To visualize the impact of routing optimization on the potential overload, we need to take all links of the network into account. Therefore, we calculate the overload values according to any mapping function R_p^x or R_q^y based on the CCDFs for all links. Then, we specify the fraction of links, whose potential overload exceeds a certain value. This leads to a CCDF of the overload values of the chosen function R_p^x or R_q^y.

Figure 7 shows CCDFs of overload values according to both mapping functions for hop-count routing and optimized USP routing as solid lines. Routing optimization redistributes the traffic in the network. On the one hand, this leads to a reduction of the worst overload values in the network. On the other hand, on some links with lower potential overload the values lightly increase. This effect is clearly visible in both graphs. It is an interesting finding, that this result holds for both mapping functions. This shows

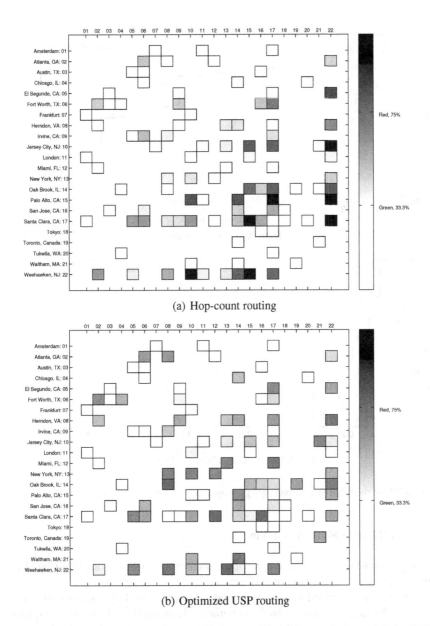

(a) Hop-count routing

(b) Optimized USP routing

Fig. 5. Adjacency matrix of the Exodus network colored according to the potential overload risk for different routings. The color of a link corresponds to the 99.999999% quantile of its CCDF of the relative link load. Darker colors indicate higher overload values.

that the link cost optimization on a small set of protected failure scenarios $\mathcal{S}_L$ is very effective because it significantly improves the resilience calculated on a large set of scenarios $\mathcal{Z}$.

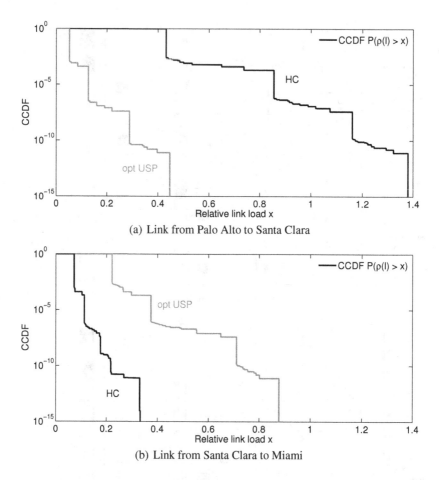

(a) Link from Palo Alto to Santa Clara

(b) Link from Santa Clara to Miami

Fig. 6. CCDF of the relative link load $\rho(l)$ for hop-count routing and optimized USP routing

4.4   IP Fast Reroute Method Not-Via

We investigate not-via IP-FRR based on hop-count routing and based on optimized USP routing in comparison to conventional IP rerouting.

We compare the overload values of the entire network for hop-count routing and optimized USP routing to unoptimized and optimized not-via IP-FRR. Figure 7 displays the overload values of not-via IP-FRR in dashed lines. The potential overload in case of unoptimized not-via FRR is even higher than for conventional IP hop-count routing. Routing optimization significantly improves these values. Optimized not-via IP-FRR reaches overload values of similar quality as optimized USP routing. This holds for both mapping functions $R_p^{0.6}$ and $R_q^{0.99999999}$. The overload values caused by not-via IP-FRR are higher than for conventional IP routing especially due to the increased load on backup paths and the longer average path lengths due to local repair. However, routing optimization can reduce the risk of overload to a secure level also for not-via IP-FRR.

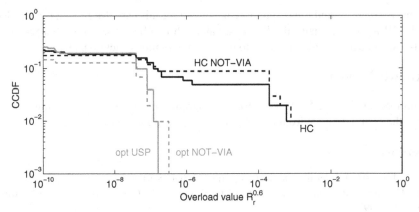

(a) CCDF over all links of the probability that a relative link load exceeds 60%

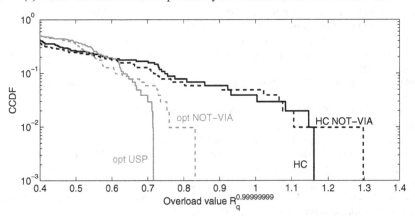

(b) CCDF over all links of the 99.999999% quantile of the relative link load

Fig. 7. Comparison of the CCDFs of the potential overload for IP rerouting and not-via IP-FRR

We have shown that not-via IP-FRR based on hop-count routing leads to even higher potential overload than conventional hop-count routing. Therefore, routing optimization is even more beneficial for not-via IP-FRR.

5   Conclusion

Resilience analysis evaluates the load conditions in communication networks for a large set of likely failure scenarios $\mathcal{Z}$ whose probabilities are at least p_{min}. Routing optimization is usually applied to improve load conditions only for a set of most likely failure scenarios $\mathcal{S}$ which is up to a thousand times smaller than $\mathcal{Z}$. Despite of this big difference in size of the considered failure sets, we have shown that routing optimization significantly reduces potential overload in networks with conventional IP routing and rerouting. Furthermore, we illustrated that without routing optimization IP fast reroute (IP-FRR) possibly causes even more overload than conventional routing and rerouting. However, routing optimization is again very effective for IP-FRR in avoiding potential bottleneck situations and thus even more beneficial for this case. Moreover, it is needed for IP-FRR anyway because the link cost values should be chosen in such a way that equal-cost paths are avoided in order to obtain unambiguous backup paths.

Acknowledgments

The authors thank David Stezenbach for his programming efforts and Prof. Phuoc Tran-Gia for the stimulating environment which was a prerequisite for this work.

References

1. ISO: ISO 10589: Intermediate System to Intermediate System Routing Exchange Protocol for Use in Conjunction with the Protocol for Providing the Connectionless-Mode Network Service (1992/2002)
2. Hock, D., Hartmann, M., Menth, M., Schwartz, C.: Optimizing Unique Shortest Paths for Resilient Routing and Fast Reroute in IP-Based Networks. In: IEEE Network Operations and Management Symposium (NOMS), Osaka, Japan (2010)
3. Martin, R., Menth, M., Hartmann, M., Cicic, T., Kvalbein, A.: Loop-Free Alternates and Not-Via Addresses: A Proper Combination for IP Fast Reroute? Accepted for Computer Networks (2010)
4. Atlas, A., Zinin, A.: RFC5286: Basic Specification for IP Fast Reroute: Loop-Free Alternates (2008)
5. Shand, M., Bryant, S.: IP Fast Reroute Framework (2009),
http://www.ietf.org/internet-drafts/
draft-ietf-rtgwg-ipfrr-framework-12.txt
6. Bryant, S., Previdi, S., Shand, M.: IP Fast Reroute Using Not-via Addresses (2009),
http://tools.ietf.org/id/
draft-ietf-rtgwg-ipfrr-notvia-addresses-04.txt
7. Menth, M., Duelli, M., Martin, R., Milbrandt, J.: Resilience Analysis of Packet-Switched Communication Networks. ToN 17(6), 1950–1963 (2009)
8. Hock, D., Menth, M., Hartmann, M., Schwartz, C., Stezenbach, D.: ResiLyzer: A Tool for Resilience Analysis in Packet-Switched Communication Networks. In: GI/ITG Conference on Measuring, Modelling and Evaluation of Computer and Communication Systems (MMB) and Dependability and Fault Tolerance (DFT), Essen, Germany (2010)
9. Hartmann, M., Hock, D., Schwartz, C., Menth, M.: Objective Functions for Optimization for Resilient and Non-Resilient IP Routing. In: 7th International Workshop on Design of Reliable Communication Networks (DRCN), Washington, D.C., USA (2009)
10. Menth, M., Hartmann, M., Martin, R.: Robust IP Link Costs for Multilayer Resilience. In: IFIP-TC6 Networking Conference (Networking), Atlanta, GA, USA (2007)
11. Dueck, G., Scheuer, T.: Threshold Accepting; a General Purpose Optimization Algorithm. Journal of Computational Physics 90, 161–175 (1990)
12. Fortz, B., Thorup, M.: Internet Traffic Engineering by Optimizing OSPF Weights. In: IEEE Infocom, Tel-Aviv, Israel, pp. 519–528 (2000)
13. Spring, N., Mahajan, R., Wetherall, D.: Measuring ISP Topologies with Rocketfuel. In: ACM SIGCOMM, Pittsburgh, PA (2002)
14. Nucci, A., Sridharan, A., Taft, N.: The Problem of Synthetically Generating IP Traffic Matrices: Initial Recommendations. ACM SIGCOMM Computer Communications Review 35, 19–32 (2005)
15. Roughan, M.: Simplifying the Synthesis of Internet Traffic Matrices. ACM SIGCOMM Computer Communications Review 35, 93–96 (2005)

Load Modeling and Generation for IP-Based Networks: A Unified Approach and Tool Support

Andrey Kolesnikov and Martin Kulas

University of Hamburg, Dept. of Computer Science, TKRN,
Vogt-Kölln-Str. 30, 22527 Hamburg
{kolesnikov,2kulas}@informatik.uni-hamburg.de

Abstract. This paper presents a unified approach to load generation in IP-based networks supported by a Unified Load Generator UNILOG which incorporates a formal automata-based load specification technique. The load specification technique is applied to two exemplarily chosen models for VoIP and MPEG-coded video traffic sources in order to use them for load generation in UNILOG. The performance characteristics of UNILOG modules, which are responsible for the injection of real traffic loads at different interfaces in IP networks, are discussed and the practical use of UNILOG is demonstrated in the context of a comprehensive QoS study of video streaming via an IEEE 802.11g WLAN under various background loads.

1 Introduction

The trend towards the convergence of media and communication services on the basis of the IP protocol strongly increases the complexity of modern communication systems. Analysis of performance and behaviour of such systems and their offered services under various load scenarios therefore have become a very important issue for owners of large networks, in particular during network planning and administration [1]. At this point, there is a strong need for tools supporting the experimenter at modeling and generation of artificial traffic loads at different network interfaces [2].

A current practical method for generation of realistic artificial loads consists in the realization of a load generator based on a load model which is inferred from a large amount of measurements in the real network. A series of dedicated model-based load generators exists, e.g. for WWW traffic (GUERNICA [3], PARASYNTG [4]), P2P and Email (LITGEN [5]), UDP and TCP (ITG [6], BRUTE [7]) or IP traffic loads (HARPOON [8], BRUNO [9]). The existing solutions are usually tailored to a particular modeling task and, therefore, they frequently do not provide an adequate flexibility in case the underlying traffic model is to be modified or a completely new model is to be used. In BRUTE, for example, a new traffic module (*T-Module*) has to be implemented in C programming language in order to define a new traffic model. Some authors (cf. [4,5,8]) consider only the generation of a trace with certain characteristics (e.g. in order to use the resulting trace for generation of traffic in network simulation or emulation

B. Müller-Clostermann et al. (Eds.): MMB & DFT 2010, LNCS 5987, pp. 91–106, 2010.

environments) and do not clearly separate between the load specification and load generation (in form of real requests injected at a particular network interface). Some existing widely used benchmarks like IPERF [10] or NETPERF [11] concentrate on measuring the UDP or TCP throughput and do not provide the possibility to exactly specify the interarrival times and the lengths of requests.

In this paper, a Unified Load Generator UNILOG is presented, which incorporates a formal automata-based load specification technique proposed in [12,13] in order to provide a unified approach for specification and flexible parameterization of traffic loads at different interfaces in IP networks. The specification of loads in UNILOG is accomplished by means of request types which are initially abstract, i.e. the experimenter can omit load attributes, which are not relevant for the given modeling study, and introduce some additional load attributes in order to enrich the semantics of the load model. The possible sequences of requests dynamically created by the users of the network services are described by means of the corresponding user behavior automaton (UBA), which is parameterized by the experimenter (e.g. by supplying the values of the request attributes and the request interarrival times). The parameterized user behavior automaton (PUBA) represents the load model to be executed by the load-generating components of UNILOG in the given modeling study.

During the execution of the PUBA, the generation of the correspondent real traffic loads at a chosen target interface (e.g. at the IP interface) is carried out by a particular interface-specific adapter (e.g. UNILOG.IP adapter, respectively). The adapter is responsible for the conversion of every individual abstract request into its real pendant in order to inject interface-conformant requests into the network. Adapters for the HTTP, UDP, TCP and IP interfaces are available for UNILOG at this moment [14,15]. So, many different traffic models (e.g. IP traffic models) can be prepared in form of a UBA and used in UNILOG in conjunction with the suitable adapter (e.g. UNILOG.IP adapter) for generation of real traffic at the chosen target interface (e.g. IP interface).

With this approach, a relatively high level of abstraction and flexibility of load specification is provided. The analyses of performance characteristics of the implemented UNILOG adapters confirm the fact, that the precise and effective generation of real traffic loads can be guaranteed at this high level of abstraction, which is the main contribution of this paper.

In this contribution we mainly aim at generating of real traffic loads which can be used, for instance, in various performance evaluation studies in real IP networks. The UNILOG approach can also be applied to generation of traffic for network simulation or emulation environments by means of a specific adapter.

The rest of the paper is organized as follows. In Section 2, the embedded formal automata-based load specification technique is introduced followed by a brief overview of the UNILOG architecture including its recent extension to a system for distributed load generation. A presentation of the UNILOG.IP adapter for generation of IP traffic loads and the discussion of its performance characteristics conclude Section 2. In Section 3, two exemplarily chosen models for VoIP and MPEG-coded video sources are presented and the load specification technique is applied to construct the correspondent automata-based models in order to use them for load generation in UNILOG. The practical use of the UNILOG load generator is demonstrated in Section 4 in the context of a comprehensive QoS study for video streaming over IEEE 802.11g WLAN under different background loads. Section 5 contains a summary and an outlook on future work.

2 Unified Load Generator UniLoG

2.1 A Formal Load Specification Technique

In order to achieve a unified and formal procedure of load generation at different interfaces in IP networks, a formal load specification technique (proposed in [12] and recently extended in [13]) has been integrated in UNILOG. The (offered) load $L = L(E, S, IF, T)$ is thereby defined as a sequence of requests $(t_i, A_i), t_i \in T$, i = 1, 2, ..., n ($t_i \in \mathbb{R}$: arrival time of request A_i; $t_i \leq t_j$ for $i < j$; n $\in \mathbb{N}$) offered by an environment E to a service system S at a well-defined interface IF during the time interval T. The specification of loads is thereafter accomplished by the following four steps LS_1-LS_4.

At the first step LS_1 the experimenter has to choose the target (network or service) interface IF for load modeling (e.g. the interface to the network service IP as presented in Fig. 1). A real network node will be conceptually decomposed into a load-generating environment E and a service system S at this step. The choice of the target interface is generally met in strict accordance to the objectives of the performance analysis study being issued. For example, the experimenter would set the target interface presumably to IP in order to evaluate different routing algorithms, but he would rather select the HTTP as a target interface for load generation in order to estimate the mean server response time under various web-server loads.

At the next step LS_2 the experimenter selects a subset of service users which are relevant for the given modeling task and substitues them by "virtual" users described by means of a finite user behaviour automaton (cf. right part of Fig. 1).

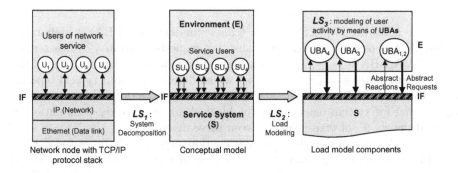

Fig. 1. An abstract approach to load modeling with UNILOG (illustrated for the case of load modeling at the network service interface IP)

Furthermore, the relevant request types RT and their corresponding request attributes as well as the possible types of system events ET (if the load model should respond to them) are identified at this step. The request types are initially *abstract*, i.e. the experimenter is allowed to skip some nonrelevant attributes of real requests as well as to introduce some new request attributes which do not exist in the real requests in order to enrich the semantics of the load model being under construction. The definition of a possible abstract IP request type `InjectPacket` to model the creation of the IP-frame by the IP protocol stack is represented in Fig. 2. In section 3, some exemplarily chosen models for voice and video traffic sources are presented and the construction of corresponding UBAs for these models is explained.

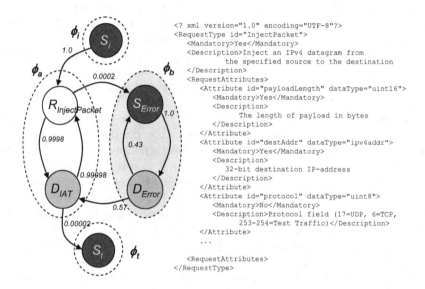

Fig. 2. An simplified user behavior automaton for a user of the IP network service (left-hand). Definition of the abstract IP request type `InjectPacket` (right-hand).

At the following step LS_3, a *user behavior automaton* (UBA) is elaborated to specify the possible sequences of abstract requests generated by the service users SU. A UBA $U = \{\phi, T_\phi\}$ is an extended finite automaton consisting of the set of macro states $\phi = \{\phi_i, \phi_a, \phi_b, \phi_t\}$ which describe the four typical types of user activity (initializaton in ϕ_i, generation of requests in the active macro state ϕ_a, waiting for system reactions in the blocked macro state ϕ_b, termination in ϕ_t) and the set T_ϕ of transitions between these macro states.

To provide for more precise load specification, especially in order to offer the possibility to model separately the generation of requests and the interarrival times (IAT) between successsive requests, the macro states are further refined by introduction of (R)equest-, (D)elay- and (S)ystem-states which have the following semantics:

(R)equest states are used to model the (conceptually timeless) generation of requests of exactly one abstract request type and appear only in the active macro state ϕ_a. The corresponding abstract request type is to be assigned by the experimenter during the creation of the UBA-model (e.g. requests of the abstract request type InjectPacket are generated in the R-state $R_{InjectPacket}$, cf. Fig. 2).

(S)ystem states imply waiting for a certain type of event to occur, e.g. the initialisation of the user in ϕ_i or termination of the user in ϕ_t. Furthermore, S-states can be introduced in the blocked macro state ϕ_b if the UBA model should respond to system events (consider the state S_{Error} in Fig. 2 to model the situation of insufficient buffer space for the next generated IP frame). The blocked macro state ϕ_b is empty, otherwise.

(D)elay states are introduced in the active macro state ϕ_a to model the inter-arrival times between successive abstract requests (cf. D_{IAT} state in Fig. 2) or to model the times needed to respond to system events in the blocked macro state ϕ_b (if ϕ_b is not empty, cf. D_{Error} state in Fig. 2).

At the last step LS_4, the experimenter has to supply a series of load model parameters, i.e. the correspondent state transition probabilities, the values of the request attributes in R-states and the interarrival times of requests in D-states. The experimenter can use constant values, various distribution functions, traces of real measurements or special procedures to complete this task in UNILOG. The resulting parameterized user behavior automaton (PUBA) presents the load model to be executed by the load generating components of UNILOG.

The input set of a UBA is provided by the different types of external events ET in S-states. The abstract request types RT in R-states in conjunction with value domains of their corresponding request attributes build up the output set of a UBA. The execution of a UBA-model constructed by the experimenter according to the steps LS_1-LS_4 for the time interval T results in the sequence of abstract requests (t_i, A_i), which represent the specified load L at IF during T.

2.2   Overview of the UniLoG Architecture

The architecture of the Unified Load Generator UNILOG has been designed according to the steps LS_1-LS_4 of the load modeling approach presented above. In a recent work [17] of the TKRN group, the UNILOG architecture has been extended towards a system for distributed load generation UNILOG-DISTRIBUTED. The basic modules of UNILOG-DISTRIBUTED are presented in Fig. 3.

Load Generators include software components, which are able to generate specific traffic loads predefined by the experimenter in form of a PUBA. The existing UNILOG components GAR and ADAPT (see below) are used in UNILOG-DISTRIBUTED in order to execute this task.

GAR (Generator for Sequences of Abstract Requests) is responsible for the execution of the PUBA model being loaded and the generation of a sequence of abstract requests $(t_i, A_i), t_i \in T, i = 1, 2, \ldots, n$ $(n \in \mathbb{N})$, which are enqueued

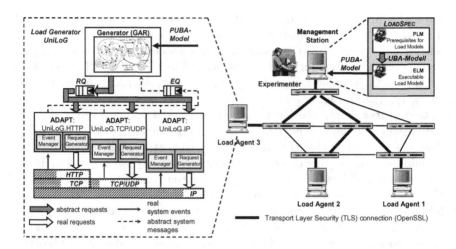

Fig. 3. Basic modules of the UNILOG-DISTRIBUTED system

in the abstract request queue RQ. During the PUBA execution, the request arrival times t_i are chosen according to the specifications in D-states of the PUBA. The attribute values of requests A_i are generated according to the specifications in R-states.

ADAPT an interface-specific adapter is responsible for the generation of real requests at the chosen target interface IF (e.g. at IP interface if the IP adapter is to be used) on the basis of abstract requests generated by GAR and enqueued into RQ. In case the PUBA model should respond to system reactions, the adapter is also responsible for capturing real system events (for example ICMP messages) and transforming them into correspondent abstract system messages, which are enqueued into the event queue EQ. Adapters for UDP/TCP [14], HTTP, and IP interfaces [15] have been implemented already for UNILOG.

Load Agents provide the load generation service to the experimenter and have the ability to control and to monitor the activities of the load generators. An experimenter has to be authenticated and authorized to be able to use the load generation service offered by the load agent. Load agents and load generators have to be installed in the nodes of the network before an experiment can be run.

Management station is set up to allow the experimenter to remotely configure, control and monitor the load generators from one central point. Transport Layer Security (TLS) connections between the management station and the associated load agents are established in order to execute these tasks securely during the whole experiment. After the successful establishment of the TLS connection, the experimenter can use the load generation service by submitting different commands to the load agents (e.g. to upload a PUBA or to start a load generator immediately or at a predefined time, see [17] for details). The graphical tool support for construction and parameterization of UBA models is provided by the LoadSpec module which is installed in the management station (cf. Fig. 3, right-hand). Generally, values of request attributes, interarrival times of requests and total load generation time have to be specified by the experimenter.

The presented UNILOG-DISTRIBUTED system provides support for specification (in LoadSpec module) and generation (in GAR module) of initially abstract loads as well as for generation of corresponding real traffic loads at a chosen target interface by means of various adapters. The use of the UNILOG-DISTRIBUTED system in conjunction with the IP adapter for generation of various IP backround loads is presented in the case study in Sec. 4 of this paper.

2.3   Adapters for Generation of Real Traffic Loads

At this moment, UNILOG adapters for HTTP, UDP and TCP (presented in [14]) as well as for IP interfaces are available. Due to the space limit, by way of example, here we shortly discuss only the UNILOG.IP adapter and its performance characteristics and refer to [15] and [16] for further details of the realization.

The injection of IP packets and the capturing of system events in UNILOG.IP is implemented using the open source libraries libnet and libpcap, respectively. The performance of UNILOG.IP is characterized mainly by the maximum packet and data rate of the generated IP streams achievable by the adapter as well as by the mean deadline missing time (MDMT) of IP packets, defined as the mean of the absolute values of differences between the desired arrival times of IP requests (specified in PUBA) and the factual injection times of IP packets (in the IP adapter).

In order to estimate the maximum packet rate achievable by UNILOG.IP, a sequence of abstract IP requests InjectPacket is generated according to the UBA model presented in Fig. 2 (without the blocking macro state ϕ_b) with a constant value of the attribute payloadLength and infinitesimal interarrival times in the D-state D_{IAT}. The abstract IP requests are handed over to the IP adapter, which is executed on the commodity PC (Intel Core 2 Duo E6400, 2.13 GHz, 1 GByte DDR2 SDRAM 667 MHz, Broadcom BCM5754 Gigabit Ethernet adapter, FreeBSD 7.2) connected to a Gigabit Ethernet testbed (IEEE 802.3ab, 1000BASE-T). The experiments were conducted in the laboratory of the TKRN group at the University of Hamburg in December 2009 for different packet lengths. Each experiment lasts about 15 seconds and is repeated at least 5 times in order to get reliable statistical results. The packet rate of the generated IP packet streams (cf. Fig. 4(a)) provides a very significant performance characteristic of the IP adapter, as the expected generation overhead per packet comes into play especially at smaller packet lengths. Comparing our results to the performance characteristics of some selected traffic generators (presented e.g. in [18], Fig. 1, left-hand) we can report a packet rate which is nearly linearly decreasing from 67000 to 60000 packets/s for IP packet lengths in the range from 46 to 1500 bytes. The small artefacts at packet lengths of 200 and 400 bytes are (as supported by the first results of further experiments not presented here)

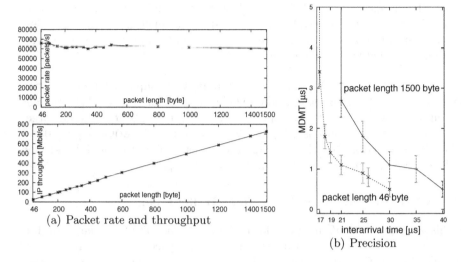

(a) Packet rate and throughput

(b) Precision

Fig. 4. Performance characteristics of the IP adapter (95% confidence intervals)

presumably due to the optimizations in memory allocation methods being used for the creation of the IP packet objects in FreeBSD 7.2 operating system.

The corresponding data rate of the generated IP packet stream exceeds 100 Mbit/s (Fast Ethernet) already at a packet length of 200 byte (cf. Fig. 4(a), at the bottom). At a packet length of 1200 byte, the data rate increases to 600 Mbit/s, which corresponds to a utilization degree of 0.6 of the experimental Gigabit Ethernet. At a packet length of 1500 byte, the resulting data rate achieved by UNILOG.IP exceeds 725 Mbit/s, while e.g. the traffic generator D-ITG can only achieve a data rate of 630 Mbit/s (cf. [18], Fig. 1, right-hand).

In order to estimate the precision of UNILOG.IP, another two series of experiments are conducted for packet lengths of 1500 byte and 46 byte, respectively. During an experiment, the interarrival times of IP requests are kept constant. In every subsequent experiment within a series, the interarrival times are reduced (in the range from 40 μs to 17 μs) and the MDMT of the injected IP packets is calculated in the adapter (cf. Fig. 4(b)). In the first series of experiments with a packet length of 1500 byte, the MDMT in the IP adapter escalates already for interarrival times in the area of 30 μs, while only 12 μs are (theoretically) required for a Gigabit Ethernet adapter to deliver an IP packet of this length to the network. So, it can be concluded, that the remaining 30 - 12 = 18 μs are required for the UNILOG.IP adapter to prepare a subsequent IP request and, therefore, can be referred to as "generation overhead". This conclusion is supported by the observation of the MDMT in the second series of experiments for the packet length of 46 byte. The MDMT escalates at interarrival times in the area of 20 μs, whereas approximately 0.5 μs are required for the delivery of an IP packet of this length in a Gigabit Ethernet.

In summary, we can conclude that UNILOG offers an astonishingly good accuracy in generating load consisting of IP packets by means of the UNILOG.IP adapter. Our tool supports interarrival times up to 20 μs, while some traffic generators (e.g. TG or MGEN with disabled *precise* feature) are not able to reproduce a given IAT accurately (cf. [18], Fig. 2). In particular, it should be noted that UNILOG is a software based solution with integrated flexible load specification technique without any dedicated hardware components.

3   Modeling of Real Application Loads with UniLoG

3.1   VoIP Application Modeling

VoIP applications are traditionally characterized by a succession of active periods (talkspurt or *ON* phases) followed by an inactive period (silence or *OFF* phase) [19]. This is due to the fact, that most of the existing voice encoding schemes (e.g. G.711 or G.729 codecs) employ the Voice Activity Detection (VAD) facility to suppress periods with no speaker activity. During the *ON* phase, the source sends packets at regular intervals of length T_p (referred to as *packetization time*). The duration of active and inactive periods is generally estimated by independent exponential laws of respective parameters α and β. A voice source may be viewed as a two state birth-death process with birth rate β and death rate α. The model is characterized by the following parameters (cf. Fig. 5):

$\bar{T}_{ON}$ [sec]: the mean duration of the *ON* phase, $\bar{T}_{ON} = 1/\alpha$, α denoting the parameter of the exponential law of the active period *ON*.

$\bar{T}_{OFF}$ [sec]: the mean duration of the *OFF* phase, $\bar{T}_{OFF} = 1/\beta$, β denoting the parameter of the exponential law of the idle period *OFF*.

T_p [sec]: the constant packet interarrival time during the *ON* phase (given by the *packetization time* of the voice coder being used).

L [byte]: the constant packet size including voice payload and additional packetization overhead (in form of RTP, UDP and IP headers, if needed).

Given this simple two-state markov model for a VoIP traffic source, the corresponding UBA is derived based on the following assumptions (cf. Fig. 5):

– After the initialization (in the S-state S_i of ϕ_i) the VoIP source switches to the *ON* phase (and not to the *OFF* phase, w.l.o.g.).

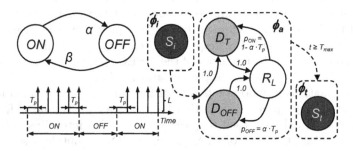

Fig. 5. ON-OFF model (left-hand) and the corresponding UBA model (right-hand) for a VoIP application

- The *ON* and *OFF* phases are covered in the active macro state ϕ_a of the UBA. The emission of voice packets during the *ON* phase is modeled in the R-state R_L by generating requests of the abstract request type `InjectPacket` (cf. Fig. 2) with `payloadLength` attribute set to L [byte].
- The constant interarrival time T_p between packets during the *ON* phase is modeled in the D-state D_T. The mean number of packets generated during the *ON* phase is $n = \bar{T}_{ON}/T_p$. The probability p_{ON} for a transition from R_L to D_T (for the source to keep in the *ON* phase) can be calculated as $p_{ON} = (n-1)/n = 1 - 1/n = 1 - T_p/\bar{T}_{ON} = 1 - \alpha * T_p$.
- The interarrival time $\bar{T}_{OFF} + T_p$ between the last packet of the actual *ON* phase and the first packet of the subsequent *ON* phase (cf. Fig. 5, left-hand) is modeled in the D-state D_{OFF}. The probability p_{OFF} for a transition from R_L to D_{OFF} (for the source to switch to the *OFF* phase) yields to $p_{OFF} = 1 - p_{ON} = T_p/\bar{T}_{ON} = \alpha * T_p$).
- The source terminates in the S-state S_t of ϕ_t when the actual simulation time t exceeds the maximum duration of the VoIP call T_{max}.
- The blocked macro state ϕ_b is empty as the underlying model does not take system reactions into account.

The illustrated UBA has to be parameterized before it can be used for load generation in UNILOG. The values of parameters T_p and L for various codecs (e.g. G.729, G.711) as well as the estimated mean durations of the *ON* phase ($\bar{T}_{ON}$) and the *OFF* phase ($\bar{T}_{OFF}$) for different types of voice applications and different languages can be found in [19,20].

3.2   Modeling of MPEG-Coded Video Sources

Several traffic models for VBR MPEG-coded video sources have been proposed in the literature. To get the necessary details of the effect of loss during transmission, frame size models (FSM) are essential. Therefore, an exemplarily FSM for a full-length video proposed by Sarkar et al. [21] is chosen and the construction of the corresponding PUBA model is illustrated in this section.

The model of Sarkar et al. assumes, that the whole movie (Crocodile Dundee) is encoded with one group-of-pictures (GOP) structure with IBBPBB sequencing of frames. In the corresponding UBA, the generation of the intra (I), predicted (P) and bidirectional (B) frames is modeled by the abstract request types `InjectI`, `InjectP` and `InjectB` with the single request attribute `FrameLength` in the R-states R_I, R_P and R_B, respectively (cf. Fig. 6). The interframe time (which is determined by the frequency of the MPEG encoder and assumed to be constant, e.g. 40 ms) is modeled in the D-states D_1-D_6.

Due to fluctuations in motion intensity of the video, a sophisticated method to determine an appropriate distribution for the size of I, B, and P frames is essential. Sarkar et al. proposed to partition the video into clips, which are identified by adding the sizes of all frames in a GOP to obtain a sequence of GOP sizes for a movie and combining the adjacent GOPs of similar size to one clip, using a moving average method. To reduce the number of resulting clips,

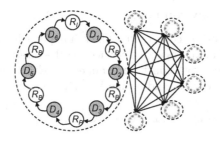

Fig. 6. A UBA model for a MPEG video encoded with a (6,3) GOP structure

the clips are grouped into seven shot classes (illustrated as dashed circles in Fig. 6), using geometrically separated class-size boundaries, so that the similar-sized I, B, and P frames are grouped together. Thereafter, each frame type in a shot class is modeled with an axis-shifted Gamma distribution, so that a total of $3 * 7 = 21$ Gamma distributions are used in the correspondent R_I, R_P and R_B states of the UBA to specify the value of the request attribute `FrameLength` (see [21] for concrete parameters of the Gamma distributions). Finally, the inter-class transition probabilities in the UBA model are computed from the relative frequency of transitions among shot classes by sequentially traversing all GOPs in the original video.

4   Case Study: QoS Evaluation of Video Streaming over a WLAN under Different Background Loads

4.1   Motivation

Wireless LANs (WLAN) according to IEEE 802.11 standard are widespread. Nearly all of the currently sold mobile devices, like notebooks or mobile phones, are equipped with WLAN adapters. Besides the ubiquitous use of WLANs at home, many congresses, air ports, etc. run public access points (so called hotspots) in order to enable their customers with WLAN capable devices to access services on the Internet. The high data rates of current WLAN products make it possible to use video on demand services (VoD) with high quality audio and video contents. However, several WLAN users often share a single wireless access point, so that a certain IP based background load exists in the WLAN from a streaming user's point of view.

This case study reproduces a typical hotspot situation where a user accesses a video on demand service by means of RTP/RTSP [23,24] over an IEEE 802.11g WLAN in order to receive a high quality audio and video stream of the movie. In addition to the movie consumer, several load generators imitate network behaviour of other WLAN stations by producing an IP based background load within the wireless network. At this point the following questions emerge: (1) At which level of background load does the quality of the movie degrade significantly? (2) Does the type of background load play an important role? (3) At which level of background load does the streaming service become "unusable"?

4.2   Experimental Environment

The case study's network is constructed like a hotspot where mobile computers equipped with WLAN adapters access services on the Internet. For that purpose, the case study uses a network consisting of one Fast Ethernet segment, with the VoD server and the load sink, and of one WLAN segment, with the VoD client and the load generators, (cf. Fig. 7). The load generators produce artificial IP based background loads by running UNILOG.IP.

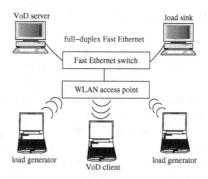

Fig. 7. Experimental setup

D-Link's access point "DWL-2100 AP" is connected to the wired network and allows WLAN stations to send packets with data rates up to 54 Mbit/s on channel 1 in the 2.4 GHz band (OFDM modulation). This access point transmits frames with the maximum transmitting power (100 mW). The distance from access point to VoD client and load generators is about 4 meter. Furthermore, the distance between all three WLAN stations is nearly 2 meter. Therefore, no hidden station problem should occur and the RTS/CTS mechanism on each WLAN station and the access point is deactivated (threshold is set to 2346 byte).

The VoD server (VLC Media Player, version 0.9.8a) streams the high quality movie "Big Buck Bunny" [22] with a high definition resolution of 1280x720 pixels, whose video is compressed as H.264/AVC and whose audio format is MPEG-4. The streaming session lasts about 10 minutes. The VoD client receives the audio and video streams from the VoD server over the WLAN while the load generators inject IP packets into the same WLAN destined to the load sink. Hence, the VoD client and the load generators compete for access to the shared communication media. During the experiments, the load sink does not send out any packets.

The series of experiments were conducted in the TKRN research group's laboratory at the University of Hamburg during the working time of the university staff (from about 9 a.m. to 6 p.m.) in September 2009. In that laboratory, beacon frames are received from eleven other active access points. Three of these external access points transmit data on the same channel as the access point of the case study. Therefore, signal collisions can occur during the experiments.

4.3   Choice of Background Load

In order to achieve various degrees of utilization in the WLAN, a set of different PUBAs based on the UBA model illustrated in Fig. 2 is prepared, which specify traffic loads for constant (CBR) and variable (VBR) throughput on the IP layer of 0.5, 1, 1.5, 2, 4, 6, 8, 10, 12 and 14 Mbit/s. Both load generators execute the same PUBA and produce aggregated background loads with 1, 2, 3, 4, 8, 12, 16, 20, 24 and 28 Mbit/s throughput on the IP layer. In the experiments with CBR traffic, the value of the request attribute `payloadLength` of the abstract IP request type `InjectPacket` is set either to 50 or to 1480 byte. The VBR experiments use constant values for the request attribute `payloadLength` of 50 or 1480 byte whereas the interarrival times between successive requests (modeled in the D-state D_{IAT}, cf. Fig. 2) are negatively exponentially distributed. In the experiments with a `payloadLength` of 50 byte, the PUBA models for the aggregated background loads up to 4 Mbit/s are used due to the fact, that IEEE 802.11g WLANs only support a maximum IP throughput of 4.9 Mbit/s for such small packet lengths [25].

4.4   Streaming Quality Metrics

The values determining the quality of the transmission of video and audio streams are extracted from the captured RTP and IP packets. This offers the advantage that no modifications to the VoD software are required. The following streaming quality metrics are considered in this case study:

jitter. The variability in the delays of the packets from the same packet stream is called jitter [24]. This case study picks the jitter from RTCP receiver reports (RR) and considers only the jitter in the audio stream as the jitter values from RR for H.264 encoded video streams are useless (RFC 3984).

packet loss. The VoD client reports (within the RR) about the difference between the number of expected and received RTP packets.

number of sequence errors. A sequence error occures in the situation, when a RTP packet arrives at the VoD client and its sequence number does not equal the increment of the last received packet.

number of duplicates. The case study defines that a RTP packet is a duplicate when at least one other packet received during the last two seconds, has the same sequence number.

IP throughput. The throughput on the IP layer is defined as the amount of data that the VoD client has sent to the VoD server and received from it (including the IP header) during the streaming session.

In order to obtain statistically significant results and to minimize the effect of outliers, each experiment for a given level of background load was conducted at least five times.

4.5   Results

The drop in streaming quality is noticeable in a quantitative way (by means of the streaming quality measurements) and in a qualitative way (the user perceived quality of the movie playback). The streaming quality becomes unacceptable when the background load reaches the WLAN's high-performance range. In that range, the VoD client receives so little audio and video data that the client is unable to playback frames and sound. As a consequence of that, the movie playback frequently stalls and the frames often contain artifacts.

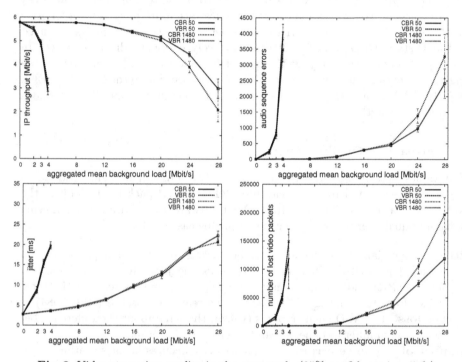

Fig. 8. Video streaming quality in the case study (95% confidence intervals)

This case study has found out that small IP packets have a disastrous impact on the performance of 802.11g WLANs. This kind of WLANs already reach their limits under loads with relatively small packet size of 70 byte and with a low mean IP throughput (4 Mbit/s). This behaviour is due to the fact, that the data-link layer and the physical layer of WLAN stations use several techniques in order to achieve a reliable data transfer. These techniques cause an overhead during data transmission and, therefore, the IP throughput degrades especially for small IP packets. The results of the case study demonstrate that UNILOG.IP pushes the WLAN into the high-performance range when it generates load starting at 16 Mbit/s with 1480 byte long payload (both CBR and VBR). From this load level on, the mean IP throughput on the VoD client side degrades undoubtfully, the jitter rises strongly and the number of sequence errors, lost packets and packet duplicates (not shown) increases heavily (cf. Fig. 8). The partially strong fluctuations are due to the only incompletely controllable experimental environment. But it is clearly evident that the streaming quality of the movie degrades with increasing IP based background loads.

Finally, the results of the case study show that the streaming quality only differs marginally when CBR and VBR experiments use levels of background load with the same mean IP throughput and the same packet lengths. Interestingly, the results demonstrate that the packet length is significantly more important than the distribution of the interarrival times because the packet length determines how long a WLAN station allocates the communication medium.

5   Summary and Outlook

In this paper, we presented a unified approach to load generation in IP based networks, supported by a Unified Load Generator UNILOG. With the embedded formal automata-based load specification technique, our tool provides a high level of abstraction and flexibility during the load modeling. The analyses of the performance characteristics of the UNILOG adapters, which are implemented by the authors for IP, UDP and TCP as well as for HTTP interfaces, confirm, that an astonishingly precise and effective generation of real traffic loads can be guaranteed by UNILOG respecting the fact, that this is a software based solution without any dedicated hardware components.

Furthermore, we illustrated the construction of the corresponding UBA for two exemplarilly chosen models for VoIP and MPEG video traffic sources. In conjunction with various UBA models, adapters and the distributed load generation facility, UNILOG provides a highly universal and effective tool for load generation in IP based networks. In the context of the comprehensive case study for a praxis-oriented WLAN scenario, we obtained concrete results for QoS parameters of video streaming under various background loads and demonstrated the practical use and the potential application fields of distributed load generators.

As a continuation of this work, the autors intend to provide additional models for aggregated VoIP and MPEG-coded video sources in the form of a UBA as well as to design adapters for other interfaces (e.g. FTP, CIFS).

Acknowledgement. The authors would like to thank Prof. Wolfinger for his great support during the preparation of this paper.

References

1. Leighton, T.: Improving Performance on the Internet. ACM Queue 6(6), 20–29 (2008)
2. Charzinski, J., Färber, J., Vicari, N.: Verkehrsmessungen und Lastmodellierung im Internet. PIK 25(2), 64–72 (2002)
3. Pena-Ortiz, R., et al.: Dweb model: Representing Web 2.0 dynamism. Computer Communications 32(6), 1118–1128 (2009)

4. El Abdouni, R., Khayari, M., Rücker, A., Lehmann, A.: Musovic, ParaSynTG: A Parameterized Synthetic Trace Generator for Representation of WWW Traffic. In: Proc. of SPECTS 2008, Edinburgh, Scotland, pp. 317–323 (2008)
5. Rolland, C., Ridoux, J., Baynat, B.: LiTGen, a lightweight traffic generator: application to P2P and mail wireless traffic. In: Proc. of PAM 2007, Louvain-la-neuve, Belgium, pp. 52–62 (2007)
6. Avallone, S., et al.: Analysis and experimentation of Internet Traffic Generator. In: Proc. of New2an 2004, St. Petersburg, Russia, pp. 70–75 (2004)
7. Bonelli, N., et al.: BRUTE: A High Performance and Extensible Traffic Generator. In: Proc. of SPECTS 2005, Philadelphia, pp. 839–845 (2005)
8. Sommers, J., Barford, P.: Self-Configuring Network Traffic Generation. In: Proc. of IMC 2004, Taormina, Sicily, pp. 68–80 (2004)
9. Antichi, G., et al.: BRUNO: A High Performance Traffic Generator for Network Processor. In: Proc. of SPECTS 2008, Edinburgh, Scotland, pp. 526–533 (2008)
10. http://iperf.sourceforge.net/
11. http://www.netperf.org/netperf/
12. Wolfinger, B.E.: Characterization of Mixed Traffic Load in Service-Integrated Networks. Systems Science Journal 25(2), 65–86 (1999)
13. Cong, J.: Load Specification and Load Generation for Multimedia Traffic Load in Computer Networks. Shaker, Aachen (2006)
14. Kolesnikov, A.: Konzeption und Entwicklung eines echtzeitfähigen Lastgenerators für Multimedia-Verkehrsströme in IP-basierten Rechnernetzen. In: Proc. of Echtzeit 2008, Boppard, pp. 91–100 (2008)
15. Kolesnikov, A., Kulas, M.: Lastgenerierung an IP-Schnittstellen mit dem Uni-LoG.IP-Adapter. In: 5. GI/ITG-Workshop MMBnet, Hamburg, pp. 24–35 (2009)
16. Kulas, M.: Entwurf und Realisierung eines Adapters für UniLoG zur Lastgenerierung an IP-basierten Schnittstellen. Diploma Thesis, University of Hamburg, Department of Computer Science (April 2009)
17. Kolesnikov, A., Wolfinger, B.E., Kulas, M.: UniLoG – ein System zur verteilten Lastgenerierung in Netzen. In: Proc. of Echtzeit 2009, Boppard, pp. 11–20 (2009)
18. Dainotti, A., Botta, A., Pescapè, A.: Do you know what you are generating? In: Proc. of CoNEXT 2007, New York, December 10-13 (2007)
19. Hassan, H., Garcia, J.M., Bockstal, C.: Aggregate Traffic Models for VoIP Applications. In: Proc. of ICDT 2006, Cap Esterel, pp. 70–75 (2006)
20. Pragtong, P., Erke, T., Ahmed, K.: Analysis and Modeling of VoIP Conversation Traffic in the Real Network. In: Proc. of ICICS 2005, Bangkok, pp. 388–392 (2005)
21. Sarkar, U., Ramakrishnan, S., Sarkar, D.: Modeling Full-Length Video Using Markov-Modulated Gamma-Based Framework. Transactions on Networking 11(4), 638–649 (2003)
22. Big Buck Bunny – free available computer animated movie from the Peach open movie project online resource, http://www.bigbuckbunny.org
23. Schulzrinne, H., Rao, A., Lanphier, R.: Real Time Streaming Protocol (RTSP), RFC 2326 (April 1998)
24. Schulzrinne, H., Casner, S., Frederick, R., Jacobson, V.: RTP: A Transport Protocol for Real-Time Applications, RFC 3550 (July 2003)
25. Rech, J.: Wireless LANs, 3rd edn. Heise (2008)

Analyzing Energy Consumption in a Gossiping MAC Protocol*

Haidi Yue, Henrik Bohnenkamp, and Joost-Pieter Katoen

Software Modeling & Verification
Department of Computer Science 2, RWTH Aachen University
D-52056 Aachen, Germany
Fax: +49 241 80 222 17
{haidi.yue,henrik,katoen}@cs.rwth-aachen.de

Abstract. In this paper, we analyze the energy-efficiency of a TDMA protocol (gMAC) for gossiping-based wireless sensor networks. In contrast to most schedule-based TDMA protocols, slot allocation in gMAC is decentralized, allowing adaptation to evolving network configurations. The protocol, modeled in the MoDeST language, is evaluated using the discrete-event simulator of the Möbius tool suite. We investigate the impact of collision-detection mechanisms, initiator positioning, and random silence on the gMAC energy efficiency. As a result, we find the number of active slots that optimize the trade-off between low energy consumption and fast information dissemination.

Keywords: TDMA, energy, wireless sensor networks, formal modeling, simulation.

1 Introduction

The Dutch company CHESS develops wireless sensor networks (WSN) comprising battery-powered mobile sensors that exchange data via gossiping-based communication. The sensors are mobile, act in a fully decentralized manner—there is, e.g., no leader—and battery recharging is not possible. CHESS WSNs are, for instance, used in the Dutch flower auction market in Aalsmeer where thousands of trolleys carrying flowers are equipped with autonomous routing capabilities.

To realize an energy-efficient communication mechanism supporting sensor mobility, CHESS developed a TDMA-variant, called gossip-based MAC [15] (gMAC, for short) to control medium access. In TDMA, the time is divided into frames which are subdivided into slots in which nodes send or receive or idle. Whereas in most TDMA protocols a central access node decides which slot is to be used by which node, in a setting with mobile nodes, a fixed schedule can no longer be maintained: ever changing neighborhood relations between

---

* This research has been funded by the EU under grant number FP7-ICT-2007-1 (QUASIMODO) and the DFG Excellence Cluster UMIC.

B. Müller-Clostermann et al. (Eds.): MMB & DFT 2010, LNCS 5987, pp. 107–119, 2010.

nodes invalidate defined schedules and cause collisions in communication. Therefore, gMAC exploits a fully decentralized slot allocation—each node decides on its own when to send and when not. Moreover, the sensors communicate with each other in an epidemic broadcast-like manner. This forms the basis of gossiping applications in which nodes continuously exchange data [10]. This all-to-all communication prevents the usage of simple (and frequently adopted) energy-conserving strategies like switching off a radio when no communication with the central access node takes place. In our setting, nodes have to listen to messages sent by all their neighbors and only idle during the non-active slots. To enable an implementation with simple (and cheap) microprocessors, CHESS designed gMAC as simple as possible. Therefore, gMAC does not incorporate techniques such as dynamic frame lengths as in EC-TDMA [16], transmission length indications as in A-MAC [12], or organizing neighbor information in a spanning tree as in TreeMAC [14].

gMAC is designed to work with a rather simple radio working in the 2.4 GHz band. Like any TDMA protocol, time is divided into frames. A frame consists of an idle and an active period. The active period is divided into equal-length slots, in which nodes send (once per frame and node) or receive. The beginning of new frames is synchronized among all neighboring nodes up to a certain precision. As nodes decide autonomously in which slot they send, collisions may occur. gMAC supports an indirect collision avoidance mechanism: node X keeps track of the slots in which it received something. This list is communicated by X to its neighbor Y as piggy-back information in the payload. If X did not receive an item in Y's send slot, Y infers that it is using the same send slot as another node, and randomly chooses a new, free one. As this mechanism cannot ensure the complete absence of collisions, a node can randomly decide to not use its send slot, and listen instead.

In this paper, we focus on the energy-efficiency of the protocol under the assumption of perfect clock synchronization. In particular, we investigate the effectiveness of the gMAC collision-detection mechanism (which fraction of real collisions is detected?), initiator positioning of gossiping messages (what is the influence of the position of the gossip initiator on latency?), and random silence on the gMAC energy efficiency (how does this protocol aspect impact collision detection?). As a result, we find the number of active slots that optimize the trade-off between low energy consumption and fast information dissemination for various system configurations. We consider first static network configurations to study the basic protocol mechanisms, and then determine the influence of node mobility. The main findings of our study that were also of interest to CHESS are (i) random silence improves collision detection significantly, (ii) the optimal number of active slots is about the number of neighbors plus one, and (iii) mobility lowers the number of failed transmissions.

Although our analysis technique is simulation, we deliberately take a drastically different approach from using standard simulation packages such as NS2, Opnet, OMNET or GloMoSim, to mention a few. Our starting point is a model of the protocol in the MoDeST language [3], a formalism that supports the modular specification of distributed systems in a mathematically rigorous, though user-friendly, manner. As MoDeST has a formal operational semantics in terms of stochastic timed automata, the simulation model obtained from the protocol models is unambiguous. The automata underlying MoDeST models are simulated using Möbius [7,5], a discrete-event simulator that has been intensively used in dependability analysis. The formality of the modeling language allows not only the integration with other formal analysis tools (such as model checkers), but, more importantly, yields semantically sound simulation runs. Together with the fact that we do not model entire protocol stacks but rather abstract from lower layer effects, this avoids many of the credibility problems of standard simulations [6,1]. This approach has, amongst others, been applied to analyze the energy consumption of Zigbee and IEEE 802.15 [8], and the analysis of a plug-and-play communication protocol [4]. Main limitation of our approach is that MoDeST models may exhibit nondeterminism, which cannot be simulated. We thus have to check our models prior to simulation on the presence of nondeterminism.

Organization of the paper. Section 2 describes the CHESS gMAC protocol. Section 3 describes the modeling assumptions and the experimental set-up. Section 4 focuses on results concerning collision detection, and Section 5 focuses on energy consumption. Section 6 concludes.

2   The gMAC Protocol

The gMAC protocol divides time in fixed-length *frames*. A frame is divided in an active and idle period, and both periods are subdivided into *slots* of equal length. A node in the network is synchronized with its immediate neighbors at the beginning of a frame. A node randomly chooses an active slot as *send slot* (the *TX slot*). All other active slots are *receive slots* (*RX slots*). During the idle period, the radio is put in idle mode to save energy. In an RX slot, a node listens for incoming messages from neighboring nodes, in its TX slot it sends a message. When the active period is over, it switches to idle mode again, and so forth.

Let S be the number of slots within a frame, and $A \leq S$ the number of active slots. A is a crucial parameter in the protocol design, as the active operation phase costs much more energy than the idle phase. The CHESS network nodes are equipped with an ATMega64 microcontroller and a Nordic nRF24L01 [13] packet radio. The energy demands of the nRF24L01 radio are summarized in Table 1. A is usually much smaller than S. In the gMAC protocol

Table 1. Energy demands of the nRF24L01 radio

mode	current
transmit	11.3 mA
receive	12.3 mA
idle	0.9 μA

implementation with the aforementioned processor, S=1129, and $A = 8$.

When a node is powered on, it randomly chooses an active slot as TX slot. In each RX slot, it can receive a message of at most one other node. The well-known *hidden node problem* describes the scenario when more than one node sends messages to the same node in the same slot.

Figure 1(a) depicts a situation where nodes X, Y, Z are positioned such that the middle node Y is within the transmission range (the circles) of both other nodes, and both X and Z are outside each others range. If X and Z select the same TX slot, then their messages will collide in the intersection of their ranges. They cannot sense this themselves, and Y will receive no message at all as it cannot distinguish a collision from the situation where no message was sent.

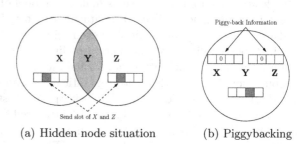

(a) Hidden node situation   (b) Piggybacking

Fig. 1. Hidden node problem and its detection

The gMAC protocol provides a piggy-back technique to make collisions detectable. With each pay-load message, the sender's perspective on the current slot allocation is also transmitted, which we call the *piggy-back information*. The piggy-back information is a sequence $(b_0, b_1, ..., b_{A-1})$, where $b_i \in \{0,1\}$ for $0 \leq i < A$. $b_i = 0$ indicates that nothing has been received in slot i, either because nobody sent something, or due to a collision or message loss. $b_i = 1$ indicates that the sender received something in slot i, or that slot i is the sender's own current send slot. In the example in Figure 1(a), since Y cannot receive anything in the second slot, it writes a 0 in its piggy-back information at the corresponding position and reports this to X and Z on its turn to send, in the third slot (*cf.* Figure 1(b)). Based on this information from Y, nodes X and Z can conclude that there was a collision in their send slot. The gMAC protocol then stipulates that X and Z pick randomly a new send slot among the free active slots, to avoid further collisions. Note that it is possible that no free slot is available when a node needs one. This can happen when the nodes are in a very crowded environment and the number of neighbors exceeds the number of active slots (some of our simulation configurations cover this situation). In this case, the node will keep the old send slot despite the detected collision in that slot.

Although the piggy-back technique helps to detect many collisions, there are still some it cannot find. In Figure 2, node Y has the same send slot as X and Z, *i.e.*, they send and receive at the same time and will therefore never receive anything from each other in this slot, hence the collisions between them will not be detected or resolved. The reason for this is that the piggy-back technique

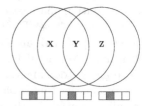

Fig. 2. Problematic scenario for piggy-back technique

requires at least one common neighbor which is not involved in the conflict, so that it can report the collision. The gMAC protocol provides one more mechanism to break this kind of conflict. When a node reaches its send slot, it can decide with a certain probability p to *not* send, but to listen. This gives a node a chance to overhear what is going on in its own send slot, and an opportunity to pick a new send slot, if necessary.

3   Experimental Setup

Modeling assumptions. In the real world, the interference range of a node's radio signal is usually larger than its effective transmission range. The magnitude of the interference range is not necessarily equal in every direction. Besides, the ranges can vary from time to time. Depending on the environment, the Nordic nRF24L01 radio has a range between $0.5m$ to $50m$. For the sake of simplicity, we adopt the approach chosen in [2] and use the closed unit disk model in which the interference range equals the transmission range, and is given by a radius r. All network nodes are assumed to have the same transmission range, which means the transmission between nodes is symmetric. We further abstract from other link layer mechanisms, i.e., message losses are assumed to be due to collisions only. gMAC incorporates a mechanism to synchronize clocks of neighboring nodes. Sufficient criteria that ensure the correctness of this clock-synchronization mechanism have recently been mathematically analyzed [9]. As our simulation models satisfy these criteria, we abstract from the clock-synchronization algorithm.

The gMAC protocol accommodates for tolerable de-synchronization by shortening the actual sending period and uses the difference to the slot length as a lead-in to and lead-out from the send period (the so-called guard times). This does of course influence the energy consumption, and therefore we incorporate the guard times in our model.

Set-up. The base model of our experiments is a 15×15 grid network of 225 nodes. Each node has a distance of 1 to its respective horizontal and vertical neighbors (*i.e.,* the distance to the diagonal neighbors is $\sqrt{2}$). A frame consists of 1129 slots. The number A of active slots is a crucial parameter in the protocol, and we analyze the behavior of the gMAC protocol for various A. Since in the real implementation $A=8$, we choose the transmission range r such that each inner node of the grid has 4 or 8 direct neighbors, respectively. We say a node is *randomly silent*, if it stays silent in its TX slot with some probability. This probability in the current implementation of the CHESS sensor node is $p = \frac{1}{16}$. We adopt this value in our model and use it for all experiments. To get insight into the influence of this parameter, we also performed experiments with other values of p, e.g. $p = \frac{1}{8}$. It turns out that the results pattern is similar to that with $p = \frac{1}{16}$, which that is with random silence, a higher percentage of collisions can be detected. The experiments focus on two major aspects: (i) the effect of the gMAC collision detection mechanism (piggy-backing and random silence), and (ii) the latency of message dissemination versus the required energy consumption. The confidence level of all simulations is set to 0.95 and the relative confidence interval is 0.1.

Collision analysis. We estimate the effectiveness of the collision detection mechanisms by counting both the real number of collisions that occurred in the network (referred to as *Failed Transmissions*, FT for short) and the number of collisions that are detected using the piggy-backing technique (the number of *Detected Collisions*, DC for short) in each frame. Note that although a node can detect collisions, it can neither distinguish with whom it collided nor how many nodes collided. Hence, when considering DC, we can only count the number of nodes that report collisions and not the real number of collisions, i.e. DC represents actually the number of nodes that detect collisions. The values for FT and DC are illustrated for different scenarios in Figure 3 where the number next to a node (small circles) indicates its TX slot. The right-most figure represents an extreme case, where the respective diagonal nodes send and receive at the same time, i.e., while the upper righthand and the lower lefthand nodes are sending, their messages collide at the upper lefthand and lower righthand nodes, and vice versa. Hence communication between all nodes fails, but no node is able to detect it. We vary the transmission range r and the number A of active slots as follows. In networks with at most 4 neighbors, A ranges from 4 to 10, and for at most 8 neighbors, A ranges from 6 to 12. Each of the experiments is run 100 times and lasts at least 1000 frames.

Latency vs. energy consumption. Second, we focus on the latency of message dissemination and the energy consumed by that. We consider the average time required and the total average energy consumed until a message is delivered to all network nodes. We say a node is *infected* if it has received a message. Initially, only one node is infected, the initiator. To get insight into the effect of the position

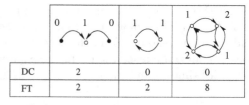

DC	2	0	0
FT	2	2	8

● : Detected Collision   : Failed transmission

Fig. 3. Three collision situations

in the network of the message initiator, we consider (cf. Figure 4): a corner node, a middle node at the border, and a center node. Again, the simulations are run for different values of r and A to investigate the influence of these parameters on gMAC's energy consumption. Each experiment is run 600 times.

Different settings. We run all aforementioned experiments for three network settings:

1. A static network without *randomly silent* nodes (for short *grid*),
2. A static network with *randomly silent* nodes (for short *grid+p*),

3. A network with node mobility but no *randomly silent* nodes (for short *grid+m*), so that we can obtain a clear comparison between static and mobile scenarios without influence of *randomly silent* nodes.

Since we want to investigate the influence of local changing of node position on the network, we model the mobility by rotating a fixed row (the fifth row) in the grid one position to the right. The node shifted out is shifted in on the other side. The row is rotated one position every 100 frames for the collision experiment, so that the network has enough time to stabilize after each shift. Since the average time required to deliver a message to all nodes is less than 30 frames, we rotate every 1 or 3 frames to investigate the influence of the moving rate on the latency.

4   Collision Analysis

The different variants of gMAC in the different scenarios have been modelled in the MoDeST modelling language [3], and simulated in the Möbius tool set [7]. The models are available from `http://moves.rwth-aachen.de/~henrik/mmb10/`.

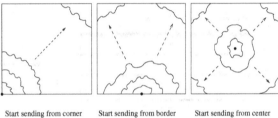

Start sending from corner   Start sending from border   Start sending from center

Fig. 4. Three different initiator positions

Static network. We consider the static grid model *grid* without *randomly silent* nodes. The transmission range is $r = 1.1 < \sqrt{2}$, *i.e.,* each inner node has 4 neighbors. Figure 5(a) shows the fraction $\frac{DC}{FT}$ versus the number of frames for different values of A. A larger percentage means that a larger fraction of collisions is detected by the gMAC piggy-backing method. The graph shows that for increasing A, a larger fraction of collisions is detected. This is confirmed for a network with 8 neighbors, cf. Figure 5(b). The almost horizontal straight lines show that for small A the randomly changing slot allocation does not reduce the number of collisions, but yields a more or less stable number of collisions. If A is large enough, $\frac{DC}{FT}$ goes to zero, as no collisions are detected anymore. This phenomenon occurs, e.g., for $A=10$ and $r = 1.1$, as can be seen in Figure 5(a). Failed transmissions may still occur, however; for $A=10$, e.g., on average 7 transmissions in the whole network fail without being detected (not depicted in Figure 5(a)). Apart from the fact that some collisions can never be detected, it is generally the case that A needs to be large—in comparison to the number of neighbors—before DC tends to go to 0. Our simulations have shown that, in the case of 4 neighbors, this is the case for $A \geq 9$; for 8 neighbors, this holds for $A \geq 23$.

Random silence. Figure 6(a) depicts the results of the same experiment run on *grid+p* with 4 neighbors. The comparison with Figure 5(a) reveals that *grid+p*

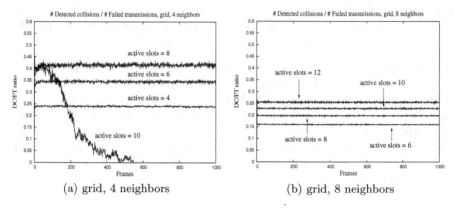

(a) grid, 4 neighbors   (b) grid, 8 neighbors

Fig. 5. Collision detection in a static network

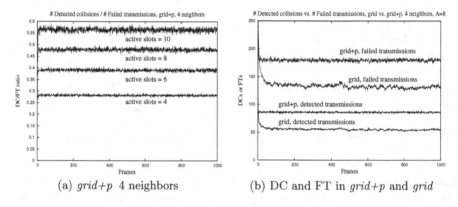

(a) *grid+p* 4 neighbors   (b) DC and FT in *grid+p* and *grid*

Fig. 6. Collision detection under random silence

can detect a significantly larger percentage of collisions than *grid*. This percentage increases for larger A. Furthermore, in *grid+p*, even with $A=10$, the fraction $\frac{DC}{FT}$ does not go to 0 anymore. Our explanation for that is that in *grid+p* nodes are more often receiving than in *grid*, and thus more collisions are detected. Indeed, for $A=8$, DC in *grid+p* is significantly higher than for *grid*, cf. Figure 6(b). Figure 6(b) also shows that FT increases compared to *grid*. This is unexpected. We believe that the reason for this phenomenon is that, when A is at least the number of neighbors, then *randomly silent* nodes can turn a good slot allocation into a bad one. Consider Figure 7 (left), with 11 nodes (the numbers indicating their TX slots) and only two neighboring nodes in conflict (in slot 2). Let $A=5$. When the boxed node is silent in slot 2, it will detect a collision, and (randomly) chooses a free send slot, which is slot 3 (all others are in use). As the right figure shows, the boxed node is suddenly in conflict with four nodes (2-hop neighbors) rather than one, causing eight failed transmissions. The new slot allocation is worse than before. Of course, the case illustrated in Figure 7 is quite extreme. In general, when A is larger than the number of direct neighbors it will probably collide only with relatively fewer 2-hop neighbors.

Node mobility. We now consider the influence of node mobility on $\frac{DC}{FT}$. Figure 8(a) shows the results for a network with $r = 1.1$ and a shifting frequency of $\frac{1}{100}$ frames. We can see for $A = 10$ that the amplitudes of the curves shortly after every 100 frames are quite significant, and between each two peaks, the curve tends to

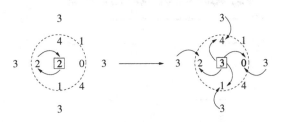

Fig. 7. Changing slot allocation by silent node

go down. For $A \leq 8$, the peaks nearly vanish. This means that for A so small that the static network can not reach a collision-free state, the influence of mobility on collision detection diminishes. In fact, when A is small, $\frac{DC}{FT}$, as well as DC and FT, especially DC, are almost unchanged under node mobility (*cf.* Figure 8(b)). For a higher rate of node shifting, *i.e.*, shifting every 30 frames, the result pattern is similar.

5   Latency vs. Energy Consumption

Static network. The second type of simulation is concerned with the energy efficiency of message propagation. By latency we mean the average time required to deliver a message to all nodes. Again, we first consider a static network. Figure 9(a) shows the experimental results for transmission range $r=1.1$, and A ranging from 4 to 7. The message initiator is positioned in the corner. The *circle-lines* show the energy consumption (right y-axis) versus the number of frames, and the black, curved lines (left y-axis) show the ratio of infected nodes (i.e., nodes that have received a message) versus the number of frames.

The results confirm that for fixed A, there is a linear dependency between the energy consumption and the number of frames, which is characteristic for TDMA protocols. The slope depends on A; the larger A, the steeper the energy curves. For the message dissemination, it can be observed that after a short warm-up phase, the fraction of infected nodes drastically grows, after which this slowly progresses to one. For increasing A, the percentage of infected nodes converges to more quickly to one, i.e., message dissemination is faster.

Obviously, the larger the A is, the lower the message latency becomes, but as a pay-off, the energy consumptions increases with larger A. In order to get insight into the trade-off between message dissemination and energy consumption, Figure 9(b) depicts an energy-percentage diagram, which shows the percentage of infected nodes versus the total energy needed to infect all nodes. One clearly sees that $A=4$ and $A=7$ are not economical and in the considered scenario, a network with 5 or 6 active slots provides the best result in terms of energy efficiency.

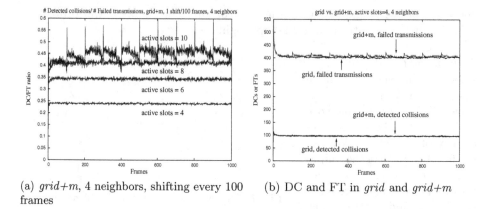

(a) *grid+m*, 4 neighbors, shifting every 100 frames

(b) DC and FT in *grid* and *grid+m*

Fig. 8. Collision detection under node mobility

Performing the experiments for $A = 8, 9$ and 10 reveals that these settings are less energy-efficient than for $A = 7$. For $A = 10$, e.g., the network tends to be collision-free, but requires twice as much energy as for $A = 5$ without offering a doubled propagation speed. We performed the experiment for three different initial sending positions and different transmission ranges. All of them exhibit a pattern similar to Figure 9(b). The optimal values of A are summarized in Table 2.

Figure 9(c) shows another effect of changing the initial sending position. We put the most energy-efficient results from a network with 4 neighbors and initial sending position at the corner or the center in one graph. Obviously, starting from the center needs only two third energy of that starting from

Table 2. Optimal A values

Position Range	corner	border	center
4 neighbors	6	5	5
8 neighbors	8	9	8

the corner. It does not come as a surprise that message dissemination from the center is more efficient than from a corner. However, when we consider the influence of network density on latency, we can see that with a fixed initiator, a network with 4 neighbors or 8 neighbors exhibits almost the same performance (*cf.* Figure 9(d)). This means, although a denser network can propagate messages faster (a result which we have not shown here), it takes still as much energy as in a less dense network to deliver a message to the whole network.

Random silence. The results for *grid+p* show a similar behavior, hence we will not present them here. Interesting is however the comparison between *grid* and *grid+p*. In Figure 9(e), we see the most economical results of *grid* and *grid+p*, both with 4 neighbors and the same initial sending position. The superiority of *grid+p* is quite clear, since roughly 15% energy can be saved if nodes are *randomly silent*. This is not self-evident, since for the used radio, receiving costs actually more energy than sending. We believe that the 15% drop in energy

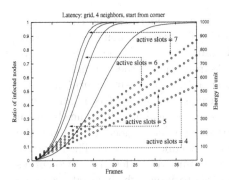

(a) grid, 4 neighbors, start sending from corner

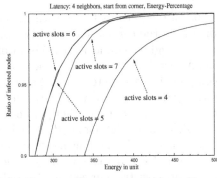

(b) Energy-percentage: grid, 4 neighbors, start sending from corner

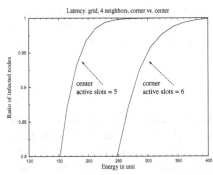

(c) corner vs. center, grid, both 4 neighbors

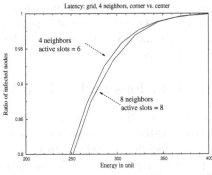

(d) 4 neighbors vs. 8 neighbors: grid, both start sending from corner

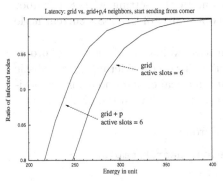

(e) *grid* vs. *grid+p*, both have 4 neighbors and start sending from corner

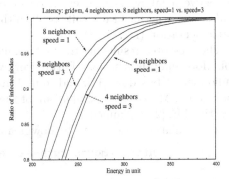

(f) different transmission ranges and shifting rates

Fig. 9. Latency vs. energy consumption

consumption is because *grid+p* has in general more opportunities to receive messages, which accelerates information dissemination.

Node mobility. For a network with mobility, we consider first the case of start sending from the corner. There are two options for transmission range (4 neighbors or 8 neighbors) and for the speed of shifting: every frame, or every third frame. As before, we combine the best results from each of these combinations in one graph (Figure 9(f)) to compare them. Recall that in the simple *grid* network, the density does not have a significant influence on the latency (see Figure 9(d)). However, in *grid+m*, if the other parameters are identical, the difference between a network with 4 neighbors and 8 neighbors cannot be neglected (compare the left-most curve with the right-most one, or the two middle curves). The influence of the speed of shifting is not very significant (compare the left-most two curves or the right-most two curves), and it is difficult to judge which speed overcome the others, for instance, speed=3 performs better than speed=1 for neighbors=4 while the trend is reversed for neighbors=8. This is due to the way we modeled mobility. In our mobility scenario, it takes circa 15 frames to deliver messages to the whole network, and a shifting of every 1 frame or every 3 frames cannot have much influence on the result. Under other mobility models, different results will be obtained.

6   Conclusions and Future Work

We reported on the simulative analysis of the CHESS gMAC protocol, aimed for gossiping-based applications in sensor networks. Our analysis reveals that randomly deciding to refrain from using send slots significantly increases the effectiveness of gMAC's collision detection mechanism, and reduces energy consumption by about 15%. Node mobility does not affect the number of detected collisions. We determined the number of active slots that optimize the trade-off between latency and energy consumption. In the setting with 8 neighbor nodes, our experimental results confirm the optimality of CHESS's current node implementation (i.e., $A=8$).

The presented results are the first quantitative evaluation of the gMAC protocol. More analysis is needed. Future work will focus on considering more realistic radio models based on [11], and to find mathematical explanations for the optimal values. Moreover, a comparison of the given results with the gMAC variant described in [2] is planned.

All simulation models can be downloaded from:

`http://moves.rwth-aachen.de/~henrik/mmb10/`

Acknowledgments

We thank Bert Bos, Frits van der Wateren, Marcel Verhoef (all of CHESS) for discussions on the gMAC protocol and suggestions on the modeling. Thanks to Daniel Klink (RWTH Aachen University), who suggested to compare latency and energy consumption.

References

1. Andel, T.R., Yasinac, A.: On the credibility of MANET simulations. IEEE Computer 39(7), 48–54 (2006)
2. Anemaet, P.A.M.: Distributed G-MAC. Master's thesis, Delft University of Technology (2008)
3. Bohnenkamp, H., D'Argenio, P.R., Hermanns, H., Katoen, J.-P.: Modest: A compositional modeling formalism for real-time and stochastic systems. IEEE Trans. on Software Engineering 32(10), 812–830 (2006)
4. Bohnenkamp, H., Gorter, J., Guidi, J., Katoen, J.-P.: Are you still there? — A lightweight algorithm to monitor node presence in self-configuring networks. In: Dependable Systems & Networks (DSN), pp. 704–709 (2005)
5. Bohnenkamp, H., Hermanns, H., Katoen, J.-P.: Motor: The MoDeST tool environment. In: Grumberg, O., Huth, M. (eds.) TACAS 2007. LNCS, vol. 4424, pp. 500–504. Springer, Heidelberg (2007)
6. Cavin, D., Sasson, Y., Schiper, A.: On the accuracy of MANET simulators. In: ACM Workshop On Principles Of Mobile Computing (POMC), pp. 38–43 (2002)
7. Deavours, D.D., Clark, G., Courtney, T., Daly, D., Derisavi, S., Doyle, J.M., Sanders, W.H., Webster, P.G.: The Möbius framework and its implementation. IEEE Trans. on Software Engineering 28(10), 956–969 (2002)
8. Gross, C., Hermanns, H., Pulungan, R.: Does clock precision influence ZigBee's energy consumptions? In: Tovar, E., Tsigas, P., Fouchal, H. (eds.) OPODIS 2007. LNCS, vol. 4878, pp. 174–188. Springer, Heidelberg (2007)
9. Heidarian, F., Schmaltz, J., Vaandrager, F.W.: Analysis of a clock synchronization protocol for wireless sensor networks. In: Cavalcanti, A., Dams, D.R. (eds.) FM 2009. LNCS, vol. 5850, pp. 516–531. Springer, Heidelberg (2009)
10. Kermarrec, A.-M., van Steen, M.: Gossiping in distributed systems. ACM SIGOPS Operating System Review 41(5), 2–7 (2007)
11. Meier, A., Rein, T., Beutel, J., Thiele, L.: Coping with unreliable channels: Efficient link estimation for low-power wireless sensor networks. In: Int. Conf. on Networked Sensing Systems (INSS), June 2008, pp. 19–26 (2008)
12. Rashid, R.A., Embong, W.M.A.E.W., Zaharim, A., Fisal, N.: Development of energy aware tdma-based MAC protocol for wireless sensor network system. European J. of Scientific Research, 571–578 (2009)
13. Nordic Semiconductors. nRF2401 Single-chip 2.4GHz Transceiver Data Sheet (2002)
14. Song, W., Huang, R., Shirazi, B.: TreeMAC: Localized TDMA MAC protocol for real-time high-data-rate sensor networks. In: IEEE Int. Conf. on Pervasive Computing and Communications (PerCom), pp. 1–10 (2009)
15. van Vessem, I.: WSN gMac protocol specification. Technical report, CHESS B. V., Haarlem, NL. Version 1.1. Patent pending US 12 / 215,040 (2008)
16. Xie, M., Wang, X.: An energy-efficient TDMA protocol for clustered wireless sensor networks. In: Computing, Communication, Control, and Management (CCCM), vol. 2, pp. 547–551 (2007)

Defining and Measuring Performance Characteristics of Current Video Games

Till Fischer[1], Axel Böttcher[1], Aaron Coday[2], and Helena Liebelt[2]

[1] Munich University of Applied Sciences
Department of Computer Science and Mathematics
Lothstr. 64
80335 München, Germany
`ab@cs.hm.edu, 9fischer@informatik.uni-hamburg.de`
[2] Intel GmbH
Dornacher Str. 1
85622 Feldkirchen/München, Germany
`{aaron.c.coday,helena.liebelt}@intel.com`

Abstract. In this paper, we provide a study of current PC video games' performance across several different metrics conducted at the Intel Labs. As a hardware manufacturer, Intel needs to look at the performance characteristics of these applications on its current hardware. The information is used to help predict future processor needs and performance characteristics. Additionally, the information can help Independent Software Vendors (ISV) understand opportunities to improve their applications in the future. Furthermore, as an educational institution we have the suggestion of a measurement set-up that we can use for practical lectures in Computer Architecture education.

The main findings are that the CPU and memory are no bottleneck for current games and that e.g. SIMD-instructions are more widely used than assumed. An important result is also that the Scalable Link Interface (SLI) does not necessarily improve performance.

1 Introduction

One goal of the study was to develop a consolidated guide providing a single standard methodology of doing measurements for all Intel engineers. Another goal was to check hypotheses, the Intel performance engineers had on the performance effects of their hardware features. Concretely we wanted to check the following hyptheses:

1. The memory interface is a bottleneck.
2. SLI drastically improves the performance of games.
3. SIMD instructions are not widely used.

Besides this there are several use cases for the results of this paper of common interest: Game developers can detect, where their performance bottlenecks are. Second, the results give hints to the hardware developers on where further improvements will pay off for software developers of high-end applications such as games. Game developers demand for an improvement of at least 20% of a new feature, otherwise their necessary

B. Müller-Clostermann et al. (Eds.): MMB & DFT 2010, LNCS 5987, pp. 120–135, 2010.

code changes to adapt the feature are not justifiable. Third gamers can see that they have to combine high-end CPU and high-end GPU to get a powerful PC. Finally the measurement methodology can be used in teaching Computer Architecture from a practical point of view.

This study is also interesting because it is a step towards the challenge proposed by Donald E. Knuth [1] to *Make a thorough analysis of everything your computer does during one second of computation.*

In the following we first describe our measurement environment in terms of hardware and computer game workload. Then we describe the metrics we want to measure and present tools to measure these quantities. The last section presents the most interesting results we have found so far.

2   Measurement Set-Up and Video Game Workload

This section describes our hardware environment and the workload in terms of games analyzed. As basis for our testing system we chose a current *Intel Software Development Platform* or short *SDP*. These *SDPs* are standardized i.e. a definition exists for these systems about what the exact hardware is. We switched the normal graphics board to a more recent one. For the measurements using Scalable Link Interface (SLI) we installed a second graphics board of the same type. SLI is a Multi-GPU technology by NVIDIA which can be used to connect two similiar graphics boards to the end of improving overall performance or support multiple monitors. We used the option to improve graphics performance. Besides that no other hardware changes were applied.

2.1   Hardware Configuration

Table 1 gives details about the exact hardware parts used in the testing system.

Table 1. Specification of the test system

Part	Specification
CPU	Core i7 965 @ 3.2GHz
RAM	3× 1GiB DDR3 @ 666.7MHz
Graphics Board	2× NVIDIA GeForce GTX 260 — Driver: 7.15.0011.8208
Mainboard	X58 rev. 12
BIOS	SOX5810J.86A.3504.2009.0218.0058
Hard Drive	Seagate Barracuda 7200.11 SATA – 3GiB/s 500GiB

2.2   Video Games

For this study we chose a significant set of video games. There was a certain set of criteria applied to choose this set of titles.

– A repeatable workload is available. This means that the measured games must offer the possibility to reproduce a concrete situation in the action's flow. In some games, a demo mode helps to establish this.

- The game uses either *DirectX 9* or *DirectX 10* and
- The game is a good representative of its genre.

Since most games do not have a built in benchmark or a *demo mode*, a function to record gameplay and replay it later, using not pre-calculation but doing the same calculations each time, we needed another process to have repeatable workloads. To this end we used textual descriptions, with detailed step-by-step instructions, which had to be followed to achieve repeatable results. Obviously there is a human factor involved, but we found that the results weren't deviating from one another too much.

A game is considered a good representative of its genre if it technologically is up to date, received good critics and is played by many people. As an indication of good critics we used the rating provided by `www.metacritics.com`, which aggregates many different ratings. We analyzed the following games:

First Person Shooters. Games of this action-oriented genre usually require high-end hardware. *Call of Duty 4: Modern Warfare* is a First Person Shooter that features many modern graphical features, such as High Dynamic Range (HDR) lighting effect, dynamic shadows, dynamic lighting, and depth of field effects. It was released November 2007.

Crysis Warhead is a product by *Crytek* that is one of the most performance-hungry games. The game was released in September 2008. It uses the *CryENGINE 2* that is also developed by *Crytek*.

Far Cry 2 by *Ubisoft-Montreal*. The developers of the previous *Far Cry*, *Crytek* were not involved in developing this title. The game was released in October 2008. The game engine is able to display dynamic effects such as fire that is spreading through dry grass realistically. Another fact that makes this engine interesting to us is that the game is said to take exceptional advantage of multi-core processors.

Unreal Tournament 3 (UT3) is done by *Epic Games* that is using the *Unreal Engine 3*. The game was released in November 2007 but the latest patch was released in May 2009.

Racing Games. This genre is one of the oldest gaming genres. There are still many games of this genre released every year. These games usually require the player to race against time and/or opponents. Games in this genre consistently push the envelope in terms of graphical effects.

Race Driver: GRID is a racing game that has done very well in reviews. It was released end of May 2008. *GameStar's* review, translated and condensed by *Metacritic* also mentions the technically impressive aspects of the game.

Real-Time Strategy. Real-time strategy (RTS) games is a genre of games usually having a warlike theme, that in difference to turn-based strategy do not progress in turns, but in real-time. RTSs are now one of the pillars of the gaming market. They are often graphically and computationally intense, featuring lots of models and much *AI* to calculate.

Warhammer 40,000: Dawn of War II is a *RTS* game that is set in the world of *Warhammer 40,000*, originally a tabletop war game produced by *Games Workshop*. *Dawn of War II* was developed by *Relic Entertainment*. The game was released in

February of 2009. Although the game is listed here as *RTS* some call it a *Real-time tactics* (RTT) game and consider this to be a sub-genre of *RTS*. *RTTs* have no or minimal base or unit building, do not have resource gathering as part of the game and often give greater importance to single units. This manifests in *Dawn of War II* in having a few key characters with special abilities, that need to survive each mission and have special abilities.

World in Conflict: Soviet Assault by *Massive Entertainment* is the sequel to *World in Conflict* and was released in March of 2009. It is a *RTS* belonging to the sub-genre of *RTT* games.

Role-Playing Video Games. This genre of games is characterized by the player controlling one or several characters that he usually steers through a series of quests. The characters gain more power and new abilities as the game progresses. Which powers or abilities these are is most of the time controlled by the player.

The story for these games is usually highly developed, often reaching the complexity and length of big novels. The rules of these games often derive from non-video *RPGs* like *Dungeons & Dragons* or similar gaming systems. These games have lots of different denominations, sometimes bordering into action or strategy genres.

World of Warcraft: Wrath of the Lich King for example is a first- or third-person *Massively Multiplayer Online RPG* or short *MMORPG* that has qualities usually found in action (adventure) games. The add-on was released during November 2008.

Wrath of the Lich King (WotLK) is the latest installment of *World of Warcraft*. It features a new continent to explore and also the *level-cap* has been raised. More interesting are the graphical improvements that come with *WotLK*. New shaders to render ice, new fire effects and better shadows where among those.

Since *WotLK* is a purely online game there are more aspects to look for regarding repeatability. The more other players are online in and in the sight of the player, the more objects have to be rendered. To this end we used a server located in the US and so we could measure when most people playing on it were asleep. One could think that the workload on the system could change significantly with the quality of the internet connection. We found that this is not the case. Almost all calculations are done on the machine, sending just the interactions back and forth between server and client. So even if the network experienced round-trip delays, we would see other players having a jerky movement, but still have the same workload on our machine.

2.3   General Game Settings

To be able to compare obtained results between games, a standard has to be defined as to which settings to use. A game usually lets the user choose between a bunch of different options for settings such as resolution, graphical effects, texture sizes, or sound effects and controls.

For the graphics, physics and gameplay settings of the application, we opted to let the application decide which settings are best. Most current games do have some mechanism to detect the capabilities of the system they are running on and to adopt their settings accordingly. So they would set *high quality* settings on a high end system and *low quality* settings on a low end system.

So we let the games decide the settings in the first step, if they had no such option we hand-set *high* quality were the steps usually are *low medium high* and sometimes *very high*. But we did not let the games decide on each of the resolutions seen below, but we let the game decide once and then kept to those settings. So the only variable (in the game) was the resolution.

We did have three different base configurations that we ran the measurements on, namely

1. Resolution of 1280×768,
2. Resolution of 1600×1200 and
3. Resolution of 1600×1200 with two graphics boards operating in SLI mode.

By increasing the resolution from 1280×768 to 1600×1200 we increase the amount of pixels by a factor of approximately two. This potentially increases the workload of the graphics board which needs to process more pixels. Adding another graphics board and coupling the two boards in SLI mode we then can find out how much games really benefit from SLI and what the effect on the whole system is.

3 Metrics

Here we define those metrics that are of interest for our study. We restrict our analysis to MS-Windows platforms due to the fact that Windows is the de-facto standard PC gaming platform. However, most metrics defined in this paper can also be measured on other operating systems.

There are three general types of metrics that we will look at: *Utilization metrics* that measure the utilization of system resources, *Instruction-mix metrics* that describe the percentage one specific set of instructions is being used in comparison to the overall number of instructions retired, and finally metrics that count other values of interest (called *Miscellaneous Metrics*).

3.1 Utilization Metrics

The following three utilization metrics have been considered in this project:

Utilization of the CPU. This metric covers the minimum, maximum and average percentage the CPU is utilized by the workload in total, and per physical core. This is interesting to determine how good a given application is parallelized and to what extent the CPU as an important resource is used.

Utilization of the Memory Bandwidth. This metric is helpful to find bottlenecks in the overall performance of an application [2]. We are using the unit of *giga binary byte per second*, short: GiB/s. When talking about bandwidth utilization we mean the fraction of the maximum achievable system bandwidth that an application uses.

There are three DDR3 Dual Inline Memory Modules (DIMM) installed in our testing systems (see table 1), to fully utilize the three memory channels and operate in Triple Channel Mode. Triple Channel in comparison to Dual Channel is a memory interface that was introduced with the new *Nehalem* architecture and triples the maximum transfer of a Single Channel interface. We can easily calculate the maximum theoretical bandwidth of a standard system that uses current Double Data Rate (DDR) memory.

Assuming a memory clock-frequency of 666.5 MHz, 64 data lines per DIMM, and two words that can be read or written with DDR-memory during each cycle, we get for the maximum theoretical memory bandwidth B_{max}:

$$B_{max} = \left(666.5 * 10^6 * \frac{cycles}{s}\right) * (3\ channels) * \left(64 * \frac{lines}{channel}\right) * \left(2 * \frac{bit}{\frac{line}{cycle}}\right)$$

$$\approx 29.79\ GiB/s \quad (1)$$

This theoretical maximum is most probably not the real practical system maximum. So this bandwidth is not what we wanted to use as a reference point. There is however a widely known memory benchmark called Stream to measure the real memory bandwidth of the system [3].

Using Stream compiled on the testing system with the current Intel compiler and utilizing all 4 hardware threads using OpenMP, we obtained 19.4GiB/s as the practical system maximum. This value is the result of Stream's *triad* test which is regarded as the most significant of Stream's tests [3].

To sum up, this metric is defined as the percentage of traffic, generated during the workload of the systems practical maximum bandwidth. And the pratical maximum bandwith is defined as the maximal data-rate as measured by Stream.

$$\text{Bandwidth Utilization} = \frac{\text{Measured bandwidth}[GiB/s]}{\text{Practical System Maximum}[GiB/s]} \quad (2)$$

Utilization of the Hard Disk. The other I/O that can potentially be a bottleneck for a game's overall performance is the hard disk drive (HDD). For this metric we are interested in the sum of read and write operations per second averaged over the runtime of the workload. This again needs to be put into relation to the system maximum.

There are measurement results available on http://ht4u.net. They tested the exact same mainboard and chipset that we used and even used the same hard drives as we did (see table 1).

Their results are:

$$\text{Average Reads} = 89.4\text{MiB/s} \quad (3)$$

$$\text{Average Writes} = 80.5\text{MiB/s} \quad (4)$$

Since we do not know the distribution of reads and writes in a workload, we simply use the average of these values (84.95MiB/s) as an approximation for the maximum disk utilization and define:

$$\text{Utilization of Disk} = \frac{\text{Measured Reads per second} + \text{Measured Writes per second}}{84.95\ \text{MiB/s}} \quad (5)$$

3.2 Instruction-Mix Metrics

Here we are interested in the fraction a certain set of instructions is used with respect to the total number of instructions retired. The classes of instructions that are of main interest are:

1. Floating point operations. These calculations are computationally intensive. On some CPUs a single floating point division can take more than 24 cycles for execution.
2. SIMD instructions. In 1997 Intel introduced the first set of Single Instruction Multiple Data instructions (SIMD) branded as MMX. In the following years, Streaming SIMD Extensions (SSE), SSE2, SSE3 and SSE4 followed. A common scenario for the use of these vector instructions in multimedia applications is the simultaneous manipulation of several pixels in a digital picture.

The metric for each instruction class is defined as the percentage of instructions of the respective instruction class during the workload:

$$\text{Percentage of instructions of the class} = \frac{\sum \text{Instructions of the class}}{\sum \text{All Instructions}} * 100 \quad (6)$$

In case of the SIMD instructions it is important to know if this feature of our CPU is accepted and valued or disregarded by game developers. Together with data on SIMD usage in other areas, such as multi-media applications or high-performance computing, this could or could not be a reason for a change in effort on this topic. We might decide to encourage and help developers, to be able to use these kinds of special instructions, thereby increasing the performance of their software.

Similar to this metric we are looking at floating point instructions with the interest shifted from the total percentage of floating point instruction executed to their distribution on the four cores The reason for this is to find out if the Windows scheduler happens to put computationally expensive threads of the workload on the same core, therefore potentially negatively influencing the overall performance of the application. This metric is defined as percentage of floating point operations on each core.

3.3 Miscellaneous Metrics

The metrics listed in this section don't fit directly in either of the above described categories. However, they are neither less significant nor less interesting.

Frames Per Second. Frames per second (FPS – not meaning First Person Shooter here!) is one of the most common metrics for evaluation of video game performance, because it is the most important performance metric to the end user [4].

A rule of thumb is that most games are enjoyable with a frame rate beyond 30 FPS. There are, however, games that try to achieve exactly 60 FPS and thus are able to synchronize with the refresh-rate of most modern displays. But it is also possible to obtain FPS rates higher than the refresh-rate of the display.

How many frames can be produced per second is a direct result of the whole system performance and the settings of a game. The higher the graphics quality settings are, the fewer FPS will be produced.

Another aspect of this metric is that the fraction can be easily inverted, resulting in *time per Frame*, the so called the *frame-budget*. A game running at 60 FPS gives a frame-budget of 16.67ms. So the FPS-metric is a direct measure for what a certain performance increase is worth in terms of better effects, higher quality textures, more calculations for the game logic.

The metrics that we are looking for regarding FPS are minimum, maximum and average FPS of the workload.

Instructions and Clock Cycles per Module. It is interesting to find out how much work each part of a workload generates. We call these parts *modules*. The term module may summarize a bundle of binaries that belong to the same part of the system. A *module* consists at least of a library, a driver or an executable. For example the Windows module is a bundle consisting of hal.dll, ntkrnlpa.exe, ntdll.dll, kernel32.dll, and several others.

There are four key modules required to run a video game. These are:

1. The Game itself
2. The Graphics driver
3. The Direct 3d runtime library
4. The Windows operating system together with the Windows API

4   Measurement Tools

Some of the tools used for this project are only for use by Intel employees. And these private tools can not be mentioned or described here. However details as to what is measured will be given.

Fraps. We used the tool Fraps^{TM}(www.fraps.com) for measuring Frames per Second. Fraps is not an open source project. It probably works by hooking into the graphic modules and listening for either swap-buffer or draw-function calls. Fraps does therefore have a minimal but existing impact on the performance.

To use Fraps^{TM}for measuring FPS one has to start the program and to go to the FPS tab. There one can set a hot-key that can in turn be used inside the game to start the measurement. Every game measurement has a description as when to start benchmarking and for how long it should last. This time can also be entered in Fraps^{TM}so that the recording of FPS automatically stops after a defined time.

There are two potential problems measuring FPS in a game.

1. Games sometimes lock the framerate at 60 or 30 frames per second. If this is not optional, no FPS measurement beyond this limit can take place.
2. Games often allow V-Sync to be enabled, which at todays 60 Hertz, flat screens, locks the framerate at 60 FPS. This, however, is optional in almost all titles and one just has to take care not to activate it. Most graphics boards' drivers will allow to override the games settings and turn V-Sync off globally, if it can not be turned off in the game. This was never necessary and could cause bad side effects in a game expecting to have fixed FPS.

Perfmon. For measuring CPU and disk utilization, we decided to make use of *perfmon*, a tool that is installed by default on all Windows machines.

Perfmon offers the following counters that are of interest for our measurements:

- The counter `% Processor Time` measures the total processing time
- and `% Processor Time` measures the processing time per core
- The counter `Disk Write bytes/s` measures the total number of disk reads
- and `Disk Read bytes/s` measures the total number of disk writes

These counters were measured each second for the workloads duration of each game. The measurement was set up to save the resulting data in csv-format for later analysis.

Performance Tuning Utility. The next tool to use is the Intel® Performance Tuning Utility, Intel® PTU. We used Intel® PTU for measuring of Cycles and Instructions per Module.

For these modules named above, we restricted ourselves to the top 95% of binaries in a measurement. Top 95% means that if we sort the list of binaries by the amount of cycles spent in them and in descending order, we cut off the list after 95% of all cycles during the sampling were accounted for. That is done because usually the 5% of least cycle contributing modules amount to over 80% percent of the binaries. Not cutting off the list would make the task of bundling modules together much harder while not changing the overall result significantly. This is acceptable for us, but needs to be kept in mind.

Intel® PTU can also be used to measure the total percentage of floating point instructions, but not the percentage of these instructions per core.

Sampling Collector (SEP). For the measurements of the Percentage of SIMD Instructions we used Intel's sampling and profiling tool. SEP is part of the Intel® VTune™ - Performance Analyzer, but can be used as a command-line tool. This is used to generate text files that contain the exact instructions executed in each module together with the count of how often the instructions were executed. It also prints a summary of each module and again an overall summary. These summaries already are grouped by instruction type and show the sum of instructions each type accounts for.

Some Proprietary Tools. were used in this study. The events we measure however are documented publicly[1] and one could write his own tool to measure those. Most of them can also be collected with SEP but this is a little bit more difficult. The proprietary tools are used for convience and for some of the data sorting that they provide.

As mentioned above, we are interested in the number of floating point instructions per core. The tool used for measuring this is an Intel proprietary application.

Counting memory accesses became quite easy on current Intel hardware. The memory controller was put into the CPU, in a section Intel calls the *Uncore* area. This integrated memory controller (IMC) also offers counters to measure its performance. We used counters `UNC_IMC_NORMAL_READS.ANY` and `UNC_IMC_WRITES.FULL.ANY`. These counters count the number of 64-byte-cache-lines being transferred between memory and IMC.

---

[1] See the developer guides: http://www.intel.com/products/processor/manuals/

To get the transfer rate however, the duration in seconds of the measurement needs to be known. The tool used for measuring is also not public, but what we essentially do is to also measure the clock cycles spent during the measurement, from this one can calculate the time spent measuring.

Table 2 provides an overview of which tool was used to measure the desired metrics.

Table 2. Tools used to measure the metrics listed in section 3

Metric	Used Tool
CPU Utilization	Perfmon
Memory Bandwidth Utilization	Intel proprietary
Harddisk Utilization	Perfmon
Floaing Point OPs	Intel proprietary
Percentage of SIMD instructions	SEP
Frames Per Second	Fraps™
Cycles Per Module	Intel®PTU

5   Measured Data and Analysis

In this section we present the top findings we got from our measurements. I.e. those results that are considered to be most significant and that will probably influence how we are looking at game-workloads in general.

5.1   The CPU Is Not a Bottleneck

The first important result is that the CPU cannot be considered a bottleneck. As can be seen from Figure 1 the average CPU utilization varies between 26.5 and 64 percent.

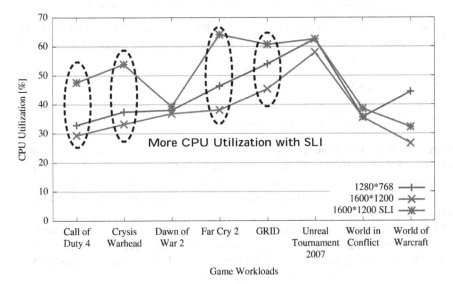

Fig. 1. Average CPU loads; Profiteers of SLI encircled

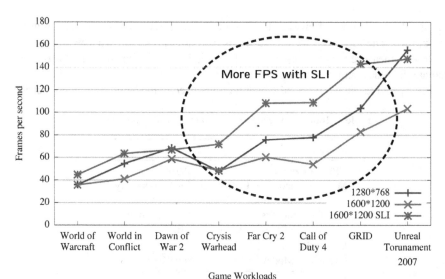

Fig. 2. Average FPS; Profiteers of SLI regarding CPU utilization encircled – Sorted by FPS with SLI

Table 3. Impact of increased resolution and SLI on Framerate and CPU Utilization – Averaged over all workloads

	Impact on CPU utilization	Impact on Framerate
Increased resolution by factor 1.95	0.86×	0.78×
SLI	1.32×	1.56×

The maximum of 64% utilization was achieved by *Far Cry 2* which is said to be very well parallelized. At least in this study it is the best parallelized – regarding utilization, not necessarily effectiveness. We found an average CPU utilization of

- 43.95% for 1280×768,
- 37.65% for 1600×1200 and
- 49.78% for 1600×1200 with SLI enabled.

Figure 2 shows that the same games that displayed increased CPU utilization also show increased FPS when using SLI compared to the case without SLI. What this essentially means is that if the processing power of the GPU is increased, more performance is gained from the total system, while at the same time showing that the CPU can do more work without a problem.

Note that this is not meant exclusive, as can be seen in the same figures, some more games also benefit from SLI. In fact we found no game performing worse when SLI was used[2]. The encircled games however benefit the most in both regards, CPU and FPS.

---

[2] Comparing 1600x1200 SLI with 1600x1200 without SLI.

When we scanned the data, we also found that not all four available cores were utilized evenly. We found that two cores always showed roughly 50 to 70 percent utilization while two others only showed roughly 30 to 50 percent utilization. So there is some potential to optimize games in that regard.

Table 3 shows in the first line what impact the step up in resolution has regarding CPU utilization and framerate. In the second line it shows the impact that SLI has in relation to the 1600×1200 setting without SLI. These are averages over all workloads.

5.2 The Game Module Only Accounts for 50% of Cycles

Although there is a high variance between the different games in that regard, the results show that the game modules very rarely are accountable for more than 50% of all cycles during the workload. The minimum is *Race Driver: GRID* at 1600×1200 pixels spending 30.84% of total cycles in the game module. The maximum is *World in Conflict: Soviet Assault* with 56.86% closely followed by *Crysis Warhead* with roughly 55.52% of cycles spent in the game module. The average is 44.85% over all titles.

Figure 3 shows how each of the four modules changed its footprint in every game and all configurations.

Taking a look at Section 5.1 the conclusion can be drawn that if the CPU is roughly utilized 50% and the game module is accountable for $\frac{4}{10}$ of these cycles, then the game module uses less than 25% of the processor capacity (i.e. available cycles) on the average.

Figure 4 shows data for the metric "Instructions and Clock Cycles per Module" with SLI enabled at 1600×1200 pixels. From this figure we see that the game module is responsible for roughly 40-60% of the CPU's work. When looking at Figure 4 the set of instructions named "Unaccounted" summarizes all binaries that we have not been able to uniquely assign to a module.

5.3 No Significant Difference in Instruction Mix between the Configurations

We found that interestingly most games' instruction mix did not significantly change at all. Only *World in Conflict: Soviet Assault* showed variance in the SIMD usage. Figures 5 and 6 show these data. Figure 6 shows the average percentage of Floating Point Instructions. Furthermore it shows the minimum and maximum measured percentage of Floating Point Instructions measured on a single CPU core.

This is of great interest because we believed games to dynamically adjust the precision and amount of certain calculations based on their self profiling. This believe needs to be revised now. At least games do not 'change' what they do, perhaps they still do more of what they normally do, but this can not be proven or disproven here.

5.4 Disk and Memory Bandwidth Utilization

The measured utilization of disk and memory is much less than the system maximum. The memory bandwidth utilization is also much less than the Practical System Maximum determined using the Stream benchmark. Table 4 shows the maximum disk and memory utilization we measured.

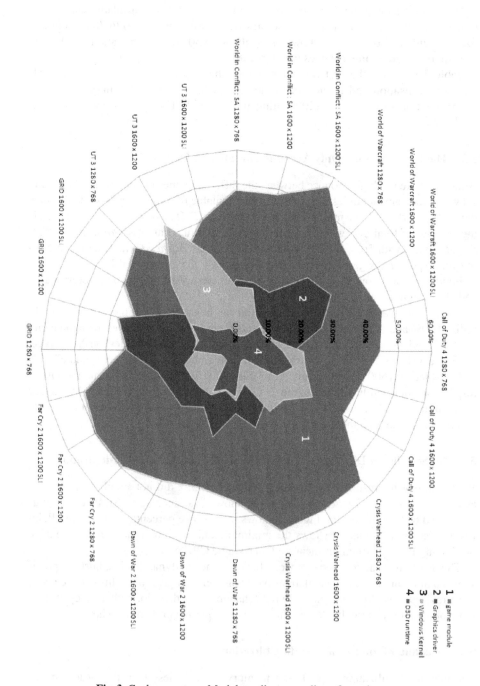

Fig. 3. Cycles spent per Module – all games, all configurations

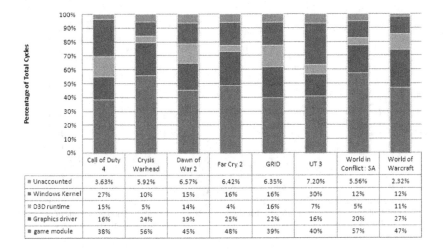

Fig. 4. Cycles per Module – 1600×1200 with SLI enabled

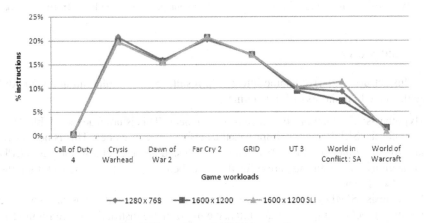

Fig. 5. Percentage of SIMD Instructions

Table 4. Maximum measured memory and disk bandwidth utilization per game

Game	Bandwidth Utilization	
	Memory	Disk
Call of Duty	19.9%	0.4%
Crysis Warhead	12.4%	25.9%
Dawn of War	12.7%	7.7%
Far Cry 2	26.9%	2.23%
GRID	20.0%	0.6%
Unreal Tournament 3	16.8%	1.7%
World in Conflict	14.7%	1.5%
World of Warcraft	37.5%	6.4%

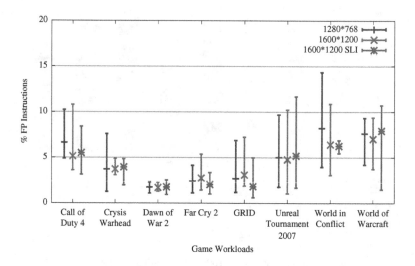

Fig. 6. Average, minimum and maximum measured percentage of Floating Point Instructions per CPU core

6   Conclusions

Using this set-up we derived some interesting results. Some results did and some did not confirm the hypotheses of Intel engineers:

1. Hypothesis: The memory interface is a bottleneck. This is not true (see Table 4).
2. Hypothesis: SLI drastically improves the performance of games. This is not generally true. SLI increase the FPS of half of the tested games, but also increases CPU utilization. This is an indication for the GPU being more of a bottleneck than the CPU (see Figure 2).
3. Hypothesis: SIMD instructions are not widely used. This also has proven to be wrong. In fact most games make intensive use of these instructions (see Figure 5).

From an educational point of view the measurement methodology proves to be very helpful. In a course on Computer Architecture at Munich University of Applied Sciences our students will have to do measurements and performance comparisons using the tools described here.

Finally we must mention that Computer games have been attracting an increasing amount of attention during the last years. One driving force is the emergence of Serious Gaming. This is the use of games and gaming technology for educational purposes. Becoming more serious, there is an increasing scientific interest in this area [5].

References

1. Knuth, D.E.: Theory and practice, iv. In: Selected Papers in Computer Science, 1st edn., pp. 149–167. CSLI lecture notes, Stanford (1996)
2. Hennessy, J.L., Patterson, D.A.: Computer Architecture – A Quantitative Approach, 3rd edn. Morgan Kaufmann Publishers, San Francisco (2003)

3. Stiller, A.: Apfel und satsuma – apple xserve 3.1 kontra fujitsu primergy rx200 s5. c't Magazin für Computer Technik (13), 156–159 (2009)
4. Claypool, M., Claypool, K.: Perspectives, frame rates and resolutions: it's all in the game. In: FDG 2009: Proceedings of the 4th International Conference on Foundations of Digital Games, pp. 42–49. ACM, New York (2009)
5. Yusoff, A., Crowder, R., Gilbert, L., Wills, G.: A conceptual framework for serious games. In: Ninth IEEE International Conference on Advanced Learning Technologies, ICALT 2009, July 2009, pp. 21–23 (2009)

Traffic Properties, Client Side Cachability and CDN Usage of Popular Web Sites

Joachim Charzinski

Nokia Siemens Networks, D-81541 Munich, Germany
j.charzinski@ieee.org

Abstract. Web traffic measurement and modeling have contributed to understanding the effect of Web traffic on Internet resources since the 1990s. In the past years, a number of new Web features have gained more and more importance, e.g. content delivery networks (CDNs), increased amount of advertisement, personalization, usage tracking, client scripting and Web 2.0 style "mashups". This paper uses active Web measurements to assess the efficiency of client side caching for modern Web sites, investigating some Web features in detail. As expected, we see that more than 50 % of the average downstream traffic volume is saved when loading a page using client side caching. More unexpected results comprise the actual distribution of cache effectiveness, varying between extreme and no reduction of traffic, the cachability of "Web bugs" and the variance between sites in cachable image pixels and CDN based files.

1 Introduction

1.1 Evolution of Web Applications

Since the early 1990s the World Wide Web (the Web) has evolved from a network of files allowing links from information in one file to information in another file to a network of sites and services that is generating substantial economic revenue and has become indispensable for most of our everyday business.

Web site structure has changed from static to dynamic pages, from pages consisting of only a single file to pages made up of hundreds of files, including latest news, advertisements, personalized pages, highly distributed Web services ("mashups"). Client side scripts allow browsers to perform certain operations locally without any delay from retrieving further content or re-loading pages over the network. Content delivery networks (CDNs) such as the Akamai service [3,22] now bring frequently requested files closer to users' networks to improve availability and reduce page loading latency.

Those changes are driven by a number of interests, such as increasing company value by attracting more customers, increasing turnover on Internet sales platforms with well performing sites or collecting end customer knowledge using excessive tracking and data mining to increase advertisement value. Service hosting, CDNs and mashups also simplify the creation of new services and sites.

Correspondingly, it is not straightforward how all those changes affect the client side cachability of Web contents, which has been one of the early but

B. Müller-Clostermann et al. (Eds.): MMB & DFT 2010, LNCS 5987, pp. 136–150, 2010.

drastic performance improvements for browsing required when the Web spread from high capacity academic network onto the general public parts of the Internet dominated by low speed dial-up access. Personalized pages will look different to different visitors. Tracking requires browsers to retrieve information again and again just for the server to know that the site has been visited again. Latest news are updated frequently, and advertisement companies make sure that every time a page is redisplayed the user receives another advertisement banner.

In this paper we make an attempt at investigating the client side cachability of popular Web pages. For a well-defined and reasonably representative set of pages to visit, we compare the client side traffic from loading the page the first time with an empty cache and for loading the page again after a short time.

1.2   Overview of the Paper

Section 2 presents an excerpt of related work in the fields of Web measurement and caching touched by this paper. In Section 3, the selection of measurement targets, measurement and evaluation methodology and measured quantities are described. Results on the effect of client side caching on basic page characteristics are presented in Section 4. The relation between client side caching and further mechanisms (CDNs, Web 2.0 methods, graphics, "Web bugs", cookies and cache expiry distributions) are investigated in Section 5.

2   Related Work

A large number of papers assessed Web traffic characteristics in the past. Due to the Web 2.0 and contents tracking developments on Web sites, however, some characteristics of Web traffic have changed. Williams et al. [23] characterize Web workload from the point of view of a Web server and find that a number of characteristics such as the median transfer size, ratio of distinct requests, the percentage of files accessed only once, the file size distribution, the ratio of busiest files to all files, inter-reference time distributions and the ratio of remote to local requests did not change significantly over that period of time. Williams et al. study one server and a large number of requests to different resources on that one server whereas in this paper we study requests from one client to a large number of different servers, which limits the amount of comparable results to the document size and type distributions. Bent et al. [6] studied properties of commercial Web sites hosted by one ISP on a large server farm to estimate the potential performance benefits of CDNs, finding that a large degree of responses is not cachable in the network (mostly due to cookies), that CDNs can benefit most Web sites and that inappropriate usage of cookies and cache control limit the possible benefit from caching.

There are some studies which explicitly cover the effects of selected Web 2.0 mechanisms on Web traffic. Kiciman and Livshits [15] look at Web 2.0 applications from a client side profiling point of view with a focus on scripting. By remotely instrumenting browsers through scripts provided on their Web pages, the authors explore performance properties and problems of different browsers. Duarte et al. [10] explore another aspect of Web 2.0, blogging. They analyze the new communication patterns from blog-related traffic such as the one-to-many broadcast-like dissemination of new blog contents and the many-to-one registration-like traffic.

Also, the topic of caching has been intensively studied in the past, however, mostly with an emphasis on network based cache architectures and management strategies. Rabinovich and Spatschek [20] give an extensive overview of different Web caching and replication technologies and their potential impact on traffic, mostly from a network point of view. Barish and Obraczka [13] give an overview of caching architectures, designs and cache management for the World Wide Web. While they do not show performance results, they review the state of the art of available cache mechanisms. A 1997 study of Duska et al. [11] shows that with a proper cache server structure, 24–45 % of Web elements can be served from caches if serving a sufficiently large population. The authors also give cache dimensioning guidelines and expected hit rates for cache hierarchies.

Most client side studies focused on proactive caching (prefetching) of elements. Eden et al. [12] show the effect of client prefetching on Web latencies. They used a combination of anonymized passive traces and instrumented Web pages to measure latencies, concluding that prefetching can significantly reduce page loading latency. Balamash and Krunz [4] focus on an analytical model for the gain from prefetching or proactive caching on the client side and investigate the effect of a combination of prefetching and proxy caching. The traffic model is purely synthetic.

Mahanti et al. [18] used proxy access logs to analyze transfer size distributions, document popularity, proxy cachability and rate of change of documents.

Saroiu et al. [21] analyze characteristics of the Akamai CDN and peer-to-peer (P2P) mechanisms for content distribution. Their emphasis is on capacity consumption from different traffic types, finding that it is mainly the larger average size of files available through P2P networks that is responsible for the large P2P share in overall traffic and transfer durations.

Logical locality properties of popular Web services and dedicated mashup services have been investigated by the author of this paper in a previous study [8], analyzing application properties and logical locations such as domain ownership and routing towards the large number of different servers that make up a single Internet service such as *google maps, weather.com* or *myspace.com.* The study in [8] was based on active measurements while using each site's service for 2–5 minutes, which included following links on the site beyond the main page. In this way, the results described part of the real service usage beyond home pages[1] but are difficult to repeat. In contrast, in [9] and in this paper, site usage is restricted to the sites' home pages, but in turn the number of sites investigated is increased, and more Web page properties are analyzed. Whereas in [9] the focus

---

[1] The term "home page" is used to denote the page that is loaded when only the host part of a URL is entered.

is on the static properties of the sites, this paper analyzes mainly the impact of local caching and statistics related to the usage of CDNs.

3   Measurements

In order to obtain replicable results per site, an approach of *actively initiated observations* similar to [5,16] was chosen for this paper. Unlike classical *active measurements* concerning the Internet infrastructure, e.g. [7], which generate traffic on IP level and observe metrics related to delay, loss or path through the network, actively initiated observations of Web traffic use a defined set of URLs to make a browser download everything that is required to display the corresponding Web pages. All traffic sent and received by a client machine while downloading the whole Web page including all elements for a given page URL was recorded in a set of trace files per page. The complete workload is defined by the set of URLs to visit and client side cache control.

Compared to *passive observations* of a number of users, which create a larger amount of traffic and potentially more representative workloads, our approach allowed us to correctly associate traffic to Web pages and to have full access to all transmitted contents without the hassle of anonymization that comes with real user traces. On the other hand, defined workloads are always artificial and do not represent any user group's real usage of the Web. Despite this, they do yield valuable insight into some properties of Web applications.

For this paper, the URLs to visit were selected as the home pages of the worldwide top 500 Web sites as extracted from the Alexa [1] Web statistics service which ranks Web sites based on popularity among a large number of users. This list of home page URLs includes a mixture of search, news, trading, contents sharing, adult services and social networking sites. Only the home pages on the URL list were visited and no further browsing on the sites was performed.

For each site on the list, a Web browser was started with empty cache and cookies list, and all traffic between the client and the network was traced. After a timeout of one minute, (to limit the effect of quasi-streaming services on some sites), the browser was closed using wmctrl -c in order to simulate normal client re-start and the trace file saved. A new trace file was opened and the browser was started to visit the same page again (this time with contents and cookies from the first visit), again recording traffic for one minute before stopping the browser process and tracing, clearing the cache and moving on to the next site. This process was fully automated using shell scripts on a Linux machine running kernel 2.6.25, using firefox 3.0 as Web browser and tcpdump [19] for tracing. In order to prevent firefox from clearing its cache when being stopped from a shell script, the wmctrl -c command was used instead of the kill command after the first session. Data were recorded in February 2009 using an Arcor (Germany) DSL connection with a maximum of 6 Mbit/s downstream and 640 kbit/s upstream.

Restricting the pages to visit to services' home pages only allows simple replication of the same measurement in other places and at other times and does not introduce personal bias with respect to navigation preferences. A large number of sites has home pages which are of the same degree of complexity as the rest of the site (e.g. yahoo.com). On the other hand, it is clear that there are also a large number of sites where the home page is much less complex than the rest of the site (e.g. google.com, where the pages returned e.g. by an image search are significantly more complex than the home page, or some access restricted sites which require login or age verification before giving access to contents).

The properties presented in Section 4 and 5 were extracted from the recorded traces using tcpdump [19] and a number of special purpose shell scripts. In the following, "S1" denotes the session where a given page was loaded the first time (with empty cache) and "S2" denotes the session when the page was loaded the second time, utilizing the data available in the browser's disk cache. As an unmodified standard firefox browser was used for the measurements, the interpretation of cachability in the measurements is exactly the same that firefox applies under normal usage. It should be noted that other browsers may have different caching efficiency.

Table 1. Key characteristics of the collected traces

	pages visited	unique hosts	conns.	bytes received	elements retrieved	unique NPs	unique ASs
total	2x500	2683	17734	297MB	39.7k	941	532
S1	500	2291	12377	249MB	31.8k	891	512
S2	500	1696	5357	48MB	7.9k	770	476

Table 1 summarizes the key characteristics of the measured traces. NPs are network prefixes determined by looking for the longest matching prefix from the OIX route-views BGP table [2]. The AS numbers (ASNs) for a server's IP addresses were taken from the same table. Note that there are quite a number of hosts, NPs and ASs contacted by more than one site, so the per-site statistics cannot be derived from Table 1.

4   Main Results and Effects of Client Side Caching

Table 2 gives the minimum, average and maximum values per site visited for the traffic characteristics. 9 of the 500 sites did not transfer anything in S1 and were excluded from the evaluations. 17 of the remaining 491 sites (mainly Chinese sites) allowed complete client side caching of their home pages, bringing the minimum values for the "S2" sessions to zero. The largest average reductions from caching are in the number of elements per page (75 %) and the number of bytes received per page (81 %). Maximum values as well as the locality measures (number of ASs or network prefixes contacted) show much less reduction from caching.

Figure 1 shows the correlation between the downstream volume received in S1 sessions (empty cache) and S2 (second attempt) for each Web site. Most

Table 2. Minimum, average and maximum of the traffic and locality properties per Web site in S1 (initial session from empty cache) and S2 (repeated session with cache filled from S1). 9 sites where nothing was loaded in S1 were omitted.

	hosts	connections	bytes received	elements retrieved	NPs	ASs
S1 min.	1	1	897	2	1	1
S1 avg.	7.6	25.2	507k	64.7	4.8	4.1
S1 max.	38	172	6.9M	314	18	18
S2 min.	0	0	0	0	0	0
S2 avg.	5.5	10.9	98.5k	16.1	4.1	3.5
S2 max.	27	82	3.5M	162	16	14

sites require between 10 % and 100 % of the initial volume when being visited again, nearly independent of the original size. However, smaller pages are unlikely to require less than 10 % of their original volume in S2 whereas this still occurred fairly frequently for pages that originally were between 100 kB and 1 MB in size. Six pages actually were slightly larger in the S2 session than in the cache-less S1 session, probably due to different pictures being shown. A complementary distribution function for the S2/S1 ratio of volumes is given later in Figure 10.

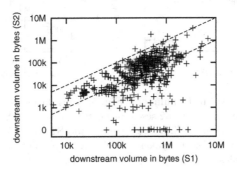

Fig. 1. Correlation between the downstream volume received in S1 sessions (empty cache) and S2 (second attempt) for each Web site, one point per site. Helper lines are at $y = x$ and $y = x/10$.

Figure 2 depicts the cumulative complementary distribution functions (ccdf) of received traffic volume per home page for S1 and S2. The effect of volume reduction from caching is clearly visible. There are even cases where in S2 the page is completely displayed from the cache without network traffic.

The number of connections in S1 and S2 is depicted as a scatter plot in Figure 3. The plot clearly shows that almost all sites require between 10 % and 100 % of the connections initially used in S1 when navigating again to the site in S2 except for the cases where in S2 the page is rendered completely from the cache without any network activity.

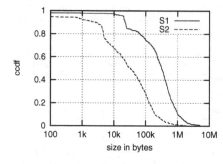

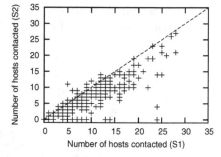

Fig. 2. Cumulative complementary distribution functions (ccdf) of bytes received in S1 and S2 sessions (empty cache/second attempt) per site

Fig. 3. Correlation between the number of TCP connections in S1 and S2 sessions for each site, one point per site. Helper lines are at $y = x$ and $y = x/10$. Log scale broken to include $y = 0$ samples.

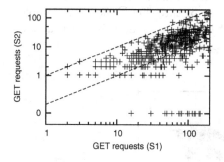

Fig. 4. Correlation between the number of HTTP GET requests in S1 and S2 sessions, one point per site. Helper lines are at $y = x$ and $y = x/10$. Log scale broken to include $y = 0$ samples.

Fig. 5. Correlation between the number of hosts contacted in S1 sessions (empty cache) and S2 (second attempt) for each Web site, one point per site. Helper line is at $y = x$.

The number of elements that make up a complete page is visible in the number of HTTP GET requests issued by the browser. The scatter plot in Figure 4 shows this number for the S1 and S2 sessions per site visited. Again, except for the cases where in S2 the pages were rendered directly from the disk cache, most home pages required between 10 % and 100 % of the initially required elements again when visited in S2.

As shown in Table 2, the number of hosts contacted per home page varied between 1 and 38 in S1. Caching introduces less reduction here than in the number of elements or bytes. This is a clue for a certain type of sites being constructed in such a distributed fashion (e.g. as Web 2.0 "mashups" or making use of a lot of classically included advertisement banners) that the structural complexity is nearly immune to caching, even though the site's main elements are cachable. Figure 5 shows that there is also a number of sites that made the browser contact one or two more distinct hosts at the second attempt (S2) than at the first (S1). This may be due to dynamic load balancing and parallel loading schemes where elements can be loaded from a number of equivalent hosts.

Similar to the number of hosts, also the number of Autonomous Systems (ASs) those hosts are located in is only slightly reduced when loading a cached page, see Figure 6. Among the 500 home pages visited, only those consisting of data from less than eight different ASs allowed being completely cached. More distributed services always required nearly the same degree of distribution in S2 as in S1. The corresponding graph for the number of network prefixes (NPs) shows the same properties and has therefore not been included here.

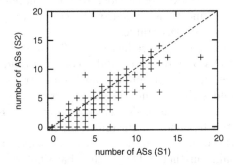

Fig. 6. Correlation between the number of Autonomous Systems (ASs) contacted in S1 sessions (empty cache) and S2 (second attempt) for each Web site, one point per site. Helper line is at $y = x$.

5 Effects of Web Site and Delivery Design

In this section, we take a closer look at correlations between the traffic properties observed in the caching experiments and some advanced features of Web site and delivery design, such as the usage of CDNs for improving contents delivery, scripting and page design associated with "Web 2.0" services, the handling of images and "Web bugs" – tiny 1 pixel images designed with no other function than tracking visitors as browsers have to load the images to render a page.

5.1 Content Delivery Networks (CDNs)

For each host contacted by the browser, the following steps were taken to determine a DNS (Domain Name System) domain name: (a) the corresponding DNS A query and response as recorded in the trace was evaluated, (b) the host's IP address was used for a reverse (in-addr.arpa) DNS lookup and (c) a DNS NS record was requested for the network prefix that the host's IP address belonged to. All three domain names were matched against a list of CDN services. Table 3 summarizes the characteristic data for those CDNs that had a data volume share

Table 3. CDN services with at least 1 % volume share identified in the traces

CDN service	DNS domains	Byte ratio S1	Byte ratio S2	ASNs	used by sites
Akamai	akamai.net, akadns.net, akam.net, akamaitechnologies.com	22.3 %	25.8 %	14779, 20940 + various	218/500
Limelight	llnw.net, llnwd.net, llns.net	5.2 %	2.8 %	8068, 22822	41/500
Footprint	footprint.net	3.1 %	1.0 %	3356	16/500
Panther Express	panthercdn.com	2.5 %	6.8 %	36408	43/500
Google	l.google.com	2.1 %	1.9 %	15169, 36561 (youtube)	258/500
Cotendo	cotcdn.net	2.0 %	1.1 %	46281	1/500

of at least 1 % in S1 or S2[2]. All connections to hosts matching a CDN service were counted as CDN connections, similarly the traffic transferred within such connections was counted as CDN traffic.

Figure 7 shows the ratio of CDN traffic to all traffic in session S2 versus session S1 for each site. If CDNs only delivered static contents (and allowed clients to cache it), the S2 traces should not contain much CDN traffic any more and all points in Figure 7 would gather around the lower part of the plot. Instead, nearly the full heterogeneity of combinations is actually observed. There are some sites that show the expected behavior of turning from high CDN byte ratio in S1 to low CDN byte ratio in S2, but most sites show a behavior around the main diagonal, i.e. they maintain their CDN traffic share before and after caching. There are even some sites that cause the browser to load mostly CDN based elements in S2 while the rest is effectively cached (top left corner of the plot).

The above observation is further substantiated by the cumulative complementary distribution functions of the CDN byte ratio (ratio of traffic volume

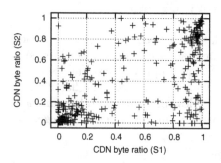
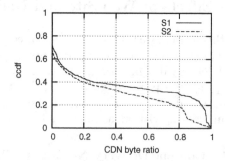

Fig. 7. Correlation of the CDN byte ratios (ratio of CDN traffic to all traffic) for initial (S1) visit to a site and second visit (S2). One data point per site visited.

Fig. 8. Cumulative complementary distribution functions (ccdf) of per site CDN byte ratio (ratio of CDN traffic to all traffic) in S1 and S2

[2] The further CDNs with less volume share were: mirrorimage/instacontent, voxcdn, fastwebcdn, tomcdn, txcdn, cdnetworks.net, fastcdn, tecache.china.com, edgecastcdn, cdn20.com, cachefly, cdn.hiido.cn, cdn.allyes.com, viacdn.net.

delivered via CDN hosts versus all traffic) plotted in Figure 8. A slightly over-proportional caching effect is visible at high CDN byte ratios: Sites that have a high portion of their traffic delivered via CDNs in S1 will see that portion slightly decreased in S2. In numbers this means e.g. that while 30 % of the sites got more than 80 % of their traffic delivered through a CDN if nothing is cached, it is only 36 % of the traffic in the cached case. However, it has to be noted that the overall traffic in the cached case is lower, so this does not mean that the non-cached traffic increased.

5.2   Web 2.0 Scripting and Interactivity

Of the 500 home pages surveyed, 100 employed the XmlHttpRequest (XHR) primitive to improve direct user interaction by dynamically changing parts of a page. 107 used the JSON (JavaScript Object Notation) data exchange format that is used to enable client-side *mashups* [24] where clients are instructed by the visited site to collect raw information from several servers and build the page to be displayed on their own. 48 sites used the Google Web Toolkit (GWT) that supports writing AJAX (asynchronous Javascript and XML) applications linking into services such as Google Maps or Gmail. As some of the sites employed multiple mechanisms, the total number of sites employing at least one of the three mechanisms (XHR, JSON or GWT) is only 167. Those three mechanisms are characteristic for technical aspects of the "Web 2.0" development. There are a lot of other components (blogging, social networks, tagging, folksonomies, etc.) that are part of Web 2.0, but those do not have the same kind of directly observable impact on Web traffic.

The cumulative complementary distribution functions of downloaded traffic volume are plotted in Figure 9 for S1 and S2 both for all sites and for those sites that were identified to employ at least one of the Web 2.0 mechanisms (XHR, JSON, GWT). The graphs show that Web 2.0 sites have a tendency to transmit more traffic than the overall ensemble, they have a much smaller probability to be fully cachable but they profit from caching roughly by the same factor as all sites. This effect is also visible in the corresponding mean sizes summarized in Table 4. Care must however be taken not to confuse correlation with causality. It cannot be determined from the measurements if it is the Web 2.0 mechanisms that make Web pages larger (or make it easier to create large sites) or if large Web pages are more likely to employ Web 2.0 mechanisms or if there is a common driver behind both the size and the mechanisms employed. Another quick conclusion to be avoided is that the 333 sites not identified as employing Web 2.0 mechanisms on their home pages are not Web 2.0 enabled. Many of them may employ those mechanisms behind the site's home page. On the other hand, one may safely assume that a site that already employs Web 2.0 mechanisms on the home page will continue using those mechanisms on other pages of the site.

Figure 10 takes a closer look at the traffic volume reduction due to caching. The distributions show that Web 2.0 sites have a slightly higher probability of showing less volume savings than the whole ensemble of sites. The distributions shows roughly negative exponential shape (note the single logarithmic scaling).

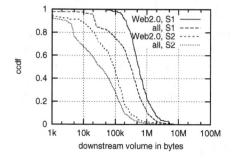 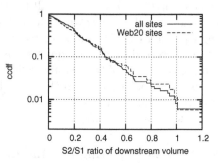

Fig. 9. Ccdf of per site downstream volume in S1 and S2. All sites ("all") vs. those 167 sites ("Web2.0") that were seen to employ Web 2.0 mechanisms (XHR, JSON, GWT).

Fig. 10. Cumulative complementary distribution functions (ccdf) of downstream traffic volume ratio (traffic in S2 divided by traffic in S1 per site) compared between all sites and Web 2.0 sites

Table 4. Mean page sizes and usage of Web 2.0 mechanisms

	mean S1 volume	mean S2 volume
all sites	498 kB	97 kB
Web 2.0 sites	859 kB	165 kB
other sites	307 kB	97 kB

5.3   Image Files

Hardly any modern Web page can afford to present its contents without images. In some cases (e.g. flickr.com), images are the primary contents and often they support identification of other contents (videos, news stories). Many advertisement banners are images and a lot of navigation elements are designed as images to give Web pages a certain look and feel.

In order to get a first estimate on the amount of page space occupied by the downloaded images, the following exercise was conducted: GIF and JPEG images were extracted from the files using a slightly modified version of the `driftnet` tool [17]. Properties of the extracted image files were then collected using the `identify` tool (part of ImageMagick, available on many Linux and Unix distributions). The number of pixels in all pictures contained in a trace was summed up and taken as representative of the screen area covered by images. This approach is very coarse because flash animations, videos and some image file types (png, bitmap) were not counted and some images could not be correctly read by the `identify` tool. Correspondingly, the given numbers are lower bounds, and there can be more image information in the traces than actually analyzed here.

Figure 11 shows a plot of the cumulative complementary distribution functions of the total screen size occupied by the sum of all images received per page (in pixels). A typical screen size of 1280x1024 corresponds to 1.31 M pixels, which is exceeded by 16 % of the sites in S1. Those sites can take unnecessarily long

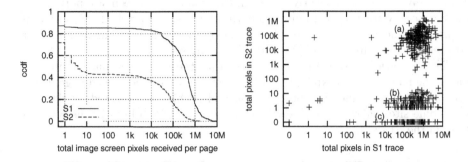

Fig. 11. Cumulative complementary distribution functions (ccdf, left) and correlation between S1 and S2 sessions (right) of total screen pixels received in images per site. For annotations (a)–(c) see text.

to load. In S2 in contrast, only one site actually loaded more than 1.3 M pixels. The jump at 33 k pixels in both distributions is due to the Google logo which has 301x110 = 33110 pixels. Note that the global top 500 Web sites include 50 national versions of the Google home page.

The scatter plot in Figure 11 shows the resulting relation between screen pixels loaded per page in the corresponding S1 and S2 sessions. There are three distinct areas showing different site behavior. (a) in the top right corner there are that load a large amount of image space and allow caching only for parts of it, or replace the images on the page at the second loading, e.g. to cycle through different advertisements. (b) below that there is a region where the amount of image pixels in S2 is drastically less than in S1. Here all real images are cached but the so-called "Web bugs" (see Section 5.4) are not cached. (c) at $y = 0$ there are a number of sites that allow complete caching of all (recognized) images.

5.4 "Web Bugs" and Cookies

"Web bugs" are single pixel images employed by Web site designers to track user behavior. They mainly serve two purposes: Every time a page is loaded, the tiny but usually not cachable picture also needs to be loaded, so the server serving the image can log a request to the image that can be used e.g. to count page views. In addition, the server serving the image can set and check cookies to personalize tracking, i.e. to correlate page views among different pages (and sites!) with users. Even if users instruct their browsers to accept and send cookies only for the same domain as the related contents, sites can include Web bug images from third party tracking providers that cover multiple sites but get their (tracking provider site specific) cookies accepted and sent within the same origin policy [14]. Another trick often employed in conjunction with Web bugs is to personalize URLs instead of or in addition to using cookies. This allows even cross-application tracking between personal links or image URLs in e-mails and the Web server serving the Web bug.

In 11, Web bugs were clearly visible in the small total screen size portions of the S2 data. With each file only accounting for a single pixel, the S2 curve in Figure 11 indicates that 58 sites (12 %) transmit a single Web bug and another 80 sites (16 %) transmit 2–10 Web bugs in the S2 session.

The correlation plot in Figure 12 shows that the more Web bugs a site employs, the more are also explicitly loaded when rendering the cached page. However, surprisingly some Web bugs are cachable, which is indicated by the fact that some sites show a significantly lower number of Web bugs in the S2 data than in the S1 data.

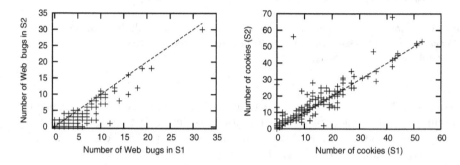

Fig. 12. Correlation of the number of Web bugs (left) downloaded and cookies set (right) per site for initial (S1) visit to a site and second visit (S2)

Figure 12 (right) depicts the number of cookies set per home page at initial (S1) and following (S2) visits. Although the total traffic is reduced in S2, the number of cookies rather has a tendency to increase. This is a further indication for a large part of the S2 traffic being due to user tracking.

5.5   Cache Expiry

The cache expiry information per element as indicated in the HTTP headers, is plotted as a ccdf in Figure 13 for large ($\geq$ 1kB) and small (< 1kB) elements.

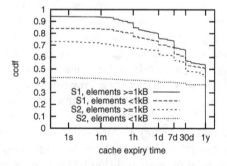

Fig. 13. Cumulative complementary distribution functions (ccdf) of cache expiry time per element for large and small elements in S1 and S2 sessions

Expiry times were limited to one year in line with to the HTTP standard. Non-cachable elements were recorded as if they had zero expiry time. There is a general tendency for larger elements to have longer cachability than smaller elements and for elements in S1 to be more cachable than elements in S2. As could be expected, the ratio of non-cachable elements in S2 is much higher than in S1, but even the S2 sessions still contain a significant amount of cachable elements due to sites exchanging the URLs to embedded elements (e.g. for advertisements).

6 Conclusions

When designing systems and networks to transport Internet traffic, it is important to have a precise knowledge about the properties of the traffic to be transported. As the Web evolved, Web traffic locality and cachability have changed.

Using actively initiated measurements on the Web's most popular sites, a number of properties of modern Web sites' traffic were explored. It was shown that while client side caching significantly reduces the volume and number of elements loaded at a second visit to a page, other measures such as the number of hosts contacted and the number of networks they belong to are much less reduced. An investigation of the graphics files loaded for each page showed that each 6th page loads more images than required to fill a full computer screen, and that Web bugs (single pixel images used for user tracking) are in widespread use. As Web bugs are loaded before a page is displayed, they are an example of low volume traffic that requires low latency treatment. Personalization (via cookies), changing contents and rotating advertisements are responsible for a large part of the traffic observed when pages are loaded again. While a lot of elements are cachable, this does not mean they are actually re-used when a page is loaded again because many sites change the contents to be displayed from visit to visit. This is no problem for PCs which usually have abundant space for caching (if properly configured) but can be critical for handheld terminals. ISPs will usually be able to cache less than what was found in this study, as cookies restrict cross-user caching and some contents may not be stored in the network for copyright reasons.

References

1. Alexa: top 1,000,000 sites updated daily,
   http://s3.amazonaws.com/alexa-static/top-1m.csv.zip (visited February 18, 2009)
2. OIX Route Views, http://archive.routeviews.org/oix-route-views/2008.05/ (visited 28 May 2008)
3. Akamai home page, http://www.akamai.com/ (visited September 26, 2008)
4. Balamash, A., Krunz, M.: Performance Analysis of a Client-Side Caching/Prefetching System for Web Traffic. Computer Networks 51(13), 3673–3692 (2007)

5. Barford, P., Crovella, M.: Measuring Web Performance in the Wide Area. ACM Performance Evaluation Review 27(2), 37–48 (1999)
6. Bent, L., Rabinovich, M., Voelker, G.M., Xiao, Z.: Characterization of a Large Web Site Population with Implications for Content Delivery. In: Proc. WWW 2004, New York, NY, USA (May 2004)
7. Bolot, J.C.: End-to-end packet delay and loss behavior in the internet. In: SIG-COMM 1993: Conference proceedings on Communications architectures, protocols and applications, pp. 289–298. ACM, New York (1993)
8. Charzinski, J.: Locality Analysis of Today's Internet Web Services. In: Proc. 19th ITC Specialist Seminar, Berlin, Germany (October 2008)
9. Charzinski, J.: Traffic, structure and locality characteristics of the Web's most popular services' home pages. In: Proc. KiVS 2009, Kassel, Germany (March 2009)
10. Duarte, F., Mattos, B., Bestavros, A., Almeida, V., Almeida, J.: Traffic Characteristics and Communication Patterns in Blogosphere. In: Proc. international conf. on Weblogs and Social Media (2007)
11. Duska, B.M., Marwood, D., Feeley, M.J.: The Measured Access Characteristics of World-Wide-Web Client Proxy Caches. In: Proc. Usenix Symp. on Internet Techn. and Systems, Monterey, CA (December 1997)
12. Eden, A.N., Joh, B.W., Mudge, T.: Web latency reduction via client-side prefetching. In: Proc. IEEE Int. Symp. on Perf. Analysis of Systems and Softw., ISPASS 2000, Austin, TX, USA, pp. 193–200 (2000)
13. Greg Barish, K.O.: World Wide Web Caching: Trends and Techniques. IEEE Communications Magazine 38, 178–184 (2000), http://citeseer.ist.psu.edu/454956.html
14. Jackson, C., Boneh, D., Bortz, A., Mitchell, J.C.: Protecting Browser State from Web Privacy Attacks. In: Proc. WWW 2006, Edinburgh, Scotland (May 2006)
15. Kiciman, E., Livshits, B.: AjaxScope: A Platform for Remotely Monitoring the Client-Side Behavior of Web 2.0 Applications. In: Proc. SOSP 2007, Stevenson, WA, USA (October 2007)
16. Krishnamurthy, B., Wills, C.E.: Analyzing factors that influence end-to-end Web performance. Computer Networks 33(1), 17–32 (2000)
17. Lightfoot, C.: driftnet, http://www.ex-parrot.com/~chris/driftnet/ (visited January 27, 2009)
18. Mahanti, A., Williamson, C., Eager, D.: Traffic Analysis of a Web Proxy Caching Hierarchy. IEEE Network, 16–23 (May/June 2000)
19. McCanne, S., Leres, C., Jacobson, V.: tcpdump. LBNL Network Research Group, ftp://ftp.ee.lbl.gov/tcpdump.tar.Z
20. Rabinovich, M., Spatschek, O.: Web Caching and Replication. Addison-Wesley, Reading (2002)
21. Saroiu, S., Gummadi, K.P., Dunn, R.J., Gribble, S.D., Levy, H.M.: An Analysis of Internet Content Delivery Systems. In: Proc. Usenix OSDI 2002, Boston, MA, USA, December 2002, pp. 315–328 (2002)
22. Sherman, A., Lisiecki, P.A., Berkheimer, A., Wein, J.: ACMS: The Akamai configuration management system. In: Proc. USENIX NSDI 2005 (May 2005)
23. Williams, A., Arlitt, M., Williamson, C., Barker, K.: Web workload characterization: Ten years later. Springer, Heidelberg (2005)
24. Yee, R.: Pro Web 2.0 Mashups: Remixing Data and Web Services. Apress (2008)

Investigation of the Multimedia Adaptive Threshold Strategy for Mobile Integrated Services Networks

Vittoria de Nitto Personè[1], Andreas Pillekeit[2], and Matteo Iacari[1]

[1] University of Rome Tor Vergata,
Faculty of Engineering, Department of Computer Science and Systems,
Via del Politecnico 1, 00133 Roma, Italy
denitto@info.uniroma2.it
[2] University of Duisburg-Essen, ICB, Research Group Systems Modelling,
Schützenbahn 70, 45127 Essen, Germany
Andreas.Pillekeit@icb.uni-due.de

Abstract. We present and investigate the multi class extension of the recently proposed analytical model for performance evaluation of a bandwidth allocation and admission control scheme in mobile integrated services networks – called MATS. The proposed model allows for a prioritization of different service classes and for considering different levels of QoS requirements. The MATS scheme is based on bandwidth units and it implements an upgrade / degrade (u-d) mechanism. This mechanism maintains the negotiated QoS levels of connections as good as possible and prevents connections from getting lost (blocked, dropped) at the same time. Instead of focusing only on the traditional metrics, we propose two new metrics to evaluate the relative frequency of the u-d mechanism and to measure the provided QoS level. A comparison with other recently published schemes concludes that our proposed scheme is mandatory if it is essential to respect the priority among classes and shows good performance from both user and service provider perspectives. Simulation results counter check the results of the Markov model and show its applicability for non-Markovian service time distributions.

Keywords: Call admission control, handoff, bandwidth allocation, flexible QoS.

1 Introduction

The rapid growth of multimedia service networks has forced the network providers to consider flexibility as a key issue [1-21]. Managing multimedia streams with different QoS requirements on the one hand and minimizing resource wastage on the other, has renewed the importance of the resource allocation problem in the new context. This could also become more critical in the advent of networks where service providers have SLAs to guarantee and the possibility of incurring penalties [13, 17]. In this scenario, analytical modeling can be viewed as a powerful tool to investigate different resource allocation algorithms to highlight future directions. Originally, the concept of adaptive multimedia networking was introduced for the wired network. It is well known that in comparison to wired networks, the fluctuation in resource availability

B. Müller-Clostermann et al. (Eds.): MMB & DFT 2010, LNCS 5987, pp. 151–167, 2010.
© Springer-Verlag Berlin Heidelberg 2010

in wireless/mobile networks is much more severe. Therefore the multimedia wireless network is one of the most challenging application fields of the "adaptive paradigm". Bandwidth is the most important resource and an adaptive allocation mechanism has to instantly adapt the network to changing conditions within the system while maintaining the negotiated QoS.

Over the past ten years and more the literature has been full of contributions with regards to flexible resource allocation, for both wireless mobile networks and fixed ones. See two recent surveys and references therein [18, 19]. Many papers deal with the flexible quality case [1, 2, 3, 4, 5, 6, 7, 8, 9, 10, 11, 12, 13, 15] at different levels and with different approaches. In the following, we briefly sketch their contribution.

In [1] an adaptive bandwidth allocation scheme is proposed, based on user quality satisfaction curves provided by each application. The curves are used by the adaptation algorithm to achieve global fairness. In [2] an analytical model for an adaptive bandwidth allocation for a QoS provisioning scheme is proposed. Groups of different QoS level users are considered, and the analytical model includes user mobility. The authors define two performance metrics to deal with flexibility: the fraction of time a user receives degraded QoS, and the frequency of QoS changes for each user. CDMA cellular networks are considered in [3], where a CAC scheme is introduced with the aim of performing online management of QoS and provider revenue. Two classes of calls are considered, with two different priority levels. A complete analytical model, incorporating specific features like soft handover, is provided. A provider revenue function for the cell is presented in [4], by deriving formulas for calculating the revenue of each call, based on priorities and degradation tolerance. By maximizing this function, the degradation framework evaluates the optimal call mix that can be accommodated by the system. An adaptive resource allocation based on a genetic algorithm is proposed in [5]. Different QoS levels for each stream are considered, and degradation is activated to achieve a maximum utilization of the resources. The optimization problem is solved by using genetic algorithms. In [6] a multilayer resource management architecture is presented for real and non-real time traffic classes. The multilayer interaction of different algorithms for adaptation and reservation is described to deal with scarce and dynamic resources. Network, service and revenue models are also provided. Again, two classes of traffic, real and non-real time, are considered in [7]. A "degraded mode" of operation for a call is described, in which the call releases one channel. A bandwidth degradation policy is introduced with the aim of maximizing a cost function based on QoS parameters. An investigation on the tradeoff between the overhead due to network messages and the fairness criteria of adaptive schemes is presented in [8], where an adaptation scheme is proposed which reconciles the two properties. A fair bandwidth allocation algorithm for multiple classes of adaptive multimedia services is proposed in [9]. Fairness between classes and between calls of the same class is considered, the bandwidth requirement of each call is defined in terms of multimedia layers for the respective class (layered coding approach). The authors define two QoS measures to characterize the degradation: the frequency and the degree of the degradation. In [10] an analytical model for the combined graceful degradation and traffic restriction mechanism is proposed. A simplified scheme, where a call receives either a full or degraded service depending on the system load, and its extension to a generic multilevel degradable service are both described in the model. In [11] a distributed CAC and bandwidth adaptation algorithm

(BAA) is proposed for a single class of calls taking a discrete quantity of bandwidth units from a set of possible values. The CAC algorithm guarantees the upper bound of the cell overload probability, while the BAA seeks to minimize the cell overload probability. A CAC and bandwidth adaptation algorithm is proposed in [12]. All calls belong to a single class and they take varying bandwidth values from the same set. Only real-time streaming services are considered. The bandwidth degradation is performed by means of evaluating the system "adaptability", that is the number of calls that can be degraded. A threshold-based admission control algorithm with negotiation for two priority classes of requests is proposed in [13], where a reward-penalty scheme is adopted. The server capacity is partitioned, and each request has a reward and a penalty (related to the acceptance of the call in the system) as high as its priority. The analytical model aims to find the best partitions (i.e. the thresholds) optimizing the system performance based on the objective function of the total reward minus the total penalty. An integrated analytical framework for analyzing the QoS performance is presented in [15]. The framework integrates the physical, the data link and the network layer to analyze call-level and packet-level performances. CAC and Adaptive Channel Allocation algorithms are proposed. Three different types of traffic, real-time, non real-time and best-effort are considered.

Very few papers offer an analytical approach for handling multimedia services with flexible quality demands. In [14, 16] the authors use an analytical approach for handling multimedia services with priority, but they don't include the flexible resource allocation. An adaptive channel reservation scheme for multiclass traffic is proposed in [14]. In this particular guard channel scheme, a new call can access the reserved handoff channels with a certain probability that depends on the current number of occupied channels and the mobility of the user. Access probability is evaluated with heuristic formulas. Note that in this case the "adaptive" characteristic is related to the fractional threshold for guard channels. Two different dynamic bandwidth allocation strategies, based on guard channel schemes, are proposed in [16]. A single cell accessed by two of traffic classes is considered. In the first scheme (Guard Channel Fixed Reservation), bandwidth is divided into fixed groups, while in the second scheme (Guard Channel Dynamic Reservation) one group is allowed to have a variable number of channels and a special rule for its channel allocation.

An adaptive bandwidth allocation and admission control scheme for wireless integrated service networks, called MATS, was proposed in [20] for the two classes case. MATS was derived by extending the scheme in [14] to include adaptive bandwidth allocation inspired by [15]. In this paper we extend the MATS scheme and its analytical Markov model to any number of classes. As introduced above, the contribution of our proposed scheme is combining the multiclass characteristics and priorities with adaptive bandwidth allocation. To deal with the integrated services characteristic of the considered networks, the scheme allows the inclusion of different classes and each request of a given class can be served according to different service levels [5]. For each class a reservation scheme is used to prefer handoff calls over new calls by means of a threshold defined for that class. We define an analytical model to investigate the efficiency of the proposed scheme. Additionally, we used a simulation framework [21] to counter check the results of the analytical approach. Thus the main contribution of the paper is twofold: the extension of the MATS scheme to the multiclass characteristic of actual multimedia wireless networks and the investigation of the robustness of the traditional analytical assumptions compared to more realistic scenarios.

The paper is organized as follows. The system characteristics and the proposed MATS scheme are presented in the following sections 2 and 3 respectively. The analytical model and the performance indices are defined in section 4. Section 5 presents the model and the simulation framework. Section 6 presents the investigation of the model behavior through the comparison with other schemes and via simulation results (section 6.1), the investigation of the analytical assumptions robustness (section 6.2) and the results for a realistic scenario case (section 6.3). Finally section 7 concludes the paper.

2   The Network and the Resource Allocation Problem

We consider a wireless network with a cellular infrastructure that carries different classes of traffic, for example voice and data traffic, or classes of real-time traffic with different QoS requirements. We assume the system uses Fixed Channel Allocation (FCA), which means each cell has a fixed capacity that is equal to B basic bandwidth units (bbu). The bandwidth units can be interpreted as system capacity slices. The definition of the amount of needed bbu for each service is based on the QoS demand of the service and the used radio access technology (FDMA, TDMA, or CDMA).

The infrastructure can support mobile users running multimedia services that demand a wide range of bandwidth allocations. The bandwidth of a multimedia call can be dynamically adjusted depending on the network load situation during the call's lifetime. Moreover, since the mobile user can freely roam within a network's coverage area, he/she may undergo a number of handoff events during a typical session. The number of handoffs mainly depends on the cell layout and the mobility of the user. During the lifetime of the service it may experience low and high loaded cells. In case of high loaded cells the "adaptive" allocation of bandwidth prevents the call from being dropped but instead it will suffer from bandwidth degradation. Most multimedia services like video, voice or radio can be described as realtime services. Therefore we concentrate our modeling efforts on realtime services for which service times can be seen as independent from the received bandwidth.

QoS requirements of the users can be quantitatively expressed in terms of probabilistic connection-level QoS parameters [22, 23] related to connection establishment and management: blocking probability P_B of a new call and dropping probability P_D of a handoff call. While minimizing these QoS parameters is very desirable from the user's point of view, this often comes at the expense of the resource utilization, which is extremely undesirable from the service provider's perspective. This proves the importance of providing a balance between the user's connection-level QoS satisfaction and system utilization. Two major components in multimedia wireless networks (MWN) contribute in solving the above problems. The first is a Call Admission Control (CAC) algorithm. It is performed at the connection-level whenever a mobile initiates communication in a new cell, either through a new or handoff call. The CAC algorithm accepts or rejects an arriving request according to the amount of available resources versus QoS requirements. The second component is the Adaptive Bandwidth Allocation (ABA) algorithm which is responsible for bandwidth management of ongoing calls in the system. In MWNs it is possible to overcome cell overload situations by dynamically adjusting the bandwidth of individual ongoing calls. In this process "fairness" amongst users is an important issue.

3 The MATS Scheme

3.1 The Threshold Reservation Scheme

A MWN with C classes of requests is considered. Class i is assumed to have priority over class i-1, i= 1, 2, ..., C. A radio resource management entity (RRM) manages a fixed amount B of bandwidth per cell. The bandwidth is partitioned into basic bandwidth units (bbu). To give priority to class i, the RRM adopts a bandwidth partition: $B_{i-1}<B_i$ bbu can be used for class i-1 requests, while B_i bbu can be used for class i requests. Finally all available bandwidth B can be used for the highest priority class C, that is $B_C=B$. It is well known that blocking a new call is more tolerated than dropping a handoff call. This is the motivation of the traditional Guard Channel (GC) scheme which uses thresholds to reserve bandwidth to the handoff calls. Let us define $T_i < B_i$ as the threshold for the class i new calls. As a consequence, the class i handoff calls have B_i-T_i bbu exclusively reserved in respect to the class i new calls. Despite these class i calls have to share these reserved bbu with higher class j calls, with i <j ≤ C, without regarding the type of the class j calls (new or handoff). Similarly, the class C handoff calls have $B-T_C$ bbu exclusively reserved according to the highest priority characteristic of class C. Without loss of generality, in this paper we assume $T_i<T_{i+1}$ and $T_{i+1}=B_i$. Figure 1 illustrates the threshold reservation scheme for the case with C=3 classes.

Each class has flexible QoS requirements. Let us define $L_i=\{l_{1,i}, l_{2,i},... l_{max_i,i}\}$ the QoS levels for a call of class i, i=1, 2, ..., C. We assume that, for class i, $l_{1,i}$ is the minimum number of bbu to maintain the connection, and $l_{max_i,i}$ is the amount of bbu which provides the highest QoS level for the connection. The proposed Multimedia Adaptive Threshold Strategy (MATS) accepts new calls at the maximum possible

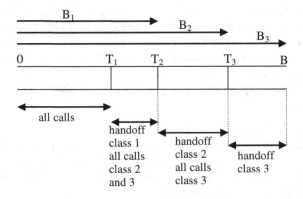

Fig. 1. The threshold reservation scheme

QoS level. So, if the bandwidth is available, $l_{max_j,i}$ bbu are allocated to an incoming call (new or handoff) of class i, otherwise the available amount l_i^* is allocated, with $l_i^* = \max\{l \mid l \in L_i, l < l_{max_j,i}\}$.

The threshold mechanism of the GC scheme yields a reduction of the dropping probabilities at the cost of increased blocking probabilities. To overcome this problem, we propose an upgrade-degrade (u-d) mechanism which allows the acceptance of a class i incoming call at its minimum QoS level $l_{1,i}$ by degrading the quality level of the ongoing calls in the cell. The degradation mechanism is performed fairly among all the ongoing calls and by taking into account the priority characteristic. As soon as some bbu are released by a departure, an upgrade mechanism is activated for allocating these released bbu, thus increasing the QoS offered to the users and maintaining a higher system utilization. For the multiclass case, we generalize and optimize the u-d mechanism presented in [20] for the two classes case. In [20] the admission control algorithm, used by the MATS scheme, is defined for a generic class i. So it can be immediately used for the multiclass case. In the following, we just sketch the admission control behavior. The MATS algorithm takes into account the class and the type (new or handoff) of the incoming call. In case of a new call arrival of class i the RRM checks if there are less than T_i bbu occupied. In this case, the RRM checks if the call can be admitted at the maximum possible level as described above. If the available number of free bbu is not sufficient for admitting the call even at its minimum level $l_{1,i}$, the degradation mechanism is activated. If the degradation is successful the new call is admitted at the minimum level $l_{1,i}$ and within the threshold T_i, otherwise it is refused.

If T_i bbu are occupied then the RRM starts the degrade mechanism for the ongoing calls to admit the new one within the limit threshold T_i. If the degradation is successful the new call is admitted at the minimum level $l_{1,i}$, otherwise it is refused.

If the arrival call is a handoff, the scheme proceeds as for the case of a new call just by using the appropriate threshold B_i instead of T_i.

3.2   The Upgrade-Degrade Mechanism

This section describes the above mentioned MATS u-d mechanism in more detail. For an incoming call of class i, the mechanism starts to degrade the calls of the minimum priority class 1, and subsequently proceeds in increasing order of priority. The degradation stops after it is applied to the ongoing calls of class i itself. Note that, with respect to the hierarchy among classes, an ongoing call of class j with j>i cannot be degraded to admit an incoming call of class i.

Assume that a class i request arrives. The *degrade mechanism* is performed according to the following steps:

d0. Start from the minimum priority class j=1.
d1. If j≤i, the class j ongoing calls at the maximum available QoS level k such that $l_{k,j} > l_{1,j}$, are selected. For fairness purposes the calls are selected in a random way (uniform). The QoS level of the calls is degraded to $l_{(k-1),j}$, until $l_{1,i}$ bbu have been released or there are no more calls to degrade.
d2. If the released bbu are sufficient to allocate the incoming call and the thresholds T_i and B_i are preserved (for the new and handoff calls respectively), the algorithm

stops. Otherwise, step d1 is repeated for the class j QoS level k-1, if k-1>1. If k-1=1, step d1 is repeated for higher priority classes j+1.

Note that if all class j ongoing calls are at the minimum level, for all j≤i, or the released bbu are not enough (released bbu < $l_{1,i}$) the degradation is not possible and the incoming call is lost (blocked or dropped for new or handoff respectively).

When a class i departure occurs, an upgrade mechanism is activated. Let us denote by f_{bbu} the bbu released by the class i departure. The *upgrade mechanism* is performed in the following steps:

u0. Select the maximum class j≤C such that there are ongoing calls to be upgraded.
u1. Let k≥1 be the minimum QoS level such that $l_{k+1,j} - l_{k,j} ≤ f_{bbu}$. A class j ongoing call at the QoS level k is selected. For fairness purposes the call is selected in a random way (uniform). The QoS level is upgraded to $l_{(k+1),j}$ whenever the threshold B_j is preserved. On the contrary step u1 is repeated for k+1<max$_j$.
u2. If the bbu released from the departure are not completely utilized, step u1 is repeated until all the released bbu are allocated or the level $l_{max_j,j}$ is reached for all the ongoing class j calls, j=1, ..., C (the B_j thresholds are preserved).

Note that when a call is accepted into the system it is becoming an ongoing call and the distinction between new or handoff is meaningless. As a consequence, in step u1 of the upgrade mechanism, we use only the threshold B_i. It is worth noting that, with respect to the priority criterion, while the degrading process starts from the minimum priority class and proceeds (j=1 in step d0), the upgrading process starts from the maximum priority class that has ongoing calls to be upgraded (j≤C in step u0). Analogously, to be consistent with the "highest-QoS policy" of MATS, while the degrading mechanism starts from the maximum possible QoS level, the upgrading mechanism starts from the minimum possible QoS level. This yields a minimized number of calls served at the minimum QoS level.

4 The Analytical Model

In this section the analytical model we use to evaluate the proposed MATS scheme is defined. For simplicity, a homogenous cellular network is considered. In other words, all cells are assumed to be statistically identical so that we can focus on one particular cell.

The arrivals for each class are assumed to follow a Poisson process with mean rates $\lambda_{n,i}$ and $\lambda_{h,i}$ for new and handoff calls respectively. The service time for each class i is assumed to be exponentially distributed with a mean rate μ_i. Note that the service time represents both the call holding time and the cell residence time. For the memoryless property, it is easy to extend the model to include two different mean rates.

Under these assumptions, the model is a continuous time Markov chain with a finite state space. The system state space E is defined as follows: E={ s={($n_{1,1}$, ..., $n_{max_1,1}$), ..., ($n_{1,C}$, ..., $n_{max_C,C}$)} | 1≤ $n_{k,i}$ ≤B_i, 1≤ k ≤max$_i$, 1≤ i ≤C}. In a generic system state s, the subset ($n_{1,i}$, ..., $n_{max_i,i}$) represents the number of class i ongoing calls for each QoS level, that is $n_{k,i}$ being the number of class i ongoing calls at QoS level $l_{k,i}$

with $l_{k,i} \in L_i = \{l_{1,i}, l_{2,i}, \ldots l_{max_j,i}\}$. The interested reader can refer [20] for an illustrative example of the Markov process. Let $\pi(s)$ denote the equilibrium probability of state s and $\pi = [\pi(s_1), \ldots, \pi(s_{|E|})]$ the steady state probability vector. The system solution can then be expressed as: $\pi S = 0$, $\sum_{\forall s:\, s \in E} \pi(s) = 1$. where S is the generator matrix of the model.

The performance indices considered in the paper for the evaluation of the proposed scheme are opportunely defined from the steady state probability vector. The blocking and dropping probabilities for each class are traditionally used as a measure of the QoS received by the user of mobile networks. They are defined simply as the sum of the steady state probabilities in which the request is lost (new call = blocked; ongoing call = dropped).

The system utilization is a QoS measure from the service provider's point of view. It is defined as the mean percentage of the used bbu. The following two less traditional metrics are defined in order to capture the cost of the proposed upgrade-degrade mechanism and the QoS delivered to the users.

For each class i, the quality level QL_i is a measure of the probabilities in which calls are served at the maximum QoS level. This is defined as follows:

$$QL_i = \sum_{\forall s \in E:\, y_{max_i} > 0} \pi'(s)\frac{y_{max_i}}{y_{tot}} \quad i = 1, \ldots, C.$$

where s is a given state and y is the state component related to class i, that is, for example, for class 1: $y_{max_1} = n_{max_1,1}$ and

$$y_{tot} = \sum_{j=1}^{max_1} n_{j,1}.$$

$\pi'(s)$ is the steady state probability distribution normalized to the subspace with class i ongoing calls.

A measure of the relative frequency of application of the u-d mechanism F_{u-d} can be defined as follows:

$$F_{u-d} = \sum_{\forall s:\, s \in E} \pi(s)\frac{t_{u-d}}{t_{tot}}$$

where t_{u-d} is the transition rate from state s for effect of the application of u-d mechanism, t_{tot} is the total out-transition rate from state s.

Note that the mechanism application yields a cost for the system that is dependent on the underlying technology and the system implementation. Of course this "flexibility cost" grows with F_{u-d}.

5   The Simulation Model

We used a common radio resource management (CRRM) model and simulation framework [21] to counter check the results of our Markov model. This framework was developed to represent the fundamental structure of wireless systems of different radio access technologies. The simulator is designed for the fast creation and evaluation of different scenarios and algorithms via a hybrid simulation approach, where a simulation model and an analytic model operate in parallel over time [24]. All submodels of the scenario showing dynamic process behavior (like mobility or information transfer) are described by discrete event simulation. The analytic submodels are parameterized during run time via the simulation state variables and provide stationary performance results (like mean response times) that are again used by the simulation model. Since the Markov model is based on an analytical bbu-model (to describe radio access technologies as well as QoS demands) and CAC algorithms are a subclass of CRRM algorithms, the simulation framework is well suited to model and test different scenarios implementing the MATS scheme. Please refer to [21] for a more comprehensive description of the framework.

The MATS algorithm is implemented into the radio access system (RAS) component of the simulation framework. The RAS consists of cells which use the bbu radio access technology model. For each cell a maximum number of bbu and the B and T thresholds of the different service classes are defined. The service class characteristics are defined in the user equipment (UE) component. The services are defined as real time services, since their service times don't depend on the allocated number of bbu. For each service class a priority and the quality level demands in bbu are defined; additionally their arrival and service time distribution are described via the type of distribution, mean value and coefficient of variation.

A special characteristic of the analytical MATS Markov model described in section 4, is the assumption of a homogenous cellular network. All cells are assumed to be statistically identical so that only one cell is considered with new and handoff connections incoming into the cell. Hence only handoffs towards the cell are modeled; handoffs away from the cell are not considered. In contrast to that the simulation framework needs at least two cells to generate handoffs. The underlying random waypoint mobility model produces handoffs towards and away from the cells. The distribution of this handoff process is based on the parameters of the mobility model and the cell layout. However, our aim was to reproduce the analytical Markov model assumptions as closely as possible in the simulation model to be able to counter check the Markov model results. Therefore we used a workaround to reproduce the Markov model assumptions for the single cell simulation scenarios. For each service class in the original scenario definition for the Markov model we defined two classes (sim-classes) in the simulation model with identical priorities. One sim-class represents the new connections; the other sim-class represents handoff connections. The parameter definition (bbu demands, thresholds etc.) is based on their type (new, handoff) and service class. This workaround has the disadvantage that handovered connections appear everywhere (uniformly distributed) in the cell, not mostly at cell borders as one would expect. This is becoming a problem if the modeled cell supports different signal quality areas. Therefore we do not use different signal quality areas in the presented scenarios. The advantage of this workaround is that we can reproduce the Markov model assumptions and we are able to directly define the handoff process.

All the simulated scenarios cover a scenario time of 14 days (excluding the transient phase) and results are derived from 70 repetitions. The simulation framework is based on OMNeT++ which uses the Mersenne Twister pseudo random generator and provides means for the generation of non-correlated random number streams.

6 Investigation of Model Behavior

In this section we present several experiments to investigate the model behavior. The first set of results (section 6.1) gives a comparison of the MATS scheme with other CAC algorithms presented in the literature.

For the aim of comparison, we consider among the proposed schemes those that are more consistent with our approach. In particular, we consider the Multi-Guard Channel Scheme (MGC) proposed in [14] and the Guard Channels with Fixed Reservation (GCFR) recently proposed in [16]. It is worth noting that while the MGC scheme uses the same criterion of priority as we consider, the GCFR uses a less stringent concept of priority since it allows handoff calls of all types to completely share the reserved guard channels (bbu). Note that both MGC and GCFR schemes consider no adaptive bandwidth allocation algorithm, in other words they assume only one QoS level for each class of requests. On the other hand, this is the main contribution of the MATS scheme. To some extend the proposed MATS scheme is the extension of the MGC scheme for providing more flexibility by including the u-d mechanism. The next scenarios (section 6.2) are based on the scenario descriptions in 6.1 and investigate the accuracy of the system behavior forecast of the analytical MATS Markov model if we deviate from the stated assumptions in section 4. Hence the scenarios show the influence of different distributions for the service and arrival process on blocking, dropping and the cell utilization. The last scenarios (section 6.3) describe the transfer of real world situations into input parameters for the MATS Markov model and show the applicability of the MATS scheme. We evaluate the blocking and dropping probability under MATS for three service classes representing radio, video and voice connections. The state space of the MATS Markov model for this scenario comprises only 3307 states. This shows that the Markov modeling approach is well suited for investigating applications of the MATS scheme.

6.1 The Comparison with Other Schemes

In the first set of experiments, the proposed MATS scheme is compared to the MGC and GCFR schemes. Note that the used parameter set doesn't originate from any particular application but is conform with the blocking probability and utilization levels investigated in [14, 16] for illustrating the scheme behavior.

A single-cell with B=100 bbu is considered. Three classes of calls are assumed, with class 3 having strict priority over both classes 2 and 1, and with class 2 having strict priority over class 1. The three classes have the following flexible QoS levels: $L_1= \{6, 10\}$, $L_2= \{8, 10\}$, $L_3= \{20\}$. Note that the highest priority class 3 has the most stringent QoS with a sole level. We select the different QoS levels for investigating the effect of the adaptability on more (class 1) or less (class 2) flexible requirements and on non-flexible requirement (class 3).

The bandwidth partition allows the three classes to use the following bandwidth portions: $B_1=70$ bbu, $B_2=80$ bbu and $B_3=100$ bbu. To guarantee that dropping probabilities are as low as possible, the following thresholds are assumed: $T_1= 60$, $T_2= 70$ and $T_3= 80$. For each class, we assume $\lambda_{h,i} = \lambda_{n,i}/2$ [15, 16], with $\lambda_i = \lambda_{n,i}+ \lambda_{h,i}$. We consider the following values for the total arrival rates: $\lambda_{tot} = \lambda_1+ \lambda_2+ \lambda_3 = 0.135, 0.27, 0.405, 0.54, 0.675, 0.81$ calls/min. For example for the first value 0.135, we assume arrival rates $\lambda_{n,1} = 0.04$, $\lambda_{n,2} = 0.03$ and $\lambda_{n,3}=0.02$, and we use the increment $\Delta_i = \lambda_{n,i}$ to obtain the next values. By that we assume decreasing values of arrival rates versus increasing priorities, thus limiting the dominant effect of the higher priorities classes. The following figures report the performance measures as a function of the total arrival rates (λ_{tot} on the x-axis). Finally, we assume μ_i=0.05 calls/min for each class.

Figures 2-(a), (b) and (c) show the blocking and dropping probabilities for the three classes according to the different schemes. These are the QoS measures from the user perspective. It is worth noting that since the other two schemes don't allow different levels for each class, we use the maximum level for this experiment. In other words for MGC and for GCFR the levels L_1= {10}, L_2= {10}, L_3= {20} are assumed for the three classes.

The results suggest that the MATS scheme performs better than the other two schemes for each class of request for new and handoff calls. We believe the reason is the u-d mechanism of the MATS: incoming call requests, that are probably blocked / dropped according to the other schemes are accepted according to the MATS by means of degradation. This is even true for the highest priority class 3 that has a sole level, but it can benefit from the degradation of the other two classes to free bandwidth. In particular, regarding the dropping probabilities, note the worsening of the behavior of GCFR scheme from class 1 until class 3. This is probably the consequence of allowing handoff calls of any class to fully share the bandwidth region reserved for handoff calls. So for example class 3, according to GCFR, shares the 20 bbu which are strictly reserved for handoff with the other two classes. Instead, according to MATS and MGC, the 20 bbu would be strictly reserved for class 3 handoff. Regarding the difference in performance between MATS and MGC, in our experience (see also [20]) the results are strongly dependent on the combination of the values of QoS levels and thresholds for each class. However, we can conclude that MATS shows in general better performance than MGC.

Figure 2-(d) shows the bandwidth utilization under the three schemes. The MGC scheme shows the lowest utilization, while the GCFR and MATS schemes show the highest utilization.

As stated in section 3.1, we define a less traditional metric to measure the percentage of time the highest QoS is delivered to the users. Figure 2–(e) shows the QL_i delivered to class i calls according to the MATS scheme. We omit class 3 because of its sole QoS level. We can conclude that class 1 calls receive the highest quality level more than 75% of the time, while class 2 calls receive the highest quality level more than the 87% of the time.

Figure 2–(f) shows the relative frequency of the application of the upgrade-degrade mechanism. It is not surprising that this is increasing, because the u-d mechanism is activated more frequently for higher utilization levels. Note that as we stated in section 4, the real cost of the mechanism application will be of course dependent on its relative frequency besides on system implementation and characteristics.

Finally, as introduced in section 5, to counter check the Markov model results, we used a simulation framework for simulating a comparable single cell scenario. The results would show virtually no difference in the graphs, therefore we omit them in figure 2 for the sake of clarity. Just to give an example, in the following table we display the blocking P_B / dropping P_D probability values in % for class 1 which we obtained for the above scenario by the analytical and simulation approach respectively. The simulation results are given with their respective 95% confidence intervals.

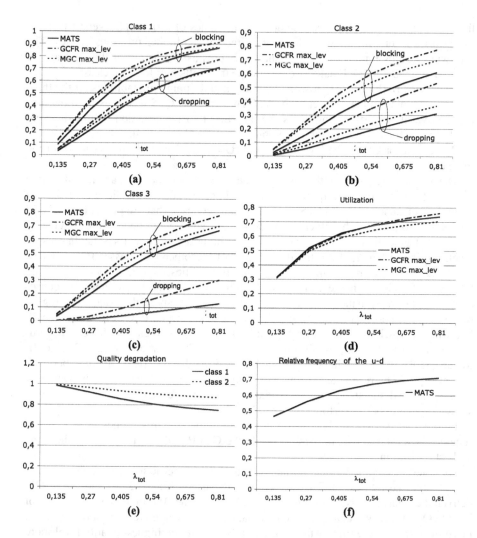

Fig. 2. Comparison among the MATS, MGC and GCFR schemes: (a), (b), (c) blocking and dropping probabilities for the three classes respectively; (d) utilization; (e) quality degradation; (f) relative frequency of the adaptive mechanism application

Table 1. Check of simulation and Markov model results

λ_{tot}	class 1 P_B [± 95%]	class 1 P_B Markov model	class 1 P_D [± 95%]	class 1 P_D Markov model
0.135	8.60 [0.40]	8.81	3.47 [0.27]	3.55
0.27	36.90 [0.67]	36.63	20.19 [0.61]	20.22
0.405	59.51 [0.74]	59.49	39.02 [0.88]	38.85
0.54	73.37 [0.72]	73.48	53.17 [0.84]	53.31
0.675	81.85 [0.68]	81.83	64.13 [0.83]	63.70
0.81	87.00 [0.68]	87.00	71.10 [0.76]	71.16

6.2 Influence of the Markov Model Assumptions

In this section we deviate from the assumptions made in the section 4 and investigate their influence on the accuracy of the Markov model results for the scenarios presented in the section 6.1. The Markov model assumes exponentially distributed interarrival and service times (or session times) which corresponds to an M/M/-model. In real systems the service times most likely will deviate from the memoryless property whereas the arrival process of new connections most likely could be seen as a Poisson process. Therefore we setup scenarios with different coefficients of variations for the service times of the service classes, which leads to an M/G/-like model. We did investigate service times with coefficients of variations (c_S) of 2.0 (two phase Hyperexponential distribution: H2) and 0.5 (Erlang-4 distribution: E4) to model more and less variable service times. Note that all services in one scenario have identical service time distributions. The results showed no significant difference in the blocking/dropping probability of the different service classes as well as an identical utilization for the M/G/- system compared to the Markov model results (all the Markov model results are within the 95% confidence interval of less than 1 % of the simulated M/G/- model results). This is consistent with the results in [25] that blocking probabilities are independent of the service time distribution for M/G/m/m systems. Our results confirm that this is even true for different thresholds and adaptable bbu demands per service class. Thus the Markov model results can be used in case of an M/G/- like system, which is most likely the case at the session level in communication systems. We do not show the detailed result tables here for the sake of briefness.

Additionally we also investigate the influence of the arrival process distribution in conjunction with the service time distribution. Thus the next scenarios model a G/G/-system and therefore they deviate from the Markov model assumption for the interarrival time and service time distribution. The results are presented in table 2. for the low and high utilization case. For each class we show the blocking P_B and dropping P_D probability together with a 95% confidence interval. The results show that if the arrival process also violates the memory less property the Markov model results for MATS can not be used any more. The results for the different distributions differ sometimes greatly not only in absolute numbers but also in general behavior for low and high system utilizations. For example the results for λ_{tot} =0.135 1/min show a higher blocking probability of class 1 connections for the H2/H2/- case in comparison to the Markov model results. In case of λ_{tot} =0.81 1/min this is reversed (see bold numbers in column "class 1 P_B" in table 4). We highlighted some other cases in italic and bold plus underlined which illustrate the change in behavior for the different distributions and utilization levels. In column "class 2 P_B" the results for different distributions change for low and high utilization levels. The bold plus underlined results show a change in behavior for different distributions at the same utilization level.

The G/M/- model scenario results also differ significantly from the Markov model results. We again omit them for the sake of briefness.

Table 2. Results for G/G/- system scenarios

Scenario λ_{tot} model	Class 1 P_B [± 95%]	Class 1 P_D [± 95%]	Class 2 P_B [± 95%]	Class 2 P_D [± 95%]	Class 3 P_B [± 95%]	Class 3 P_D [± 95%]	Utilization [± 95%]
0.135 M/M/-	**8.60** **[0.40]**	3.47 [0.27]	*2.65* *[0.20]*	0.73 [0.12]	3.54 [0.32]	0.11 [0.05]	31.54 [0.18]
0.135 E4/E4/-	5.22 [0.21]	1.43 [0.12]	*0.60* *[0.06]*	0.10 [0.04]	0.43 [0.07]	0.00 [0.00]	32.41 [0.09]
0.135 H2/H2/-	13.00 **[1.00]**	6.39 [0.81]	*6.63* *[0.60]*	2.77 [0.53]	15.60 [1.56]	4.27 [0.79]	29.47 [0.39]
0.81 M/M/-	87.00 [0.68]	<u>71.10</u> **[0.76]**	*61.07* *[0.56]*	31.15 [0.56]	<u>66.69</u> **[0.88]**	12.91 [0.40]	72.67 [0.05]
0.81 E4/E4/-	89.67 [0.39]	75.00 [0.47]	*61.87* *[0.35]*	29.36 [0.38]	65.67 [0.39]	2.82 [0.11]	74.04 [0.03]
0.81 H2/H2/-	82.22 **[1.44]**	<u>64.58</u> **[1.41]**	*60.81* *[1.17]*	35.26 [1.16]	<u>72.03</u> **[1.40]**	34.84 [1.17]	68.19 [0.11]

6.3 MATS Application Scenario

The scenario in this section illustrates the transfer of real world situations into input parameters for the MATS Markov model. Numbers for cell capacities are derived from results published in [26 p. 167] for the uplink direction of a WCDMA cell. The approximate cell capacities given in this reference for the data rates of different services are transferred into bbu demands for different service classes. Please note that this bbu-model is simplified and neglects the influence of different interference situations for different service mixes, user locations and neighbor cell utilization levels. A capacity of 100 bbu is assumed for the cell. Common realtime services in today's wireless wide area networks are voice, radio and video connections. We assume that voice is the most important service to the provider followed by video and radio. In table 3 we show the assumed high and low quality level data rates (DH, DL) for the services, the respective capacities of the cell and the transfer into the input parameters of the Markov model. For all services we assume that the user mobility creates a handoff rate $\lambda_{h,i}$ of half the arrival rate for new connections ($\lambda_{h,i} = \lambda_{n,i} / 2$). Our tests with multi cell scenarios show that this ratio corresponds to a pedestrian mobility pattern. Table 4 presents the performance comparison of the MATS scheme with MGC and GCFR schemes. As we mentioned above, these two schemes don't allow for the multilevel characteristic. Hence, for the aim of consistency with the "highest-QoS policy" of MATS, we consider the maximum levels of QoS for all classes in case of both MGC and GCFR schemes (MGC_max, GCFR_max). From the results, one can be convinced that the lack of flexibility dramatically worsens the performance from both the point of views of the users (blocking and dropping probabilities) and of the service provider (utilization of system/network components). For the aim of completeness, we extend the two schemes MGC and GCFR to include the multilevel characteristic (MGC_ext, GCFR_ext). Hence the two schemes behave similarly to MATS by starting to accept a call at the highest possible level. If this is not possible, the call will be accepted at the minimum level (for example the arriving call at the maximum level would not be within the right threshold). It is obvious that the multi-level characteristic improves the performance from all points of view. However, it is the flexibility of MATS with the upgrade-degrade mechanism that yields the best results. This claim is further confirmed by the last experiment, where we enhance the GCFR scheme with flexibility (GCFR_flex). Now, the behavior of the two schemes (MATS and GCFR_flex) is quite similar except for the fully shared channels for handoff in the GCFR.

Table 5 shows the two less traditional metrics defined in section 3.1 ("na" stands for not available). First of all, note that class 3, when it is present in the system, receives always the highest quality. This is obvious since the voice traffic has a stringent sole QoS level, in particular $L_3= \{2\}$. Similarly, all calls in MGC_max and in GCFR_max receive the highest quality, since in this case only the maximum level for each class is considered. In case of the MATS scheme one can be easily convinced that the gain in performance showed in Table 4, is reached at a very modest cost. Indeed, the radio traffic suffers the quality degradation only in about 1% of time, while the video traffic is degraded in about 9% of time. The relative frequency of the application of the upgrade-degrade mechanism is about 4%.

Table 3. Transfer into MATS Markov model input parameters

Service type	Data rates (kbit/s)	Cell-capacities (channel)	Input paramters	
			Cell thresholds (%)	Service parameters
radio	DL = 32	20	T1 = 70	L_1 {5,13}; $\lambda_{n,1}$ = 1/60 1/min;
	DH = 128	8	B1 = 80	μ_1= 1/20 1/min; Prio = 1
video	DL = 144	6	T2 = 80	L_2 {17,50}; $\lambda_{n,2}$ = 1/30 1/min;
	DH = 384	2	B2 = 90	μ_2= 1/5 1/min; Prio = 2
voice	DH=DL=12	60	T3 = 90	L_3 {2}; $\lambda_{n,3}$ = 2 1/min;
			B3 = 100	μ_3= 2/3 1/min; Prio = 3

Table 4. The realistic case: performance comparison

	P_B in %			P_D in %			Utilization
	radio	video	voice	radio	video	voice	
MATS	6.49	0.08	0.00	1.77	0.01	0.00	26.59
MGC_max	14.66	25.64	0.04	5.42	20.54	0.00	24.25
GCFR_max	14.75	25.87	0.11	5.58	20.63	0.01	24.39
MGC_ext	8.13	9.48	0.09	2.14	3.11	0.00	24.99
GCFR_ext	8.28	9.61	0.24	2.36	3.30	0.01	25.14
GCFR_flex	6.52	0.09	0.00	1.79	0.01	0.00	26.63

Table 5. The realistic case: quality levels and cost

	Quality levels			u-d relative frequency
	radio	video	voice	
MATS	0.990	0.912	1	0.043
MGC_max	1	1	1	na
GCFR_max	1	1	1	na
MGC_ext	0.930	0.830	1	na
GCFR_ext	0.946	0.828	1	na
GCFR_flex	0.990	0.912	1	0.044

7 Conclusions

In this paper, we considered an adaptive resource allocation problem, which is a very critical issue in the new framework of differentiated services in heterogeneous networks. In particular, we considered wireless mobile integrated service networks and proposed the MATS (CAC and ABA algorithm) for a multiclass environment with flexible QoS requirements and priority. Despite the fact of extensive research in the field of admission control and resource allocation in wireless networks, very few papers combine the multiclass characteristic with the adaptive issue [3, 15]. This combination is the main contribution of MATS. We developed a general analytical model to include the characteristics of the considered services and networks. We considered traditional performance metrics and we also defined two additional metrics for measuring the relative frequency of the ABA algorithm activation and to scale the amount of high level service time received by users.

We compared MATS with schemes recently proposed in the literature that are consistent with our assumptions. It is worth noting that these schemes do not include an adaptive mechanism for flexible QoS. From the first set of experiments one can conclude that an adaptive mechanism is mandatory for efficient resource utilization and for respecting the priority criterion.

Our simulation experiments confirm the results of the Markov model and show that they are even valid in the presence of non-Markovian service times. Future simulations will investigate the influences of multi cell scenarios, the user mobility and more sophisticated radio access technology models on the applicability of the Markov model results. Additionally we investigate means of increasing the cell utilization and to improve the control of blocking/dropping probabilities for different service classes via MATS.

Acknowledgement

The authors are thankful to the anonymous referees and to Bruno Müller-Clostermann for sharing their valuable time and expertise, which were useful in improving the quality of the presentation of the paper.

References

1. Aljadhai, A.R., Znati, T.F.: A Bandwidth Adaptation Scheme to Support QoS Requirements of Mobile Users in Wireless Environments. In: IEEE 9th ICCCN, Las Vegas, Nevada, October 16-18, pp. 34–39 (2000)
2. Chou, C.T., Shin, K.G.: Analysis of Adaptive Bandwidth Allocation in Wireless Networks with Multilevel Degradable Quality of Service. IEEE T Mobile Comput. 3(1), 5–17 (2004)
3. Lindemann, C., Lohnmann, M., Thummler, A.: Adaptive call admission control for QoS/revenue optimization in CDMA cellular networks. Wirel. Netw. 10(4), 457–472 (2004)
4. Zaruba, G.V., Chlamtac, I., Das, S.K.: A Prioritized Real-Time Wireless Call Degradation Framework for Optimal Call Mix Selection. Mobile Netw. Appl. 7, 143–151 (2002)

5. Sherif, M.R., Habib, I.W., Nagshineh, M., Kermani, P.: Adaptive Allocation of Resources and Call Admission Control for Wireless ATM Using Genetic Algorithms. IEEE J. Sel. Area Comm. 18(2) (February 2000)
6. Bharghavan, V.B., Lee, K.-W., Lu, S., Ha, S., Li, J.-R., Dwyer, D.: The TIMELY Adaptive Resource Management Architecture. IEEE Pers. Commun., 20–31 (August 1998)
7. Sen, S., Javanda, J., Basu, K., Das, S.: Quality-of-Service Degradation Strategies in Multimedia Wireless Networks. In: IEEE VTC 1998, pp. 1884–1888 (1998)
8. Talukdar, A.K., Badrinath, B.R., Acharya, A.: Rate Adaptation Schemes in Networks with Mobile Hosts. In: ACM MobiCom 1998, Dallas, Texas, USA (1998)
9. Xiao, Y., Chen, C.L.P., Wang, Y.: Fair bandwidth allocation for multi-class for adaptive multimedia services in wireless/mobile networks. In: IEEE VTC 2001, vol. 3, pp. 2081–2085 (2001)
10. Chou, C.T., Shin, K.G.: Analysis of combined adaptive bandwidth allocation and admission control in wireless networks. In: IEEE INFOCOM 2002, vol. 2, pp. 676–684 (2002)
11. Kwon, T., Choi, Y., Bisdkian, C., Naghshineh, M.: QoS provisioning in wireless / mobile multimedia networks using an adaptive framework. Wirel. Netw. 9(1) (2003)
12. Nasser, N.: Real-time service adaptability in multimedia wireless networks. In: ACM Q2SWinet 2005, Montreal, Quebec, Canada (2005)
13. Cheng, S.T., Chen, C.M., Chen, I.R.: Performance evaluation of an admission control algorithm with dynamic threshold with negotiation. Perform Evaluation 52, 1–13 (2003)
14. Salamah, M.: An adaptive multi-guard channel scheme for multi-class traffic in cellular networks. In: ACS/IEEE AICCSA 2006, pp. 716–723 (2006)
15. Niyato, D., Hossain, E.: A novel analytical framework for integrated cross-layer study of call-level and packet-level QoS in wireless mobile multimedia networks. IEEE T Mobile Comput. 6(3), 322–335 (2007)
16. Mohamed, N.A., Deniz, D.Z.: Fixed and dynamic bandwidth allocation strategies for wireless mobile integrated services networks. Wirel. Netw. 14(1), 121–131 (2008)
17. ITU-T E.860 Framework of a service level agreement (2002)
18. Ghaderi, M., Boutaba, R.: Call admission control in mobile cellular networks: a comprehensive survey. Wirel. Commun. Mob. Com. 6(1), 69–93 (2006)
19. Falowo, O.E., Chan, H.A.: Joint call admission control algorithms: requirements, approaches and design considerations. Comput. Comun., 1200–1217 (2008)
20. de Nitto Personè, V., Campagna, E.: Adaptive bandwidth allocation and admission control for wireless integrated services networks with flexible QoS. In: SIMUTools/QoSim 2009, 2nd International Workshop on the Evaluation of Quality of Service through Simulation in the Future Internet, Rome, Italy, March 2-6 (2009)
21. Pillekeit, A., Müller-Clostermann, B.: A Simulation Framework for the Evaluation of Scenarios and Algorithms for Common Radio Resource Management. In: SIMUTools 2009, Rome, Italy, March 3-6 (2009)
22. International Standard: Information Technology-Quality of Service: Framework. Reference number ISO/IEC 13236:1998(E)
23. ITU-T Recommendation G.1000 - Communications quality of service: a framework and definitions (2001)
24. Shanthikumar, J.G., Sargent, R.G.: A Unifying View of Hybrid Simulation/Analytic Models and Modeling. Operations Research 31(6), 1030–1052 (1983)
25. Bose, S.K.: An Introduction to Queueing Systems, 1st edn. Kluwer Academic/Plenum Publishers, New York (2002)
26. Holma, H., Toskala, A.: WCDMA for UMTS - Radio Access for Third Generation Mobile Communications. Revised edn. John Wiley and Sons, New York (2001)

Setting the Parameters Right for Two-Hop IEEE 802.11e Ad Hoc Networks

Anne Remke[1,*], Boudewijn R. Haverkort[1,2], Geert Heijenk[1], and Jesper Bax[1]

[1] University of Twente
Design and Analysis of Communication Systems
Enschede, The Netherlands
http://dacs.cs.utwente.nl/
[2] Embedded Systems Institute
Eindhoven, The Netherlands
http://www.esi.nl

Abstract. Two-hop ad-hoc networks, in which some nodes forward traffic for multiple sources, with which they also compete for channel access suffer from large queues building up in bottleneck nodes. This problem can often be alleviated by using IEEE 802.11e to give preferential treatment to bottleneck nodes. Previous results have shown that differentiation parameters can be used to allocate capacity in a more efficient way in the two-hop scenario. However, the overall throughput of the bottleneck may differ considerably, depending on the differentiation method used. By applying a very fast and accurate analysis method, based on steady-state analysis of an QBD-type infinite Markov chain, we find the maximum throughput that is possible per differentiation parameter. All possible parameter settings are explored with respect to the maximum throughput conditioned on a maximum buffer occupancy. This design space exploration cannot be done with network simulators like NS2 or Opnet, as each simulation run simply takes to long.

The results, which have been validated by detailed simulations, show that by differentiating TXOP it is possible to achieve a throughput that is about 50% larger than when differentiating AIFS and CW_{min}.

1 Introduction

The availability of cheap yet powerful wireless access technology, most notably IEEE 802.11 ("wireless LAN"), has given an impulse to the development of wireless ad hoc networks. In such networks, the stations (nodes) that are in reach of each other, help each other in obtaining and maintaining connectivity. At the same time they are also competitors, as they all contend for the same resource, i.e., the shared ether as transmission medium. The medium access control of IEEE 802.11 (based on CSMA/CA) is commonly referred to as the distributed

---

* The work presented in this paper has been performed in the context of the MC=MC project (612.000.311), financed by the Netherlands Organization for Scientific Research (NWO).

B. Müller-Clostermann et al. (Eds.): MMB & DFT 2010, LNCS 5987, pp. 168–182, 2010.

coordination function (DCF) [6,12]. Research has shown that, effectively, the DCF tends to equally share the capacity among contending stations [2,7]. Although this appears to be a nice fairness property, this fairness does lead to undesirable situations in case one of the nodes that functions as bridge toward either another group of nodes, or via an access point to the wired internet, as illustrated in Figure 1. In such cases, it appears fair to allocate more bandwidth to the bridging node.

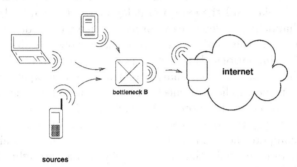

Fig. 1. Bottleneck in a two-hop ad hoc network

Recently, a quality-of-service (QoS)-extension of the IEEE 802.11 standard, the so-called EDCA ("e") version has been released [1]. Roughly speaking, this extension provides mechanisms to provide preferential treatment of certain traffic classes (or nodes) over others. Four different parameters can be used to reallocate the amount of radio capacity given to each station, corresponding to a large number of different parameter settings.

The current paper analyzes how we can optimize IEEE 802.11e parameter settings such that maximum throughput is obtained for a given buffer size in this 2-hop ad hoc network scenario?

Even though single parameter settings can be simulated with network simulators like NS2 or Opnet, it is practically impossible to find the optimal parameter setting for a given scenarios using costly and slow simulations. In contrast to the simulations a very fast analytical approach has been proposed in [10], where we presented a new model for analyzing IEEE 802.11e access mechanism in a two-hop ad hoc network. Our high-level model is flow-based, and uses results from packet-based models (such as those proposed by Bianchi and Engelstad et al. [2,4]), and allows for the numerical evaluation of the buffer occupancy at the bottleneck node, the system throughput, as well as provides information on the mean number of active sources. This analytical approach has been verified by extensive simulations.

However, the key result of the current paper is that we use these models in a variety of scenarios, and show how they can be used to optimize system parameters. By exploring the parameter choices for all stations and the chosen threshold for the buffer occupancy, we obtain the maximum load parameter λ for which the buffer occupancy still remains below the threshold and then compute the throughput that corresponds to this load. Note that we only differentiate one parameter at a time.

This cannot be achieved with detailed simulation models, simply because they are too time-consuming to be executed so often. We do, however, show that also for the optimized parameter scenarios, the results obtained with the analytical models, do coincide very well with detailed simulation studies.

The only paper we are aware of explicitly addressing an analytical evaluation of the two-hop case is [13]. They obtain explicit (closed-form) equations for the expected overall delay and the expected delay at the bottleneck by translating the model at hand into a generalized processor sharing model, as studied by Cohen [3]. Although the analysis is approximate, good results are obtained, as confirmed by simulations. However, this evaluation approach is limited in that it only allows for an equal sharing of transmission capacity between all active stations (including the bottleneck). They do not address the differentiation parameters introduced in the protocol IEEE 802.11e.

In this paper, the system of interest and the modeling approach is described in Section 2. We compare the maximum throughput that can be obtained with the different QoS parameters with the maximum obtainable throughput in the basic setting in Section 3. Conclusions and future work are discussed in Section 4.

2   System of Interest and Modeling Approach

In Section 2.1 we describe the scenario of interest, in Section 2.2 the quality of service parameters are described and in Section 2.3 the analytical modeling approach is discussed.

2.1   Bottleneck Scenario

The scenario under study, as illustrated in Figure 1, has a varying number N of active nodes, the so-called sources, which are all within reach of each other. Additionally there is the bottleneck node B, that is the only node that can reach via an access point the wired internet. Hence, all traffic originating from the sources and the traffic passing through the bridge has to share the same radio transmission capacity. It has been shown that the DCF access mechanism effectively shares the radio capacity equally over all competing nodes [2,7]. Clearly, this situation benefits the sources as a group, as they can use a relatively large share of radio capacity to send their packets, whereas the bottleneck only gets the same share as every other individual node. Because it has to support the traffic of all other nodes, fairness leads to a very high buffer occupancy in B, eventually also buffer overflow, and in any case, long delays.

2.2   IEEE 802.11e

The Enhanced Distributed Channel Access Function (EDCA) of IEEE 802.11e allows multiple contention instances to be simultaneously active in a single station, each supporting a certain access category (AC). Furthermore, the standard introduces four differentiation parameters (EDCA parameters), as discussed below, which can be set individually for each access category of each individual station to enable QoS provisioning [11].

We facilitate adaptive capacity sharing between stations by letting each station have a single access category, and using the EDCA parameters for differentiating between the source stations and the bottleneck station. In principle the EDCA parameters are meant for service differentiation, while we apply it here for node differentiation. Another relevant scenario for such node level differentiation is the case of uplink versus downlink transfer in an infrastructure-based WLAN, where the access point should get a bigger share of the resources to achieve fairness between both directions [9,5]. In the remainder of this paper we will analyze the following four scenarios:

1. With standard IEEE 802.11, the medium needs to be idle for at least one distributed inter-frame spacing (DIFS) period before stations can start to contend for medium access. A station then needs to wait a random number of slots, drawn from the so-called contention window ($\{0, CW\}$), before starting to transmit if the medium is still idle. After winning contention a station is allowed to send exactly one packet. The range of the window grows with every collision (until the maximum is reached) and is reset to its minimum after a successful transmission.

In the IEEE 802.11e QoS extension, two contention-based methods are proposed to change the above procedure:

2. The initial value of the *contention window* ($CW_{min} - 1$) and/or the maximum value of the contention window ($CW_{max} - 1$) are set smaller for a given station, thus, this station draws its backoff from a smaller contention window, hence, has a higher probability to win contention.
3. With so-called *arbitration inter-frame spacing* (AIFS) it is possible to assign different inter-frame spacings for different service classes (or nodes) instead of the fixed DIFS. Thus, high-priority nodes can be assigned shorter AIFS, so that they can start counting off their backoff earlier, hence, have an advantage when contending for medium access.

A way to adapt the capacity sharing that does not alter the actual contention mechanism is the following:

4. The transmission opportunity limit ($TXOP_{limit}$) provides a time period during which a station may send packets after having won a contention. Thus, a station with a sufficiently high $TXOP_{limit}$ is able to send several packets and will thus be able to grab a larger share of the channel capacity than a station with a smaller $TXOP_{limit}$.

The above four parameters (CW_{min} and CW_{max}, AIFS and $TXOP_{limit}$) in the IEEE 802.11e standard can be used to reallocate the amount of radio capacity given to the sources and to the bottleneck.

2.3 An Abstract Analytical Model

In this section we briefly recall the analytical model, for a more detailed description please refer to [10].

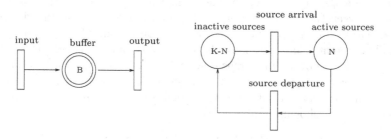

Fig. 2. High-level model as iSPN

We model the bottleneck B, cf. Figure 1, using an infinite-state stochastic Petri net (iSPN), as given in Figure 2. The left part of this figure contains an unbounded place (double circle) *buffer* that models the (buffer of the) bottleneck of the system. Transition *input* models the total arrival stream of packets from all active sources, whereas transition *output* models the transmission of packets leaving the bottleneck B. We limit the maximum number of active sources to some finite number K and do not distinguish between individual active sources, modeled by the right part of the iSPN in Figure 2. An inactive source becomes active after a negative exponentially distributed amount of time (with mean $1/\lambda$) and immediately instantiates a flow, which has a geometrically distributed length, measured in packets. The average size of a data packet is assumed to be $E[P] = 1500$ bytes, with exponentially distributed length. The duration of a flow does not only depend on its size but also on the radio capacity a source can use to transmit the flow. Note that the duration of a flow implicitly gives the source departure rate, as well. Hence, the behavior of the sources depends on the system behavior. This traffic model is realistic for interactive applications, such as web browsing. Following the parametric assumptions made in [13], the expected amount of work put forward per flow (the amount of packets comprising the flow) equals $E[F] = 500$ packets; the other values for the key system parameters are summarized in Table 1.

Table 1. Values for the system parameters

parameter	
arrival rate	$\lambda \in [0.1, 0.4]$ sec^{-1}
average flow size	$E[F] = 500$ packets
overall radio capacity	$C = 917$ packets/sec
maximum of active sources	$K = 10$

Table 2. State-dependent transition rates for the iSPN

transition rates	
input:	if $N = 0$ then 0 else $C \cdot S_s(\cdot)$;
output:	if $B = 0$ then 0 else $C \cdot S_b(\cdot)$;
source departure:	$C \cdot S_s(\cdot)/E[F]$;
source arrival:	$(K - N)\lambda$;

In Table 2 we list the four state-dependent transition rates of the iSPN, where N refers to the current number of active sources (i.e., the number of tokens in place *active sources*), and B to the current number of packets queued in the bottleneck (i.e., the number of tokens in place *buffer*). Note that the transitions *input* and *output* in fact make use of the same medium, hence, they have to share the available capacity; this is exactly what the IEEE 802.11e access mechanism is for! The functions $S_b(\cdot)$ and $S_s(\cdot)$ (for bottleneck and source) now give the normalized data rate at which the bottleneck and all sources can transmit, respectively. Note that $S_b(\cdot)$ and $S_s(\cdot)$ depend on the number of currently active sources (N), as well as whether or not the bottleneck has packets queued, or not ($B > 0$).

The explicit expressions for the functions $S_s(\cdot)$ and $S_b(\cdot)$ that express the share of the wireless capacity that sources and the bottleneck receive, resp., for each of the QoS enhancements are taken from Engelstad's model [4], which proposes an analytical evaluation of the throughput, for a *fixed* number of independent stations, including the impact of the QoS enhancements on the effectively available capacity in IEEE 802.11e.

Hence, we have obtained one generic model at the iSPN level, that can be specialized toward different QoS enhancements, by "plugging in" the appropriate bandwidth sharing functions $S_b(\cdot)$ and $S_s(\cdot)$.

3   Setting the Parameters Right

In this section, we compute the maximum throughput that can be achieved for a given constraint on the buffer occupancy, per differentiation parameter. Note that we only differentiate one parameter at a time but allow for different choices for the sources as opposed to the bottleneck. For AIFS, this is discussed in Section 3.1, in Section 3.2 for CW_{min} and in Section 3.3 for TXOP. Finally, we compare the maximum throughput that can be obtained for the different QoS settings with the maximum throughput obtained with basic IEEE 802.11 in Section 3.4. Moreover, for each setting that has been found to be optimal, we compare the results with Opnet simulations [8].

3.1   Throughput for Different AIFS

The constrained maximum throughput of a given combination of $AIFS_b$ (the chosen value for the bottleneck) and $AIFS_s$ (the chosen value for the sources) is obtained as illustrated in Figure 3. First the value of λ is identified for which the buffer occupancy equals the maximum of the buffersize that has been set as threshold (step 1). In Figure 3 the buffer occupancy for $\lambda = 0.024$ equals the threshold of 50 packets (steps 2). Then the corresponding throughput of 108 packets per second for this value of λ is computed (step 3).

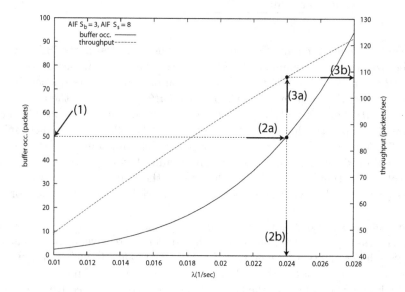

Fig. 3. Average buffer occupancy versus throughput for a given parameter setting

Modeling the buffer in the bottleneck with infinite capacity facilitates our analysis approach, however, bounding the maximum buffer occupancy to a given threshold when computing the maximum throughput results in more realistic results and additionally keeps the maximum delay low.

Figure 4 shows the maximum throughput that can be achieved per parameter setting when the buffer occupancy is bound to be at most 50. $AIFS_b$ is between 2 and 9 and $AIFS_s$ is between 5 and 12. Note that this value has been chosen to realistically model the buffer size of an ad hoc node. Evaluating the system for other values can be done without additional modeling and analysis effort.

For combinations of large $AIFS_b$ and small $AIFS_s$ the bound on the average buffer occupancy can only be met for $\lambda = 0$. Clearly, the resulting throughput is zero as well. For increasing values of $AIFS_s$ the achievable throughput grows. The maximum throughput of 195.21 packets per second is achieved for $AIFS_b = 2$ and $AIFS_s = 10$, as marked with x in Figure 3. If $AIFS_s$ is increased above 10 and $AIFS_b$ above 2, the achieved throughput declines. This is due to a waste of capacity, as stations have to wait longer before they can start decrementing their backoff. Too high values for AIFS reveal an inherent inefficiency in the MAC protocol.

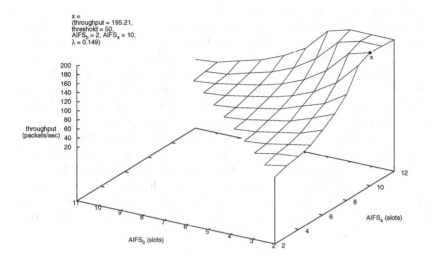

Fig. 4. Maximum throughput for different combinations of $AIFS_b$ and $AIFS_s$

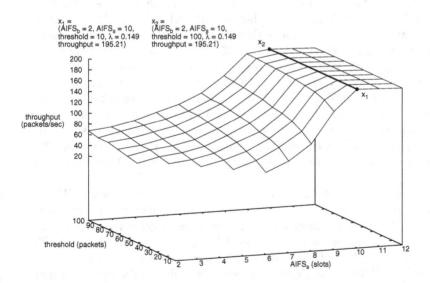

Fig. 5. Maximum throughput for different combinations of $AIFS_s$ and the threshold on the average buffer occupancy

Figure 5 shows the maximum throughput that can be achieved for $AIFS_b = 2$, when $AIFS_s$ ranges between 2 and 12 slots and the threshold on the average buffer occupancy ranges between 10 and 100.

Again, the maximum throughput is 195 packets per second. This throughput is obtained for $AIFS_s = 10$ and $AIFS_b = 2$, independent of the bound on the threshold. When $AIFS_s$ is increased beyond 10, the throughput decreases due to the waste of capacity, evenly for all considered thresholds. When $AIFS_s$ is set smaller than 10, the throughput decreases overall and even faster for smaller thresholds. Only with small values of λ, the low threshold on the average buffer occupancy can be met. This, of course, keeps the throughput low. For several combinations of small $AIFS_s$ and low thresholds the value of λ even has to be zero to match the constraint on the buffer occupancy, resulting in zero throughput.

Concluding, we can state that a maximum throughput of 195 packets per second can be achieved, when differentiating AIFS. Moreover, this maximum appears independent of the threshold on the average buffer occupancy. Regarding the throughput and the buffer occupancy, $AIFS_s$ should be chosen rather too big than too small, whereas $AIFS_b$ should be set to 2.

3.2   Throughput for Different CW_{min}

Figure 6 shows the maximum throughput that can be achieved for different combinations of $CW_{min,b}$ and $CW_{min,s}$, when the average buffer occupancy is, again, bounded to 50. $CW_{min,b}$ ranges between 31 and 287 and $CW_{min,s}$ ranges between 31 and 447. The maximum throughput of 193 packets per second is obtained for $CW_{min,b} = 31$ and $CW_{min,s} = 255$ (point x in Figure 6). For higher values of $CW_{min,b}$ the throughput decreases due to several reasons: first, capacity is wasted as randomly chosen backoffs become unnecessarily large, second the difference between $CW_{min,b}$ and $CW_{min,s}$ is too small, resulting in already high buffer occupancy for still small values of λ. Consequently the throughput remains small. For the same reason, several combinations of high $CW_{min,b}$ and low $CW_{min,s}$ result in zero throughput. When $CW_{min,s}$ is increased above 255, the throughput decreases slowly, as capacity is wasted due to large backoffs in the sources.

Figure 7 shows the maximum throughput that can be achieved when $CW_{min,s}$ ranges from 31 to 447 and the bound on the average buffer occupancy ranges from 10 to 100. The throughput increases evenly for larger values of $CW_{min,s}$. The maximum throughput is obtained for $CW_{min,b} = 31$ and $CW_{min,s} = 255$ and a threshold on the buffer occupancy of at least 40 packets. For values of $CW_{min,s}$ above 255 the throughput decreases slowly, due to the waste of capacity. We can conclude that maximum throughput is obtained for $CW_{min,b} = 31$ and $CW_{min,s} = 255$ and a threshold of at least 40 packets. As for $AIFS_s$, the parameter $CW_{min,s}$ should be chosen rather too big than too small.

Note that we only use CW_{min} and not CW_{max} to differentiate, as we found CW_{max} to have little influence on the performance results.

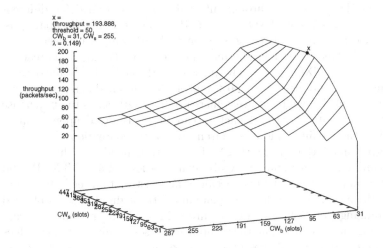

Fig. 6. Maximum throughput for different combinations of CW_b and CW_s

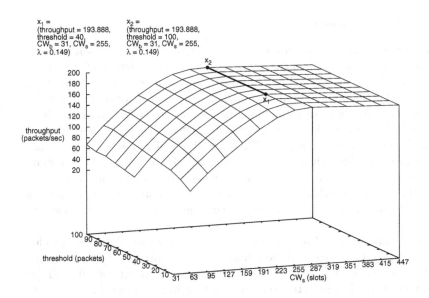

Fig. 7. Maximum throughput for different combinations of CW_s and the threshold on the average buffer occupancy

3.3   Throughput for Different TXOP

Figure 8 shows the maximum throughput that can be obtained for different combinations of $TXOP_b$ and $TXOP_s$, when the average buffer occupancy is, again, bound to be at most 50 packets. When $TXOP_b$ ranges between 1 and 30 and $TXOP_s$ between 1 and 15 the maximum of 281.103 packets is reached for $TXOP_b = 30$ and $TXOP_s = 4$. The maximum throughput, obtained when differentiating via TXOP is almost 50% higher than when differentiating via AIFS or CW_{min}. On the one hand every increase in $TXOP_b$ leads to an increase in the effective capacity as several packets can be transmitted upon winning contention, i.e., the medium is idle less often due to less contention.

On the other hand the choice of $TXOP_s$ highly depends on the value of $TXOP_b$, as can be seen in Figure 8. Again, combinations of small $TXOP_b$ and large $TXOP_s$ lead to zero throughput, because the constraint on the buffer occupancy cannot be met. Figure 9 shows the maximum throughput that is obtained for $TXOP_b$ ranging from 1 to 30 and the threshold on the average buffer occupancy ranging from 10 to 100. The throughput increases evenly for larger values of $TXOP_b$ and for larger thresholds, and the maximum throughput of 283 packets per second is achieved for the largest considered $TXOP_b = 30$ and the largest considered threshold of 100 packets. This is due to the fact that every increase in $TXOP_b$ leads to an increased capacity.

3.4   Overall Comparison

To conclude this case study, we compare the maximum throughput that can be obtained for a given threshold on the buffer occupancy per differentiation parameter. Figure 10 shows this throughput as a function of λ under the constraint that the average buffer occupancy is smaller than 100 packets. All three differentiation parameters are able to keep the buffer occupancy below the given threshold of 100 packets for all considered values of λ. However, the throughput that can be obtained when differentiating via $TXOP_b$ and $TXOP_s$ is about 50% higher for large values of λ than when differentiating via AIFS or CW_{min}. Differentiating AIFS and CW_{min} results in approximately the same maximum throughput. Note that the throughput that can be obtained with standard EDCA parameters is not included in this figure, as the buffer occupancy constraint is only met for $\lambda < 0.015$.

To validate our analytical results, Figure 10 also shows simulation results for the three parameter settings that we found in our optimization in the previous section. Simulation results are derived with the network simulator OPNET [8] using the included IEEE 802.11e model, which take into account the full details of the MAC protocols. Except for AIFS differentiation with load larger than 0.6 all analytical results lie well within the confidence intervals. This discrepancy is probably due to the inaccuracy of the AIFS approximation in Engelstad's model.

Figure 11 shows the maximum throughput that can be obtained for the three differentiated settings and for basic IEEE 802.11 as a function of the threshold on

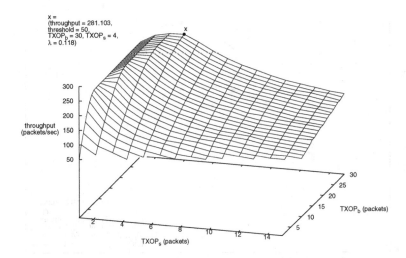

Fig. 8. Maximum throughput for different combinations of TXOP$_b$ and TXOP$_s$

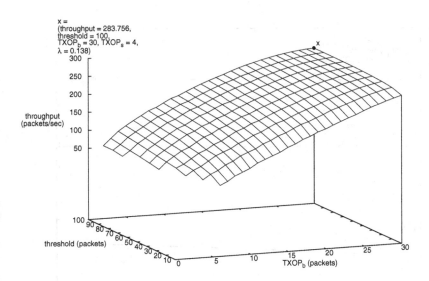

Fig. 9. Maximum throughput for different combinations of TXOP$_b$ and the threshold on the average buffer occupancy

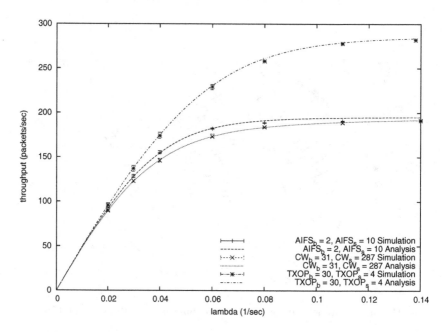

Fig. 10. Maximum obtainable throughput per differentiation parameter as a function of λ, validated by simulations

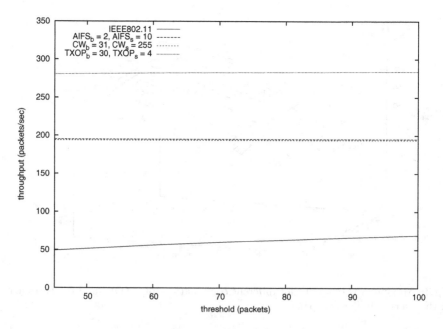

Fig. 11. Maximum obtainable throughput per differentiation parameter for different bounds on the expected buffer occupancy

the buffer occupancy. As one would expect, the smallest throughput is obtained in the non-differentiated setting. The throughput that can be obtained when differentiating via AIFS and CW_{min} is about the same. The highest throughput is obtained when differentiating via $TXOP_b$ and $TXOP_s$. Note that we only consider thresholds between 45 and 100 packets, as smaller threshold constraints cannot be met with non-differentiated EDCA parameters. The throughput in the differentiated cases is almost independent of the chosen threshold, whereas the throughput in the basic setting grows slightly with growing thresholds on the buffer occupancy.

We conclude that in a two-hop bottleneck scenario it is advisable to differentiate, using $TXOP_b$ and $TXOP_s$, as increasing these differentiation parameter results in an increase of the effective capacity. Differentiating $TXOP_b$ and $TXOP_s$ results in a maximum throughput that is 300% larger than the throughput in the non-differentiated setting and about 50% larger than when differentiating AIFS and CW_{min}. However, note that differentiating TXOP may affect performance metrics not considered by our models, especially delay jitter, since the traffic is more and more served in bursts.

4   Conclusions

Previous results have shown that all IEEE 802.11e EDCA parameters can be used to allocate capacity in a better way between the bottleneck and the sources. However, as we have shown, the overall throughput of the bottleneck differs, significantly, depending on the differentiation method used.

Exploiting a very fast and accurate analysis method, we explore all possible parameter settings to find the setting that provides the maximum throughput conditioned on a maximum buffer occupancy, in order to make the results more realistic and to provide a bound on the induced delay.

We have shown that the largest throughput can be obtained when using differentiation parameters $TXOP_b$ and $TXOP_s$. The resulting throughput is about 50% larger than when differentiating using AIFS of CW_{min}. This is due to the fact that a larger TXOP increases the effective capacity, whereas differentiating CW and AIFS decreases the effective capacity. Even though the conclusions drawn from this case study may seem rather evident we can quantify the impact of the choices relative to each other, quantitatively.

We have compared our results for the optimal parameter settings per parameter with simulations (using Opnet [8]) and show that our models provide very accurate results at almost negligible cost in comparison to the simulations. No other analytical models that allow for similar evaluations have been proposed so far.

Future work will analyze the possibilities of efficiently modelling and optimizing multi-hop networks with several bottlenecks. Furthermore, our analytical approach will be compared to a control-theoretic approach for simulating the scenario under study [14].

References

1. IEEE 802.11e/D13.0. Wireless LAN Medium Access Control (MAC) and Physical layer (PHY) specifications: Medium Access Control Enhancements for Quality of Service (QoS). IEEE 802.11 std. (2005)
2. Bianchi, G.: Performance analysis of the IEEE 802.11 Distributed Coordination Function. IEEE Journal on Selected Areas in Communications 18, 535–547 (2000)
3. Cohen, J.W.: The multiple phase service network with Generalized Processor Sharing. Acta Informatica 12, 245–284 (1979)
4. Engelstad, P.E., Osterbo, O.N.: Non-saturation and saturation analysis of IEEE 802.11e EDCA with starvation prediction. In: Proc. 8th ACM Int. Symposium on Modeling, Analysis and Simulation of Wireless and Mobile Systems (MSWiM 2005), pp. 224–233. ACM Press, New York (2005)
5. Jeong, J., Choi, S., Kim, C.: Achieving Weighted Fairness between Uplink and Downlink in IEEE 802.11 DCF-Based WLANs. In: Proc. 2nd Int. Conference on Quality of Service in Heterogeneous Wired/Wireless Networks (QSHINE 2005), p. 22. IEEE Press, Los Alamitos (2005)
6. Kurose, J.F., Ross, K.W.: Computer Networking. Addison-Wesley, Reading (2005)
7. Litjens, R., Roijers, R., van den Berg, J.L., Boucherie, R.J., Fleuren, M.J.: Analysis of flow transfer times in IEEE 802.11 wireless lans. Annals of Telecommunications 59, 1407–1432 (2004)
8. Opnet modeler software, http://www.opnet.com/products/modeler
9. Pilosof, S., Ramjee, R., Raz, D., Shavitt, Y., Sinha, P.: Understanding TCP fairness over Wireless Lan. In: Proc. 29th Conference on Computer Communications (INFOCOM 2003), pp. 863–872. IEEE Press, Los Alamitos (2003)
10. Remke, A., Haverkort, B.R., Heijenk, G., Cloth, L.: Bottleneck Analysis for Two-Hop IEEE 802.11e Ad hoc Networks. In: Al-Begain, K., Heindl, A., Telek, M. (eds.) ASMTA 2008. LNCS, vol. 5055, pp. 279–294. Springer, Heidelberg (2008)
11. Roijers, F., van den Berg, J.L., Fan, X., Fleuren, M.: A performance study on service integration in IEEE 802.11e wireless LANs. Computer Communications 29, 2621–2633 (2006)
12. Schiller, J.: Mobile Communications. Addison-Wesley, Reading (2003)
13. van den Berg, H., Mandjes, M., Roijers, F.: Performance modeling of a bottleneck node in an IEEE 802.11 ad-hoc network. In: Kunz, T., Ravi, S.S. (eds.) ADHOC-NOW 2006. LNCS, vol. 4104, pp. 321–336. Springer, Heidelberg (2006)
14. Yang, Y., Haverkort, B.R.H.M., Heijenk, G.J.: A control-theoretic modeling approach for service differentiation in multi-hop ad-hoc networks. In: Proc. 5th Int. Conference on the Quantitative Evaluation of Systems (QEST 2008). IEEE Press, Los Alamitos (2008)

CrossTrace: Cross-Layer Measurement for IEEE 802.11 Wireless Testbeds

Simon Frohn, Sascha Gübner, and Christoph Lindemann

University of Leipzig,
Department of Computer Science,
Johannisgasse 26
04103 Leipzig,
Germany
{frohn,guebner,cl}@rvs.informatik.uni-leipzig.de

Abstract. In this paper, we introduce and evaluate CrossTrace, a framework for performing cross-layer measurements in IEEE 802.11 based wireless networks. CrossTrace allows tracing of parameters at MAC-, routing and transport layer in a controlled environment and in a repeatable manner. Possible areas of application include network performance analysis and protocol optimization. Using CrossTrace, we conduct a comprehensive measurement study in a miniaturized testbed, in which we analyze the behavior of the IEEE 802.11 MAC-layer with respect to signal strength and bit error rate. We derive the delivery probability and bit error rate dependent on signal strength and MAC-layer data rate with and without interfering background traffic. We show that even moderate background traffic can significantly degrade network performance.

Keywords: Design and implementation of wireless mesh testbeds, IEEE 802.11 wireless networks, performance evaluation, real-world experiments.

1 Introduction

With the emergence of the IEEE 802.11 standard, wireless networking has experienced a rapid growth. In this context design and evaluation of wireless networking protocols becomes increasingly important. Wireless testbeds provide a real-world platform for implementing and evaluating next-generation network protocols. Such testbeds allow more accurate evaluations than network simulators such as ns-2 [16] and Qualnet [17]. The latter are often build on simplified wireless channel models and rely on optimistic assumptions compared to the real world. Such models typically neglect wireless characteristics such as multipath fading and spatial diversity. As a consequence, simulations do not always deliver accurate results. Therefore simulation is only applicable in the early design phase of new protocols and needs to be reinforced by testbed studies.

Opposed to wired networks, in IEEE 802.11 networks the wireless channel is a scarce resource shared among nodes within their radio range. Furthermore, hidden and exposed terminal effects [6], interference-aware routing [9], security [12] and QoS deficiencies [18] are features of wireless networks. However these features have

B. Müller-Clostermann et al. (Eds.): MMB & DFT 2010, LNCS 5987, pp. 183–197, 2010.

not been considered in the design of classic network protocol stack with its rigid layer architecture.

Cross-layer design has been becoming increasingly popular within the research community due to the described deficiencies of the classic network protocol stack. Instead of incremental and isolated improvements new network protocols are designed from scratch levering the strict boundaries between different layers of the protocol stack. For example a routing protocol may access information available at MAC-layer to estimate interference and identify high throughput paths. Also a routing protocol may select paths according to the QoS constraints of a transport protocol. Such cross-layer design approaches require a comprehensive understanding of the parameters observable at MAC-, routing and transport layer.

In this paper we introduce and evaluate CrossTrace, a framework for performing cross-layer measurements in IEEE 802.11 based wireless networks. CrossTrace allows tracing of parameters at MAC-, routing and transport layer in a controlled environment and in a repeatable manner. We give a detailed description of the design of CrossTrace and the underlying testbed architecture and its miniaturization technology. Possible areas of application include network performance analysis and protocol optimization. Using CrossTrace we conduct a comprehensive measurement study in a miniaturized wireless testbed, in which we analyze the behavior of the 802.11 MAC-layer with respect to signal strength and bit error rate. In this study we focus on the behavior of single hop links. We derive the transmission probability dependent on signal strength and MAC-layer data rate with and without interfering background traffic.

The remainder of this paper is organized as follows. Section 2 summarizes related work on real deployments of wireless mesh networks as well as testbed prototypes. Section 3 describes the architecture of CrossTrace as well as the architecture of the underlying testbed infrastructure and outlines potential application scenarios, whereas in Section 4 we present an experimental cross-validation of our framework and results from a measurement study. Finally, concluding remarks are given.

2 Related Work

Bicket et al. [1] evaluated a 37-node 802.11b community mesh network over an area of approximately four square kilometers in Cambridge, Massachusetts. The mesh network, denoted as MIT Roofnet, adopts off-the-shelf equipment, e.g. IEEE 802.11 wireless cards and standard omni-directional antennas. The authors evaluated multiple aspects of the architecture such as the effect of node density on connectivity and throughput as well as the characteristics of wireless links.

Camp et al. [2] deployed a two-tier mesh network in Houston, Texas, that aims at providing Internet access over a wide area with minimal infrastructure. The deployed network comprises an access tier and a backhaul tier. The access tier connects mobile clients with mesh nodes, whereas the backhaul tier interconnects the mesh nodes and forwards traffic to and from the Internet. Using this network, the authors presented a measurement driven deployment strategy and a data driven model to study the impact of design and topology decisions on network-wide performance.

Opposed to [1] and [2], we introduce a miniaturized wireless testbed and a measurement framework rather than a large-scale wireless network. Using our testbed, networks such as [1] and [2] can be emulated within a miniaturized experimentation area.

De et al. [4] proposed a mobile 12-node testbed for multihop wireless networks. Each node in the testbed comprises a wireless computing device and a mobile robot. Fixed signal attenuators are used to limit the transmission range of the mobile nodes.

Eriksson et al. [8] evaluated the feasibility of an all-wireless office mesh network consisting of 21 multi-radio mesh nodes. The authors captured user traffic on office PCs with wired ethernet connectivity and replayed them on the mesh network. A set of parameters, such as different routing metrics and hardware settings were evaluated.

Krop et al. presented JiST/MobNet [10] an approach for the quantitative evaluation of wireless multi-hop networks, using simulation, emulation and real-world measurements.

Lundgren et al. reported in [11] on their experience in designing and deploying the UCSB MeshNet, a 30-node wireless mesh testbed which covers several floors inside a building.

Ott et al. [14] proposed an open access research testbed called Orbit for evaluating next-generation wireless network protocols. The testbed consists of an indoor radio grid for experiments and an outdoor field trial software for end user evaluations.

Su et al. introduced and evaluated IvyNet [15] a miniaturized IEEE 802.11 testbed using fixed attenuators. They also presented initial measurement results.

Zimmermann et al. introduced the UMIC wirelss testbed [19], which allows parallel execution of experiments using a virtualization approach.

Similar to [4], [8], [10], [14], [15] and [19], our testbed aims at emulating large-scale wireless networks in a controlled environment. Opposed to [4], [8], [10], [14], [15] and [19] our testbed comprises variable attenuators to variably adjust the transmission range and thus flexibly emulate large-scale networks. Deploying fixed signal attenuators significantly limits the spectrum of network topologies which can be considered due to the fixed transmission range associated with the attenuators.

We introduced a miniaturization approach for wireless testbeds [7] and presented initial measurement results regarding transport-layer performance. Opposed to [7], in this paper we focus on the measurement framework and provide comprehensive measurement results regarding MAC-layer performance in the presence of interfering background traffic.

3   CrossTrace Architecture

CrossTrace is build upon a miniaturized wireless testbed. In the following section a detailed description of the hard- and software components is given.

3.1 Hardware Components

The testbed comprises 20 wireless mesh nodes. Each node consists of a PC with an Intel Celeron 3.2 GHz processor and two IEEE 802.11b/g Netgear WG311T wireless PCI network interface cards (NICs) with Atheros chipsets. Each wireless card is connected to a variable signal attenuator and a 2.1dBi low-gain antenna. The deployment of the testbed is shown in Figure 1, the architecture is shown in Figure 2.

The variable attenuators are connected to the wireless PCI cards through 50 Ohm, 7m long, highly shielded aircell5 coaxial cables, whereas the antennas are connected to the signal attenuators through a 50 Ohm, 3m long RG-174 coaxial cable. According to the technical specifications, Both cables add a total of 12.5dB signal attenuation.

Testbed nodes run a SuSE Linux 10.2 operating system with a standard kernel version 2.6.26. As driver for the wireless PCI cards, we employ the Linux Madwifi kernel device driver version 0.9.4.1 for Atheros chipsets.

Fig. 1. Deployment of miniaturized wireless testbed

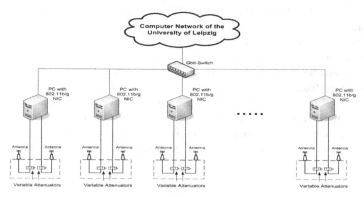

Fig. 2. Architecture of the miniaturized wireless testbed

Each wireless node further possesses a Gigabit ethernet NIC, which is connected to the subnet of the University of Leipzig through a Gigabit switch. This allows a remote management of the wireless nodes from any wired host in the subnet. Hence, wireless experiments can be managed from a remote computer and traces can be copied and evaluated through the wired network. Table 1 shows a detailed description of hardware and software components of the miniaturized testbed.

Multi-hop topologies can be emulated by adjusting the positions of the antenna-stations according to the desired topology. An antenna-station is a joint magnetic board, on which every two antennas of each mesh node are mounted. Such antenna-stations define the logical structure of a mesh node. Since ScaleMesh is deployed in an indoor environment, the shadowing and fading characteristics of wireless signals correspond to the indoor propagation model, which takes into account reflections on walls and floors. For all-wireless office mesh networks as introduced in [8], these indoor shadowing characteristics are identical.

To scale down a distance $d^{non-scaled}$ to a distance d^{scaled} assuming a path loss exponent p the required attenuation can be calculated as follows:

$$\Omega_{sum} = -\log\left(\frac{d^{scaled}}{d^{non-scaled}}\right) 10p \tag{1}$$

A detailed derivation and validation of this formula can be found in [7].

For mesh networks operating in free space, different shadowing characteristics apply. These different characteristics may as well be considered using outdoor instead of indoor propagation models for downscaling mesh networks. While the signal-to-noise ratio in the testbed may not deliver one-to-one identical results as in a free space mesh network, the acquired results are representative due to the identical characteristics of the IEEE 802.11 wireless link (opposed to simulations). Furthermore, while a large-scale free space multi-hop network has a fixed topology, nodes in our testbed are variably adjustable, making it more convenient for evaluating network protocols. A more comprehensive discussion of our miniaturization approach and its limitations can be found in [7].

Table 1. Hardware and software componentes of the miniaturized wireless testbed

HARDWARE	
Component	Description
PC	Fujitsu-Siemens P2510 3.2 GHz, 512 Mbytes RAM, 80 Gbytes HDD
Wireless NIC	Netgear IEEE 802.11b/g wireless PCI card WG311T with Atheros chipset
Variable attenuator	Broadwave variable attenuator, attenuation range 0-30dB in 1 dB steps
Coaxial cable	7m aircell5 + 3m RG-174, 50 Ohm with SMA / RPSMA connectors
Antenna	Maldol mini 2.1dBi antenna with magnetic mount and 3m SMA cable
SOFTWARE	
Component	Description
Operating System	SuSE Linux 10.2 with standard kernel version 2.6.26
Wireless NIC driver	Madwifi Linux kernel device driver for Atheros chipsets version 0.9.4.1
Routing protocol	OLSR for Linux version 0.5.5 with ETX support

3.2 Software Components

To allow cross-layer performance studies we developed CrossTrace, a software framework for tracing various parameters at MAC-, routing and transport layer. CrossTrace possesses a multi-layer interface and allows tracing of parameters such as MAC retransmission count, per packet receive signal strength and number of bit errors in received frames. These parameters are essential for the understanding of the interaction of layers in IEEE 802.11 based wireless networks. However these parameters cannot be traced using standard network measurement tools such as ping and iperf. CrossTrace consists of a central control and storage instance (trace server) and local node clients (trace client).

The trace server is responsible for preparing and controlling the testbed nodes, including configuration of the wireless network cards and setting up static routes if required. The trace server also provides a web interface for experiment definition and to obtain experiment results. Figure 3 shows the architecture of CrossTrace.

The trace clients are responsible for local data collection at each node. For this purpose the Linux libpcap library is used to trace all frames within transmission range of the wireless network interface. The amount of collected frames can be limited by applying a filter according to certain criteria, such as source address, target address and protocol type.

To allow tracing of MAC-layer parameters, the wireless interface operates in a special monitor mode to allow tracing of frames destined for other nodes in the testbed. Each trace client is connected to the trace server and to a central database where a record for every collected frame is stored. Communication with the trace server and the database is handled by the wired Ethernet interface of the testbed node, therefore running experiments in the wireless testbed are not biased.

To allow tracing of routing layer parameters, the trace client possesses an interface to the OLSR routing client [3] running on the same node. Using this interface the whole topology information known to the OLSR client can be obtained. This includes hop count and ETX metric [5] to any known host.

For traffic generation, CrossTrace contains a module, which starts and controls diverse generator programs. The tracing of the transport layer information is independent of the chosen traffic generator, because it is done through packet header analyzing, currently for UDP and TCP packets.

A challenge in the design of the trace client was the processing of the high-volume trace data. Consider a broadcast experiment with $N = 20$ nodes, where one node is transmitting and the remaining nodes are receiving. For a detailed description of such an experiment refer to section 5.2. Given a MAC-layer data rate $R = 54$ MBit/s and a frame size $D = 1500$ Byte an upper bound for the number of traced frames P_{node} at a single node can be calculated as follows:

$$P_{node} = \left\lceil \frac{R*1s}{D*8\frac{Bit}{Byte}} \right\rceil \approx 4400 \tag{2}$$

Overall $P = N * P_{node} \approx 88000$ entries per second are generated and have to be stored in the database. To allow such high volume processing we introduced a local queue at each testbed node where each record is temporally stored. When the queue length reaches a certain threshold (approx. 1000 records) we transmit the whole record as a batch to the database.

A further goal in the design of CrossTrace was to ensure repeatability of experiments. Therefore metadata is stored for each experiment, alleviating the reconstruction of the experiments environment. Metadata includes among others time of day, used nodes, used attenuation and the average signal strength between nodes at the beginning of the experiment.

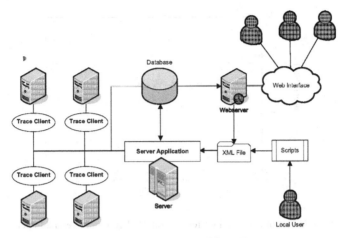

Fig. 3. Software architecture of CrossTrace

3.3 Application Scenarios

Currently CrossTrace is mainly employed for performance studies of IEEE 802.11 based wireless networks, particularly focusing on MAC-layer performance. Further application scenarios include protocol optimization. Using CrossTrace, protocols such as TCP can be analyzed with respect to a broad set of parameters, allowing to setup completely passive network traffic measurement experiments. Furthermore the protocol program code does not need to be altered (eg. adding debug code), because packets are directly captured at the wireless interface. The remote access capability also provides the opportunity that the testbed is made available to other research groups as well as students for educational use.

4 Performance Study

Using CrossTrace we conduct a comprehensive performance study, in which we analyze the behavior of the 802.11 MAC-layer with respect to signal strength, frame delivery probability and bit error rate. We derive the transmission probability and MAC-layer bit error rate dependent on signal strength and MAC-layer data rate with and without interfering background traffic. If not stated otherwise experiments are performed with a MAC-layer data rate for unicast and broadcast transmissions set to 11 Mbit/s and rate adaption turned off. This eliminates undesired effects that may be caused by the rate adaption algorithm, which can influence the results when evaluating and comparing certain performance aspects. Moreover, prior work such as [13] showed that the rate adaptation functionality of 802.11 can influence the throughput of other hosts that share the same radio channel. That is, a host with a lower bit rate can pull down bit rates of other hosts in the vicinity, degrading their performance. The

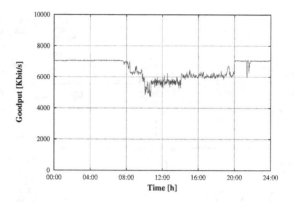

Fig. 4. Effect of external interference on TCP goodput over a 24h period

RTS/CTS mechanism is disabled for all experiments. The default payload size for TCP/UDP packets is set to 1000 bytes, unless otherwise stated.

Due to the increased number of IEEE 802.11 access points as well as other devices operating in the ISM 2.4 GHz band, external interference within the testbed's environment (i.e. in nearby offices) may affect running experiments. In order to eliminate such external interference, we conduct a 24-hour experiment to identify time slots with the least external interference. Figure 4 shows the TCP goodput for a single hop link over a 24h interval. We see that during the core working time between 8am and 8pm, the measured goodput is influenced by external interference, especially due to students who access the web wirelessly through their IEEE 802.11 equipped laptops. Therefore, experiments in this paper are conducted in the time with the least external interference, between 8pm and 8am.

4.1 Framework Validation

To assure that the measurements retrieved from our trace data are consistent with measurements obtained using standard tools, we conducted a cross validation with ping and iperf. A validation of the miniaturization approach can be found in [7].

In a first experiment we compare the Round Trip Time (RTT) of an ICMP Echo Request respectively ICMP Echo Response packet measured with ping to the RTT calculated by CrossTrace. To obtain a more representative scenario, we introduced bursty background traffic to provoke RTT fluctuations. Although we are currently focusing on the characterization of IEEE 802.11 single hop behavior, we also considered a multi hop path. Figure 5 shows the result of our validation. We observe that the RTT values measured with CrossTrace are qualitatively and quantitatively comparable to the values obtained with ping. We note that the average RTT value calculated by CrossTrace is slightly lower compared with ping. This is due to the fact that CrossTrace measures the time a packet enters or leaves the MAC-Layer, while ping measures the time a packet enters or leaves the application layer.

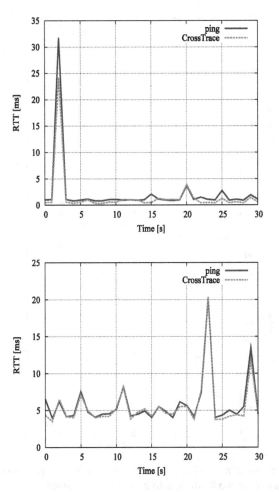

Fig. 5. Round Trip Time (RTT) measured at MAC-layer with our framework and at application layer with the standard tool ping for a one-hop (top) and four-hop (bottom) path in the wireless testbed

In a second experiment we compare the throughput measured with iperf to the throughput calculated by CrossTrace. Therefore we use iperf to establish a TCP connection. Again, this validation is conducted for both a single hop and a multi hop path. Figure 6 shows the result of our validation. We observe that there is a slightly higher fluctuation of throughput values when using iperf than CrossTrace. This is due to the fact that iperf measures the number of bytes arriving at application layer. This process shows more burstiness than the arrival of frames at MAC-layer, because of the involved buffering and processing of frame data by the operating system.

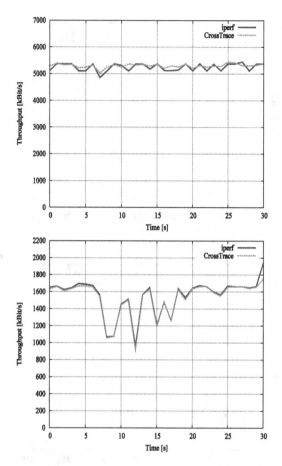

Fig. 6. Throughput measured at MAC-layer with CrossTrace and at application layer with iperf for a one-hop (top) and four-hop (bottom) path in the wireless testbed

4.2 One-Hop Link-Level Measurements

Using CrossTrace we conduct a comprehensive measurement study in which we analyze the behavior of the IEEE 802.11 MAC-layer with respect to signal strength and bit error rate with and without interfering background traffic.

4.2.1 Delivery Probability

In this experiment we analyze the correlation of signal-to-noise ratio and delivery probability in the wireless testbed. We set up a random topology where each node is in the transmission of each other node. Due to the varying inter-node distance the signal strength varies over the different node pairs. During this experiment one node starts a broadcast transmission with a batch of 500.000 frames and the remaining nodes listen to this transmission and record the percentage of correctly received frames and the average signal-to-noise ratio. The experiment is repeated 20 times. In each round a different one of the 20 testbed nodes is chosen as transmitting node. The use of broadcast transmission is required to prevent automatic retransmission, which is used for unicast transmissions by the IEEE 802.11 standard. The experiment is conducted using 11 Mbit/s and 54 Mbit/s MAC-layer data rate.

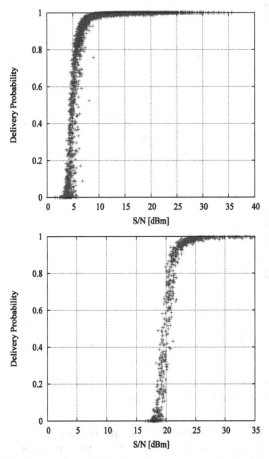

Fig. 7. Signal-to-Noise Ratio versus delivery probability for an 11 Mbit/s (top) and 54 Mbit/s (bottom) link in the wireless testbed

Figure 7 shows the delivery probability dependent on the signal-to-noise ratio. We observe that at a MAC-layer data rate of 11Mbit/s all links with signal-to-noise ratio of 10dbm or greater have a delivery probability of at least 90%. We note that at a MAC-layer data rate of 54 Mbit/s the situation changes drastically. At a signal-to-ratio of 16dbm there is no successful frame transmission at all. Only links with a signal-to-noise ratio of 23dbm or greater have a delivery probability of at least 90%.

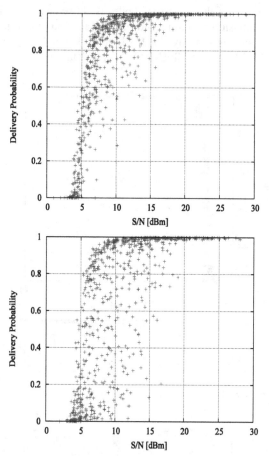

Fig. 8. Signal-to-noise ratio versus delivery probability with 2 Mbit/s (top) and 6 Mbits/s (bottom) interfering background traffic in the wireless testbed

4.2.2 Delivery Probality in the Presence of Interference

In this experiment we use CrossTrace to analyze the correlation of signal-to-noise ratio and delivery probability in presence of interfering background traffic. We vary the aforementioned broadcast experiment and introduce an interfering node. We use the variable attenuators to attenuate the output signal of the interfering node, such that interfering and transmitting node are out of carrier sensing range but within interference range. Hence both nodes cannot synchronize their transmissions resulting in frame collisions at the receiving nodes. We repeat this experiment 2 times considering background traffic intensities of 2 Mbit/s and 6 Mbit/s, while the MAC-layer data rate of all nodes is set to 11 Mbit/s.

Figure 8 shows the delivery probability dependent on the signal-to-noise ratio for 2 different background traffic intensities. We observe that opposed to Figure 7 the scatterplot is much more diffuse. Note that in Figure 7 the delivery probability given a certain signal-to-noise ratio lies within a small interval. For example, all links with a signal-to-noise ratio of 10dbm have a delivery probability between 90% and 100%.

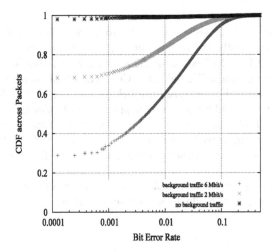

Fig. 9. Log plot showing Cumulative Distribution Function (CDF) of Bit Error Rate with interfering background traffic over a one-hop link in the wireless testbed

In the presence of interfering background traffic this interval is increasing significantly. For example, with a traffic intensity of 6 Mbit/s links with a signal-to-noise ratio of 10dbm or greater have a delivery probability between 2% and 100%. We conclude that interfering background traffic significantly degrades network performance with respect to delivery probability. We conclude further that signal-to-noise ratio in presence of interfering background traffic only is a weak indicator for delivery probability.

4.2.3 Bit Error Rate in the Presence of Interference

To gain deeper insight at the effect of interfering background traffic we use Cross-Trace to analyze the Bit Error Rate (BER). Therefore we modified the software driver of the wireless cards to also accept packets for which the IEEE 802.11 CRC checksum check failed. We setup a one hop unicast connection between two nodes and transmit UDP packets with a random payload. We also setup an interfering node, which transmits with a given traffic intensity. Again, we use the variable attenuators to attenuate the output signal of the interfering node, such that interfering and transmitting node are out of carrier sensing range but within interference range. At the end of the experiment we compared the payload of the transmitted and received packet and calculated the bit error rate for each packet. We repeat this experiment 3 times accounting for different intensities of background traffic.

Figure 9 shows a log plot of the Cumulative Distribution Function of BER with and without interfering background traffic. We observe that consistent with our findings in section 5.2.1 the BER with no background traffic is close to 0% for almost all packets. However with interfering background traffic the BER significantly increases indicating overlapping transmissions at the receiver due to the hidden terminal effect.

5 Conclusion

We introduced the software architecture of CrossTrace, as well as the underlying miniaturized wireless testbed. The current focus of CrossTrace is on cross-layer measurements in IEEE 802.11 based wireless networks. Further areas of application include protocol optimization. We validated CrossTrace and conducted a comprehensive measurement study. We analyzed the behavior of the 802.11 MAC-layer with respect to signal strength and bit error rate in presence of hidden terminals. Further we derived the delivery probability dependent on signal strength and MAC-layer data rate with and without interfering background traffic. Our results indicate that even moderate background traffic can significantly degrade network performance with respect to delivery probability.

Potential areas of future research include the extension of our measurement study to consider multi-hop paths and dual-radio communication.

References

1. Bicket, J., Aguayo, D., Biswas, S., Morris, R.: Architecture and Evaluation of an Unplanned 802.11b Mesh Network. In: Proceedings MobiCom., pp. 31–42. ACM, New York (2005)
2. Camp, J., Robinson, J., Steger, C., Knightly, E.: Measurement Driven Deployment of a Two-tier Urban Mesh Access Network. In: Proceedings MobiSys., pp. 96–109. ACM, New York (2006)
3. Clausen, T., Jacquet, P.: Optimized Link State Routing Protocol. RFC 3626 (2003), http://www.ietf.org/rfc/rfc3626.txt
4. De, P., Raniwala, A., Krishnan, R., Tatavarthi, K., Modi, J., Syed, N.A., Sharma, S., Chiueh, T.c.: Mint-m: an Autonomous Mobile Wireless Experimentation Platform. In: Proceedings MobiSys., pp. 124–137. ACM, New York (2006)
5. De Couto, D.S.J., Aguayo, D., Bicket, J., Morris, R.: A High-throughput Path Metric for Multi-hop Wireless Routing. Wireless Networks 11(4), 419–434 (2005)
6. ElRakabawy, S.M., Klemm, A., Lindemann, C.: TCP with Adaptive Pacing for Multihop Wireless Networks. In: Proceedings MobiHoc, pp. 288–299. ACM, New York (2005)
7. ElRakabawy, S., Frohn, S., Lindemann, C.: ScaleMesh: A Scalable Dual-Radio Wireless Mesh Testbed. In: Proceedings IEEE WiMesh., pp. 1–6 (2008)
8. Eriksson, J., Agarwal, S., Bahl, P., Padhye, J.: Feasibility Study of Mesh Networks for All-wireless Offices. In: Proceedings MobiSys., pp. 69–82. ACM, New York (2006)
9. Karbaschi, G., Fladenmuller, A., Wolfinger, B.E.: Link-quality Measurement Enhancement for Routing in Wireless Mesh Networks. In: International Symposium on a World of Wireless, Mobile and Multimedia Networks, pp. 1–9 (2008)
10. Krop, T., Bredel, M., Hollick, M., Steinmetz, R.: Jist/mobnet: Combined Simulation, Emulation, and Real-world Testbed for Ad Hoc Networks. In: Proceedings WinTECH, pp. 27–34. ACM, New York (2007)

11. Lundgren, H., Ramachandran, K., Belding-Royer, E., Almeroth, K., Benny, M.: Experiences from the Design, Deployment, and Usage of the UCSB MeshNet testbed. IEEE Wireless Communications 13(2) (2006)
12. Martinovic, I., Zdarsky, F.A., Bachorek, A., Jung, C., Schmitt, J.B.: Phishing in the Wireless: Implementation and Analysis. In: SEC, pp. 145–156 (2007)
13. Munaretto, A., Fonseca, M., Agha, K., Pujolle, G.: Fair Time Sharing Protocol: A Solution for IEEE 802.11b Hot Spots. In: de Souza, J.N., Dini, P., Lorenz, P. (eds.) ICT 2004. LNCS, vol. 3124, pp. 1261–1266. Springer, Heidelberg (2004)
14. Ott, M., Seskar, I., Siraccusa, R., Singh, M.: ORBIT Testbed Software Architecture: Supporting Experiments as a Service. In: Proceedings TridentCom, pp. 136–145 (2005)
15. Su, Y., Gross, T.: Validation of a Miniaturized Wireless Network Testbed. In: Proceedings WiNTECH, pp. 25–32. ACM, New York (2008)
16. The network simulator - ns-2, http://www.isi.edu/nsnam/ns/
17. The Qualnet Simulator, http://www.scalable-networks.com/
18. Zapotoczky, J., Wolter, K.: Increasing Performance of the 802.11e Protocol Through Access Category Shifting. In: Proc. MMB, pp. 61–76 (2008)
19. Zimmermann, A., Wenig, M., Meis, U.: Construction and Evaluation of a Wireless Mesh Network Testbed. In: Misra, S., Misra, S.C., Woungang, I. (eds.) Guide to Wireless Mesh Networks, pp. 497–519. Springer, London (2009)

The Total Overflow during a Busy Cycle in a Markov-Additive Finite Buffer System

Lothar Breuer

Institute of Mathematics and Statistics
University of Kent
Canterbury CT2 7NF, UK
L.Breuer@kent.ac.uk

Abstract. We consider a finite buffer system where the buffer content moves in a Markov-additive way while it is strictly between the buffer boundaries. Upon reaching the upper boundary of the buffer the content is not allowed to go higher and for every additional input into the system a penalty must be paid (to negotiate buffer overflow). At the lower boundary (empty buffer) the process terminates. For this system we determine the joint distribution of the total overflow and the last time of being at the upper boundary. The analysis is performed using excursion theory for Markov-additive processes.

1 Introduction

We shall consider a finite buffer system where the buffer content changes according to a Markov-additive process (MAP) while it is strictly between the buffer boundaries. Upon reaching the upper boundary of the buffer the content is not allowed to go higher and for every additional input into the system a penalty must be paid (to negotiate buffer overflow). At the lower boundary (empty buffer) the process terminates.

Such a system plays an important role in different areas of applied probability. It might represent a dam and its storage (or capacity) process. It is also used in insurance mathematics to model dividend payments. In queueing theory a penalty for buffer overflow is a standard consequence and termination once the buffer is empty is a natural restriction to the busy cycle. The content of the buffer is often called work load or virtual waiting time in queueing applications.

The model to be analysed in this paper is general enough to encompass a large variety of popular modelling approaches. Among them are Markovian single server queues (with BMAP input, see [17] for definition and [10] for estimation, and phase-type service time distributions, see [18] for definition, [7] for estimation, and [11] for a recent continuity result) or stochastic fluid flows with possible Brownian perturbation (see the seminal paper [3] or [1,9] for recent related results without perturbation). An algorithmic solution for the time to buffer overflow in a Markov-additive framework is given in [6], section 6, see also [2]. An algorithmic solution for the expectation of the total overflow during a cycle is presented in [13], albeit in terms of insurance risk.

B. Müller-Clostermann et al. (Eds.): MMB & DFT 2010, LNCS 5987, pp. 198–211, 2010.

Assuming that the penalty to be paid is simply the amount of system input while the buffer is full (the total buffer overflow), we shall determine the joint distribution of this penalty and the last time of being at the upper boundary. We do not assume necessarily that the system starts with an empty buffer.

The analysis is performed mainly by matrix-analytic methods using probabilistic arguments wherever possible. This naturally results in formulas containing matrices which are to be computed via fixed point iterations. We shall present examples for the simple cases allowing explicit scalar solutions. This restriction is due to the circumstance that only for these there are solutions in the literature which can be compared with results in the present paper.

The paper is structured as follows. Section 2 contains an exact definition of the model to be analysed and the performance measures we wish to determine. Section 3 presents preparatory results from recent literature that will be needed in this paper. Section 4 finally contains the main result. Examples will be developed throughout the paper in subsequent stages.

2   The Model

Let $\tilde{\mathcal{J}} = (\tilde{J}_t : t \geq 0)$ be an irreducible Markov process with finite state space $\tilde{E}$ and infinitesimal generator matrix $\tilde{Q} = (\tilde{q}_{ij})_{i,j \in \tilde{E}}$. We call $\tilde{J}_t$ the phase at time $t \geq 0$ (another common name is regime). Define the real–valued process $\tilde{\mathcal{X}} = (\tilde{X}_t : t \geq 0)$ as evolving like a Lévy process $\tilde{\mathcal{X}}^{(i)}$ with parameters $\tilde{\mu}_i$ (drift), $\tilde{\sigma}_i^2$ (variation), and $\tilde{\nu}_i$ (Lévy measure) during intervals when the phase equals $i \in \tilde{E}$. For the sake of a more concise presentation we exclude the case of $\tilde{\mu}_i = \tilde{\sigma}_i^2 = 0$, i.e. a pure jump process or the constant zero process, for any phase $i \in \tilde{E}$. Whenever $\tilde{\mathcal{J}}$ jumps from a state $i \in \tilde{E}$ to another state $j \in \tilde{E}$, this may be accompanied by a jump of $\tilde{\mathcal{X}}$ with some distribution function F_{ij}. Then the two–dimensional process $(\tilde{\mathcal{X}}, \tilde{\mathcal{J}})$ is called a Markov–additive process (or shortly MAP). In short, a MAP is a Markov-modulated Lévy process with possible jumps at phase changes. For a textbook introduction to MAPs see [4], chapter XI.

We now turn to define our model $\mathcal{B} = (B_t : t \geq 0)$ for the buffer content, where B_t shall denote the content level at time t. Let $b \geq 0$ denote the upper buffer boundary beyond which overflow occurs and penalty must be paid. As long as $0 < B_t < b$, the process $\mathcal{B}$ equals $\tilde{\mathcal{X}}$. Upon passing the upper boundary b from below, $\mathcal{B}$ does not increase above b and any additional buffer input is recorded as overflow. If a positive jump of size x occurs at time t and $b - x < B_{t-} < b$, then we agree upon the rule that the buffer content rises up to b and the overflow increases by $B_{t-} - (b - x)$. Upon passing the lower boundary 0 from above, the busy cycle concludes and we stop our examination. Thus we consider $\mathcal{B}$ as a MAP that is reflected at the upper boundary b and terminates upon passing the lower boundary 0. In exact terms,

$$B_t := \tilde{X}_t - \left(\sup_{s \leq t} \tilde{X}_s - b \right)^+$$

for all $t < \tau_B(0)$, where $(V)^+ := \max(V, 0)$ and

$$\tau_B(0) := \inf \left\{ t \geq 0 : \tilde{X}_t - \left(\sup_{s \leq t} \tilde{X}_s - b \right)^+ \leq 0 \right\} \tag{1}$$

For the sake of defining $\mathcal{B}$ at all times, say $B_t := 0$ for all $t \geq \tau_B(0)$.

Denote the initial buffer content by $u := B_0 \geq 0$. We may assume $u \leq b$ without loss of generality, since $b < u$ would entail an immediate pay-out of a penalty of $u - b$ and the buffer content process would continue with initial surplus b.

Let D denote the total overflow during a busy cycle. This can be defined as follows. First, let

$$\tilde{S}(t) := \left(\sup_{s \leq t} \tilde{X}_s - b \right)^+$$

denote the overflow until time $t \in [0, \tau_B(0)]$. Then $D := \tilde{S}(\tau_B(0))$ is the total overflow during a busy cycle. Define the generalised inverse of the function $\tilde{S}(t)$ by

$$\tilde{S}^{-1}(x) := \inf\{t \geq 0 : \tilde{S}(t) \geq x\}$$

for $x \geq 0$. Then $\tilde{S}^{-1}(D)$ is the last time of overflow before the end of the busy cycle.

In this paper we shall determine the joint distribution of D and $\tilde{S}^{-1}(D)$ in the form of an expression for

$$\bar{F}(x, \gamma) := \mathbb{E} \left(e^{-\gamma \tilde{S}^{-1}(x)}; D > x \right)$$

where $x \geq 0$ and $\gamma \geq 0$. Note that $\tilde{S}^{-1}(D)$ signifies the time of the last overflow and may be strictly smaller than $\tau_B(0)$, the end of the busy cycle. Further note that the process $\mathcal{B}$ and hence $\bar{F}(x, \gamma)$ is completely determined by $\tilde{X}$.

Example 1. We consider the classical M/M/1 queue. Inter–arrival and service times are iid exponential with parameter $\lambda > 0$ and $\beta > 0$, respectively. The total work load at time $t \geq 0$ (including the overflow) within a busy cycle starting with a buffer content $u > 0$ is given by

$$\tilde{X}_t = u + \sum_{n=0}^{N_t} C_n - t \tag{2}$$

where $(N_t : t \geq 0)$ is a Poisson process with intensity λ and the C_n, $n \in \mathbb{N}$, are iid random variables with exponential distribution of parameter β.

The total work load process can be analysed as a MAP with exponential (and hence phase–type) positive jumps with parameter β. For this, we would need only one phase, i.e. $|\tilde{E}| = 1$. This phase governs a Lévy process with parameters $\tilde{\sigma} = 0$, $\tilde{\mu} = -1$, and $\tilde{\nu}(dx) = \lambda e^{-\beta x} \beta dx$ for all $x > 0$.

Before we can proceed by analysing our model, we first need to collect some necessary preliminary results for MAPs. This shall be the purpose of the next section.

3   Preliminaries

3.1   Markov–Additive Processes with Phase–Type Jumps

In this section we introduce the restriction that all jumps have a phase-type distribution. Then we construct a new MAP $(\mathcal{X}, \mathcal{J})$ from the given MAP $(\tilde{\mathcal{X}}, \tilde{\mathcal{J}})$ without losing any information. This new MAP will have continuous paths, which simplifies the one- and two-sided exit problems (cf. sections 3.2 and 3.3) considerably.

Denote the indicator function of a set A by $\mathbb{I}_A$. We assume that the Lévy measures $\tilde{\nu}_i$ have the form

$$\tilde{\nu}_i(dx) = \lambda_i^+ \mathbb{I}_{\{x>0\}} \, \alpha^{(ii)+} \exp(T^{(ii)+}x)\eta^{(ii)+} dx$$
$$+ \lambda_i^- \mathbb{I}_{\{x<0\}} \, \alpha^{(ii)-} \exp(-T^{(ii)-}x)\eta^{(ii)-} dx \qquad (3)$$

for all $i \in \tilde{E}$, where $\lambda_i^{\pm} \geq 0$ and $(\alpha^{(ii)\pm}, T^{(ii)\pm})$ are representations of phase–type distributions without an atom at 0. The $\eta^{(ii)\pm} := -T^{(ii)\pm}\mathbf{1}$ are called the exit vectors, where $\mathbf{1}$ denotes a column vector of appropriate dimension with all entries being 1. This means that the jump process induced by the Lévy measure ν_i is compound Poisson with jump sizes of a doubly phase–type distribution. Denote the order of $PH(\alpha^{(ii)\pm}, T^{(ii)\pm})$ by $m_{ii}^{\pm}$. Further write $\lambda_i := \lambda_i^+ + \lambda_i^-$.

Likewise, let p_{ij}^+ (resp. p_{ij}^-) denote the probability that a positive (resp. negative) jump is induced by a phase change from $i \in \tilde{E}$ to $j \in \tilde{E}$, and assume that these jumps have a $PH(\alpha^{(ij)\pm}, T^{(ij)\pm})$ distribution without an atom at 0. Note that $p_{ij}^+ + p_{ij}^- \leq 1$ for all $i, j \in \tilde{E}$. Let $m_{ij}^{\pm}$ denote the order of $PH(\alpha^{(ij)\pm}, T^{(ij)\pm})$ and define $\eta^{(ij)\pm} := -T^{(ij)\pm}\mathbf{1}$.

The class of Markov–additive processes with these assumptions of phase–type jumps is dense within the class of all MAPs, see [5], proposition 1. The main advantage of the phase–type restriction on the jump distributions is the possibility of transforming the jumps into a succession of linear pieces of exponential duration (each with slope 1 or -1) and retrieving the original process via a simple time change, see [8].

This is done in the following way. Without the jumps, the Lévy process $\tilde{\mathcal{X}}^{(i)}$ during a phase $i \in \tilde{E}$ is either a linear drift (i.e. $\tilde{\sigma}_i = 0$) or a Brownian motion (with parameters $\tilde{\sigma}_i > 0$ and $\tilde{\mu}_i \in \mathbb{R}$). Considering this MAP (without the jumps) we can partition its phase space $\tilde{E}$ into the subspaces E_p (for positive drifts), E_σ (for Brownian motions), and E_n (for negative drifts). We thus define

$$E_p := \{i \in \tilde{E} : \tilde{\mu}_i > 0, \tilde{\sigma}_i = 0\}, \quad E_n := \{i \in \tilde{E} : \tilde{\mu}_i < 0, \tilde{\sigma}_i = 0\} \qquad (4)$$

and $$E_\sigma := \{i \in \tilde{E} : \tilde{\sigma}_i > 0\}$$

Note that $\tilde{E} = E_p \cup E_\sigma \cup E_n$, since we have excluded the case of $\tilde{\mu}_i = \tilde{\sigma}_i^2 = 0$ for any phase $i \in \tilde{E}$. Then we introduce two new phase spaces

$$E_\pm := \{(i, j, k, \pm) : i, j \in E_p \cup E_\sigma \cup E_n, 1 \le k \le m_{ij}^\pm\} \tag{5}$$

to model the jumps. Define now the enlarged phase space $E = E_+ \cup \tilde{E} \cup E_-$. We define the modified MAP $(\mathcal{X}, \mathcal{J})$ over the phase space E as follows. Set the parameters $(\mu_i, \sigma_i^2, \nu_i)$ for $i \in E$ as

$$(\mu_i, \sigma_i^2, \nu_i) := \begin{cases} (\pm 1, 0, \mathbf{0}), & i \in E_\pm \\ (\tilde{\mu}_i, \tilde{\sigma}_i, \mathbf{0}), & i \in \tilde{E} = E_p \cup E_\sigma \cup E_n \end{cases} \tag{6}$$

This leads to the cumulant functions

$$\psi_i(\alpha) = \begin{cases} \pm\alpha, & i \in E_\pm \\ \mu_i\alpha, & i \in E_p \cup E_n \\ \frac{1}{2}\sigma_i^2\alpha^2 + \mu_i\alpha, & i \in E_\sigma \end{cases} \tag{7}$$

We shall order the new phase space $E = E_+ \cup E_p \cup E_\sigma \cup E_n \cup E_-$ such that $i_+ < i_p < i_\sigma < i_n < i_-$ for phases $i_* \in E_*$. Let $E_c := E_p \cup E_\sigma \cup E_n$ denote the subspace of E that contains all phases under which the real time movements are continuous. The modified phase process $\mathcal{J}$ is determined by its generator $Q = (q_{ij})_{i,j \in E}$. For this the construction above yields

$$q_{ih} = \begin{cases} \tilde{q}_{ii} - \lambda_i, & h = i \in E_c \\ \tilde{q}_{ih} \cdot (1 - p_{ih}^+ - p_{ih}^-), & h \in E_c, h \ne i \\ \lambda_i^\pm \alpha_k^{(ii)\pm}, & h = (i, i, k, \pm) \\ \tilde{q}_{ij} \cdot p_{ij}^\pm \cdot \alpha_k^{(ij)\pm}, & h = (i, j, k, \pm) \end{cases} \tag{8}$$

for $i \in E_c$ as well as

$$q_{(i,j,k,\pm),(i,j,l,\pm)} = T_{kl}^{(ij)\pm} \quad \text{and} \quad q_{(i,j,k,\pm),j} = \eta_k^{(ij)\pm} \tag{9}$$

for $i, j \in E_c$ and $1 \le k, l \le m_{ij}^\pm$. For later use we define $q_i := -q_{ii}$ for all $i \in E$.

The original level process $\mathcal{X}$ is retrieved via the time change

$$c(t) := \int_0^t \mathbb{I}_{\{J_s \in E_c\}} \, ds \quad \text{and} \quad \tilde{X}_{c(t)} = X_t \tag{10}$$

for all $t \ge 0$. Likewise, we obtain

$$S(t) := \left(\sup_{s \le t} X_s - b\right)^+ = \left(\sup_{s \le c(t)} \tilde{X}_s - b\right)^+ = \tilde{S}(c(t))$$

and for the generalised inverse

$$\tilde{S}^{-1}(x) = c(S^{-1}(x))$$

The inverses of the cumulant functions ψ_i can be given explicitly as

$$
\phi_i(\beta) = \begin{cases}
\pm\beta, & i \in E_\pm \\
\frac{\beta}{\mu_i}, & i \in E_p \cup E_n \\
\frac{1}{\sigma_i}\sqrt{2\beta + \frac{\mu_i^2}{\sigma_i^2}} - \frac{\mu_i}{\sigma_i^2}, & i \in E_\sigma
\end{cases}
\tag{11}
$$

We shall, however, use them only for the so–called ascending phases $i \in E_a := E_+ \cup E_p \cup E_\sigma$.

Example 2. Continuing example 1, we obtain the MAP $(\mathcal{X}, \mathcal{J})$ as follows. In equation (3) we have $\lambda_2^+ = \lambda$ and $\lambda_2^- = 0$. Further $m_{22}^+ = 1$ since the positive jumps have an exponential distribution. Hence the enlarged phase space is given by $E_+ = \{1\}$, $E_n = \{2\}$, and $E_p = E_\sigma = E_- = \emptyset$. The parameters are given by $\sigma_1 = \sigma_2 = 0$, $\mu_1 = 1$, $\mu_2 = -1$, $\nu_1 = \nu_2 = 0$, and

$$
Q = \begin{pmatrix} -\beta & \beta \\ \lambda & -\lambda \end{pmatrix}
$$

3.2   First Passage Times

Of central use in the present paper will be the recent derivation of the Laplace transforms for the first passage times of MAPs as given in [12]. We call the phases $i \in E_d := E_n \cup E_-$ descending. Define the first passage times

$$
\tilde{\tau}(x) := \inf\{t \geq 0 : \tilde{X}_t > x\} \quad \text{and} \quad \tau(x) := \inf\{t \geq 0 : X_t > x\}
$$

for all $x \geq 0$ and assume that $\tilde{X}_0 = X_0 = 0$. Note that $\tilde{\tau}(x)$ is the first passage time over the level x for the original MAP $\tilde{\mathcal{X}}$, meaning that we do not count the time spent in jump phases $i \in E_\pm$. This means that

$$
\tilde{\tau}(x) = c(\tau(x)) = \int_0^{\tau(x)} \mathbb{I}_{\{J_s \in E_c\}}\, ds
$$

according to (10). In particular, we may compute expectations over $\tilde{\tau}(x)$ using the distribution of the modified MAP $(\mathcal{X}, \mathcal{J})$ only and without needing to recur to the original MAP $(\tilde{\mathcal{X}}, \tilde{\mathcal{J}})$. For $\gamma \geq 0$ denote

$$
\mathbb{E}_{ij}(e^{-\gamma\tilde{\tau}(x)}) := \mathbb{E}(e^{-\gamma\tilde{\tau}(x)}; J_{\tau(x)} = j | J_0 = i, X_0 = 0)
$$

for all $i, j \in E$. Let $\mathbb{E}(e^{-\gamma\tilde{\tau}(x)})$ denote the matrix with these entries and write

$$
\mathbb{E}(e^{-\gamma\tilde{\tau}(x)}) = \begin{pmatrix} \mathbb{E}_{(a,a)}(e^{-\gamma\tilde{\tau}(x)}) & \mathbb{E}_{(a,d)}(e^{-\gamma\tilde{\tau}(x)}) \\ \mathbb{E}_{(d,a)}(e^{-\gamma\tilde{\tau}(x)}) & \mathbb{E}_{(d,d)}(e^{-\gamma\tilde{\tau}(x)}) \end{pmatrix}
$$

in obvious block notation with respect to the subspaces $E_a = E_+ \cup E_p \cup E_\sigma$ (ascending phases) and $E_d = E_n \cup E_-$ (descending phases).

Since a first passage to a level above cannot occur in a descending phase, we obtain first $\mathbb{P}(J_{\tau(x)} = j) = 0$ for all $j \in E_d$ and thus

$$\mathbb{E}_{(d,d)}(e^{-\gamma\bar{\tau}(x)}) = \mathbb{E}_{(a,d)}(e^{-\gamma\bar{\tau}(x)}) = \mathbf{0}$$

where $\mathbf{0}$ denotes a zero matrix of suitable dimension. Equation (6) in [12] states that

$$\mathbb{E}_{(d,a)}(e^{-\gamma\bar{\tau}(x)}) = A(\gamma)e^{U(\gamma)x}$$

and

$$\mathbb{E}_{(a,a)}(e^{-\gamma\bar{\tau}(x)}) = e^{U(\gamma)x}$$

for some sub–generator matrix $U(\gamma)$ of dimension $E_a \times E_a$ and a sub–transition matrix $A(\gamma)$ of dimension $E_d \times E_a$. Altogether we can write

$$\mathbb{E}(e^{-\gamma\bar{\tau}(x)}) = \begin{pmatrix} I_a \\ A(\gamma) \end{pmatrix} \begin{pmatrix} e^{U(\gamma)x} & \mathbf{0} \end{pmatrix} \tag{12}$$

where I_a denotes the identity matrix of dimension $E_a \times E_a$.

Write $\Delta_q := diag(q_i)_{i \in E}$ and let $P = \Delta_q^{-1}Q + I$ denote the transition matrix of phase changes. Note that $p_{ii} = 0$ for all $i \in E$.

In order to shorten notation, we shall write $A = A(\gamma)$ and $U = U(\gamma)$ unless we wish to stress dependence on γ. According to theorem 3 in [12], A and U satisfy the following equations:

$$e'_h U = \sum_{l=1}^{m^+_{ij}} T^{(ij)+}_{kl} e'_{(i,j,l,+)} + \eta^{(ij)+}_k e'_j \begin{pmatrix} I_a \\ A \end{pmatrix} \qquad \text{for } h = (i,j,k,+) \in E_+,$$

$$e'_i U = \phi_i(q_i) \sum_{j \in E} p_{ij} e'_j \begin{pmatrix} I_a \\ A \end{pmatrix} L_i(-U) - \phi_i(q_i + \gamma)e'_i \qquad \text{for } i \in E_p \cup E_\sigma,$$

$$e'_i A = \sum_{j \in E, j \neq i} q_{ij} e'_j \begin{pmatrix} I_a \\ A \end{pmatrix} ((q_i + \gamma)I_a - \psi_i(-U))^{-1} \qquad \text{for } i \in E_n, \text{ and}$$

$$e'_i A = \sum_{j \in E, j \neq i} q_{ij} e'_j \begin{pmatrix} I_a \\ A \end{pmatrix} (q_i I_a - \psi_i(-U))^{-1} \qquad \text{for } i \in E_-.$$

where e'_i, e'_j and e'_h denote canonical row base vectors with suitable dimension. For the MAP $(\mathcal{X}, \mathcal{J})$ with continuous level process, the matrix function

$$L_i(-U) = \frac{q_i}{\phi_i(q_i)} \cdot (\phi_i(q_i + \gamma)I_a + U) \cdot ((q_i + \gamma)I_a - \psi_i(-U))^{-1}$$

can be simplified considerably. For $i \in E_\sigma$, the same arguments as in [12], example 2, lead to

$$L_i(-U) = \phi_i^*(q_i) \cdot (\phi_i^*(q_i + \gamma)I_a - U)^{-1} \tag{13}$$

with

$$\phi_i^*(\beta) = \frac{1}{\sigma_i} \sqrt{2\beta + \frac{\mu_i^2}{\sigma_i^2}} + \frac{\mu_i}{\sigma_i^2} \tag{14}$$

Furthermore, $L_i(-U) = I_a$ for $i \in E_p$ (see example 3 in [12]), while according to (7) $\psi_i(-U) = -\mu_i U$ for $i \in E_n$, and $\psi_i(-U) = U$ for $i \in E_-$. Hence the equations above involve rather simple expressions only.

Considering (11), the matrices $A(\gamma)$ and $U(\gamma)$ can be determined by successive approximation as the limit of the sequence $((A_n, U_n) : n \geq 0)$ with initial values $A_0 := \mathbf{0}$, $U_0 := -diag(\phi_i(q_i + \gamma)1_{i \in E_\sigma \cup E_p} + \phi_i(q_i)1_{i \in E_+})_{i \in E_a}$, and the following iteration:

$$e'_h U_{n+1} = \sum_{l=1}^{m^+_{ij}} T^{(ij)+}_{kl} e'_{(i,j,l,+)} + \eta^{(ij)+}_k e'_j \begin{pmatrix} I_a \\ A_n \end{pmatrix} \qquad \text{for } h = (i,j,k,+) \in E_+,$$

$$e'_i U_{n+1} = -\frac{q_i + \gamma}{\mu_i} e'_i + \frac{1}{\mu_i} \sum_{j \in E, j \neq i} q_{ij} e'_j \begin{pmatrix} I_a \\ A_n \end{pmatrix} \qquad \text{for } i \in E_p,$$

$$e'_i A_{n+1} = \sum_{j \in E, j \neq i} q_{ij} e'_j \begin{pmatrix} I_a \\ A_n \end{pmatrix} ((q_i + \gamma)I + \mu_i U_n)^{-1} \qquad \text{for } i \in E_n,$$

$$e'_i A_{n+1} = \sum_{j \in E, j \neq i} q_{ij} e'_j \begin{pmatrix} I_a \\ A_n \end{pmatrix} (q_i I - U_n)^{-1} \qquad \text{for } i \in E_-, \text{ and}$$

$$e'_i U_{n+1} = \frac{2}{\sigma_i^2} \sum_{j \in E, j \neq i} q_{ij} e'_j \begin{pmatrix} I_a \\ A_n \end{pmatrix} (\phi^*_i(q_i + \gamma)I - U_n)^{-1} - \phi_i(q_i + \gamma)e'_i$$

for $i \in E_\sigma$. For the last equality the relation $\phi_i(q_i)\phi^*_i(q_i) = 2q_i/\sigma_i^2$ has been used. Note that the only difference between the iterations for E_n and E_- is the missing γ in the last factor for E_-, reflecting that we do not discount the time for phases $i \in E_-$ as they are jump phases in real time.

Example 3. Continuing example 2, first note that phase 1 represents the upwards jumps and we will not discount the time during sojourns in it. As shown in [12], example 5, the Laplace transform of the first passage time over a level $x > 0$, is given by

$$\mathbb{E}(e^{-\gamma \tilde{\tau}(x)}) = Ae^{Ux} \quad \text{where} \quad A = \frac{\beta - R}{\beta}, \quad U = -R$$

and

$$-R = \frac{1}{2}\left(\lambda + \gamma - \beta - \sqrt{(\beta - \gamma - \lambda)^2 + 4\beta\gamma}\right)$$

This coincides with equation (4.24) in [15], noting that γ is denoted as δ there and $c = 1$ in our case.

3.3 The Two-Sided Exit Problem

Define the stopping times $\tau(0, b) := \inf\{t \geq 0 : X_t < 0 \quad \text{or} \quad X_t > b\}$ and

$$\tilde{\tau}(0, b) := \int_0^{\tau(0,b)} \mathbb{I}_{\{J_s \in E_c\}} ds = \inf\{t \geq 0 : \tilde{X}_t < 0 \quad \text{or} \quad \tilde{X}_t > b\} \qquad (15)$$

which are the exit times of $\mathcal{X}$ and $\tilde{\mathcal{X}}$ from the interval $[0, b]$, respectively. For the main result we need an expression for

$$\Psi_{ij}^+(b|x) := \mathbb{E}\left(e^{-\gamma\tau(0,b)}; X_{\tau(0,b)} = b, J_{\tau(0,b)} = j | J_0 = i, X_0 = x\right)$$

where $x \in [0, b]$ and $i, j \in E$. Clearly $\Psi_{ij}^+(b|x) = 0$ for $j \in E_d$ since an exit over the upper boundary can occur only in an ascending phase. Define the matrix $\Psi^+(b|x) := (\Psi_{ij}^+(b|x))_{i \in E, j \in E_a}$. A formula for $\Psi^+(b|x)$ has been derived in [16]. In order to state it we need some additional notation.

Let $(\mathcal{X}^+, \mathcal{J})$ denote the MAP as constructed in section 3.1 and define the process $\mathcal{X}^- = (X_t^- : t \geq 0)$ by $X_t^- := -X_t^+$ for all $t > 0$ given that $X_0^+ = X_0^- = 0$. Thus $(\mathcal{X}^-, \mathcal{J})$ is the negative of $(\mathcal{X}^+, \mathcal{J})$. The two processes have the same generator matrix Q for $\mathcal{J}$, but the cumulant functions of the Lévy process governed by phase $i \in E$ are different and relate as $\psi_i^-(\alpha) = \psi_i^+(-\alpha)$. Denoting variation and drift parameters for $\mathcal{X}^\pm$ by $\sigma_i^\pm$ and $\mu_i^\pm$, respectively, this means $\sigma_i^+ = \sigma_i^-$ and $\mu_i^- = -\mu_i^+$ for all $i \in E$. This of course implies that phases $i \in E_+ \cup E_p$ (resp. $i \in E_- \cup E_n$) are descending (resp. ascending) phases for $\mathcal{X}^-$.

Let $A^\pm(\gamma)$ and $U^\pm(\gamma)$ denote the matrices that determine the first passage times in (12). We shall write $A^\pm = A^\pm(\gamma)$ and $U^\pm = U^\pm(\gamma)$ except in cases when we wish to underline the dependence on γ. Define the matrices

$$C^+ := \begin{pmatrix} \mathbf{0} & I_{E_\sigma} \\ A^+ & \end{pmatrix} \quad \text{and} \quad C^- := \begin{pmatrix} A^- & \\ I_{E_\sigma} & \mathbf{0} \end{pmatrix}$$

of dimensions $(E_\sigma \cup E_d) \times E_a$ and $E_a \times (E_\sigma \cup E_d)$, respectively. Further define

$$W^+ := \begin{pmatrix} I_{E_a} \\ A^+ \end{pmatrix} \quad \text{and} \quad W^- := \begin{pmatrix} A^- \\ I_{E_\sigma \cup E_d} \end{pmatrix}$$

which are matrices of dimensions $E \times E_a$ and $E \times (E_\sigma \cup E_d)$. Finally, let $Z^\pm := C^\pm e^{U^\pm \cdot b}$. Then equation (23) in [16] states that

$$\Psi^+(b|x) = \left(W^+ e^{U^+ \cdot (b-x)} - W^- e^{U^- \cdot x} Z^+\right) \cdot (I - Z^- Z^+)^{-1} \qquad (16)$$

for $0 \leq x \leq b$. Note that this expression depends on a choice of $\gamma \geq 0$.

Remark 1. Noting that $(I - Z^- Z^+)^{-1} = \sum_{n=0}^{\infty}(Z^- Z^+)^n$ and $Z^- Z^+$ represents a crossing of the interval $[0, b]$ from b to 0 and back, this formula has a clear probabilistic interpretation. The term $W^+ e^{U^+ \cdot (b-x)}$ simply yields the event that $\mathcal{X}$ exits from b. The correction term $W^- e^{U^- \cdot x} Z^+$ refers to the event that $\mathcal{X}$ descends below 0 before exiting from b. Multiplication by $(I - Z^- Z^+)^{-1}$ yields all possible combinations with any number of subsequent (down and up) crossings over the complete interval $[0, b]$.

Remark 2. Since $Z^+ = C^+ e^{U^+ \cdot b}$ we can write $\Psi^+(b|x)$ in the form

$$\Psi^+(b|x) = \left(W^+ e^{-U^+ \cdot x} - W^- e^{U^- \cdot x} C^+\right)\left(e^{-U^+ \cdot b} - C^- e^{U^- \cdot b} C^+\right)^{-1}$$

This comes closer to the usual expression of the exit time distribution in terms of scale functions. For instance, let $\mathcal{X}$ be a Brownian motion with variation $\sigma > 0$ and drift $\mu \in \mathbb{R}$. We then obtain

$$U^{\pm} = \frac{\pm\mu - \sqrt{\mu^2 + 2\gamma\sigma^2}}{\sigma^2}$$

Denote $-r := U^+$ and $s := U^-$. Then

$$\Psi^+(b|x) = \frac{e^{rx} - e^{sx}}{e^{rb} - e^{sb}}$$

cf. [14], (2.12 - 2.15), where the γ-scale function is given as $g(x) = e^{rx} - e^{sx}$.

Example 4. Another example is the M/M/1 queue during a busy cycle, which is the negative of the classical compound Poisson model with exponential jumps used in insurance mathematics. This continues example 3. We obtain

$$U^{\pm} = \frac{1}{2}\left(\pm(\lambda + \gamma - \beta) - \sqrt{(\beta - \gamma - \lambda)^2 + 4\beta\gamma}\right)$$

Denote $R := -U^+$ and $\rho := -U^-$ and compare this to [15], equations (3.12) and (4.24), with $\delta = \gamma$ and $c = 1$. Section 3.2 further yields $A^- = \beta/(\beta+\rho)$ and $A^+ = (\beta - R)/\beta$. Thus, starting with buffer content x in the descending phase, we obtain

$$\Psi^+(b|x) = \left(A^+ e^{-U^+ \cdot x} - e^{U^- \cdot x} A^+\right)\left(e^{-U^+ \cdot b} - A^- e^{U^- \cdot b} A^+\right)^{-1}$$

$$= \left(\frac{\beta - R}{\beta}e^{Rx} - e^{-\rho x}\frac{\beta - R}{\beta}\right)\bigg/\left(e^{Rb} - \frac{\beta}{\beta + \rho}e^{-\rho b}\frac{\beta - R}{\beta}\right)$$

$$= (\beta + \rho) \cdot \frac{\beta - R}{\beta} \cdot \frac{e^{Rx} - e^{-\rho x}}{(\beta + \rho)e^{Rb} - (\beta - R)e^{-\rho b}}$$

This is the Laplace transform of the time to buffer overflow within a busy cycle.

4 Main Result

Starting with an initial buffer content $u < b$ or with $u = b$ but in a descending phase, there is a positive probability of no overflow at all before the buffer empties. Let α denote the initial phase distribution of $(\mathcal{X}, \mathcal{J})$, i.e. $\alpha_i = \mathbb{P}(J_0 = i)$ for all $i \in E$. Then equation (16) yields, with $\gamma := 0$,

$$\mathbb{P}(D = 0) = \begin{cases} 1 - \alpha\Psi^+(b|u)\mathbf{1}, & u < b \\ 1 - \alpha\begin{pmatrix} 0 & 0 \\ 0 & I_{E_d} \end{pmatrix}\Psi^+(b|b)\mathbf{1}, & u = b \end{cases}$$

where I_{E_d} denotes the identity matrix of dimension $|E_d|$. Clearly the event $D = 0$ means that $\mathcal{X}$ exits the interval $[0, b]$ at the lower boundary first. We further observe that an overflow can occur only in ascending phases, i.e. on the time set $\{t \geq 0 : J_t \in E_a\}$.

We wish to derive an expression for the function

$$\bar{F}(x, \gamma) := \mathbb{E}\left(e^{-\gamma \tilde{S}^{-1}(x)}; D > x\right)$$

where $x, \gamma \geq 0$. The strong Markov property and the fact that an exit from $[0, b]$ at the upper boundary can occur only in an ascending phase yield together

$$\bar{F}(x, \gamma) = \Psi^+(b|u)\, \mathbb{E}\left(e^{-\gamma \tilde{S}^{-1}(x)}; D > x | X_0 = b\right)$$

where the last factor (written as an expectation) is an $E_a \times E_a$ matrix with entries

$$\mathbb{E}\left(e^{-\gamma \tilde{S}^{-1}(x)}; D > x, J_{S^{-1}(x)} = j | X_0 = b, J_0 = i\right)$$

for $i, j \in E_a$. This observation may be compared with equation (2.16) in [14]. Thus it suffices to determine the matrix-valued function

$$M(x, \gamma) := \mathbb{E}\left(e^{-\gamma \tilde{S}^{-1}(x)}; D > x | X_0 = b\right)$$

This is the content of our main result.

Theorem 1. *The distribution of the total overflow above the level b, given that $X_0 = b$ and $J_0 \in E_a$, is matrix-exponential. Specifically,*

$$M(x, \gamma) = e^{G(b) \cdot x}$$

for $\gamma, x \geq 0$, where

$$G(b) = \left(U^+ e^{-U^+ b} + C^- e^{U^- b} U^- C^+\right)\left(e^{-U^+ b} - C^- e^{U^- b} C^+\right)^{-1}$$

Proof. We employ the following approximation. Assume that the penalty for an overflow is paid out in small batches of sizes $\varepsilon > 0$ rather than continuously. More exactly, we define a process $(\mathcal{X}^\varepsilon, \mathcal{J}^\varepsilon)$ as follows. The phase process $\mathcal{J}^\varepsilon$ shall equal $\mathcal{J}$ almost surely. The level process $\mathcal{X}^\varepsilon$ behaves like $\mathcal{X}$ in the interval $[0, b]$ but may go above the level b. Whenever $\mathcal{X}^\varepsilon$ reaches the level $b + \varepsilon$, we pay a penalty of amount ε whereupon $\mathcal{X}^\varepsilon$ jumps back to the level b. The phase process $\mathcal{J}^\varepsilon$ remains unchanged by this jump. The original process $(\mathcal{X}, \mathcal{J})$ is obtained if we let ε tend to 0.

Let D^ε denote the total penalty obtained for $(\mathcal{X}^\varepsilon, \mathcal{J}^\varepsilon)$. Then D^ε has a matrix-geometric distribution, i.e.

$$M^\varepsilon(n, \gamma) := \mathbb{E}\left(e^{-\gamma T_n(\varepsilon)}; D^\varepsilon \geq n \cdot \varepsilon | X_0^\varepsilon = b\right) = \left(\Psi_{(a,a)}^+(b + \varepsilon|b)\right)^n$$

for $n \in \mathbb{N}$ and $\gamma \geq 0$, where

$$\Psi_{(a,a)}^+(b + \varepsilon|b) = \left(e^{U^+ \varepsilon} - C^- e^{U^- b} C^+ e^{U^+ \cdot (b+\varepsilon)}\right)$$
$$\times \left(I - C^- e^{U^- \cdot (b+\varepsilon)} C^+ e^{U^+ \cdot (b+\varepsilon)}\right)^{-1}$$

according to (16), and $T_n(\varepsilon)$ denotes the time of the nth payment of an ε-penalty.

Now letting ε tend to 0 we obtain that $M(x, \gamma)$ has a matrix-exponential distribution with parameter

$$
\begin{aligned}
G(b) &= \lim_{\varepsilon \downarrow 0} \frac{1}{\varepsilon} \left(\Psi^+_{(a,a)}(b + \varepsilon | b) - I \right) \\
&= \lim_{\varepsilon \downarrow 0} \frac{1}{\varepsilon} \left(e^{U^+\varepsilon} - I + C^- e^{U^-b} \left(e^{U^-\varepsilon} - I \right) C^+ e^{U^+\cdot(b+\varepsilon)} \right) \\
&\quad \times \left(I - C^- e^{U^-\cdot(b+\varepsilon)} C^+ e^{U^+\cdot(b+\varepsilon)} \right)^{-1} \\
&= \left(U^+ + C^- e^{U^-b} U^- C^+ e^{U^+b} \right) \left(I - C^- e^{U^-b} C^+ e^{U^+b} \right)^{-1}
\end{aligned}
$$

which is equivalent to the statement. $\qquad\qquad\qquad\qquad\qquad\qquad\quad\square$

Remark 3. Defining an analogue of the γ-scale function by

$$
W(x) := e^{-U^+x} - C^- e^{U^-x} C^+
$$

for $x > 0$, we see first that $G(b) = -W'(b)[W(b)]^{-1}$ where $W'(b)$ denotes the derivative of the function $W(x)$ at b. Setting $\gamma = 0$, the mean total overflow during a busy cycle can be computed as

$$
\begin{aligned}
V(b|u) &:= \mathbb{E}\left(D | X_0 = u\right) = \Psi^+(b|u)\, \mathbb{E}\left(D | X_0 = b\right) \\
&= \Psi^+(b|u) \int_0^\infty \mathbb{P}(D > x | X_0 = b)\, dx \\
&= \Psi^+(b|u) \int_0^\infty M(x, 0)\, dx = \Psi^+(b|u)\, [-G(b)]^{-1} \\
&= \left(W^+ e^{-U^+u} - W^- e^{U^-u} C^+ \right) \left(-U^+ e^{-U^+b} + C^- e^{U^-b} \left(-U^- \right) C^+ \right)^{-1}
\end{aligned}
$$

Example 5. We continue the example in remark 2 of a Brownian motion fluid flow. Since there is only one phase, we get $W^+ = W^- = \dot{C}^+ = C^- = 1$ and hence

$$
V(b|u) = \frac{e^{ru} - e^{su}}{re^{rb} - se^{sb}}
$$

which is equation (2.11) in [14]. Note that for $\gamma = 0$ we obtain

$$
(s, r) = \begin{cases} \left(-2\frac{\mu}{\sigma^2}, 0\right), & \mu > 0 \\ \left(0, -2\frac{\mu}{\sigma^2}\right), & \mu < 0 \end{cases}
$$

This implies

$$
\mathbb{E}(D) = \begin{cases} \dfrac{\sigma^2}{2\mu} \left(e^{2\mu b/\sigma^2} - e^{2\mu(b-u)/\sigma^2} \right), & \mu > 0 \\[2mm] -\dfrac{\sigma^2}{2\mu} \left(e^{2\mu(b-u)/\sigma^2} - e^{2\mu b/\sigma^2} \right), & \mu < 0 \end{cases}
$$

cf. equation (2.22) in [14] for the case $\mu > 0$.

Example 6. Another example is the M/M/1 queue. Starting in the descending phase with initial buffer content $X_0 = u$, we obtain for the mean discounted overflow during a busy cycle

$$V(b|u) = \left(A^+ e^{-U^+ u} - e^{U^- u} A^+\right)\left(-U^+ e^{-U^+ b} + A^- e^{U^- b}\left(-U^-\right) A^+\right)^{-1}$$

$$= \frac{\frac{\beta-R}{\beta} e^{Ru} - e^{-\rho u} \frac{\beta-R}{\beta}}{Re^{Rb} + \frac{\beta}{\beta+\rho} e^{-\rho b} \rho \frac{\beta-R}{\beta}}$$

$$= \frac{\beta-R}{\beta}(\beta+\rho) \frac{e^{Ru} - e^{-\rho u}}{(\beta+\rho)R \cdot e^{Rb} + (\beta-R)\rho \cdot e^{-\rho b}}$$

Note that this is different from formula (7.8) in [15], as the M/M/1 queue is the negative of the compound Poisson model in risk theory. Setting $\gamma = 0$ and assuming the stability condition $\beta > \lambda$ holds, we obtain

$$R = \beta - \lambda \qquad \text{and} \qquad \rho = 0$$

This yields

$$\mathbb{E}(D) = \frac{\lambda}{\beta \cdot (\beta - \lambda)}\left(e^{(\lambda-\beta)\cdot(b-u)} - e^{(\lambda-\beta)\cdot b}\right)$$

for the mean total overflow during a busy cycle.

References

1. Ahn, S., Badescu, A., Ramaswami, V.: Time dependent analysis of finite buffer fluid flows and risk models with a dividend barrier. Queueing Syst. 55(4), 207–222 (2007)
2. Asmussen, S., Jobmann, M., Schwefel, H.P.: Exact buffer overflow calculations for queues via martingales. Queueing Syst. 42, 63–90 (2002)
3. Asmussen, S.: Stationary distributions for fluid flow models with or without Brownian motion. Stochastic Models 11, 1–20 (1995)
4. Asmussen, S.: Applied Probability and Queues. Springer, New York (2003)
5. Asmussen, S., Avram, F., Pistorius, M.: Russian and American put options under exponential phase-type Lévy models. Stochastic Processes and their Applications 109, 79–111 (2004)
6. Asmussen, S., Kella, O.: A multi-dimensional martingale for Markov additive processes and its applications. Adv. Appl. Prob. 32, 376–393 (2000)
7. Asmussen, S., Nerman, O., Olsson, M.: Fitting phase-type distributions via the EM algorithm. Scand. J. Stat. 23(4), 419–441 (1996)
8. Badescu, A., Breuer, L., da Silva Soares, A., Latouche, G., Remiche, M.A., Stanford, D.: Risk processes analyzed as fluid queues. Scandinavian Actuarial Journal, 127–141 (2005)
9. Bean, N., O'Reilly, M., Taylor, P.G.: Hitting probabilities and hitting times for stochastic fluid flows. Probab. Eng. Inf. Sci. 23, 121–147 (2009)
10. Breuer, L.: An EM Algorithm for Batch Markovian Arrival Processes and its Comparison to a Simpler Estimation Procedure. Annals of Operations Research 112, 123–138 (2002)

11. Breuer, L.: Continuity of the M/G/c queue. Queueing Syst 58(4), 321–331 (2008)
12. Breuer, L.: First passage times for Markov–additive processes with positive jumps of phase–type. J. Appl. Prob. 45(3), 779–799 (2008)
13. Frostig, E.: On risk model with dividends payments perturbed by a Brownian motion - an algorithmic approach. Astin Bulletin 38(1), 183–206 (2008)
14. Gerber, H., Shiu, E.: Optimal Dividends: Analysis with Brownian motion. North American Actuarial Journal 8(1), 1–20 (2004)
15. Gerber, H., Shiu, E.: On the time value of ruin. North American Actuarial Journal 2(1), 48–78 (1998)
16. Jiang, Z., Pistorius, M.: On perpetual American put valuation and first-passage in a regime-switching model with jumps. Finance Stoch. 12, 331–355 (2008)
17. Lucantoni, D.M.: New results on the single server queue with a batch Markovian arrival process. Commun. Stat., Stochastic Models 7(1), 1–46 (1991)
18. Neuts, M.F.: Matrix–Geometric Solutions in Stochastic Models. Johns Hopkins University Press, Baltimore (1981)

Accuracy of Strong and Weak Comparisons for Network of Queues[*]

Hind Castel-Taleb[1] and Nihal Pekergin[2]

[1] INSTITUT TELECOM, TELECOM SudParis
9,rue Charles Fourier 91011 Evry Cedex, France
hind.castel@int-evry.fr
[2] LACL, Université Paris-Est, Val de Marne
61, av. du Général de Gaulle, 94010 Créteil Cedex, France
nihal.pekergin@univ-paris12.fr

Abstract. Quality of performance measure bounds is crucial for an accurate dimensioning of computer network resources. We study stochastic comparisons of multidimensional Markov processes for which quantitative analysis could be intractable if there is no specific solution form. On partially ordered state space, different stochastic orderings can be defined as the strong or the less constrained weak ordering. The goal of the present paper is to compare these two orderings with respect the quality of derived bounds. We propose to study a system similar to a Jackson network except that queues have finite capacity. Different bounding systems are built either in the sense of the strong ordering with hard constraints, or in the sense of the weak ordering with less ones. The proofs of the stochastic comparisons are done using the coupling and the increasing set methods, with an intuitive event based formalism. The qualities of bounding systems are compared regarding to blocking probabilities.

Keywords: Markov processes, Jackson networks, stochastic comparisons, blocking probabilities.

1 Introduction

With the complexity of network architectures, and the variety of technology it is crucial to evaluate the performance of the whole network for end to end QoS (Quality of Sercice) requirements. These systems are usually represented by multidimensional processes with very large state spaces. As a result, quantitative analysis is difficult if there is no specific solution form (product form, matrix-geometric solutions, ...). We propose to use a mathematical method based on stochastic comparisons of Markov processes [18,19]. The key idea of this method is that given a large size Markov process, we bound it by other Markov processes easier to study, and which provide bounds on performance measures. Different solutions are proposed using stochastic comparisons [18]. The bounding process either has a probability distribution with a specific form, thus we can compute

---

[*] Partially supported by french research project ANR-SETI06-02.

B. Müller-Clostermann et al. (Eds.): MMB & DFT 2010, LNCS 5987, pp. 212–226, 2010.

bounding performance measures, or it is defined on a smaller state space, thus using stochastic comparisons by mapping functions we can define aggregated bounding Markov process [4]. The advantage of this method is that it can be applied for different kinds of network architectures [17]. In [2], we apply this method on mobile networks in order to obtain dropping handover bounds, and in [3] for the loss rates packets in an IP switch. A stochastic ordering is defined as an ordering relation between random variables, or stochastic processes [19]. The most known stochastic order is the strong stochastic ordering ($\preceq_{st}$), equivalent to a sample path ordering [19]. When the state space is multidimensional, weak stochastic orderings ($\preceq_{wk}$, and $\preceq_{wk*}$) can also be defined using increasing sets families [19,15]. The goal of the present paper is to compare the strong ordering "$\preceq_{st}$" with the weak ordering "$\preceq_{wk}$", from the point of view of the applied stochastic comparison method and also for the quality of the performance measure. Each stochastic ordering generates special relations between probability distributions. The strong ordering yields to comparisons of increasing functionals (the expectations of all increasing functions of the probability distributions) while the weak ordering is equivalent to tail probability distribution comparisons. We apply stochastic comparison methods on a general queueing network similar to a Jackson network except that queues have a finite capacity. This system is very difficult to study as there is no product form for the stationnary probability distribution. In [20], tandem queueing networks with blocking have been studied. Bounding systems have been defined by modifying the behavior of the system in order to obtain product forms for steady state probabilities. In our paper, the approach is different as we define stochastic bounds for both stationnary and transient probability distributions. We define from the exact system two bounding systems by creating independence between queues. The first idea is to make infinite the queues in order to obtain a Jackson network. The second one is to cut the links between the queues in order to obtain a system with independent M/M/1/K queues [15,14]. We prove using the coupling [11,13,9] that the Jackson network represents an upper bound for the strong ordering (strong bound). We apply the increasing set formalism [5] in order to prove that the second system represents an upper bound in the sense of weak ordering (weak bound). As the strong ordering has harder conditions than the weak ordering, then it is interesting to study the quality of derived bounds. To our knowledge, there is no study which aims to compare the quality of the bounds regarding to the sense of the applied stochastic ordering. In this paper, from different input parameters values (routing probabilities, load) we compute blocking probability bounds in order to compare these values. The relevance of this paper is to propose the best bounding system according to the input parameters. This paper is organized as follows. Next, we present the studied system and the bounding systems, and we give the proofs of the stochastic comparisons using the coupling and increasing sets methods. In section 3, we present analytical results of the blocking probabilities for the different bounding systems in order to study the accuracy of bounds. As a conclusion, we explain how to choose the more precise bounding system according to the input parameters.

2   Bounding Systems and Stochastic Comparisons

The system understudy is similar to a Jackson network except that queues have finite capacities. This system may represent a telecommunication system with series of interconnected nodes. Performance evaluation of this system is crucial for end to end QoS requirements.

2.1   System Description

The system is represented by n queues, and each queue i ($1 \le i \le n$) has a finite capacity K_i, and is characterized by the following parameters:

- Exponential inter-arrival times, with parameters λ_i
- Exponential service times, with parameters μ_i, and after the service, we have two cases:
   - with the probability p_{ij} the customer transits from queue i to queue j if the queue is not full. If queue j is full, then the customer goes out.
   - with the probability d_i the customer goes out.

With the following assumptions: $p_{ii} = 0$, and $\sum_{j \ne i} p_{ij} + d_i = 1$, $\forall i = 1 \ldots n$. Let $\{X(t), t \ge 0\}$ be the Markov process representing the evolution of this system with infinitesimal generator, Q. We denote by Π the stationary probability distribution which has no product form solution. Thus its computation is very difficult due to the state space explosion with n the number of queues.

2.2   Bounding Systems

We propose to define from the exact system different bounding processes easier to analyze. We study two different ways for the definition of these systems. In order to compute easily the stationary probability distribution of $\{X(t), t \ge 0\}$ we propose to make the queues independent in order to obtain a product form. Two kinds of systems are defined: the first one is obtained by removing the links between the queues, and so the bounding system is represented by independent $M/M/1/K_i$ queues. Note that cuting links between queues is a general approach, so could be also applied in the case of multiserver stations. The system can be represented by a Markov process $\{Y(t), t \ge 0\}$, with infinitesimal Q^Y, and stationary probability distribution Π^Y. The second system is obtained by making infinite capacities, so it represents a Jackson network. This system can be represented by a Markov process $\{Z(t), t \ge 0\}$, with infinitesimal Q^Z, and stationary probability distribution Π^Z. For both systems, the stationary probability distribution can be easily computed, as they have a product form. We apply stochastic comparisons in order to prove that these systems represent really bounds. The stochastic comparison for the strong ordering called "$\preceq_{st}$"-comparison used in this paper is based on the coupling of the processes. It remains to compare the realizations by considering events happening in the systems. We apply the $\preceq_{st}$-comparison to prove that $\{Z(t), t \ge 0\}$ represents an upper bound for the system understudy. The strong ordering between processes could be very useful in performance evaluation as it generates the comparison of performance measures written as increasing functions on the stationary and transient distributions. So we can compare performance measures as : blocking probabilities, delays, and resource utilization. As the strong ordering is hard constrained, in some cases it could not be defined between the underlying processes. So it could be interesting to search if weakers orderings could be defined. In [15,14], it has been proved that cutting links between queues makes that the $\preceq_{st}$ ordering could not exists. So the strong ordering could not exist between $\{X(t), t \geq 0\}$ and $\{Y(t), t \geq 0\}$. We propose to apply the increasing sets method [15,14] to prove that the $\preceq_{wk}$ ordering exists. We call $\preceq_{wk}$-comparison the stochastic comparison based on increasing sets in order to generate the $\preceq_{wk}$-ordering. Note that in [16], others bounding systems have been defined by generalizing the approach to any partition of the set of nodes. Some interesting features will be studied in these stochastic comparison methods. For the $\preceq_{st}$-comparison, we compare a Markov process defined on a finite state space with another on an infinite state space. For the $\preceq_{wk}$-comparison, we define the increasing sets from events, in order to limit the number of increasing sets effectively used for the comparison. Another objective of the present paper is to compare the bounding systems with respect to a performance measure which is the blocking probability. Considering the quality of the bounding systems from different input parameter values could be very interesting in order to see the impact of the stochastic orderings. The processes understudy are multidimensional, defined on $E = \mathbb{N}^n$. We propose to use the component-wise partial ordering denoted by $\preceq$ on this state space:

$$\forall x, y \in \mathbb{N}^n, \ x \preceq y \Leftrightarrow x_i \leq y_i, \forall i = 1, \ldots, n \tag{1}$$

This order is widely used for multidimensional state spaces as it allows us to compare queue by queue the behavior of queueing networks. Next, we present the $\preceq_{wk}$-comparison with independent $M/M/1/K_i$ queues.

2.3 $\preceq_{wk}$-Comparisons with Independent $M/M/1/K_i$ Queues

The bounding process $\{Y(t), t \geq 0\}$ is represented by n independent $M/M/1/K_i$ queues, obtained from the exact system by removing the links between the queues [15,14]. For each pairs of queues j and i interconnected, the flow of packets leaving node j and entering node i with rate $\mu_j p_{ji}$ is forbidden. As compensation this flow is added to the flow of packets entering node i. So each queue i is an $M/M/1/K_i$ with an arrival rate $\lambda_i + \sum_{j \neq i} \mu_j p_{ji}$, and a service rate μ_i. The interest of this bounding system is that both stationary and transient behavior can be computed easily. We give the following proposition:

Proposition 1

$$\{X(t), t \geq 0\} \preceq_{wk} \{Y(t), t \geq 0\} \tag{2}$$

Proof. In [14] similar systems with infinite queues have been studied. The $\preceq_{wk}$-comparison has been presented using an operator-analytic approach. In this paper, we try to develop increasing sets using an event based formalism in order to provide a more intuitive approach for $\preceq_{wk}$-comparison. We apply theorem 2 of the Appendix, where $\preceq_\Phi$ represents $\preceq_{wk}$. There are two steps in theorem 2: first we must verify the monotonicity of one of the processes, and secondly we have to compare the transition rates of the processes in the increasing set. We can remark easily that $Y(t)$ is $\preceq_{st}$-monotone (since it is a Jackson network with null routing probabilities between queues, and Jackson networks are $\preceq_{st}$-monotone [11]) then it is also $\preceq_{wk}$-monotone from proposition 5 in the Appendix. According to theorem 2, we also have to compare the transition rates of each process using the increasing sets. So we have to check if $\sum_{z \in \Gamma} Q(x, z)$ is lower than $\sum_{z \in \Gamma} Q^Y(x, z)$, $\forall \Gamma \in \Phi_{wk}(E)$. As E is multidimensional, then $\Phi_{wk}(E)$ could be very large. So we need to define the increasing sets which are necessary for the verification of the $\preceq_{wk}$-comparison. As the transitions from a state happened due to the events, then we define the increasing sets from these events. Let e_i be a vector from N^n such that all components are null except component i which equals 1. We use e_i to represent the transitions from x when events happen. From x, we have three kinds of events in queue i ($\forall i = 1 \ldots n$) : arrivals, services, and transits to queue $j = i$. Arrivals generate transition from x to $x + e_i$, so we define the increasing set $\{x + e_i\} \uparrow$ if $x_i < K_i$. From other events we define the increasing sets $\{x - e_i\} \uparrow$, if $x_i > 0$, and $\{x - e_i + e_j\} \uparrow$, if $x_i > 0$, and $x_j < K_j$. We add also the increasing set $\{x\} \uparrow$ corresponding to the process staying in state x. We denote by $\Gamma_{x+e_i} = \{x + e_i\} \uparrow$, $\Gamma_{x-e_i+e_j} = \{x - e_i + e_j\} \uparrow$, $\Gamma_x = \{x\} \uparrow$, and $\Gamma_{x-e_i} = \{x - e_i\} \uparrow$. Let $S_{wk}(E)$ be the set of states which are necessary for the $\preceq_{wk}$-comparison. So:

$$S_{wk}(E) = \{\Gamma_{x+e_i}, \Gamma_{x-e_i+e_j}, \Gamma_x, \Gamma_{x-e_i}\}, \text{ where } S_{wk}(E) \subset \Phi_{wk}(E)$$

Table 1. Transition rates comparison

Γ	$\sum_{z \in \Gamma} Q(x, z)$	$\sum_{z \in \Gamma} Q^Y(x, z)$
Γ_{x+e_i}	λ_i	$\lambda_i + \sum_{k=1, k \neq i}^n \mu_k p_{ki}$
$\Gamma_{x-e_i+e_j}$	$\mu_i p_{ij} + \lambda_j$	$\lambda_j + \sum_{k=1, k \neq i}^n \mu_k p_{kj}$
Γ_x	$-\sum_{k=1}^n \mu_k 1_{x_k > 0}$	$-\sum_{k=1}^n \mu_k 1_{x_k > 0}$
Γ_{x-e_i}	$-\sum_{k=1, k \neq i}^n \mu_k 1_{x_k > 0}$	$-\sum_{k=1, k \neq i}^n \mu_k 1_{x_k > 0}$

It is easy to see from table 1 that:

$$\sum_{z \in \Gamma} Q(x, z) \leq \sum_{z \in \Gamma} Q^Y(x, z), \ \forall \Gamma \in S_{wk}(E)$$

So we can deduce from theorem 2 that $\{X(t), t \geq 0\} \preceq_{wk} \{Y(t), t \geq 0\}$, and we call $\{Y(t), t \geq 0\}$ a weak bounding system.

From the stochastic comparisons of the processes we have : $P(X(t) \in \Gamma) \leq P(Y(t) \in \Gamma), \forall \Gamma \in \Phi_{wk}(E)$. And so for the stationary probability distributions we have:

$$\sum_{x \in \Gamma} \Pi(x) \leq \sum_{x \in \Gamma} \Pi^Y(x), \forall \Gamma \in \Phi_{wk}(E) \tag{3}$$

As we will see after, these results could be very interesting, as the right term can be easily computed as the product of probability distributions of independent $M/M/1/K_i$ queues. In the next section, we propose to compare $\{X(t), t \geq 0\}$ with $\{Z(t), t \geq 0\}$, using $\preceq_{st}$-comparison.

2.4   The $\preceq_{st}$-Comparison with Jackson Network

We propose to bound the process $\{X(t), t \geq 0\}$ by $\{Z(t), t \geq 0\}$, in order to compute performance measure bounds. Using the coupling, we aim to prove the following proposition:

Proposition 2

$$\{X(t), t \geq 0\} \preceq_{st} \{Z(t), t \geq 0\} \tag{4}$$

Proof. In most of the cases, the coupling concerns processes which have either both infinite state space, or both finite state space [11]. Here, it is not the case as $\{X(t), t \geq 0\}$ has a finite state space, and $\{Z(t), t \geq 0\}$ an infinite. We use Theorem 1, so we prove that there exists two processes $\{\widehat{X}(t), \ t \geq 0\}$ (resp. $\{\widehat{Z}(t), \ t \geq 0\}$) with the same infinitesimal generator matrix than $\{X(t), \ t \geq 0\}$ (resp. $\{Z(t), \ t \geq 0\}$) representing two different realizations and we prove that:

$$\widehat{X}(0) \preceq \widehat{Z}(0) \Rightarrow \widehat{X}(t) \preceq \widehat{Z}(t), \ t > 0 \tag{5}$$

Let suppose that: $\widehat{X}(t) \preceq \widehat{Z}(t)$. We show if $\widehat{X}(t+\Delta t) \preceq \widehat{Z}(t+\Delta t)$ by considering the evolution from events occurring during the time interval Δt:

1. an arrival in queue i: we can see easily that the arrival rate in queue i is λ_i from $\widehat{X}(t)$ (if queue i is not full) and also from $\widehat{Z}(t)$. So if $\widehat{X}(t)$ increases with an arrival in queue i, then $\widehat{Z}(t)$ will increase also. From the component $\widehat{X}_i(t)$, we obtain $\widehat{X}_i(t + \Delta t) = min\{K_i, \widehat{X}_i(t) + 1\}$, and from $\widehat{Z}_i(t)$ as the capacity is infinite then the component always increases: $\widehat{Z}_i(t + \Delta t) = \widehat{Z}_i(t) + 1$. Since other components do not change, and $\widehat{X}(t) \preceq \widehat{Z}(t)$ then $\widehat{X}(t + \Delta t) \preceq \widehat{Z}(t + \Delta t)$.

2. a transit from queue i to queue j: as the transition rate is $\mu_i p_{ij}$ for $\widehat{X}(t)$ and $\widehat{Z}(t)$ then the evolutions are the same, and a transit with this event of one of the process can be compensated by another. The transit occurs if $\widehat{X}_i(t) > 0$ and the customer is accepted in queue j if $\widehat{X}_j(t) < K_j$, otherwise it is lost. From $\widehat{X}(t)$, we obtain $\widehat{X}_i(t + \Delta t) = max\{0, \widehat{X}_i(t) - 1\}$, and $\widehat{X}_j(t + \Delta t) = min\{K_j, \widehat{X}_j(t) + 1\}$. From $\widehat{Z}(t)$, similarly, $\widehat{Z}_i(t + \Delta t) = max\{0, \widehat{Z}_i(t) - 1\}$, and as the queue j is infinite, $\widehat{Z}_j(t+\Delta t) = \widehat{Z}_j(t)+1$. Since other components do not change, and $\widehat{X}(t) \preceq \widehat{Z}(t)$ then $\widehat{Z}(t + \Delta t) \preceq \widehat{Z}(t + \Delta t)$.

3. a service from queue i to the outside: as the service rate is $\mu_i d_i$ for the two processes, then if we have a service in queue i for $\widehat{Z}(t)$, we have also a service for $\widehat{Z}(t)$. So $\widehat{X_i}(t + \Delta t) = max\{0, \widehat{X_i}(t) - 1\}$, and $\widehat{Z_i}(t + \Delta t) = max\{0, \widehat{Z_i}(t) - 1\}$, then $\widehat{X}(t + \Delta t) \preceq \widehat{Z}(t + \Delta t)$.

As the process $\{Z(t), t \geq 0\}$ is time-homogeneous, even it is defined on an infinite state space, the coupling of the processes for the comparison of the realizations is still verified. We deduce that $\{X(t), t \geq 0\} \preceq_{st} \{Z(t), t \geq 0\}$, and so $\{Z(t), t \geq 0\}$ represents a strong bounding system.

Thus we have the comparison of transient probability distributions: $P(X(t) \in \Gamma) \leq P(Z(t) \in \Gamma)$, $\forall \Gamma \in \Phi_{st}(E)$. If the stability condition is satisfied, then the stationary probability distribution Π^Z exists. So we have the following inequality:

$$\sum_{x \in \Gamma} \Pi(x) \leq \sum_{x \in \Gamma} \Pi^Z(x), \forall \Gamma \in \Phi_{st}(E) \tag{6}$$

3   Accuracy of Bounding Systems

The goal of this section is to study the quality of bounding systems regarding to the blocking probability. As bounding systems are generated either by the strong ordering or the weak ordering then the objective is to conclude which order could provide the most precise bounds. First, we give blocking probability equations for the exact and bounding systems.

3.1   Blocking Probability

The exact blocking probability B_i on queue i for the process $\{X(t), t \geq 0\}$ is given by the following formula :

$$B_i = \sum_{x \succeq x^*} \Pi(x) \tag{7}$$

where x^* is the vector where all components are null except component i which equals K_i. We can remark that B_i is very difficult to compute because there is not a product form for Π and the state space size could be very large (equals to : $K_1 \times \ldots K_i \times \ldots \times K_n$). So we propose to compute different blocking probability bounds for queue i : the weak bound BY_i on the weak bounding system, and the strong bound BZ_i on the strong bounding system. These bounds can be computed easily as the stationary probability distributions have a product form. BY_i is given by : $BY_i = \sum_{x \succeq x*} \Pi^Y(x)$. We can remark that the set of states $\Gamma = \{x \succeq x*\}$ used for the computation of the blocking probability B_i is an increasing set such that $\Gamma \in \Phi_{wk}(E)$. Moreover, in the inequality (3), if we take $\Gamma = \{x \succeq x*\}$, then for any queue i we have : $B_i \leq BY_i$. The blocking probability BY_i is equivalent to the blocking probability in an $M/M/1/K_i$ queue:

$$BY_i = a_i^{K_i} \frac{1 - a_i}{1 - a_i^{K_i+1}} \text{ where } a_i = \frac{\lambda_i + \sum_{k=1,k \neq i}^n \mu_k p_{ki}}{\mu_i} \tag{8}$$

The blocking probability BZ_i is given by: $BZ_i = \sum_{x \succeq x^*} \Pi^Z(x)$. As $\Gamma = \{x \succeq x^*\}$ is such that $\Gamma \in \Phi_{wk}(E)$, then $\Gamma \in \Phi_{st}(E)$ (see Proposition 3). Furthermore from the comparison of stationary probability distributions (see equation (6)), we have also for any queue i : $B_i \leq BZ_i$.

We explain now how to compute BZ_i. Let Λ_i be the input traffic in queue i. It equals the sum of traffic coming from the outside λ_i and the traffic coming from other queues k $(k \neq i)$: $\Lambda_k p_{ki}$. We denote by:

$$b_i = \frac{\Lambda_i}{\mu_i} \ where \ \Lambda_i = \lambda_i + \sum_{k=1, k \neq i}^{n} \Lambda_k p_{ki} \qquad (9)$$

We suppose that the stability condition $b_i < 1$ is satisfied, so the stationary probability distribution could be computed. The blocking probability BZ_i is :

$$BZ_i = \sum_{x_i=K_i}^{\infty} b_i^{x_i}(1 - b_i) \qquad (10)$$

Since $\sum_{x_i=0}^{\infty} b_i^{x_i}(1-b_i) = 1$, then $BZ_i = b_i^{K_i}$. For the comparison of the blocking probabilities BZ_i and BY_i, first, we can compare a_i with b_i. As $\Lambda_k < \mu_k, \forall 1 \leq k \leq n$, then:

$$\lambda_i + \sum_{k=1, k \neq i}^{n} \Lambda_k p_{ki} \leq \lambda_i + \sum_{k=1, k \neq i}^{n} \mu_k p_{ki} \qquad (11)$$

thus we deduce that $b_i \leq a_i$, and also $b_i^{K_i} \leq a_i^{K_i}$. Since $\frac{1-a_i}{1-a_i^{K_i+1}} < 1$, we could not conclude for the comparison between BZ_i and BY_i.

3.2 Numerical Results

We give now some numerical results in order to study the quality of the bounds. As we need to compare the different bounds with the same input parameters, then we choose them under the stability conditions of the strong bound. First, we study a simple system in order to compare the exact blocking probabilities with bounding measures. The system is represented by two queues : queue 1 and queue 2 in tandem. The arrival rate in queue 1 is $\lambda_1 = 100$, and the service rate $\mu_1 = 110$, the probability $p_{12} = 1$, and $d_1 = 0$. So $a_2 = 0.95$, and $b_2 = 0.90$. In table 2, we give the exact blocking probabilities B_2 of queue 2 (obtained from QNAP simulator) and also upper bounding measures BY_2 and BZ_2. We can easily see that BY_2 provides better bounds for $K_2 = 20, 30, 40, 50, 60$, but for upper values of K_2, BZ_2 is better.

Next, we study a more complex system, given by figure 1. The input parameters for each queue are given in Table 3. The system is represented by 10 queues with finite capacities. We can suppose easily that this system could represent a telecommunication network with nodes as routers, and arrival and service rates given in term of bit rates. The goal of our study is to compute blocking probabilities of queue 9. As the exact blocking probability B_9 is very difficult to compute

Table 2. Blocking probabilities

K_2	B_2 (Exact)	$BY_2(Weak)$	$BZ_2(Strong)$
20	$0.137 * 10^{-1}$	$0.28 * 10^{-1}$	0.148
30	$0.485 * 10^{-2}$	$0.14 * 10^{-1}$	$0.57 * 10^{-1}$
40	$0.178 * 10^{-2}$	$0.83 * 10^{-2}$	$0.92 * 10^{-2}$
50	$0.643 * 10^{-3}$	$0.48 * 10^{-2}$	$0.8 * 10^{-2}$
60	$0.223 * 10^{-3}$	$0.29 * 10^{-2}$	$0.32 * 10^{-2}$
70	$0.14 * 10^{-3}$	$0.18 * 10^{-2}$	$0.12 * 10^{-2}$
80	$0.268 * 10^{-4}$	$0.11 * 10^{-2}$	$4.88 * 10^{-4}$
90	$0.199 * 10^{-5}$	$0.700 * 10^{-3}$	$1.88 * 10^{-4}$
100	$0.787 * 10^{-5}$	$4.377 * 10^{-4}$	$7.2565 * 10^{-5}$

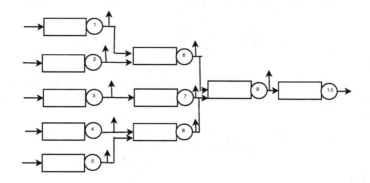

Fig. 1. Queueing system understudy

Table 3. Input parameters values

Queue : i	λ_i	μ_i	d_i	p_{ij}
1	168	170	0.2	0.8
2	40	41	0.2	0.8
3	110	112	0.2	0.8
4	82	84	0.2	0.8
5	82	84	0.2	0.8
6	0	170	0.1	0.9
7	0	91	0.1	0.9
8	0	136	0.1	0.9
9	0	480	0.8	0.2
10	0	500	1	0

due to the state space explosion, then we compute the upper bounds BY_9 and BZ_9, and we compare them. From input parameters, we obtain $a_9 = 0.743$, and $b_9 = 0.722$. In Table 4 we can see that the weak bound is better only for small buffers : 20, 30, 40. For higher buffer sizes, the strong bound is better. We suppose now that $\mu_9 = 360$, in order to increase the load of queue 9, and other input

Table 4. Blocking probability bounds : $a_9 = 0.743$, $b_9 = 0.722$

K_9	$BY_9(Weak)$	$BZ_9(Strong)$
20	$6.887 * 10^{-4}$	0.0015
30	$3.560 * 10^{-5}$	$5.9244 * 10^{-5}$
40	$1.8439 * 10^{-6}$	$2.3095 * 10^{-6}$
50	$9.5501 * 10^{-8}$	$9.0035 * 10^{-8}$
60	$4.9463 * 10^{-9}$	$3.5098 * 10^{-9}$
70	$2.5618 * 10^{-10}$	$1.3682 * 10^{-10}$
80	$1.326 * 10^{-11}$	$5.3340 * 10^{-12}$
90	$6.87 * 10^{-13}$	$2.0794 * 10^{-13}$
100	$3.559 * 10^{-14}$	$8.106 * 10^{-15}$

parameters are the same as in Table 3. We obtain $b_9 = 0.9638$, and $a_9 = 0.991$, and the blocking probability bounds are given in Table 5. In Table 5, we can see that the Weak bound gives always the most accurate blocking probability bounds. We aim to decrease more the load of queue 9. We modify the routing probabilities of queues 6,7 and 8 into queue 9. We take 0.8 instead of 0.9. We obtain $b_9 = 0.51$, and $a_9 = 0.52$. We can remark that in Table 6, the Strong bound provides better results than the weak bound, except for buffer size 20. At the end, we can conclude that when the buffer size is large, the strong bound is better, and when the load is high the Weak bound is better. Furthermore, it is difficult to generalize to other systems, and to say in the general case which ordering provides the best system. The important idea is how the original system is modified in order to obtain the bounding systems. Indeed the modification is related to the kind of the stochastic ordering. For example, cutting the links seems generate a weak ordering, and making infinite queues a strong bound.

For general systems, the most important thing to see is how bounding systems are built, and how parameters of the original systems are modified in bounding systems. So we will be able to identify the most accurate system.

In the case of the dimensioning problem, we can see the relevance of computing different bounds. For example, in the case of table 5, if the threshold

Table 5. Blocking probability bounds : $b_9 = 0.9638$, $a_9 = 0.991$

K_9	$BY_9(Weak)$	$BZ_9(Strong)$
20	0.043	0.479
30	0.028	0.331
40	0.020	0.229
50	0.0157	0.158
60	0.0126	0.11
70	0.010	0.076
80	0.0086	0.052
90	0.00736	0.0365
100	0.006	0.025

Table 6. Blocking probability bounds : $a_9 = 0.52$, $b_9 = 0.51$

K_9	$BY_9(Weak)$	$BZ_9(Strong)$
20	$1.38 * 10^{-6}$	$1.674 * 10^{-6}$
30	$2.365 * 10^{-9}$	$2.165 * 10^{-9}$
40	$4.04 * 10^{-12}$	$2.80 * 10^{-12}$
50	$6.93 * 10^{-15}$	$3.62 * 10^{-15}$
60	$1.18 * 10^{-17}$	$4.69 * 10^{-18}$
70	$2.03 * 10^{-20}$	$6.07 * 10^{-21}$
80	$3.48 * 10^{-23}$	$7.85 * 10^{-24}$
90	$5.96 * 10^{-26}$	$1.01 * 10^{-26}$
100	$1.02 * 10^{-28}$	$1.31 * 10^{-29}$

blocking probability is 0.05, then the weak bound provides a buffer size equal to 20, and the strong bound 90. So the weak bound is very interesting in this case. Furthermore, in table 6, for a threshold equals to 10^{-20}, the strong bound provides a buffer size equals to 70 and the weak bound 80.

4 Conclusion

We propose in this paper different bounding systems using different stochastic orderings for networks of queues with finite capacities. We develop a methodology based on the coupling and increasing sets for Markovian discrete event systems to establish stochastic comparisons. This leads to an intuitive way to build bounding systems having product form solutions. We compute blocking probability bounds, and we compare the values derived from the bounding systems for different input parameters. For systems with large buffers, the strong bounding system provides more accurate bounds, while when the load is large, the weak bounding system provides more accurate bounds. These results are interesting to see that even the strong stochastic ordering has more constraints than the weak ordering, they may provide more accurate bounds. This depends indeed on the bounding system and its capacity to capture the dynamic of the considered system. Therefore, one can derive both bounds and use the most accurate bound to dimension buffers in a network.

References

1. Ridder, A.: Weak stochastic ordering for multidimensionnal Markov chains. Oper. Research Letters 18, 121–126 (1995)
2. Castel-Taleb, H., Mokdad, L.: Performance measure bounds in wireless networks by state space reduction. In: 13th Annual Meeting of the IEEE International Symposium on Modeling, Analysis, and Simulation of Computer and Telecommunication Systems (MASCOTS 2005), Atlanta Georgia, September 27-29 (2005)
3. Castel-Taleb, H., Mokdad, L., Pekergin, N.: Loss rates bounds for IP switches in MPLS networks. In: ACS/IEEE International Conference on Computer Systems and Applications, AICCSA 2006, Dubai/Sharjah, UAE, March 8-11 (2006)

4. Castel-Taleb, H., Mokdad, L., Pekergin, N.: Aggregated bounding Markov processes applied to the analysis of tandem queues. In: Second International Conference on Performance Evaluation Methodologies and Tools, ACM Sigmetrics, ValueTools 2007, Nantes, France, October 23-25 (2007)
5. Castel-Taleb, H., Pekergin, N.: Weak stochastic comparisons for performability verification. In: Al-Begain, K., Fiems, D., Horváth, G. (eds.) ASMTA 2009. LNCS, vol. 5513, pp. 294–308. Springer, Heidelberg (2009)
6. Castel-Taleb, H., Pekergin, N.: Stochastic monotonicity in queueing networks. In: Bradley, J.T. (ed.) EPEW 2009. LNCS, vol. 5652, pp. 116–130. Springer, Heidelberg (2009)
7. Castel-Taleb, H., Pekergin, N.: Stochastic monotonicity for the comparison of multidimensionnal Markov chains (submitted)
8. Doisy, M.: Comparaison de processus Markoviens. PHD thesis, Univ. de Pau et des pays de l'Adour 92
9. Economous, A.: Necessary and sufficient condition for the stochastic comparison of Jackson Networks. Prob. in the Engineering and Informational Sciences 17, 143–151 (2003)
10. Fourneau, J.M., Pekergin, N.: An algorithmic approach to stochastic bounds. In: Calzarossa, M.C., Tucci, S. (eds.) Performance 2002. LNCS, vol. 2459, p. 64. Springer, Heidelberg (2002)
11. Lindvall, T.: Lectures on the coupling method. Wiley series in Probability and Mathematical statistics (1992)
12. Lindvall, T.: Stochastic monotonicities in Jackson queueing networks. Prob. in the Engineering and Informational Sciences 11, 1–9 (1997)
13. Lopez, F.J., Martinez, S., Sanz, G.: Stochastic domination and Markovian couplings. Adv. Appl. Prob. 32, 1064–1076 (2000)
14. Massey, W.: An Operator-analytic approach to the Jackson network. J. Appl. Prob. 21, 379–393 (1984)
15. Massey, W.: Stochastic orderings for Markov processes on partially ordered spaces. Mathematics of Operations Research 12(2) (May 1987)
16. Massey, W.: A family of bounds for the transient behavior of a Jackson network. J. Appl. Prob., 543–549 (1986)
17. Mokdad, L., Castel-Taleb, H.: Stochastic comparisons: a methodology for the performance evaluation of fixed and mobile networks. Computer Communications 31(17) (November 2008)
18. Shaked, M., Shantikumar, J.G.: Stochastic Orders and Their Applications. Academic Press, Boston (1994)
19. Stoyan, D.: Comparison methods for queues and other stochastics models. J. Wiley and Son, Chichester (1976)
20. Van Dijk, N.M.: Queueing networks and product forms, a system approach. John Wiley and Sons, Chichester (1993)

Appendix

The stochastic comparisons are established by means of two methods on partially ordered state spaces: increasing sets, and the coupling. The goal of stochastic comparisons is to generate stochastic orderings, which can be defined as a relation order between random variables (probability distributions), or stochastic processes.

A   Stochastic Ordering Theory

Let E be a discrete, and countable state space, and $\preceq$ be at least a preorder (reflexive, transitive but not necessarily an anti-symmetric binary relation) on E. We suppose that E is a multidimensional state space, where each component is discrete, as it is the case in the queueing models. Several stochastic orderings can be defined, the most known is the strong stochastic ordering $\preceq_{st}$, but also weaker orderings can be defined: $\preceq_{wk}$, and $\preceq_{wk*}$ [15]. The strong stochastic ordering is equivalent to a sample path ordering [19], the $\preceq_{wk}$ ordering leads to a comparison of tail distributions, and $\preceq_{wk*}$ serves the same role for cumulative distribution functions [15,14]. Different formalisms can be used to define a stochastic ordering: increasing functions, and increasing sets [19]. We focus on the increasing set formalism in this paper, as we will use it for the comparison of the processes in this paper. Let $\Gamma \subseteq E$, we denote by $\Gamma \uparrow = \{y \in E \mid y \succeq x, x \in \Gamma\}$.

Definition 1. Γ *is called an increasing set if and only if* $\Gamma = \Gamma \uparrow$

From the general definition of an increasing set, three stochastic orderings have been defined from families of increasing sets [15]. The first one is $\Phi_{st}(E)$ which is defined from all the increasing sets of E:

$$\Phi_{st}(E) = \{\text{all increasing sets on } E\} \qquad (12)$$

The other families $\Phi_{wk}(E)$ and $\Phi_{wk*}(E)$ are defined from particular kinds of increasing sets.

$$\Phi_{wk}(E) = \{\{x\} \uparrow, \ x \in E\} \ and \ \Phi_{wk*}(E) = \{E - \{x\} \downarrow, \ x \in E\} \qquad (13)$$

Where $\{x\} \downarrow = \{y \in E \mid y \preceq x\}$. We can easily derive the following inclusion relations between the families of increasing sets [15]:

Proposition 3

$$\Phi_{wk}(E) \subset \Phi_{st}(E) \ and \ \Phi_{wk*}(E) \subset \Phi_{st}(E)$$

As it is mentioned in [15], increasing sets of $\Phi_{st}(E)$ are generated by successive unions of increasing sets of $\Phi_{wk}(E)$. As it is explained in [15], a family $\Phi(E)$ of increasing sets induces a stochastic ordering if and only if it is a strongly separating family of increasing sets. Let X and Y be two random variables defined on E, and their probability measures given respectively by the probability vectors p and q where $p[i] = Prob(X = i)$, $\forall i \in E$ (resp. $q[i] = Prob(Y = i)$, $\forall i \in E$). If $\Phi(E)$ represents one of these families ($\Phi_{st}(E)$, $\Phi_{wk}(E)$, or $\Phi_{wk*}(E)$), then a stochastic ordering $\preceq_\Phi$ representing ($\preceq_{st}$, $\preceq_{wk}$, or $\preceq_{wk*}$) can be defined as follows [15]:

Definition 2

$$X \preceq_\Phi Y \Leftrightarrow \sum_{x \in \Gamma} p[x] \le \sum_{x \in \Gamma} q[x], \forall \Gamma \in \Phi(E) \qquad (14)$$

From the inclusion relations between families of increasing sets, we have the following relations between the random variables:

Proposition 4

$$X \preceq_{st} Y \Rightarrow X \preceq_{wk} Y \text{ and } X \preceq_{wk^*} Y$$

Next, we expand the stochastic ordering theory to Continuous Time Markov Chains (CTMC). As we have explained in this paper, stochastic comparison of Markov processes is very efficient for computing performance measures bounds on stationary or transient distributions. The increasing set theory could be very useful, with the different kinds of increasing sets. In fact, sometimes when the strong ordering could not be defined, then less constrained orderings called weaker orderings could be defined for deriving performance measure bounds.

B   Stochastic Comparisons of Markov Processes

Let $\{X(t), t \geq 0\}$ (resp. $\{Y(t), t \geq 0\}$) be a CTMC defined on E. We give the definition of the $\preceq_\Phi$-stochastic comparison [15]:

Definition 3. *We say that* $\{X(t), t \geq 0\} \preceq_\Phi \{Y(t), t \geq 0\}$

$$\text{if } X(0) \preceq_\Phi Y(0) \Longrightarrow X(t) \preceq_\Phi Y(t), \forall t > 0 \tag{15}$$

In the case of the $\preceq_{st}$ ordering, the coupling method can be used for the stochastic comparison of CTMCs. As presented in [11], [12], it remains to define two CTMCs: $\{\widehat{X}(t), t \geq 0\}$ and $\{\widehat{Y}(t), t \geq 0\}$ governed by the same infinitesimal generator matrix as respectively $\{X(t), t \geq 0\}$, and $\{Y(t), t \geq 0\}$, representing different realizations of these processes with different initial conditions. The following theorem establishes the $\preceq_{st}$-comparison using the coupling [11]:

Theorem 1
$$\{X(t), t \geq 0\} \preceq_{st} \{Y(t), t \geq 0\} \tag{16}$$

if there exists the coupling $\{(\widehat{X}(t), \widehat{Y}(t)), t \geq 0\}$ *such that:*

$$\widehat{X}(0) \preceq \widehat{Y}(0) \Rightarrow \widehat{X}(t) \preceq \widehat{Y}(t), \forall t > 0 \tag{17}$$

If we suppose that $\{X(t), t \geq 0\}$ (resp. $\{Y(t), t \geq 0\}$) is a CTMC with infinitesimal generator matrix A (resp. B), then we present the theorem of the $\preceq_\Phi$-stochastic comparison of CTMCs using increasing set formalism (theorem 3.4 in [15]):

Theorem 2. *If the following conditions are verified:*

1. $X(0) \preceq_\Phi Y(0)$
2. $\{X(t), t \geq 0\}$ *or* $\{Y(t), t \geq 0\}$ *is* $\preceq_\Phi$*-monotone*
3.

$$\forall x \in E, \sum_{z \in \Gamma} A(x, z) \leq \sum_{z \in \Gamma} B(x, z), \ \forall \Gamma \in \Phi(E) \tag{18}$$

then

$$\{X(t), t \geq 0\} \preceq_\Phi \{Y(t), t \geq 0\} \tag{19}$$

The monotonicity is a property used in this theorem, corresponding to an increasing (decreasing) in time of a process. Next we give the definition of the $\preceq_\Phi$-monotonicity (see definition 5.5.1 in [19]).

Definition 4. *We say that* $\{X(t), t \geq 0\}$ *is* $\preceq_\Phi - monotone$ *if:*

$$X(t) \preceq_\Phi (\succeq_\Phi) X(s), \forall t, s \in \mathbb{R}^+ \mid t < s \tag{20}$$

The $\preceq_{st}$ monotonicity of $\{X(t), t \geq 0\}$ can be proved from its generator Q as follows [15]:

Theorem 3. $\{X(t), t \geq 0\}$ *is* $\preceq_{st}$- *monotone, if and only if*
$\forall \Gamma \in \Phi_{st}(E), \ \forall x \preceq y \in E \mid x, y \in \Gamma$ *or* $x, y \notin \Gamma$ *we have :*

$$\sum_{z \in \Gamma} Q(x, z) \leq \sum_{z \in \Gamma} Q(y, z)$$

In [6], we generalize the theorem 3 to the stochastic ordering $\preceq_\Phi$. From the implication relations between stochastic orderings (see prop. 4), we can deduce the following proposition [7]

Proposition 5. *If* $\{X(t), t \geq 0\}$ *is* $\preceq_{st}$*-monotone then it is* $\preceq_{wk}$*-monotone and* $\preceq_{wk^*}$*-monotone.*

Searching for Tight Performance Bounds in Feed-Forward Networks

Andreas Kiefer, Nicos Gollan, and Jens B. Schmitt

Distributed Computer Systems Lab (DISCO), TU Kaiserslautern, Germany

Abstract. Computing tight performance bounds in feed-forward networks under general assumptions about arrival and server models has turned out to be a challenging problem. Recently it was even shown to be NP-hard [1]. We now address this problem in a heuristic fashion, building on a procedure for computing provably tight bounds under simple traffic and server models. We use a decomposition of a complex problem with more general traffic and server models into a set of simpler problems with simple traffic and server models. This set of problems can become prohibitively large, and we therefore resort to heuristic methods such as Monte Carlo. This shows interesting tradeoffs between performance bound quality and computational effort.

1   Motivation and Related Work

When designing or analyzing a network, one of the most important aspects is its performance under various load conditions. A number of methods for that kind of analysis have been devised, among them network calculus, which describes methods for calculating performance bounds, i.e., describing worst-case behavior.

Network calculus is a $(\min, +)$ system theory for deterministic queuing systems which builds on the calculus for network delay in [2,3]. The important *service curve* concept was introduced in [4,5,6,7,8] to perform efficient analysis of tandem queues. Scaling properties in the number of traversed network nodes are linear, as is shown in [9], a phenomenon also known as pay bursts only once phenomenon [10]. Detailed descriptions of the $(\min, +)$ algebra and of network calculus can be found in [11] and [10,12].

Network calculus has found numerous applications, most prominently in the Internet's Quality of Service (QoS) proposals IntServ and DiffServ [13,14], but it has also become a valuable method in other fields, such as wireless sensor networks [15,16], switched Ethernets [17], Systems-on-Chip (SoC) [18], or even to speed-up simulations [19].

However, as a relatively young theory, compared to, e.g., traditional queueing theory, there is also a number of challenges network calculus still has to master. A very tough challenge is found in the treatment of non-tandem topologies with aggregate multiplexing of multiple flows. While this has been addressed from the beginning [3], there are still many open issues. For aggregate multiplexing in general network topologies there is a very fundamental issue about

B. Müller-Clostermann et al. (Eds.): MMB & DFT 2010, LNCS 5987, pp. 227–241, 2010.
© Springer-Verlag Berlin Heidelberg 2010

the circumstances under which a finite delay bound exists at all [20,21]. In [22] a sufficient condition for stability in general network topologies and an explicit delay bound are given. Extensions of this approach are provided in [23,24]. Yet, for larger networks this severely limits the utilization of the network since the maximum allowable utilization is inversely proportional to the network diameter. The problems in the analysis of general topologies arise from cyclic dependencies between flows and the resulting difficulties in bounding their network-internal burstiness. A special class of topologies which avoids those problems are feed-forward networks, which are known to be stable for all utilizations ≤ 1 [3]. In this paper, we focus on this class of networks. While many networks are obviously not feed-forward, many important instances like switched networks, wireless sensor networks, or MPLS networks with multipoint-to-point label switched paths are, or can be made, feed-forward by using, e.g., the turn-prohibition algorithm [25].

In feed-forward networks, there has been some work on aggregate multiplexing recently: [26] treats the case of feed-forward networks under FIFO multiplexing for token-bucket constrained flows and rate-latency servers, showing that the derived left-over service curve for a flow of interest is again of the rate-latency type with minimally possible latency. [27] shows that this does not result in a tight delay bound, and derives tight delay bounds under knowledge about the arrival curve of the flow of interest for the special case of sink-trees and, again, under token bucket constrained flows and rate-latency servers. Another work [28] also investigates sink-tree networks, but now under dual token-bucket constrained flows and constant rate servers, for which delay bounds are derived by summing per-node bounds, which unsurprisingly does not yield tight bounds but is still reported as being close under practical conditions.

Besides being very specific with respect to traffic and server models, all of the above work assumes FIFO aggregate multiplexing. However in practice, as argued in [29], many devices cannot be accurately described by FIFO because packets arriving at the output queue from different input ports may experience different delays when traversing a node. This is due to the fact that many networking devices like routers are implemented using input-output buffered crossbars and/or multistage interconnections between input and output ports. Hence, packet reordering on the aggregate level is a frequent event (unlike on the flow level) and should not be neglected in modelling. Therefore, in this work we drop the FIFO multiplexing assumption and make essentially no assumptions on the way aggregates are multiplexed at servers, i.e. we assume arbitrary multiplexing also known as general or blind multiplexing [2,10]. On the level of a single flow, however, we still assume FIFO. This assumption is sometimes called FIFO-per-microflow [30] or locally FCFS multiplexing [2].

Work on bounds for networks with arbitrary multiplexing has become frequent only recently, but there are already several important results. Some older results are reported in [10] (see Section 2), and there is some work on the burstiness increase due to arbitrary multiplexing at a single node [31]. Adversarial queueing theory [32] provides results for general networks, however it is more concerned with network stability than with the determination of performance bounds. In previous work related to network calculus tool support, we have proposed and implemented a number of network calculus analysis methods for arbitrary multiplexing in feed-forward networks [33], but as will be demonstrated here, they were not the ultimate solution. A similar approach has been taken in [34], regarding a wider class of traffic and service specifications.

The goal of our work is to search for tight delay bounds in feed-forward networks of arbitrary multiplexers. With respect to traffic and server models we address a more general case than previous work on FIFO multiplexing, in particular we assume piecewise linear concave arrival curves and convex service curves, which encompass the majority of practical traffic and server models. Compared to our previous work in [35], we now try to solve an issue that arises from the algebra used in network calculus, which, while allowing for an easy analysis, hides certain properties, and may lead to pessimistic bounds.

After a short introduction to network calculus, we present an approach to network analysis based on an optimization problem, and show how a solution to that problem can be approximated by heuristics. We show how the quality of the performance bounds obtained by that new method compares with traditional results.

2 Network Calculus Background

As network calculus is built around the notion of cumulative functions for input and output flows of data, the set of real-valued, non-negative, and wide-sense increasing functions passing through the origin plays a major role:

$$\mathcal{F} = \{f : \mathbb{R}^+ \to \mathbb{R}^+ \,|\, \forall t \geq s : f(t) \geq f(s), f(0) = 0\}$$

In particular, the input function $F(t)$ and the output function $F'(t)$, which cumulatively count the number of bits that are input to, respectively output from, a system $\mathcal{S}$, are in $\mathcal{F}$. Throughout the paper, we assume in- and output functions to be continuous in time and space. Note that this is not a general limitation as there exist transformations between discrete and continuous time models [10].

Definition 1. *(Min-plus Convolution and Deconvolution) The min-plus convolution* $\otimes$ *and deconvolution* $\oslash$ *of two functions* $f, g \in \mathcal{F}$ *are defined as*

$$(f \otimes g)(t) = \inf_{0 \leq s \leq t} \{f(t-s) + g(s)\}$$

$$(f \oslash g)(t) = \sup_{u \geq 0} \{f(t+u) - g(u)\}$$

It can be shown that the triple $(\mathcal{F}, \wedge, \otimes)$, where $\wedge$ denotes the pointwise minimum operator, constitutes a dioid [10]. Also, the min-plus convolution is a linear operator on the dioid $(\mathbb{R} \cup \{+\infty\}, \wedge, +)$, whereas the min-plus deconvolution is not. These algebraic characteristics result in a number of rules that apply to those operators, many of which can be found in [10,12]. Let us now turn to the performance characteristics of flows which can be bounded by network calculus means:

Definition 2. *(Backlog and Delay) Assume a flow with input function F that traverses a system S resulting in the output function F'. The backlog of the flow at time t is defined as*

$$x(t) = F(t) - F'(t)$$

Assuming FIFO delivery, the virtual delay for a bit input at time t is defined as

$$d(t) = \inf \{\tau \geq 0 : F(t) \leq F'(t + \tau)\}$$

Next, the arrival and departure processes specified by input and output functions are bounded based on the central network calculus concepts of arrival and service curves:

Definition 3. *(Arrival Curve) Given a flow with input function F a function $\alpha \in \mathcal{F}$ is an arrival curve for F iff*

$$\forall t, s \geq 0, s \leq t : F(t) - F(t - s) \leq \alpha(s) \Leftrightarrow F \leq F \otimes \alpha$$

A typical example of an arrival curve is given by an affine arrival curve $\gamma_{r,b}(t) = b + rt, t > 0$ and $\gamma_{r,b}(t) = 0, t \leq 0$ which corresponds to token-bucket traffic regulation.

Definition 4. *(Service Curve) If the service provided by a system S for a given input function F results in an output function F' we say that S offers a service curve β iff*

$$F' \geq F \otimes \beta$$

A typical example of a service curve is given by a so-called rate-latency function $\beta_{R,T}(t) = R [t - T]^+$, where $[x]^+ := x \vee 0$, and $\vee$ denotes the maximum operator. A number of systems fulfill, however, a stricter definition of the service curve [10], which is particularly useful as it permits certain derivations that are not feasible under the more general minimum service curve model.

Definition 5. *(Strict Service Curve) Let $\beta \in \mathcal{F}$. System S offers a strict service curve β to a flow if during any backlogged period of duration u, the output of the flow is at least equal to $\beta(u)$.*

Note that any strict service curve is also a service curve, but not the other way around. Many schedulers offer strict service curves, for example most of the generalized processor sharing-emulating schedulers offer a strict service curve of the rate-latency type. Strict service curves will play a crucial role in this paper, since they, in contrast to service curves, allow to bound the maximum backlogged period of a system. More specifically, that bound $\bar{d}$ is given as the non-zero intersection point between arrival and service curve, i.e. $\alpha(\bar{d}) = \beta(\bar{d})$.

Using those concepts it is possible to derive *tight* performance bounds on backlog, (virtual) delay and output:

Theorem 1. *(Performance Bounds) Consider a system S that offers a service curve β. Assume a flow F traversing the system has an arrival curve α. Then we obtain the following performance bounds:*

Fig. 1. General network topology. Arrival processes and service characteristics are labeled as described in Section 2. Flows are specified as $F_{i,j}$, where i and j denote the ingress and egress nodes. The analysis covers all nodes that the flow of interest F_{int} passes through.

Backlog: $\forall t : x(t) \leq (\alpha \oslash \beta)(0) =: v(\alpha, \beta)$
Delay: $\forall t : d(t) \leq \inf \{t \geq 0 : (\alpha \oslash \beta)(-t) \leq 0\} =: h(\alpha, \beta)$
Output (arrival curve α' for F'): $\alpha' = \alpha \oslash \beta$

One of the strongest results of network calculus (albeit being a simple consequence of the associativity of $\otimes$) is the concatenation theorem that enables us to investigate tandems of systems as if they were single systems:

Theorem 2. *(Concatenation Theorem for Tandem Systems) Consider a flow that traverses a tandem of systems S_1 and S_2. Assume that S_i offers a service curve β_i, $i = 1, 2$ to the flow. Then the concatenation of the two systems offers a service curve $\beta_1 \otimes \beta_2$ to the flow.*

Using the concatenation theorem, it is ensured that an end-to-end analysis of a tandem of servers still achieves tight performance bounds, which in general is not the case for an iterative per-node application of Theorem 1.

So far we have only covered the single flow case, the next result factors in the existence of other interfering flows. In particular, it states the minimum service curve available to a flow at a single node under cross-traffic from other flows at that node.

Theorem 3. *(Left-over Service Curve under Arbitrary Multiplexing) Consider a node multiplexing two flows 1 and 2 in arbitrary order. Assume that the node guarantees a* strict *minimum service curve β to the aggregate of the two flows. Assume that flow 2 has α_2 as an arrival curve. Then*

$$\beta^1 = [\beta - \alpha_2]^+$$

is a service curve for flow 1 if $\beta^1 \in \mathcal{F}$, often also called the left-over service *curve for the* flow of interest. *Note that we require the service curve to be strict. In [10], an example is given showing that the theorem otherwise would not hold.*

3   Optimization-Based Approach

To analyze a network as shown in Figure 1, conventional methods are the Separated Flow Analysis (SFA) and the Pay Multiplexing Only Once analysis, abbreviated PMOO-SFA since it is an extension of the SFA. A detailed discussion

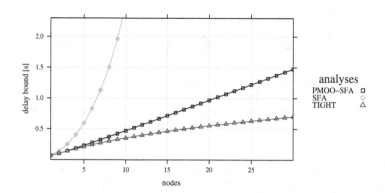

Fig. 2. Bound quality comparison. Results are taken from a feed-forward network at 50% utilization. "TIGHT" shows results of the method presented in [36].

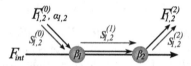

Fig. 3. Sample topology that exposes the weakness of the PMOO-SFA. Also shown are the slack variables $s_{i,j}^{(n)}$ that are used by the optimization-based approach. The indices i, j denote the ingress and egress servers of a flow, and (n) denotes the hop.

of those methods can be found in [33]. Those methods, as mentioned, offer relatively simple algebraic means to calculate delay bounds for a given feed-forward network, but as shown in [36,37], those bounds can be made arbitrarily pessimistic by choosing an antagonistic network topology. An example of numerical results comparing different analysis methods is shown in Figure 2. It is obvious that the delay bounds obtained by the SFA are exceedingly pessimistic, while PMOO results at least expose a saner growth behavior. In a similar manner, it can be shown that for some traffic characteristics, the PMOO yields arbitrarily worse results than the SFA, even for very simple topologies like the one shown in Figure 3.

We now introduce an approach based on the transformation of the problem to a system of linear programs that was first presented in [36]. The motivation for this new approach becomes obvious when exploring a weakness of the PMOO-SFA. While that analysis looks like a perfect application of network calculus principles, it can be shown that applying the convolution to obtain an end-to-end service curve for the flow of interest destroys information about the sequence of servers. While the commutativity of the convolution is algebraically nice, it also means that the burstiness of the traffic is always paid for at the rate of the slowest server, even if the structure of the network and the cross-traffic do not require it. While that is not a serious shortcoming in rather homogeneous networks, it becomes more of an issue in networks where servers are successively faster towards the sink.

To work around that shortcoming, we need to find a way to distribute the burst to the servers where it has to be paid, as opposed to the slowest server. To allow for that, slack variables are introduced to represent the accumulated burstiness up to a given server. Those variables are shown as $s_{i,j}^{(n)}$ in Figure 3.

From those slack variables and with constraints resulting from the traffic and service specifications, it is possible to construct a linear program that finds the left-over service curve for the flow of interest. A thorough discussion of generating the linear programs for a given network, as well as an example can be found in [37]. We will present the core result for analyzing networks with traffic adhering to arrival curves composed from a number of token-buckets, and service curves composed from a number of rate-latency curves, the *decomposition theorem*, along with a method to use it, as well as numerical results in the following sections.

4   Heuristic Search

When looking at the results so far, we are facing a dilemma: we can either choose to use computationally cheap algorithms at the expense of potentially highly pessimistic bounds, or we can achieve tight bounds at the cost of possibly prohibitively high costs.

As is often the case in such a situation, a heuristic approach seems promising, so we propose a new approach to search for tight bounds based on the following decomposition theorem (see [36] for the proof):

Theorem 4. *(Decomposition theorem) Let* $\bigwedge C$ *and* $\bigvee C$ *denote the minimum and maximum over a set* C *of curves. Then given piecewise linear concave arrival curves* $\alpha_i = \bigwedge_{k_i=1}^{n_i} \gamma_{r_{k_i}, b_{k_i}}$ *for each interfering flow* $i = 1, \ldots, n$ *and piecewise linear convex service curves* $\beta_j = \bigvee_{l_j=1}^{m_j} \beta_{R_{l_j}, T_{l_j}}$ *for each node* $j = 1, \ldots, m$ *on the path of the flow of interest, the left-over service curve for the flow of interest is given by*

$$\beta^{l.o.} \geq \bigvee_{i=1}^{n} \bigvee_{j=1}^{m} \bigvee_{k_i=1}^{n_i} \bigvee_{l_j=1}^{m_j} \beta_{\{k_i\},\{l_i\}}^{l.o.} \tag{1}$$

where $\beta_{\{k_i\},\{l_j\}}^{l.o.}$ *are end-to-end left-over service curves for a specific combination of a single token bucket per interfering flow and a single rate-latency curve per node.*

This leads to a set of linear programs that have to be solved, since each combination of arrival and service segment generates one. For piecewise linear curves, we get systems of $\prod_{i=1}^{n} \prod_{j=1}^{m} n_i m_j$ programs. So if we assume for example arrivals adhering to a T-Spec curve (i.e., two segments), and m_j-segment service curves for two flows ($n = 2$) over m servers, we get $(2m)^{2m_j}$ linear programs, so the problem size is polynomial in the number of nodes, but exponential in the number of segments in the arrival and service curves. This means a large number of linear programs with a discrete search space.

Since a complete coverage of such a huge search space would mean an extreme expense of computational resources, we decided on a heuristic approach.

4.1 Monte Carlo Search

For reference, we implemented a pure Monte Carlo search. That method does not make any assumptions about the structure of the search space, and is relatively easy to implement. The search space consists of the token-bucket and rate-latency segments the arrival and service curves are composed of, and one iteration of the Monte Carlo method just picks a random segment of each arrival curve and service curve, and calculates a delay for the resulting left-over service curve.

While that approach may lead to some intermediate infinite delay values when the arrival curve segments have a higher rate than the service curve segments, those results will be discarded as soon as a feasible combination is encountered.

4.2 Hooke and Jeeves "Direct Search"

For our heuristic search, we combined the Monte Carlo search with a local search algorithm, the "Direct Search" by Hooke and Jeeves [38] (H-J). This search minimizes a function $S(\phi)$ of several arguments $\phi = (\phi_1, \ldots, \phi_k)$ that can be interpreted as a k-dimensional space. The strategy is to vary the arguments of ϕ until a minimum of $S(\phi)$ is found. Here, we are minimizing the delay bound.

The algorithm is separated into two important phases. The first phase is to acquire knowledge of the behaviour of $S(\phi)$. Therefore, the neighbourhood of a point is explored to establish a pattern of movement for which it is likely to find a lesser value. Each exploratory move is expected to be simple, that means each move varies only a single argument ϕ_i at a time by first increasing and afterwards decreasing it by the current step size Δ.

The second phase applies the resulting pattern to the point with the lowest value of $S(\phi)$ found up to that point. If that pattern move is successful, i.e., the corresponding functional value is lower, then the new point is the base point for the next exploration. Otherwise, the exploration starts from the point with the minimal functional value so far. The regularly performed exploration revises the pattern continually. If the exploration is a failure, the current step size Δ is reduced by a reduction factor $\rho < 1$ until the minimum step size δ is reached.

Figure 4 illustrates the process. Starting at an arbitrarily chosen base point, both the increase of the first and second dimension ϕ_1 and ϕ_2 are successful. The acquired pattern is used for the following pattern move to get to the next base point. At each base point, the exploration phase starts again to revise the pattern and, in this example, leads to a changed direction and a new base point. The revised pattern is applied, but the move is a failure, so the next base point is set to the last successful move, and the exploration phase continues from there. The search now stops because no successful move can be made.

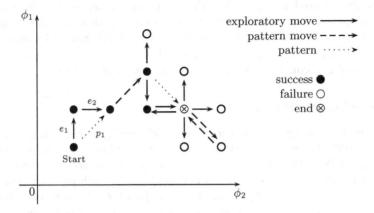

Fig. 4. Illustration of the moves taken by the Hooke and Jeeves optimization method. Exploratory moves to the top/right are steps of size $+\Delta$, and $-\Delta$ towards the bottom/left. The first two exploratory moves e_1 and e_2 establish the pattern p_1 which is then used for the first pattern move.

To apply the H-J algorithm to our workspace, we need to map the arrival and service curves to the k dimensions ϕ_i and define how to increase and decrease it by the step size Δ. Each dimension will contain a list composed of segments of individual curves. If, for example, a dimension consists of two arrival curves, α_1 with 2 token-bucket components and α_2 with 3 token-bucket components, then the dimension is made up from lists $[i_1, i_2]$ with $i_1 \in \{0, 1\}$ and $i_2 \in \{0, 1, 2\}$ as the zero-based indices of the token-bucket components of the individual curves. Stepping through such a dimension is implemented through an appropriate enumeration scheme.

We analyze the Optimization-Based Approach (OBA) with two mappings of curves to dimensions:

- A two-dimensional mapping (OBA-HJTwo), using one dimension to represent all arrival curves, and the other for the services.
- A multi-dimensional mapping (OBA-HJMulti) with still only one dimension for the services, but the arrivals are handled as one dimension for each ingress node.

5   Results

For the numerical experiments, our network calculus tool, the DISCO Network Calculator [39,40] was extended significantly to perform the decomposition and generation of the linear programs. The generated programs were handed off to lp_solve [41], but other linear solvers can also be used by implementing an interface. The implementation involved major refactoring, and we are planning to make that implementation publicly available with an upcoming new release.

The hardware used for the calculations was similar to commonly available desktop computers, running on Intel's Core 2 architecture Xeons. An optimization run with 15 nodes used only up to $1.1GB$ of RAM. Since the implementations of the DNC and lp_solve are single-threaded, a single instance of the problem would run comparably on common off-the-shelf hardware.

5.1   Experimental Design

For our experiments, we used the general network topology as shown in Figure 1. This is a simplified view of the network from the flow of interest's perspective and implies that all flows that share the same ingress and egress node are seen as only one flow. We assumed a fully occupied network – so for each pair of nodes (i, j) with $i \leq j$ there was a flow $F_{i,j}$ – and realistic data flow characteristics for our workload. Hence, to generate arrival curves for the cross-traffic, we have chosen the following setup. At first arbitrary T-SPECs [42] (M, p, r, b) are generated to simulate realistic envelopes. Each T-SPEC is constrained by the following constant parameters burst size $b = 1Mb$, maximum packet size $M = 1500bit$, and sustained rate $r = 1Mbps$. The peak rate p is arbitrarily chosen amongst 18 fixed values between $p_{max} = 10Mbps$ and $p_{min} = 1.5Mbps$. For each flow $F_{i,j}$, 32 random T-SPECs are added up.

Each node offers a strict rate-latency service curve with a latency of $0.1ms$ and a service rate dimensioned so that a target utilization of 50% is achieved. The flow of interest is constrained by a token-bucket with a burstiness of $b = 8Mb$ and a rate of $r = 1Mbps$.

In the experiment we compare, under a varying number of server nodes, the SFA as a representative of the traditional methods, and the heuristic methods OBA-MC (Monte Carlo), OBA-HJTwo, and OBA-HJMulti as described in Section 4.

For the runtime, there is a tradeoff to be made between the search space and the number of points sampled by the heuristics. Regardless of the maximum number of combinations, MC samples always 5000 points, even in topologies with less than three nodes (in those cases, we achieve a maximum coverage of over 100%). Since the "intelligent" optimization methods can stop early if they get trapped in a local minimum, there would be a disparity if we had strict limits for the number of starting points and the maximum number of steps. We decided to let the H-J methods run for the same number of points as the MC search with a maximum of 50 steps from a given starting point, and repeat this until it did 5000 steps, so those methods sample upwards of 100 starting points.

All experiments were repeated 20 times with new randomly generated traffic and service characteristics.

5.2   Evaluation

The delay bounds for different methods over number of nodes are shown in Figure 5, connecting the mean values for visual reference. Overall, the results of the heuristic methods look very promising, and expose similar growth properties for

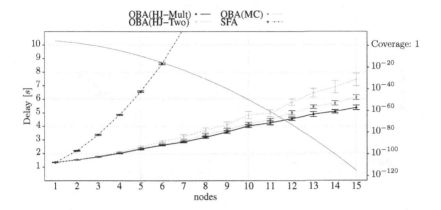

Fig. 5. Comparison of delay bound quality stating 95% confidence level. Also shown is the coverage of the search space on a logarithmic scale (decreasing series). From best to worst, the delay bounds are: multi-dimensional H-J, Monte Carlo, 2-dimensional H-J, and SFA.

the delay bound as the delay bounds obtained by complete coverage in Figure 2, even though they only cover a small part of the search space.

When comparing the results of the Direct Search methods with the pure Monte Carlo search, we see two trends:

It can be said with 95% confidence, that from 12 nodes on, the HJMulti method does significantly better than Monte Carlo. For 8 to 11 nodes the mean differs, but we cannot make a clear statement with 95% confidence. The figure also shows, that there is a difference between H-J with two and multiple dimensions, which is significant with 95% confidence for 4 nodes and up.

However, the two-dimensional direct search has a tendency to yield worse results than Monte Carlo. This can be explained by taking a look at the different structure or the search spaces. Because in our setting, each service curve has only one rate-latency component, that dimension will not change during exploration. Grouping all arrival curves in only one dimension in the two-dimensional approach will then severely restrict the exploration steps.

The figure also shows another metric: coverage of the search space. For each number of nodes, the mean coverage of the corresponding replications is drawn. It becomes obvious that with an increasing number of nodes, only a miniscule portion of all possible combinations can be examined; the runtime savings compared to a thorough search for the best bound can be estimated from that fraction when looking at the runtime behavior.

Figure 6 shows a comparison between the median values of the computation time of the analysis methods over the number of nodes: since the calculations are very much the same for the optimization-based methods, the runtime only varies slightly. Overall, SFA has an advantage in that regard, since it does not suffer from combinatorial explosion like the other methods do. Although the runtime scales quadratically, the increase is irrelevant for the networks examined here.

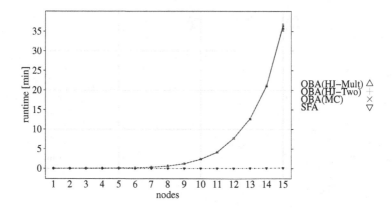

Fig. 6. Comparison of calculation time over the number of nodes with 95% confidence level

Table 1. Delay bound and runtime comparison for 15 nodes

analysis	mean delay bound [s]	median runtime [min]
SFA	81.360	0.162
OBA-HJTwo	7.443	36.950
OBA-MC	6.140	36.784
OBA-HJMulti	5.386	36.389

The important question is how much of an advantage the intelligent methods can draw from the increased amount of runtime. The comparison of the mean delay bound with 15 nodes in Table 1 shows, that we can achieve an about 76 seconds better delay bound with HJMulti, but for about 36 minutes longer runtime.

When judging that trade-off, it has to be considered that such a network analysis will likely be performed offline to help in the dimensioning of a network. In such a case, the quality of the results will be more important than a quick calculation, since a pessimistic bound would have to be countered with over-provisioning of the infrastructure. That would mean deploying more expensive hardware, or just hardware with a higher energy consumption, making projects more expensive to deploy and to maintain.

In that light, the proposed heuristics all appear very capable of providing good-quality bounds in an acceptable timeframe. The multi-dimensional Hooke and Jeeves direct search yields the best results of the methods we examined, at no runtime overhead.

6   Conclusion

We have presented a novel method for finding performance bounds in feed-forward networks that does not make overly restrictive assumptions about arrival and server models. While tight bounds still remain elusive, this new approach shows far better behavior for the performance bounds as network size increases. Furthermore, only very general assumptions are made about the characteristics of data arrivals and server models, keeping it compatible with previous applications of network calculus. In the course of the work, our DISCO Network Calculator tool was extended to allow integration of new analysis methods more easily.

Numerical experiments show a good scaling behavior with respect to the delay bounds and calculation time in relation to the network size. Even though the computational complexity increases exponentially if the traffic and service specifications become complex, it remains polynomial with the network diameter. The heuristics used for finding the best bounds hold up favorably while only searching a diminuitive portion of the search space, and fairly simple methods such as Monte Carlo can be used to achieve good results.

An interesting point that came up during experimentation was a highly irregular structure of the search space of the optimization problem that does not lend itself very well to local optimization schemes. More work towards an optimization scheme that suits the search space better, or a way to restructure it, would thus be advised to reach global optimization and thus better bounds.

Another area of interest is to find ways to simplify traffic curves as much as possible by culling completely irrelevant segments, or without impacting the resulting bounds too much. Since the overall complexity is exponential in the number of curve segments, such a reduction could massively speed up computation, but would require a careful error analysis when relevant segments are removed.

References

1. Bouillard, A., Jouhet, L., Thierry, E.: Tight performance bounds in the worst-case analysis of feed-forward networks. Tech. Rep. RR-7012, Unité de recherche INRIA Rennes (2009)
2. Cruz, R.L.: A calculus for network delay, Part I: Network elements in isolation. IEEE Transactions on Information Theory 37, 114–131 (1991)
3. Cruz, R.L.: A calculus for network delay, Part II: Network analysis. IEEE Transactions on Information Theory 37, 132–141 (1991)
4. Cruz, R.L.: Quality of service guarantees in virtual circuit switched networks. IEEE Journal on Selected Areas in Communications 13, 1048–1056 (1995)
5. Sariowan, H., Cruz, R.L., Polyzos, G.C.: Scheduling for quality of service guarantees via service curves. In: Proc. IEEE ICCCN, September 1995, pp. 512–520 (1995)
6. Chang, C.-S.: On deterministic traffic regulation and service guarantees: A systematic approach by filtering. IEEE Transactions on Information Theory 44, 1097–1110 (1998)
7. Le Boudec, J.-Y.: Application of network calculus to guaranteed service networks. IEEE Transactions on Information Theory 44, 1087–1096 (1998)
8. Agrawal, R., Cruz, R.L., Okino, C., Rajan, R.: Performance bounds for flow control protocols. IEEE/ACM Transactions on Networking 7, 310–323 (1999)

9. Ciucu, F., Burchard, A., Liebeherr, J.: A network service curve approach for the stochastic analysis of networks. In: Proc. ACM SIGMETRICS, June 2005, pp. 279–290 (2005)
10. Le Boudec, J.-Y., Thiran, P.: Calculus A Theory of Deterministic Queuing Systems for the Internet. LNCS, vol. 2050. Springer, Heidelberg (2001)
11. Baccelli, F., Cohen, G., Olsder, G.J., Quadrat, J.-P.: Synchronization and Linearity: An Algebra for Discrete Event Systems. Probability and Mathematical Statistics. John Wiley & Sons Ltd., Chichester (1992)
12. Chang, C.-S.: Performance Guarantees in Communication Networks. Telecommunication Networks and Computer Systems. Springer, Heidelberg (2000)
13. Braden, R., Clark, D., Shenker, S.: Integrated Services in the Internet Architecture: an Overview. RFC 1633, Informational (June 1994)
14. Blake, S., Black, D., Carlson, M., Davies, E., Wang, Z., Weiss, W.: An Architecture for Differentiated Service. RFC 2475 (Informational). Updated by RFC 3260 (December 1998)
15. Schmitt, J., Roedig, U.: Sensor network calculus - a framework for worst case analysis. In: Prasanna, V.K., Iyengar, S.S., Spirakis, P.G., Welsh, M. (eds.) DCOSS 2005. LNCS, vol. 3560, pp. 141–154. Springer, Heidelberg (2005)
16. Koubaa, A., Alves, M., Tovar, E.: Modeling and worst-case dimensioning of cluster-tree wireless sensor networks. In: Proc. IEEE RTSS, pp. 412–421 (2006)
17. Skeie, T., Johannessen, S., Holmeide, O.: Timeliness of real-time ip communication in switched industrial ethernet networks. IEEE Transactions on Industrial Informatics 2, 25–39 (2006)
18. Chakraborty, S., Kuenzli, S., Thiele, L., Herkersdorf, A., Sagmeister, P.: Performance evaluation of network processor architectures: Combining simulation with analytical estimation. Computer Networks 42(5), 641–665 (2003)
19. Kim, H., Hou, J.: Network calculus based simulation: theorems, implementation, and evaluation. In: Proc. IEEE INFOCOM (March 2004)
20. Chang, C.-S.: Stability, queue length and delay of deterministic and stochastic queueing networks. IEEE Transactions on Automatic Control 39, 913–931 (1994)
21. Andrews, M.: Instability of fifo in session-oriented networks. In: Proc. SODA, March 2000, pp. 440–447 (2000)
22. Charny, A., Le Boudec, J.-Y.: Delay bounds in a network with aggregate scheduling. In: Crowcroft, J., Roberts, J., Smirnov, M.I. (eds.) QofIS 2000. LNCS, vol. 1922, pp. 1–13. Springer, Heidelberg (2000)
23. Jiang, Y.: Delay bounds for a network of guaranteed rate servers with fifo aggregation. Computer Networks 40(6), 683–694 (2002)
24. Zhang, Z.-L., Duan, Z., Hou, Y.T.: Fundamental trade-offs in aggregate packet scheduling. In: Proc. ICNP, November 2001, pp. 129–137 (2001)
25. Starobinski, D., Karpovsky, M., Zakrevski, L.A.: Application of network calculus to general topologies using turn-prohibition. IEEE/ACM Transactions on Networking 11(3), 411–421 (2003)
26. Fidler, M., Sander, V.: A parameter based admission control for differentiated services networks. Computer Networks 44(4), 463–479 (2004)
27. Lenzini, L., Martorini, L., Mingozzi, E., Stea, G.: Tight end-to-end per-flow delay bounds in fifo multiplexing sink-tree networks. Performance Evaluation 63(9), 956–987 (2006)
28. Urvoy-Keller, G., Hébuterne, G., Dallery, Y.: Traffic engineering in a multipoint-to-point network. IEEE Journal on Selected Areas in Communications 20, 834–849 (2002)

29. Le Boudec, J.-Y., Charny, A.: Packet scale rate guarantee for non-fifo nodes. In: Proc. IEEE INFOCOM, June 2002, pp. 23–26 (2002)
30. Le Boudec, J.-Y., Rizzo, G.: Pay bursts only once does not hold for non-fifo guaranteed rate nodes. Performance Evaluation 62(1-4), 366–381 (2005)
31. Echagüe, J., Cholvi, V.: Worst case burstiness increase due to arbitrary aggregate multiplexing. In: Proc. of VALUETOOLS. ACM, New York (2006)
32. Rajagopal, S., Reisslein, M., Ross, K.W.: Packet multiplexers with adversarial regulated traffic. In: Proc. IEEE INFOCOM, March 1998, pp. 347–355 (1998)
33. Schmitt, J., Zdarsky, F.: The DISCO Network Calculator - a toolbox for worst case analysis. In: Proc. of VALUETOOLS. ACM, New York (2006)
34. Bouillard, A., Thierry, E.: An algorithmic toolbox for network calculus. Tech. Rep. RR-6094, Unité de recherche INRIA Rennes (2007)
35. Schmitt, J.B., Zdarsky, F.A., Martinovic, I.: Improving Performance Bounds in Feed-Forward Networks by Paying Multiplexing Only Once. In: 14th GI/ITG Conference on Measurement, Modeling, and Evaluation of Computer and Communication Systems (MMB 2008), Dortmund, Germany, GI/ITG (March 2008)
36. Schmitt, J.B., Zdarsky, F.A., Fidler, M.: Delay Bounds under Arbitrary Multiplexing: When Network Calculus Leaves You in the Lurch... In: 27th IEEE International Conference on Computer Communications (INFOCOM 2008), Phoenix, AZ, USA (April 2008)
37. Schmitt, J., Zdarsky, F., Fidler, M.: Delay bounds under arbitrary multiplexing. Technical Report 360/07, University of Kaiserslautern, Germany (July 2007)
38. Hooke, R., Jeeves, T.A.: "'Direct Search"' Solution of Numerical and Statistical Problems. J. ACM 8(2), 212–229 (1961)
39. Gollan, N., Zdarsky, F.A., Martinovic, I., Schmitt, J.B.: The DISCO Network Calculator. In: 14th GI/ITG Conference on Measurement, Modeling, and Evaluation of Computer and Communication Systems (MMB 2008), Dortmund, Germany, GI/ITG (2008)
40. Zdarsky, F., Schmitt, J., Gollan, N.: The DISCO Network Calculator, http://disco.informatik.uni-kl.de/content/Network_Calculator (last accessed 2009-10-09)
41. Eikland, K., Notebaert, P., et al.: lp_solve: A Mixed Integer Linear Programming (MILP) solver, http://sourceforge.net/projects/lpsolve/ (last accessed 2009-10-09)
42. Shenker, S., Partridge, C., Guerin, R.: Specification of Guaranteed Quality of Service. RFC 2212 (Proposed Standard) (September 1997)

An EM Algorithm for Markovian Arrival Processes Observed at Discrete Times

Lothar Breuer and Alfred Kume

University of Kent, Canterbury, UK
{l.breuer,a.kume}@kent.ac.uk

Abstract. The present paper contains a specification of the EM algorithm in order to fit an empirical counting process, observed at discrete times, to a Markovian arrival process. The given data are the numbers of observed events in disjoint time intervals. The underlying phase process is not observable. An exact numerical procedure to compute the E and M steps is given.

1 Introduction

Markovian arrival processes have been introduced by [25] and [21]. They have extensively been used as models for input streams to queueing systems (for a survey see [22]). Their appealing feature is that they are Markovian (and hence analytically tractable) on the one hand but very versatile (even dense in the class of point processes, see [3]) on the other hand. Although the concept of Markovian arrival processes (MAPs[1]) has gained widespread use in stochastic modelling of communication systems and other application areas, the quest for the best statistical methods of parameter estimation is far from finished yet.

A survey of estimation methods is given in [2]. His emphasis is on maximum likelihood estimation and its implementation via the EM algorithm (see [12]). [4] derived a fitting procedure for phase-type distributions via the EM algorithm. Markov chain Monte Carlo methods for the estimation of phase-type distributions (and functionals of these) are given in [5]. For a special case of MAPs, the Markov–modulated Poisson Process (MMPP), an EM algorithm has been developed in [27]. [6] specify the EM algorithm for the case of discretely observed Markov jump processes (MJPs). We will have to deal with discretely observed MJPs, for which even the observations at discrete times are partial only. [13] provide a simulation method for MMPPs. Our results extend this paper in so far in that we provide a maximum likelihood approach for a more general class of processes.

Statistical model fitting depends of course on the type of data observation that is available. In practice, we think of essentially two types of data:

(a) Exact times are recorded for each observed event.
(b) The arrival process is observed at a grid of discrete times only. This yields only the information of how many arrivals have occurred in each interval of the grid.

---

[1] There is some confusion in the literature about this acronym. It is used also for Markov–additive processes, which form a much more general class than Markovian arrival processes. However, since MAP is the most common abbreviation for Markovian arrival processes, we will use it in this article.

B. Müller-Clostermann et al. (Eds.): MMB & DFT 2010, LNCS 5987, pp. 242–258, 2010.
© Springer-Verlag Berlin Heidelberg 2010

We always assume that the underlying phase process is unobservable. An EM algorithm for case (a) has been given in [7]. The present paper contains a specification of the EM algorithm for MAPs in the case (b) of discrete time observation. One of the referees brought to our attention that a similar approach to ours is also considered in [28]. Our approach here differs essentially from theirs in the method of calculating the elementary steps of the EM algorithm. One of the methods proposed here is based on the matrix exponential function which is easily implementable. Other contributions in this area are either based on the method of moments approach or EM for data of type (a). See for example [8], [9], [11] [15] and [18].

In section 2, we review shortly the main definitions and notations for MAPs. The EM algorithm is specified to discretely observed MAPs with hidden phases in section 3. Exact expressions for the integrals appearing in the E–step are given in sections 4 and 5. In the remainder of this section, we describe the kind of data available from observations and give a short remark on estimating the order of the MAP which is to fit the empirical time series.

We assume to be in the following, for many applications typical, situation of data retrieval: An empirical counting process is observed at discrete times t_n, $n = 0, \ldots, N$, where $t_0 := 0$. To simplify later notation we assume that $t_n := n$. It will be apparent that this assumption of equidistant observation points is not necessary. We further assume that the observed point process is stationary in time. The only information that can be measured is the number of observed events in the interval $]t_{n-1}, t_n]$, denoted by z_n, $n = 1, \ldots, N$. Thus the given data has the form $z = (z_1, \ldots, z_N)$. Due to the result that MAPs are dense in the class of all point processes on the positive real axis (see [3]), the approach of model fitting by a MAP is reasonable. By the nature of the problem, no information is given on the underlying phase process, not even the number of phases.

Throughout this article, we fix the number of phases for the MAP model to be a known integer $m \geq 1$. Procedures for estimating the number m of phases are discussed in [29] for the MMPP.

Since the adaptation of the model increases with the assumed number of phases m, the likelihood gain at the ML estimates is always positive if we increase m by 1. If this gain is not bigger than some threshold value, we can assume that we have found the right value for m. This incremental method was proposed by [16]. The threshold value reflects the limit of accuracy beyond which the gain in model adaptation is not worth the additional computation time.

2 Markovian Arrival Processes

A Markovian arrival process is a homogeneous Markov process $\mathcal{Y} = (Y_t : t \geq 0)$ with state space $E = \mathbb{N}_0 \times \{1, \ldots, m\}$, where m is some positive integer, and a generator matrix of the (block) form

$$G = \begin{pmatrix} D_0 & D_1 & & \\ & D_0 & D_1 & \\ & & \ddots & \ddots \end{pmatrix}$$

In this generator, only the main and the first upper block diagonals have non–zero entries. Apart from that there are no restrictions for the matrices D_0 and D_1, except of course the generator conditions

$$(D_0 + D_1)\mathbf{1} = \mathbf{0}, \quad D_{0;ij} \geq 0 \quad \text{for } i \neq j, \quad D_{1;ij} \geq 0 \quad \text{for all } i, j$$

where $\mathbf{1}$ and $\mathbf{0}$ denote the vectors with all entries being ones and zeroes, respectively. In order to avoid absorbing states, we assume that $D_{0;ii}$ is strictly negative for all $i = 1, \ldots, m$.

As Y_t is two–dimensional, it is natural to write $\mathcal{Y} = (\mathcal{N}, \mathcal{J}) = ((N_t, J_t) : t \geq 0)$. The marginal processes $\mathcal{N}$ and $\mathcal{J}$ are called the counting process and the phase process associated with $\mathcal{Y}$. For any state $(n, i) \in E$, the first dimension is called the level and the second one is called the phase.

Under this interpretation, the entries $D_{0;ij}$ of D_0 give the infinitesimal transition rates among phases $\{1, \ldots, m\}$ without an arrival if $i \neq j$. The entries $D_{1;ij}$ of D_1 give the infinitesimal transition rates among phases accompanied by an arrival. The diagonal entries $D_{0;ii}$ are the negative parameters of the exponential sojourn times in any state (n, i), independently of $n \in \mathbb{N}_0$.

The special case of a Markov–modulated Poisson Process (MMMP), also called a Cox process, arises if D_1 is chosen to be a diagonal matrix. This has of course a large impact on the modelling power. The matrix D_1 governs correlations between inter–arrival times (which are crucial in many applications). If D_1 is restricted to be diagonal, there is no way to control these. This is the main reason why MMPPs can be employed only in special modelling situations.

The process has stationary increments if it starts in phase equilibrium π, which is determined as the stationary distribution of the phase process, i.e. by $\pi(D_0 + D_1) = \mathbf{0}$. As we wish to fit a stationary empirical point process by a MAP, we can hence assume that $\mathbb{P}(Y_0 = (0, i)) = \pi_i$.

The likelihood of a complete sample path x on $[0, t_N]$ under parameters $D_0 = (D_{0;ij})$ and $D_1 = (D_{1;ij})$ is given by

$$l(x|D_0, D_1) = \prod_{i=1}^{m} \exp\left(D_{0;ii} Z_i\right) \prod_{i=1}^{m} \prod_{j=1, j \neq i}^{m} D_{0;ij}^{B_{ij}} \prod_{i=1}^{m} \prod_{j=1}^{m} D_{1;ij}^{A_{ij}} \tag{1}$$

where $Z_i = Z_i(x)$ denotes the total time spent in phase i, $B_{ij} = B_{ij}(x)$ the number of jumps from phase i to phase j without arrival, and $A_{ij} = A_{ij}(x)$ the number of jumps from phase i to phase j with accompanying arrival. These variables form a sufficient statistic for likelihood based estimations. They can of course be decomposed into the sum of the respective variables over all the intervals $]t_{n-1}, t_n]$, $n = 1, \ldots, N$. Thus we can write

$$Z_i = \sum_{n=1}^{N} Z_i^n, \qquad B_{ij} = \sum_{n=1}^{N} B_{ij}^n, \qquad A_{ij} = \sum_{n=1}^{N} A_{ij}^n$$

where Z_i^n, B_{ij}^n, and A_{ij}^n refer to the nth interval.

Acknowledging the relation $D_{0;ii} = -\left(\sum_{j=1}^{m} D_{1;ij} + \sum_{j=1, j\neq i}^{m} D_{0;ij}\right)$, the maximum likelihood estimators $\hat{D}_0$ and $\hat{D}_1$ for the matrices D_0 and D_1 are then given by

$$\hat{D}_{0;ij} = \frac{B_{ij}}{Z_i}, \qquad \hat{D}_{1;ij} = \frac{A_{ij}}{Z_i}, \tag{2}$$

$$\hat{D}_{0;ii} = -\left(\sum_{j=1}^{m} \hat{D}_{1;ij} + \sum_{j=1, j\neq i}^{m} \hat{D}_{0;ij}\right) \tag{3}$$

for $1 \leq i, j \leq m$, see [1].

Remark 1

The above equation (1) shows that under the complete statistics, written as a row vector

$$T(x) = (Z_i(x) : i \leq m; B_{ij}(x) : i \neq j; A_{ij}(x) : i, j \leq m)$$

we are dealing with an exponential family in T and a parameter column vector

$$\zeta(D_0, D_1) = (D_{0;ii} : i \leq m; \log D_{0;ij} : i \neq j; \log D_{1;ij} : i, j \leq m)^T$$

where we define by natural extension $\log 0 := -\infty$ and $(-\infty) \cdot 0 := 0$. Under this setting we obtain

$$l(x|D_0, D_1) = \exp(T(x)\zeta(D_0, D_1)) \tag{4}$$

This shows that results obtained by [30] are applicable to the problem studied here. If for example, we have some missing information and we only observe $z = (z_1, \ldots, z_N)$ indicating the number of observed arrivals within each interval. The likelihood function is then obtained as

$$f(z|D_0, D_1) = \int_{\Omega_z} l(x|D_0, D_1)dx \tag{5}$$

where Ω_z is the set of all the possible paths with z_i arrivals at ith interval. Note that $f(z|D_0, D_1)$ is a likelihood with respect to the counting measure on N^{N_0}, all possible values for z. EM algorithm is based on maximizing with respect to D_0, D_1:

$$\int \log l(x|D_0, D_1)dF(x|z, (\hat{D}_0, \hat{D}_1)) = \frac{\int_{\Omega_z} T(x)\zeta(D_0, D_1)l(x|\hat{D}_0, \hat{D}_1)dx}{f(z|\hat{D}_0, \hat{D}_1)} \tag{6}$$

where $F(x|z, (\hat{D}_0, \hat{D}_1))$ is the conditional distribution of the full data x given the observed data z and $(\hat{D}_0, \hat{D}_1)$ are the current estimates of D_0, D_1.

One can easily maximize (6) with respect to D_0, D_1 by equating their partial derivatives to zero and by transferring the derivative sign inside the integration sign and proceeding as in [1]. We obtain similar equations as in (2) as in (3) with the only difference that Z_i, A_{ij} and B_{ij} there are replaced by $E_{(\hat{D}_0, \hat{D}_1)}(Z_i)$, $E_{(\hat{D}_0, \hat{D}_1)}(A_{ij})$ and $E_{(\hat{D}_0, \hat{D}_1)}(B_{ij})$: the corresponding conditional expectations with respect to $dF(x|z, \hat{D}_0, \hat{D}_1)$. This observation has two implications:

1. These expectations are proportional to the partial derivatives of the likelihood (5). Differentiating (5) with respect to $D_{0;ii}$ we obtain

$$\frac{\partial}{\partial D_{0;ii}} \int_{\Omega_z} l(x|D_0, D_1)dx = \int_{\Omega_z} Z_i(x)l(x|D_0, D_1)dx$$
$$= E_{(D_0,D_1)}(Z_i|z)f(z|D_0, D_1) \qquad (7)$$

Other expectations are similarly obtained. For example,

$$\frac{\partial}{\partial D_{0;ij}} \int_{\Omega_z} l(x|D_0, D_1)dx = \int_{\Omega_z} \frac{B_{ij}(x)}{D_{0;ij}} l(x|D_0, D_1)dx$$
$$= E_{(\hat{D}_0,\hat{D}_1)}(B_{ij}|z)\frac{f(z|D_0, D_1)}{D_{0;ij}}, \quad i \neq j \quad (8)$$

and analogously for $E_{(\hat{D}_0,\hat{D}_1)}(A_{ij})/D_{1;ij}$.

2. The ratios (as in (2) and (3)) of expectations $E_{(\hat{D}_0,\hat{D}_1)}(Z_i)$, $E_{(\hat{D}_0,\hat{D}_1)}(A_{ij})$ and $E_{(\hat{D}_0,\hat{D}_1)}(B_{ij})$ generate the expressions for the update steps needed for the EM algorithm. As indicated above, the EM steps are involving only the partial derivatives of the likelihood function. Hence EM in this case is a version of a gradient optimization.

In a more detailed approach, the explicit calculations of these EM steps are explained below. They can also be obtained using probabilistic arguments analogous to those in in [4].

3   The EM Algorithm

The typical property of observing time series derived from a MAP is that only the arrivals but not the phases can be seen. If the phases were observable, then one could apply the maximum likelihood estimators for finite state Markov processes (see [1]). To make things worse, we cannot even observe the exact arrival times. Thus we have a problem of estimation from incomplete data. For this type of statistical problems, the so–called EM algorithm has proven to be a good means of approximating the maximum likelihood estimator (see [12], [23] or [24]). The name EM algorithm stems from the alternating application of an expectation step (for E) and a maximization step (for M) which yield successively higher likelihoods of the estimated parameters.

In our case, the incomplete sample consists only of the sequence $z = (z_1, \ldots, z_N)$ indicating the number of observed arrivals within each interval. Denote the the maximal observed number of arrivals within one interval by M.

Given the parameters D_0 and D_1 as well as the stationary phase distribution π (which is determined by $D_0 + D_1$), the likelihood of the incomplete sample z is

$$f(z|D_0, D_1) = \pi \prod_{n=1}^{N} g(z_n|D_0, D_1)\mathbf{1} \qquad (9)$$

with $g(0|D_0, D_1) = e^{D_0}$ and

$$g(i|D_0, D_1) = \int_{u_0+\ldots+u_i=1} \left(\prod_{n=0}^{i-1} e^{D_0 u_n} D_1 \right) e^{D_0 u_i} \, du_0 \ldots du_{i-1}$$

for $i \geq 1$.

Assume that the estimates after the kth EM iteration are given by the matrices $(\hat{D}_0^{(k)}, \hat{D}_1^{(k)})$. Then in the first step of the $k+1$st cycle, the conditional expectations of the variables Z_i, A_{ij} and B_{ij} given the incomplete observation and the current estimates $(\hat{D}_0^{(k)}, \hat{D}_1^{(k)})$ are computed.

In order to simplify notations, define the column vectors

$$\eta_N := 1 \quad \text{and} \quad \eta_{n-1} := g(z_n|\hat{D}_0^{(k)}, \hat{D}_1^{(k)}) \, \eta_n = \prod_{i=n}^{N} g(z_i|\hat{D}_0^{(k)}, \hat{D}_1^{(k)})1 \quad (10)$$

iteratively for $2 \leq n \leq N$.

Since the empirical time series is observed in a stationary regime, we can set the phase distribution α_0 at time 0 to be the estimated phase equilibrium, i.e. satisfying $\alpha_0(\hat{D}_0^{(k)} + \hat{D}_1^{(k)}) = 0$. Then we define iteratively the row vectors

$$\alpha_{n+1} := \alpha_n \, g(z_{n+1}|\hat{D}_0^{(k)}, \hat{D}_1^{(k)}) = \pi \prod_{i=0}^{n} g(z_i|\hat{D}_0^{(k)}, \hat{D}_1^{(k)}) \quad (11)$$

for $0 \leq n \leq N-2$. Clearly $f(z|\hat{D}_0^{(k)}, \hat{D}_1^{(k)}) = \alpha_n \eta_n$.

We begin the E–step with the accumulated sojourn times in a phase i. These are given by

$$Z_i^{(k+1)} := E_{(\hat{D}_0^{(k)}, \hat{D}_1^{(k)})}(Z_i|z) = \sum_{n=1}^{N} E_{(\hat{D}_0^{(k)}, \hat{D}_1^{(k)})}(Z_i^n|z)$$

where $i = 1 \leq m$ and Z_i^n denotes the random variable of the total amount of time spent in phase i within the nth interval. The terms in the sum are given by

$$E_{(\hat{D}_0^{(k)}, \hat{D}_1^{(k)})}(Z_i^n|z) = \frac{\alpha_{n-1} \, c_{z_n}(i, i|\hat{D}_0^{(k)}, \hat{D}_1^{(k)}) \, \eta_n}{f\left(z|\hat{D}_0^{(k)}, \hat{D}_1^{(k)}\right)} \quad (12)$$

for all $0 \leq n \leq N$, where the matrix–valued functions c_n are defined as

$$c_0(i,j|\hat{D}_0^{(k)}, \hat{D}_1^{(k)}) := \int_0^1 \exp(\hat{D}_0^{(k)}u)e_i \cdot e_j^T \exp(\hat{D}_0^{(k)}(1-u))\, du \qquad (13)$$

$$c_n(i,j|\hat{D}_0^{(k)}, \hat{D}_1^{(k)}) := \int_{u_0+\ldots+u_n=1} \sum_{h=0}^{n} \left(\prod_{l=0}^{h-1} \exp(\hat{D}_0^{(k)}u_l)\hat{D}_1^{(k)} \right) \qquad (14)$$

$$\int_0^{u_h} \exp(\hat{D}_0^{(k)}v)e_i \cdot e_j^T \exp(\hat{D}_0^{(k)}(u_h-v))\, dv$$

$$\left(\prod_{l=h+1}^{n} \hat{D}_1^{(k)} \exp(\hat{D}_0^{(k)}u_l) \right) du_0 \ldots du_{n-1}$$

for $1 \leq i, j \leq m$ and $1 \leq n \leq M$. Here e_i denotes the ith canonical column base vector and e_i^T its transpose, i.e. the row vector. The empty products $\prod_{l=0}^{-1} \ldots$ and $\prod_{l=n+1}^{n} \ldots$ are defined as the identity matrix. The values for $c_n(i,j|\hat{D}_0^{(k)}, \hat{D}_1^{(k)})$ can be rewritten in terms of the $n+2$-dimensional simplex as

$$\sum_{h=0}^{n} \int_{u_0+\ldots+u_{n+1}=1} \left(\prod_{l=0}^{h-1} \exp(\hat{D}_0^{(k)}u_l)\hat{D}_1^{(k)} \right) \exp(\hat{D}_0^{(k)}u_h)e_i \cdot e_j^T \exp(\hat{D}_0^{(k)}u_{h+1})$$

$$\left(\prod_{l=h+2}^{n+1} \hat{D}_1^{(k)} \exp(\hat{D}_0^{(k)}u_l) \right) du_0 \ldots du_h \ldots du_n \qquad (15)$$

The derivation of (12) is completely analogous to the one in [4], p.439. Likewise,

$$B_{ij}^{(k+1)} := E_{(\hat{D}_0^{(k)}, \hat{D}_1^{(k)})}(B_{ij}|z) = \sum_{n=1}^{N} E_{(\hat{D}_0^{(k)}, \hat{D}_1^{(k)})}(B_{ij}^n|z)$$

with

$$E_{(\hat{D}_0^{(k)}, \hat{D}_1^{(k)})}(B_{ij}^n|z) = \frac{\hat{D}_{0;ij}^{(k)} \cdot \alpha_{n-1}\, c_{z_n}(i,j|\hat{D}_0^{(k)}, \hat{D}_1^{(k)})\, \eta_n}{f\left(z|\hat{D}_0^{(k)}, \hat{D}_1^{(k)}\right)} \qquad (16)$$

for $1 \leq n \leq N$ is derived using completely the same arguments as in [4], p.440. The E–step is completed by

$$A_{ij}^{(k+1)} := E_{(\hat{D}_0^{(k)}, \hat{D}_1^{(k)})}(A_{ij}|z) = \sum_{n=1}^{N} E_{(\hat{D}_0^{(k)}, \hat{D}_1^{(k)})}(A_{ij}^n|z)$$

with

$$E_{(\hat{D}_0^{(k)}, \hat{D}_1^{(k)})}(A_{ij}^n|z) = \begin{cases} 0, & z_n = 0 \\ \dfrac{\hat{D}_{1;ij}^{(k)} \cdot \alpha_{n-1}\, c_{z_n-1}(i,j|\hat{D}_0^{(k)}, \hat{D}_1^{(k)})\, \eta_n}{f\left(z|\hat{D}_0^{(k)}, \hat{D}_1^{(k)}\right)}, & z_n > 0 \end{cases} \qquad (17)$$

for $1 \leq n \leq N$.

Remark 2

It can be seen from the general expression of the likelihood function (9) that its partial derivatives with respect to the (i,j) entry of D_0 and D_1 respectively are

$$\frac{\partial f}{\partial D_{0;ij}} = \sum_{k=1}^{N} \alpha_{k-1} \frac{\partial g(z_k|D_0, D_1)}{\partial D_{0;ij}} \eta_k \quad \text{and} \quad \frac{\partial f}{\partial D_{1;ij}} = \sum_{k=1}^{N} \alpha_{k-1} \frac{\partial g(z_k|D_0, D_1)}{\partial D_{1;ij}} \eta_k.$$

Based on the fact that (see [14])

$$\frac{\partial \exp(D_0^{(k)} u_h)}{\partial D_{0;ij}^{(k)}} = u_h \int_0^1 \exp(t D_0^{(k)} u_h) e_i e_j^T \exp((1-t) D_0^{(k)} u_h) dt$$

$$= \int_0^{u_h} \exp(D_0^{(k)} v) e_i e_j^T \exp(D_0^{(k)} (u_h - v)) dv$$

and by transferring the derivative inside the integration sign one can easily see that

$$\frac{\partial g(n|D_0^{(k)}, D_1^{(k)})}{\partial D_{0;ij}^{(k)}} = c_n(i,j|D_0^{(k)}, D_1^{(k)}) \quad \text{and} \quad \frac{\partial g(n|D_0^{(k)}, D_1^{(k)})}{\partial D_{1;ij}^{(k)}} = c_{n-1}(i,j|D_0^{(k)}, D_1^{(k)}).$$

Therefore

$$\frac{\partial f(z|D_0^{(k)}, D_1^{(k)})}{\partial D_{0;ij}^{(k)}} = \sum_{r=1}^{N} \alpha_{r-1} c_{z_r}(i,j|, D_0^{(k)}, D_1^{(k)}) \eta_r$$

and

$$\frac{\partial f(z|D_0^{(k)}, D_1^{(k)})}{\partial D_{1;ij}^{(k)}} = \sum_{r=1}^{N} \alpha_{r-1} c_{z_r-1}(i,j|D_0^{(k)}, D_1^{(k)}) \eta_r.$$

Similarly, one could easily obtain the second or higher order derivatives of the likelihood. These derivatives can be easily adopted for the cases when there is some simple functional relationship between the entries of the parameter matrices $D_0^{(k)}$ and $D_1^{(k)}$.

Now, the next step of the $k + 1$st cycle of the EM consists of the computation of maximum likelihood estimates given the new (conditional but complete) statistic computed in the E–step. This can be done by simply replacing the variables in equations (2) and (3) by the conditional expectations computed above. This leads to re-evaluated estimates

$$\hat{D}_{0;ij}^{(k+1)} = \frac{B_{ij}^{(k+1)}}{Z_i^{(k+1)}}, \qquad \hat{D}_{1;ij}^{(k+1)} = \frac{A_{ij}^{(k+1)}}{Z_i^{(k+1)}},$$

and

$$\hat{D}_{0;ii}^{(k+1)} = -\left(\sum_{j=1}^{m} \hat{D}_{1;ij}^{(k+1)} + \sum_{j=1,j\neq i}^{m} \hat{D}_{0;ij}^{(k+1)} \right)$$

for $1 \leq i, j \leq m$.

Using these, one can compute the likelihood $f(z|\hat{D}_0^{(k+1)}, \hat{D}_1^{(k+1)})$ of the empirical time series under the new estimates according to equation (9). If the likelihood ratio

$$\rho = \frac{f(z|\hat{D}_0^{(k+1)}, \hat{D}_1^{(k+1)})}{f(z|\hat{D}_0^{(k)}, \hat{D}_1^{(k)})}$$

remains smaller than a threshold $1+\varepsilon$, then the EM iteration process can be stopped, and the latest estimates may be adopted. The threshold value reflects the limit of accuracy beyond which the gain in model adaptation is considered not to be worth the additional computation time.

4   Implementation of EM

In this section we focus on the implementation of the EM algorithm.

It is clear that in order to evaluate the update rules we need to be able to calculate the value of the matrix integral of the type

$$\mathcal{I} = \int_{u_0 + \cdots + u_k = 1} e^{D_0 u_0} P_1 e^{D_0 u_1} \cdots P_k e^{D_0 u_k} d\mathbf{u}$$

where D_0 is our parameter square matrix of order m and P_r's are equal to D_1 except for calculating the elementary terms for $c_{k-1}(i, j|\hat{D}_0, \hat{D}_1)$ in (15) where one P_r needs to replaced with $e_i e_j^T$. Note that the true likelihood function is also constructed in terms of such expectations.

In the following, we show two ways to calculate $\mathcal{I}$. The first operates with the matrices of the same dimension as D_0 and D_1 and the second is based on the matrix exponentials of some large dimension depending on k and m. The choice of these approaches for practical implementation will depend on the computing limitations related to large values of m and k.

4.1   Direct Evaluation

The purpose of this sub-section is two fold:

First, to demonstrate a direct method of evaluating the density function of a convolution of Erlang distributions. To our knowledge this is not reported before and we show it to be closely related to the normalizing constant of a particular spherical distribution.

Secondly, the expression of the density function of the convolutions of Erlang's is shown to be closely related to the close form expression of $\mathcal{I}$. In particular, if the Jordan decomposition of D_0 is known, we have a closed-form expression for evaluating both the likelihood function and the EM update steps.

Convolutions of Erlang Distributions: Let assume that the random variables X_i have distribution $Gamma(n_i + 1, \lambda_i)$ for $i = 0, \cdots, k$. Since we will obtain the pdf of $Y = X_0 + X_1 + \cdots + X_k$, we can assume without loss of generality that all λ_i's are distinct.

It is now clear that the pdf of Y at point s is

$$f_Y(s) = \prod_{i=0}^{k} \frac{\lambda_i^{n_i+1}}{n_i!} \int_{v_0+\cdots+v_k=s} e^{-\sum_{i=0}^{k} v_i\lambda_i} \prod_{i=0}^{k} v_i^{n_i} d\mathbf{v}$$

where $d\mathbf{v} = \prod_{i=1}^{k} dv_i$. A change of variables $u_i = v_i/s$ leads to

$$f_Y(s) = \prod_{i=0}^{k} \frac{\lambda_i^{n_i+1}}{n_i!} s^{k+\sum_{i=0}^{k} n_i} \int_{u_0+\cdots+u_k=1} e^{-\sum_{i=0}^{k} u_i s\lambda_i} \prod_{i=0}^{k} u_i^{n_i} d\mathbf{u} \qquad (18)$$

Integrals of the type $\int_{u_0+\cdots+u_k=1} e^{-\sum_{i=0}^{k} u_i\lambda_i} \prod_{i=0}^{k} u_i^{n_i} d\mathbf{u}$ are obtained in the closed-form in [19]. The authors provide the value of the normalizing constant for Complex Bingham Distributions (see [17]) with multiplicities in the eigenvalues of the parameter matrix. In particular, provided that all λ_i's are distinct, it is shown in Proposition 2 there that

$$\int_{u_0+\cdots+u_k=1} e^{-\sum_{i=0}^{k} u_i\lambda_i} \prod_{i=0}^{k} u_i^{n_i} d\mathbf{u}$$

$$= \sum_{i=0}^{k} \sum_{|J_0(i)|=n_i} \frac{(-1)^{n_i+j} e^{-\lambda_i} n_i!}{j! j_0! \ldots j_{i-1}! j_{i+1}! \ldots j_k!} \prod_{r\neq i} \frac{(n_r+j_r)!}{(\lambda_r - \lambda_i)^{n_r+j_r+1}} \qquad (19)$$

where the second summation is performed along all $J_0(i) = (j, j_0 \ldots, j_{i-1}, j_{i+1}, \ldots, j_k)$, which are integer partitions (including zeros) of n_i in $k+1$ components. A simple algorithm which generates such partitions is given on page 49 of [26] where the number of such partitions is shown to be $C_{n_i+k}^{n_i}$. Replacing λ_i's in (19) by $s\lambda_i$'s we have

$$\int_{u_0+\cdots+u_k=1} e^{-\sum_{i=0}^{k} u_i s\lambda_i} \prod_{i=0}^{k} u_i^{n_i} d\mathbf{u}$$

$$= s^{-k-\sum_{i=0}^{k} n_i} \sum_{i=0}^{k} \sum_{|J_0(i)|=n_i} \frac{(-1)^{n_i+j} e^{-s\lambda_i} s^j n_i!}{j! j_0! \ldots j_{i-1}! j_{i+1}! \ldots j_k!} \prod_{r\neq i} \frac{(n_r+j_r)!}{(\lambda_r - \lambda_i)^{n_r+j_r+1}} \qquad (20)$$

which implies that

$$f_Y(s) = \prod_{i=0}^{k} \frac{\lambda_i^{n_i+1}}{n_i!} \sum_{i=0}^{k} e^{-s\lambda_i} \sum_{|J_0(i)|=n_i} \frac{(-1)^{n_i+j} s^j n_i!}{j! j_0! \ldots j_{i-1}! j_{i+1}! \ldots j_k!} \prod_{r\neq i} \frac{(n_r+j_r)!}{(\lambda_r - \lambda_i)^{n_r+j_r+1}}$$

$$\qquad (21)$$

The expression (19) is also valid for complex values of λ_i. This fact is important in calculating our expectations if the eigenvalues of D_0 are complex.

Evaluating $\mathcal{I}$: Assume that D_0 has p distinct eigenvalues with Jordan decomposition

$$D_0 = O\Delta O^{-1} = O \begin{pmatrix} \Delta_1(r_1) & & \\ & \ddots & \\ & & \Delta_p(r_p) \end{pmatrix} O^{-1} \quad \text{with} \quad \Delta_j(r_j) = \begin{pmatrix} \lambda_j & 1 & & \\ & \lambda_j & \ddots & \\ & & & 1 \\ & & & \lambda_j \end{pmatrix}$$

where r_j is the dimension of $\Delta_j(r_j)$ and O is an invertible matrix. Without loss of generality we can assume that O is the identity matrix. This can easily be seen from the fact that $e^{xD_0} = Oe^{x\Delta}O^{-1}$ and so

$$\mathcal{I} = O \int_{u_0+\cdots+u_k=1} e^{\Delta u_0} Q_1 e^{\Delta u_1} \cdots Q_k e^{\Delta u_k} d\mathbf{u} \; O^{-1} \quad Q_j = O^{-1}D_jO.$$

We need to make the following remarks

Remark 1

$$e^{x\Delta} = \begin{pmatrix} e^{x\Delta_1(r_1)} & & \\ & \ddots & \\ & & e^{x\Delta_p(r_p)} \end{pmatrix}$$

Remark 2. From the decomposition $\Delta_j(r_j) = \lambda_j I + N(r_j)$ with

$$N(r_j) = \begin{pmatrix} & 1 & & \\ & & \ddots & \\ & & & 1 \\ & & & \end{pmatrix}$$

and noting that $N(r_j)$ is a nilpotent matrix of order r_j, it follows that

$$e^{x\Delta_j(r_j)} = e^{x\lambda_j} \sum_{w=0}^{r_j-1} \frac{x^w N(r_j)^w}{w!}.$$

with $N(r_j)^0 = I$.

Let denote by $M(j,w)$ the $p \times p$ matrix related to the block matrix $N(r_j)$ defined as

$$M(j,w) = \begin{pmatrix} & & \\ & \frac{N(r_j)^w}{w!} & \\ & & \end{pmatrix}$$

It is now easy to see that the required value of $\mathcal{I}$ is given in terms of a finite sum of elementary integrals of the type

$$\mathcal{I} = \sum_{j_0=1}^{p} \sum_{w_{j_0}=1}^{r_{j_0}-1} \cdots \sum_{j_k=1}^{p} \sum_{w_{j_k}=1}^{r_{j_k}-1} \mathcal{J}(j_0 \ldots j_k; w_{j_0} \ldots w_{j_k})$$

where

$$\mathcal{J}(j_0 \ldots j_k; w_{j_0} \ldots w_{j_k}) = \int\limits_{u_0 + \cdots + u_k = 1} e^{u_0 \lambda_{j_0}} u_0^{w_{j_0}} M(j_0, w_{j_0}) \prod_{l=1}^{k} P_l e^{u_l \lambda_{j_l}} u_l^{w_{j_l}} M(j_l, w_{j_l}) d\mathbf{u}.$$

In the summation above each of $j_0, j_1, \cdots, j_k$ take values independently of $1, 2, \cdots, p$ and for each j_l the corresponding w_{j_l} takes values in $1, 2, \cdots, r_{j_l}$. Note that p is the number of distinct eigenvalues of D_0 and r_{j_l} denotes the multiplicity of the eigenvalue λ_{j_l}.

It can be seen that the integrating factors in $\mathcal{J}(j_0 \ldots j_k; w_{j_0} \ldots w_{j_l})$ are only scalars which can be grouped together such that

$$\mathcal{J}(j_0 \ldots j_k; w_{j_0} \ldots w_{j_l}) = M(j_0, w_{j_0}) \prod_{l=1}^{k} P_l M(j_l, w_{j_l}) \int\limits_{u_0 + \cdots + u_k = 1} e^{\sum_{l=0}^{k} u_l \lambda_{j_l}} \prod_{l=0}^{k} u_l^{w_{j_l}} d\mathbf{u}$$

It is now clear that we only need to evaluate the value of $\int\limits_{u_0 + \cdots + u_k = 1} e^{\sum_{l=0}^{k} u_l \lambda_{j_l}}$

$\prod_{l=0}^{k} u_l^{w_{j_l}} d\mathbf{u}$. Using the result (19) we can exactly evaluate $\mathcal{I}$. Note that for implementing directly (19) in this case we need all λ_{j_l}'s distinct, otherwise, we then need to initially collapse to a single u_i all those u_l's such that λ_{j_l}'s share the same value.

4.2 Matrix Exponential Approach

A novel idea for calculating $\mathcal{I}$ is reported in [10] who describe a method for calculating the matrix integrals of the type

$$\int\limits_{u_0 + \cdots + u_k = t} e^{A_0 u_0} P_1 e^{A_1 u_1} \cdots P_k e^{A_k u_k} d\mathbf{u}$$

where A_i's and P_i's are square of dimension $m \times m$. Their method relies heavily on the matrix exponential function and expands to any k the approach of [31] for $k \leq 4$. In particular, they show that the resulting matrix above is in fact the top-right $m \times m$ sub-matrix of $\exp(t\mathcal{A})$, where $\mathcal{A}$ is a two-diagonal square matrix of dimension $(k + 1)m$ defined as

$$\mathcal{A} = \begin{pmatrix} A_0 & P_1 & 0 & \cdots & & 0 \\ 0 & A_1 & P_2 & 0 & \cdots 0 \\ \vdots & & \ddots & & & \vdots \\ 0 & \cdots & 0 & A_{k-1} & P_k \\ 0 & \cdots & 0 & 0 & A_k \end{pmatrix}.$$

Our expectation $\mathcal{I}$ is the top-right $m \times m$ sub-matrix of $\exp(\mathcal{A})$ where all A_i's are equal to D_0.

The implementation of this approach is straightforward, but rather inefficient since we need to calculate the $(k+1)m \times (k+1)m$ matrix $\exp(\mathcal{A})$ and extract only a small part. If its dimension however is unmanageably large for the computer we can apply the same result to low order matrices as shown below.

Applying the result of [10] for a scalar case i.e. all $A_i = \lambda_i$ are numbers and $P_i = 1$ see that the corresponding integral in (19) for $n_i = 0$ is simply the top right entry of $\exp(\mathcal{A})$, where

$$
\mathcal{A} = \begin{pmatrix}
\lambda_0 & 1 & 0 & \cdots & & 0 \\
0 & \lambda_1 & 1 & 0 & \cdots & 0 \\
\vdots & & \ddots & & & \vdots \\
0 & \cdots & 0 & \lambda_{k-1} & 1 \\
0 & \cdots & 0 & 0 & \lambda_k
\end{pmatrix}.
$$

One can easily show that the values in (19) for $n_i \neq 0$ can be similarly obtained by expanding each dimension of $\mathcal{A}$ to $\sum_{i=0}^{k} n_i + k + 1$ such that each λ_i is repeated $n_i + 1$ times and the resulting value obtained after evaluating $\exp(\mathcal{A})$ needs re-scaling by $\prod_{i=0}^{k} \Gamma(n_i + 1)$. We can use this method to then evaluate the elementary integrals $\mathcal{J}(j_0 \ldots j_k; w_{j_0} \ldots w_{j_l})$ in the direct approach in subsection 4.1.

5   Numerical Examples

The purpose of this section is to show that the proposed algorithm can indeed be implemented in a tractable way on a normal PC. We utilized the first matrix exponential approach of subsection 4.2 where $\mathcal{A}$ has matrix blocks and performed the calculations in the Statistical package R.

Example 1. We consider an application where we know that all inter–arrival times have an exponential distribution. This makes an estimation simpler as we can set the off–diagonal elements of $\hat{D}_0$ as zero. The EM algorithm guarantees that initial estimates of zero remain zero, see equations (16) and (17). We set the original parameters as

$$
D_0 = \begin{pmatrix} -0.2 & 0 \\ 0 & -5 \end{pmatrix} \quad \text{and} \quad D_1 = \begin{pmatrix} 0 & 0.2 \\ 0.5 & 4.5 \end{pmatrix}
$$

With these parameters we ran a simulation of 500 arrivals, yielding a time series of $N = 353$ intervals. This served as the input to our EM algorithm. The initial estimates were set as

$$
\hat{D}_0^{(0)} = \begin{pmatrix} -N/d & 0 \\ 0 & -M \end{pmatrix} \quad \text{and} \quad \hat{D}_1^{(0)} = \begin{pmatrix} N/2d & N/2d \\ M/2 & M/2 \end{pmatrix}
$$

where $M = \max\{z_n : n \leq N\}$ is the maximal number of arrivals within one interval, d is the total number of intervals without arrivals, and N is the total number of intervals in the time series. After 28 EM steps, the estimates for D_0 and D_1 are

$$
\hat{D}_0 = \begin{pmatrix} -0.207 & 0.000 \\ 0.000 & -4.727 \end{pmatrix} \quad \text{and} \quad \hat{D}_1 = \begin{pmatrix} 0.000 & 0.207 \\ 0.555 & 4.172 \end{pmatrix}
$$

The likelihood of the time series under these estimates is $\hat{l} = 2.017871e - 203$ as compared to the likelihood $l = 6.151147e - 204$ under the original parameters. Note that the qualitative entry $D_{0;11} = 0$ has been found by the algorithm on its own.

Example 2. The second example is a Markov–modulated Poisson process (MMPP). The original parameters were set as

$$D_0 = \begin{pmatrix} -1 & 0.5 \\ 0.5 & -2 \end{pmatrix} \quad \text{and} \quad D_1 = \begin{pmatrix} 0.5 & 0 \\ 0 & 1.5 \end{pmatrix}$$

Again, we used these parameters to run a simulation of 500 arrivals, yielding a time series of $N = 479$ intervals. This served as the input to our EM algorithm. The initial estimates were set as

$$\hat{D}_0^{(0)} = \begin{pmatrix} -N/d & N/2d \\ M/2 & -M \end{pmatrix} \quad \text{and} \quad \hat{D}_1^{(0)} = \begin{pmatrix} N/2d & 0 \\ 0 & M/2 \end{pmatrix}$$

with M and d as defined in example 1. After 142 steps, the algorithm produced the following estimates for D_0 and D_1:

$$\hat{D}_0 = \begin{pmatrix} -1.509 & 1.130 \\ 1.370 & -3.220 \end{pmatrix} \quad \text{and} \quad \hat{D}_1 = \begin{pmatrix} 0.378 & 0.000 \\ 0.000 & 1.850 \end{pmatrix}$$

The likelihood of the time series under these estimates is $\hat{l} = 7.820401e - 285$, under the original parameters it is $l = 7.218375e - 285$.

Example 3. Now a full Markovian arrival process with two phases: Original parameters are

$$D_0 = \begin{pmatrix} -2.5 & 1 \\ 2.5 & -5 \end{pmatrix} \quad \text{and} \quad D_1 = \begin{pmatrix} 1 & 0.5 \\ 1.5 & 1 \end{pmatrix}$$

Again, we used these parameters to run a simulation of 500 arrivals, this time yielding a time series of $N = 293$ intervals. The initial estimators were set as

$$\hat{D}_0^{(0)} = \begin{pmatrix} -N/d & N/3d \\ M/3 & -M \end{pmatrix} \quad \text{and} \quad \hat{D}_1^{(0)} = \begin{pmatrix} N/3d & N/3d \\ M/3 & M/3 \end{pmatrix}$$

After only two steps, the estimates for D_0 and D_1 are

$$\hat{D}_0 = \begin{pmatrix} -2.432 & 0.992 \\ 2.521 & -4.948 \end{pmatrix} \quad \text{and} \quad \hat{D}_1 = \begin{pmatrix} 0.961 & 0.479 \\ 1.458 & 0.970 \end{pmatrix}$$

The likelihood of the time series under these estimates is $\hat{l} = 6.623291e - 209$, under the original parameters it is $l = 4.625924e - 209$.

If we apply the same algorithm to the first part of the same data such that there are $N = 200$ intervals only, we obtain after 28 steps

$$\hat{D}_0 = \begin{pmatrix} -2.323 & 1.175 \\ 3.361 & -6.757 \end{pmatrix} \quad \text{and} \quad \hat{D}_1 = \begin{pmatrix} 0.576 & 0.572 \\ 1.635 & 1.761 \end{pmatrix}$$

Here the likelihoods are $\hat{l} = 9.80752e - 147$ under the estimates and $l = 2.817786e - 147$ under the original parameters.

Example 4. The last example deals with real data taken from measurements of fetal lamb movements. They have been analysed in [20] via discrete time hidden Markov models. Here we apply our continuous time model to these data. In [20] the assumption was that in each interval the number of counts follows a Poisson distribution. The equivalent assumption in a continuous time model is that of exponential inter-arrival times. We can model this by setting D_0 to be diagonal, which means that the underlying phase can change only upon an arrival (i.e. together with an observed movement). In order to find the most suitable number m of phases, we just try increasing values of m until the likelihood gain does not appear to be worthwhile anymore.

The estimates for $m = 2$ are

$$\hat{D}_0 = \begin{pmatrix} -0.243 & 0.000 \\ 0.000 & -2.775 \end{pmatrix} \quad \text{and} \quad \hat{D}_1 = \begin{pmatrix} 0.222 & 0.021 \\ 0.435 & 2.340 \end{pmatrix}$$

where the achieved likelihood is $3.638315e - 78$. For $m = 3$ the estimates are

$$\hat{D}_0 = \begin{pmatrix} -0.096 & 0.000 & 0.000 \\ 0.000 & -0.548 & 0.000 \\ 0.000 & 0.000 & -3.631 \end{pmatrix} \quad \text{and} \quad \hat{D}_1 = \begin{pmatrix} 0.059 & 0.028 & 0.009 \\ 0.044 & 0.504 & 0.000 \\ 0.221 & 0.000 & 3.410 \end{pmatrix}$$

They generate a likelihood of $1.264017e - 73$. The estimates for $m = 4$ yield a likelihood of $1.275225e - 72$. This last likelihood gain appears as too small to justify an extra phase. Hence we stop here and decide for the model with three phases.

It is remarkable that the qualitative entries $\hat{D}_1(2,3) = \hat{D}_1(3,2) = 0$ have been picked up by the discrete time model in [20], table 4 under $m = 3$, too. The interpretation is that phase 1 serves as an intermediate phase, over which also changes between phases 2 and 3 need to occur.

Acknowledgement

We are obliged to Dr. Rolando Biscay from the Instituto de Cibernética, Matemática y Física in Habana, Cuba, for sending us the manuscript [10], which contains a crucial result for the computational part of this paper. We further thank Martin Ridout from the University of Kent at Canterbury, UK, for providing the suitable data set for example 4.

References

1. Albert, A.: Estimating the infinitesimal generator of a continuous time, finite state Markov process. Ann. Math. Stat. 33, 727–753 (1962)
2. Asmussen, S.: Phase-type distributions and related point processes: Fitting and recent advances. In: Chakravarthy, Alfa (eds.) Matrix-analytic methods in stochastic models. Lect. Notes Pure Appl. Math, vol. 183, pp. 137–149. Marcel Dekker, NY (1997)
3. Asmussen, S., Koole, G.: Marked point processes as limits of Markovian arrival streams. J. Appl. Probab. 30(2), 365–372 (1993)
4. Asmussen, S., Nerman, O., Olsson, M.: Fitting phase-type distributions via the EM algorithm. Scand. J. Stat. 23(4), 419–441 (1996)

5. Bladt, M., Gonzalez, A., Lauritzen, S.: The estimation of phase-type related functionals using Markov chain Monte Carlo methods. Scandinavian Actuarial Journal 2003(4), 280–300 (2003)
6. Bladt, M., Soerensen, M.: Statistical inference for discretely observed Markov jump processes. Journal of the Royal Statistical Society: Series B 67(3), 395–410 (2005)
7. Breuer, L.: An EM Algorithm for Batch Markovian Arrival Processes and its Comparison to a Simpler Estimation Procedure. Annals of Operations Research 112, 123–138 (2002)
8. Buchholz, P.: An EM-Algorithm for MAP Fitting from Real Traffic Data. In: Kemper, P., Sanders, W.H. (eds.) TOOLS 2003. LNCS, vol. 2794, pp. 218–236. Springer, Heidelberg (2003)
9. Buchholz, P., Kriege, J.: A Heuristic Approach for Fitting MAPs to Moments and Joint Moments. In: 2009 Sixth International Conference on the Quantitative Evaluation of Systems, pp. 53–62. IEEE Computer Society, Los Alamitos (2009)
10. Carbonell, F., Jimenez, J.C., Pedroso, L.M.: Computing multiple integrals involving matrix exponentials. Journal of Computational and Applied Mathematics 213, 300–305 (2007)
11. Casale, G., Zhang, Z., Smirni, E.: KPC-Toolbox: Simple Yet Effective Trace Fitting Using Markovian Arrival Processes. In: International Conference on Quantitative Evaluation of Systems, pp. 83–92. IEEE Comp. Soc., Los Alamitos (2008)
12. Dempster, A., Laird, N., Rubin, D.: Maximum likelihood from incomplete data via the EM algorithm. Discussion. J. R. Stat. Soc., Ser. B 39, 1–38 (1977)
13. Fearnhead, P., Sherlock, C.: An exact Gibbs sampler for the Markov–modulated Poisson process. J. R. Statist. Soc. B 68(5), 767–784 (2006)
14. Horn, R.A., Johnson, C.R.: Topics in Matrix Analysis. Cambridge University Press, Cambridge (1991)
15. Horvath, G., Telek, M., Buchholz, P.: A MAP fitting approach with independent approximation of the inter-arrival time distribution and the lag correlation. In: QEST 2005: Proc Sec. Inter. Conf. Quant. Eval. Syst., p. 124. IEEE Comp. Soc., Los Alamitos (2005)
16. Jewell, N.P.: Mixtures of exponential distributions. Ann. Stat. 10, 479–484 (1982)
17. Kent, J.: The complex Bingham distribution and shape analysis. J.R. Statist. Soc. Series B 56, 285–289 (1994)
18. Klemm, A., Lindemann, C., Lohmann, M.: Modeling IP traffic using the batch Markovian arrival process. In: Perform. Eval., pp. 149–173. Elsevier Science Publishers B. V., Amsterdam (2003)
19. Kume, A., Wood, A.T.A.: On the normalising constant of the Bingham distribution. Statistics and Probability Letters 77, 832–837 (2007)
20. Leroux, B.G., Puterman, M.L.: Maximum-Penalized-Likelihood Estimation for Independent and Markov-Dependent Mixture Models. Biometrics 48, 545–558 (1992)
21. Lucantoni, D.M.: New results on the single server queue with a batch Markovian arrival process. Commun. Stat., Stochastic Models 7(1), 1–46 (1991)
22. Lucantoni, D.M.: The BMAP/G/1 Queue: A Tutorial. In: Donatiello, L., Nelson, R. (eds.) SIGMETRICS 1993 and Performance 1993. LNCS, vol. 729, pp. 330–358. Springer, Heidelberg (1993)
23. McLachlan, G.J., Krishnan, T.: The EM algorithm and extensions. John Wiley & Sons, New York (1997)
24. Meng, X.-L., van Dyk, D.: The EM algorithm - an old folk-song sung to a fast new tune. J. R. Stat. Soc., Ser. B 59(3), 511–567 (1997)
25. Neuts, M.F.: A versatile Markovian point process. J. Appl. Probab. 16, 764–774 (1979)
26. Nijenhuis, A., Herbert, S.W.: Combinatorial Algorithms. Academic Press, London (1978)
27. Ryden, T.: An EM algorithm for estimation in Markov-modulated Poisson processes. Comput. Stat. Data Anal. 21(4), 431–447 (1996)

28. Okamura, H., Dohi, T., Trivedi, S.K.: Markovian arrival process parameter estimation with group data. IEEE/ACM Trans. Netw. 17(4), 1326–1339 (2009)
29. Ryden, T.: Estimating the order of continuous phase-type distributions and Markovmodulated Poisson processes. Commun. Stat., Stochastic Models 13(3), 417–433 (1997)
30. Sundberg, R.: Maximum Likelihood Theory for Incomplete Data from an Exponential Family. Scand. J. Statist. 1, 49–58 (1974)
31. Van Loan, C.F.: Computing integrals involving the matrix exponential. IEEE Transactions on Automatic Control 23, 395–404 (1978)

An Empirical Comparison of MAP Fitting Algorithms

Jan Kriege and Peter Buchholz

Informatik IV, TU Dortmund
D-44221 Dortmund, Germany
{jan.kriege,peter.buchholz}@udo.edu

Abstract. The paper presents an empirical comparison of different methods to fit the parameters of a MAP according to the quantities derived from three different real traces. The results indicate that for two of the three traces an adequate fitting with low order MAPs is possible whereas almost all approaches failed for the third trace. Apart form this the question for the best approach for fitting MAPs is still open although there seems to be a tendency that the most costly EM algorithms provide the best fitting results.

1 Introduction

In stochastic modeling, the appropriate representation of arrival and service processes is of major importance to build realistic models. It turns out that many real processes include some correlation which implies that random variables that are identically and independently distributed are not sufficient to describe real behavior, instead stochastic processes have to be used to model the distribution and the autocorrelation structure. Markovian arrival processes (MAPs) [17] are stochastic processes which can be applied to capture a wide range of different stochastic behaviors and can be used in queuing network models as arrival or service processes. Queuing networks with MAPs can be analyzed numerically by solving the global balance equations [23], if the state space is not too large, they can be analyzed with matrix analytical methods [18], if they are of the MAP/MAP/m type, they may as well be analyzed approximately [9] or by simulation.

To capture real behavior by MAPs, the parameters of a MAP have to be fitted according to some trace resulting from observations or measured behavior. The fitting problem of MAPs is a nonlinear optimization problem which becomes even more complex since the matrix representation of MAPs is redundant [24] and a canonical representation is only available for MAPs of order two [3]. Different fitting approaches have been proposed in the literature which all have their pros and cons. The most general approach is to find a MAP that maximizes the likelihood according to the available trace. The EM algorithm [2] can be used for this purpose and many specific variants of the algorithm for MAP fitting are available [4,5,14,22]. However, EM algorithms have several disadvantages since

B. Müller-Clostermann et al. (Eds.): MMB & DFT 2010, LNCS 5987, pp. 259–273, 2010.

they have a slow convergence, may converge towards local minima and require a huge effort that grows linearly in the length of a trace. Since for MAP fitting very long traces are required to adequately match the autocorrelation structure, in practice, EM approaches are not sufficient to obtain good fitting result with an acceptable effort. Alternative approaches first derive some quantities from a trace, like higher order moments, joint moments or lag-k autocorrelations and then fit the parameters of a MAP according to these quantities. This implies that fitting becomes independent of the trace length. As shown in [24], a non redundant MAP of order n which is characterized by $2n^2 - n$ free parameters is completely determined by n^2 parameters, e.g., by the first $2n - 1$ moments and $(n - 1)^2$ joint moments. Thus, one may fit a MAP according to the empirical moments and joint moments of a trace as done in [7]. Other approaches use the lag-k autocorrelation instead of the joint moments for fitting [10,13].

However, all these approaches have their limitations since in practice n^2 parameters of a trace hardly define a MAP. In [7] we used least square fitting to obtain the *nearest* MAP of order n according to some measured moments and joint moments. It turns out that it is hard to fit even approximately in the range of n^2 parameters of a real trace with a MAP of order n. Another problem which is also considered in [7] is the reliability of quantities derived from a trace. In general, a trace is only a sample of the behavior of a system such that the quantities computed from the trace are only estimates. If one computes confidence intervals for these quantities, it turns out that confidence intervals become very wide for higher order moments or joint moments of traces from the Internet archive [1] which already contain more than a million entries. This observation implies that for MAP fitting long traces are required.

Although many approaches for MAP fitting are available, it is completely unclear which is the best approach and it is not even clear how to measure whether one approach is better than another. It seems that a lot of empirical work is necessary to find reliable and efficient fitting methods. In this paper we perform such empirical observations by comparing different fitting approaches and different quantities that are fitted. We apply a standard EM approach and two classes of fitting methods that fit first order quantities like joint moments and higher order quantities like lag-k autocorrelations. For this purpose we slightly extend available fitting methods that are based on a two step approach which first fits a phase type (PH) distribution, then possibly do some equivalence transformation on the representation and finally fit a MAP that leaves the distribution unchanged.

The paper is structured as follows. In the next section we introduce the basic notation and recall some basic results for PH distributions and MAPs. In chapter 3 we present several MAP fitting approaches. We start with a brief introduction of EM based MAP fitting and present afterwards two classes of approaches that expand an available PH distribution into a MAP. In the first case, the expansion is done by a least squares approach to fit joint moments. Then we consider the fitting of lag-k autocorrelations. In the following section we use the different fitting methods to fit MAPs according to specific quantities derived from real

traces and we compare MAPs fitted with different approaches. The paper ends
with the conclusions.

2   Background

We first introduce the basic notation and define PH distributions, then we briefly
outline fitting methods for PH distributions and, finally, we present basic results
for MAPs.

2.1   Basic Definitions and Results for PH Distributions

A PH distribution [18] of order n is defined by a non-singular $n \times n$ matrix $\mathbf{D}_0$
with $\mathbf{D}_0(i, j) \geq 0$ for $i \neq j$, $\mathbf{D}_0(i, i) \leq -\sum_{j=1, j\neq i}^{n} \mathbf{D}_0(i, j)$ and a row vector π
with $\pi(i) \geq 0$ and $\pi\, \mathbb{I} = 1$ where $\mathbb{I}$ is the unit column vector of length n. Let
$\mathbf{M} = (-\mathbf{D}_0)^{-1}$, the so called moment matrix. The distribution function, density
and the moments of a random variable X with a PH distribution $(\mathbf{D}_0, \pi)$ are
given by

$$F_X(t) = 1 - \pi e^{t\mathbf{D}_0}\, \mathbb{I} \tag{1}$$

$$f_X(t) = \pi e^{t\mathbf{D}_0}(-\mathbf{D}_0\, \mathbb{I}) \tag{2}$$

$$\mu_k = E(X^k) = k!\pi\, (\mathbf{M})^k\, \mathbb{I} . \tag{3}$$

It has been shown [19] that every non negative random variable with a continuous
density that is non-zero in $(0, \infty)$ can be approximated arbitrarily close by a PH
distribution.

2.2   Fitting Methods for PH Distributions

The task of fitting PH distributions is to choose the parameters of a PH distribution in such a way that some measured quantities are matched. Usually these
quantities result from a trace which is an observation of some real behavior.
From a trace different quantities like moments, joint moments, lag-k coefficients
of autocorrelation or values of the empirical distribution function or density can
be computed. Since a trace is only a sample of some real behavior, all values
are estimates. The goal of a fitting approach is to find a PH distribution that
matches the quantities of the trace as good as possible. A large number of fitting
methods for PH distributions exist, an overview can be found in [11].

   We only outline a few approaches which we later use as a first step for MAP
fitting. In general one can distinguish between fitting methods that work on
the whole trace and those that try to match some quantities derived from the
trace. Methods of the former type usually maximize the likelihood value which
is defined for a trace $t_1, \ldots t_m$ as

$$L_{(\mathbf{D}_0, \pi)}(t_1, \ldots, t_m) = \prod_{k=1}^{m} \pi e^{t_k \mathbf{D}_0}(-\mathbf{D}_0\, \mathbb{I}) . \tag{4}$$

Maximization is done with the so called EM algorithm [2]. However, the general variant of this algorithm is rather inefficient but if one restricts the class of PH distributions, much more efficient variants can be defined. In [25] an EM algorithm which fits the parameters of a generalized Erlang distribution is shown to be rather efficient. We will use this approach as a first step for MAP fitting.

Alternatively, one may fit the PH distribution according to the moments of the trace. In this case acyclic phase type distributions are used since for this subclass a canonical representation exists. Methods for moment fitting which we also apply as a first step for MAP fitting are proposed in [7,12].

2.3   Basic Definitions and Results for MAPs

A MAP [17] of order n is a stochastic process defined by two $n \times n$ matrices $(\mathbf{D}_0, \mathbf{D}_1)$ where $\mathbf{D}_0$ is as defined for a PH distribution above and $\mathbf{D}_1 \geq 0$ such that $\mathbf{Q} = \mathbf{D}_0 + \mathbf{D}_1$ and $\mathbf{Q}\,\mathbb{1} = \mathbf{0}$. Matrix $\mathbf{D}_0$ contains the rates of internal transitions without an arrival and matrix $\mathbf{D}_1$ contains the rates of transitions generating an arrival. We assume that $\mathbf{Q}$ is an irreducible generator matrix. Define $\mathbf{P} = -\mathbf{D}_0^{-1}\mathbf{D}_1$ as the transition matrix of the embedded discrete time Markov chain after an arrival. The stationary vector $\pi\mathbf{P} = \pi$, $\pi\,\mathbb{1} = 1$ includes the distribution just after an arrival. Consequently, $(\mathbf{D}_0, \pi)$ describes the inter-arrival time distribution of a MAP. Similarly each PH distribution $(\mathbf{D}_0, \pi)$ can be expanded into a MAP by defining $\mathbf{D}_1 = -\mathbf{D}_0\,\mathbb{1}\pi$.

The joint moments of consecutive arrivals of a MAP $(\mathbf{D}_0, \mathbf{D}_1)$ are given by

$$\mu_{k,l} = E(X_i^k X_{i+1}^l) = k!\; l!\pi\mathbf{M}^k\mathbf{P}\mathbf{M}^l\,\mathbb{1}\;, \tag{5}$$

the lag-k autocorrelation equals

$$\rho_k = \frac{\mu_1^{-2}\pi(-\mathbf{D}_0)^{-1}\mathbf{P}^k(-\mathbf{D}_0)^{-1}\,\mathbb{1} - 1}{2\mu_1^{-2}\pi(-\mathbf{D}_0)^{-1}(-\mathbf{D}_0)^{-1}\,\mathbb{1} - 1} \tag{6}$$

and the joint density of the first m interarrival times is defined as

$$f(\tau_1, \ldots, \tau_m) = \pi\left(\prod_{i=1}^{m} e^{\tau_i\mathbf{D}_0}\mathbf{D}_1\right)\,\mathbb{1}\;. \tag{7}$$

Fitting methods as introduced in the subsequent section try to approximate the empirical measures of a trace by a MAP. As for fitting PH distributions either the complete trace may be used resulting in the maximization of the likelihood

$$L_{(\mathbf{D}_0,\mathbf{D}_1)}(t_1, \ldots, t_m) = \pi\left(\prod_{k=1}^{m} e^{t_k\mathbf{D}_0}\mathbf{D}_1\right)\,\mathbb{1}\;. \tag{8}$$

or some derived quantities like joint moments or lag-k autocorrelations may be used for fitting.

One approach which has been applied successfully [7,8,13] is to separate distribution and dependency fitting. In a first step, a PH distribution is generated that captures the distribution of the elements in the trace and in a second step the distribution is expanded into a MAP by considering the dependencies in the trace. This expansion implies that matrix $\mathbf{D}_0$ remains unchanged and $\mathbf{D}_1$ is chosen such that $-\mathbf{D}_0 \, \mathbb{I} = \mathbf{D}_1 \, \mathbb{I}$ and $\pi \mathbf{M} \mathbf{D}_1 = \pi$ which puts $2n$ constraints for the elements of $\mathbf{D}_1$.

3   MAP Fitting Approaches

3.1   Expectation Maximization

We begin with a brief look on EM algorithms for MAP fitting and refer for the details of the approaches to the literature [2,4,5]. All EM algorithms perform an alternating sequence of expectation (E) and maximization (M) steps which improve the likelihood values in each step. Due to the structure of the M-step zero values in the matrices remain zero which implies that no fill in occurs if the algorithm is initially started with sparse matrices. The effort of a single iteration depends linearly on the length of the trace and the number of non-zero elements in the $\mathbf{D}_1$ matrix. Furthermore, it depends on the values in the trace in relation to the matrix entries since $e^{t_i \mathbf{Q}_0}$ has to be evaluated for each entry t_i in the trace and the effort depends on the number of non zero entries in $\mathbf{D}_0$ and the relation between transition rates and time steps. Unfortunately, the convergence of EM algorithms is very slow such that a large number of iterations is required.

If the likelihood is the measure to be maximized, then EM algorithms are currently the best alternative. However, one should start the EM algorithm with a MAP that has already been fitted to the trace using one of the approaches presented in the following two subsections. In this case, the EM algorithm improves the likelihood value but may reduce the fitting quality according to other measures like joint moments or lag-k autocorrelations which have been used to fit the initial MAP. The effort of EM algorithms applied to real traces is usually very high, e.g. for $LBL\text{-}TCP\text{-}3$, one of the traces we use later, the EM algorithm from [5] requires about 5 minutes per iteration with a MAP of order 5 and about 100 iterations are needed to reach convergence.

3.2   Fitting of Joint Moments

If fitting of the distribution and the autocorrelation structure are done separately, then the matrix $\mathbf{D}_0$ and vector π result from distribution fitting. Since we use the moment fitting approach from [7] or the EM algorithm of [25] for distribution fitting, the result is in both cases an acyclic PH distribution with an upper triangular matrix $\mathbf{D}_0$. Acyclic PH distributions of order n have $n(n+1)/2+(n-1)$ free parameters but only $2n - 1$ parameters are necessary to characterize the distribution such that different representations of the same distribution exist. [6] summarizes three methods to perform equivalence transformations that generate different acyclic representations of the same distribution. For MAP fitting the number of non zero entries in π and $\mathbf{D}_0 \, \mathbb{I}$ has to be maximized to maximize the number of possible non zero entries in $\mathbf{D}_1$. However, even with this goal the transformation is non unique and different approaches may be tried.

Define $\mathbf{v}^k = \pi \mathbf{M}^{k+1}$ and $\mathbf{w}^k = \mathbf{M}^k \, \mathbb{I}$, then

$$\mu_{k,l} = k! \; l! \; \mathbf{v}^k \mathbf{D}_1 \mathbf{w}^l \; . \tag{9}$$

Now assume that $\mathcal{J}$ is a set of joint moments that should be matched by the MAP and let for $(k, l) \in \mathcal{J}$ $\nu_{k,l}$ be the joint moments of the trace. Then the following constrained non negative least squares problem has to be solved to find the nearest MAP.

$$\min_{\mathbf{D}_1 : \mathbf{D}_1 \geq 0, \; \mathbf{D}_1 \, \mathbb{I} = -\mathbf{D}_0 \, \mathbb{I}, \; \pi \mathbf{M} \mathbf{D}_1 = \pi} \left(\sum_{(k,l) \in \mathcal{J}} \left(\beta_{k,l} \frac{\mu_{k,l}}{\nu_{k,l}} - \beta_{k,l} \right)^2 \right) \tag{10}$$

$\beta_{k,l}$ are some weights which allow one to discriminate higher order joint moments. In our experiments we present later, all weights are set to 1. However, if the resulting MAP cannot match the required moments adequately, it is often appropriate to set the weights such that lower order joint moments get a higher weight, e.g., by choosing $\beta_{k,l} = 2^{-(k-1)(l-1)}$. In this case, lower order joint moments are often matched exactly or almost exactly with the price of a bad fit for higher order moments.

The least squares solution can be computed with available algorithms [15]. The major advantage of joint moment fitting is the efficiency. I.e., to fit the joint moments $\nu_{k,l}$ with $1 \leq k, l \leq 3$ for *LBL-TCP-3* with a MAP of order 5 requires less than 1 second which is negligible compared to the fitting times of EM-algorithms.

3.3   Fitting of Autocorrelations

The approach for the fitting of autocorrelation works similarly to joint moment fitting. In a first step, the initial probability vector π and the matrix $\mathbf{D}_0$ are determined by a PH fitting algorithm like [7] or [25] and are transformed such that the number of non zero entries is maximized. Then matrix $\mathbf{D}_1$ is generated such that the autocorrelations $\rho = (\rho_1, \cdots, \rho_n)$ of the MAP $(\mathbf{D}_0, \mathbf{D}_1)$ (cf. Eq. 6) approximate the autocorrelations $\hat{\rho} = (\hat{\rho}_1, \cdots, \hat{\rho}_n)$ that have been estimated from the trace, i.e. we have to solve the following minimization problem:

$$\min_{\mathbf{D}_1 : \mathbf{D}_1 \geq 0, \; \mathbf{D}_1 \, \mathbb{I} = -\mathbf{D}_0 \, \mathbb{I}, \; \pi \mathbf{M} \mathbf{D}_1 = \pi} \left(\sum_{i=1}^{n} (\beta_i | \rho_i - \hat{\rho}_i |) \right) \tag{11}$$

where the β_i are weights which again may be used to privilege lower lag autocorrelations.

In this paper, we use a slightly modified approach of the two step algorithm presented in [13]. For minimizing Eq. 11 we use the Nelder-Mead algorithm [16]. An implementation can for example be found in [21]. For a MAP of order n we have n^2 variables from matrix $\mathbf{D}_1$ and Nelder-Mead requires $n^2 + 1$ initial solutions $D_1^{(i)}, i = 1, \cdots, n + 1$. The first initial solution is the MAP representation of the given PH distribution $(\pi, \mathbf{D}_0)$, i.e. $\mathbf{D}_1^{(1)} = (-\mathbf{D}_0\,\mathbb{I})\pi$. The possible range for other valid initial solutions is bounded by the constraints on the row sums $(-\mathbf{D}_0\,\mathbb{I} = \mathbf{D}_1\,\mathbb{I})$ and on the steady-state vector $(\pi\mathbf{P} = \pi)$. Let $\mathbf{x}$ be a vector that contains the first row of matrix $\mathbf{D}_1$ in positions $1, \cdots, n$, the second row in positions $n + 1, \cdots, 2n$ etc. Then we can define a linear system of equations using the conditions on row sums and steady-state vector (cf. [13]):

$$
\underbrace{\begin{bmatrix} 1 & 1 \cdots & 1 & 0 \cdots 0 & 0 & 0 \cdots & 0 \\ \vdots & \vdots \ddots & \vdots & \ddots & \vdots & \vdots \ddots & \vdots \\ 0 & 0 \cdots & 0 & 0 \cdots 0 & 1 & 1 \cdots & 1 \\ \pi'(1) & 0 \cdots & 0 & \cdots & \pi'(n) & 0 \cdots & 0 \\ \vdots & \vdots \ddots & \vdots & \ddots & \vdots & \vdots \ddots & \vdots \\ 0 & 0 \cdots \pi'(1) & & \cdots & 0 & 0 \cdots & \pi'(n) \end{bmatrix}}_{A}
\underbrace{\begin{bmatrix} \mathbf{D}_1(1,1) \\ \mathbf{D}_1(1,2) \\ \vdots \\ \mathbf{D}_1(1,n) \\ \mathbf{D}_1(2,1) \\ \mathbf{D}_1(2,2) \\ \vdots \\ \mathbf{D}_1(n,n) \end{bmatrix}}_{x}
=
\underbrace{\begin{bmatrix} \begin{bmatrix} -\mathbf{D}_0\,\mathbb{I} \end{bmatrix} \\ \pi(1) \\ \pi(2) \\ \vdots \\ \pi(n) \end{bmatrix}}_{b}
\tag{12}
$$

where $\pi' = \pi(\mathbf{M})$.

If initial solutions of the Nelder-Mead algorithm differ only slightly, the algorithm gets stuck at a local minimum close to one of the starting points. Therefore we apply the simplex algorithm to find the initial solutions for Nelder-Mead: For each x_i of Eq. 12 we solve

$$\max x_i \,, Ax = b \,, \text{ and } x \geq 0$$

which ensures that the Nelder-Mead algorithm has initial solutions with a large stepwidth for each x_i.

Fitting according to autocorrelations is not as efficient as fitting according to joint moments, since the minimization problem is not a simple least squares problem. Depending on the number of lag-k autocorrelations that are considered the approach takes between some seconds and few minutes, e.g. to fit the first 30 lags for *LBL-TCP-3* with a MAP of order 5 the algorithm required less than 10 seconds, for the first 100 lags it took 2 minutes.

4   Experimental Results

To compare the different fitting algorithms we use three different traces. The trace *BC-pAug89* contains a million packet arrivals observed at the Bellcore Morristown Research and Engineering facility in August 1989. The trace *LBL-TCP-3* [20] contains two hours of TCP traffic from the Lawrence Berkeley Laboratory and was recorded in January 1994. Both traces are taken from the Internet Traffic Archive [1]. The third trace *TUDo* contains the interarrival times of one million packets that have been measured from the Squid proxy server at the Computer Science Department of TU Dortmund in 2006.

We fitted MAPs of different order (from $n = 2$ to $n = 6$) with the three fitting approaches from Sec. 3. Since fitting according to joint moments and autocorrelations both require a given distribution that is fitted in the first step, we used Gfit [25] and a moment matching approach [7]. In a first step of our empirical evaluation we will compare the joint moments, lag-k autocorrelations and the likelihood of MAPs that have been fitted according to one of the characteristics with MAPs for which other properties have been used in the fitting process. The second part of our empirical evaluation compares the queueing behavior. In the following we will present the results for some of the fitted MAPs.

4.1   Comparison of Quantities

We start with the comparison of the fitted MAPs for the trace *BC-pAug89*. Figs. 1 and 2 show the results for MAPs of order 4 and 6 that we obtained for the different fitting algorithms. The curves resulting from autocorrelation fitting are labeled with AC and the number of lags that have been considered for fitting.

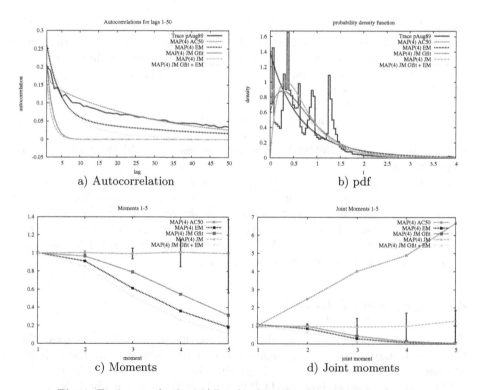

Fig. 1. Fitting results for MAPs of order 4 for the trace *BC-pAug89*

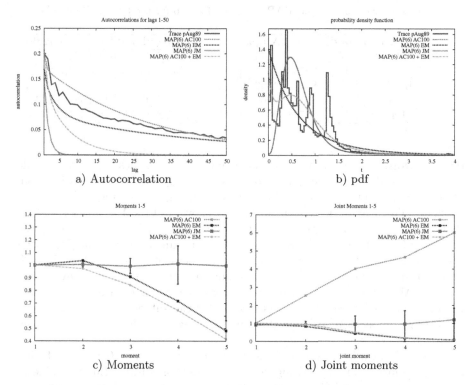

a) Autocorrelation   b) pdf

c) Moments   d) Joint moments

Fig. 2. Fitting results for MAPs of order 6 for the trace $BC\text{-}pAug89$

Curves from joint moment fitting and expectation maximization are labeled with
JM and EM, respectively. For moment matching we used the first five moments
$\nu_k, (k = 1...5)$ and for joint moment fitting 25 joint moments $\nu_{k,l}, (k, l = 1...5)$
and set all weights β_k and $\beta_{k,l}$ to 1. Usually we used moment matching [7] to
obtain the distribution for joint moment and autocorrelation fitting. In cases
where Gfit [25] was used this is denoted in the plots. In addition to the pure
EM algorithm that starts with a random MAP to improve the likelihood we
used the MAPs resulting from AC and JM fitting as initial solutions for the EM
algorithm as mentioned in Sec. 3.1. These MAPs are labeled with JM + EM or
AC + EM. The likelihood values for the MAPs are shown in Table 1.

The MAPs resulting from joint moment fitting failed to capture the autocorrelations, while both autocorrelation fitting and EM algorithm resulted in
a much better approximation of the lag-k autocorrelations, although the latter
tends to underestimate the autocorrelation. In contrast EM and AC fitting do
not capture the joint moments of the trace, while, of course, JM fitting provides a
good approximation as one can see from Figs. 1 d) and 2 d). The curves show the
joint moments $\mu_{k,k}$ of the MAPs relative to the joint moments of the trace. Joint
moments $\mu_{k,l}(k \neq l)$ are not shown but are similar. Additionally the confidence
intervals of the joint moments are printed in red. For all the MAPs we fitted with

Table 1. Likelihood for the MAPs of order 4 and 6 for the trace *BC-pAug89*

Likelihood	Trace pAug89	Likelihood	Trace pAug89
MAP(4) AC50	-891757.644354	MAP(6) AC100	-1138434.529730
MAP(4) EM	-857368.761951	MAP(6) EM	-850032.779585
MAP(4) JM Gfit	-833728.156640		
MAP(4) JM	-879217.986678	MAP(6) JM	-1142582.505733
MAP(4) JM Gfit + EM	-806247.089218	MAP(6) AC100 + EM	-804071.232488

the EM algorithm the joint moments are smaller than the ones of the trace, while AC fitting resulted in larger joint moments. Similarly the MAPs resulting from the EM algorithm underestimated the higher moments of the trace (cf. Figs. 1 c) and 2 c)). The distributions of the MAPs are shown in Figs. 1 b) and 2 b). Note, that AC fitting and JM fitting used the same PH distribution. Regarding the likelihood EM fitting provides a larger likelihood than AC fitting and JM fitting that used a PH distribution obtained from the moment matching algorithm (cf. Table 1). Interestingly, using a PH distribution that has been fitted by Gfit as basis for MAP fitting resulted in a very high likelihood. As a drawback those PH distributions showed to be less flexible for the subsequent AC fitting and JM fitting compared to PH distributions resulting from the moment matching approach.

As already mentioned we used the MAPs resulting from AC and JM fitting as initial solution for the EM algorithm. In these cases EM fitting was able to improve the likelihood significantly, although the fitting quality according to other measures was reduced as one can see from Figs. 1 and 2.

Figs. 3 and 4 and Table 2 show fitting results for the trace *LBL-TCP-3*. The results are similar to the previous trace: JM fitting and to a lesser degree EM fitting underestimate the autocorrelations, while AC fitting over- and EM fitting underestimate the joint moments.

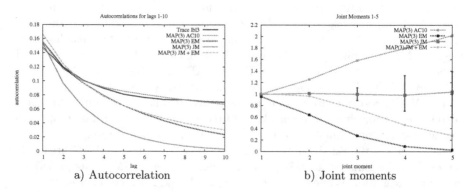

a) Autocorrelation   b) Joint moments

Fig. 3. Fitting results for MAPs of order 3 for the trace *LBL-TCP-3*

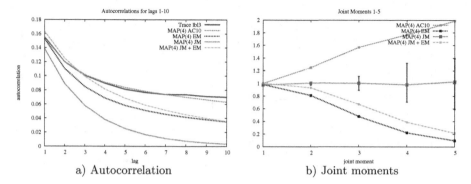

a) Autocorrelation b) Joint moments

Fig. 4. Fitting results for MAPs of order 4 for the trace *LBL-TCP-3*

Table 2. Likelihood for the MAPs of order 3 and 4 for the trace *LBL-TCP-3*

Likelihood	Trace lbl3	Likelihood	Trace lbl3
MAP(3) AC10	-1652039.018594	MAP(4) AC10	-1654146.788752
MAP(3) EM	-1637813.770617	MAP(4) EM	-1627420.100721
MAP(3) JM	-1639440.176623	MAP(4) JM	-1647272.298004
MAP(3) JM + EM	-1626938.629808	MAP(4) JM + EM	-1626267.526219

Table 3. Likelihood for the MAPs of order 2 and 4 for the trace *TUDo*

Likelihood	Trace TUDo	Likelihood	Trace TUDo
MAP(2) AC30 Gfit	409209.247942	MAP(4) AC30 Gfit	450455.635351
MAP(2) AC5	17874.468130	MAP(4) AC10	297622.747212
MAP(2) EM	34339.840111	MAP(4) EM	134878.147095
MAP(2) JM	33220.591429	MAP(4) JM	285171.814999
MAP(2) AC30 Gfit+EM	487457.907053	MAP(4) AC10 + EM	385977.643978

The last trace we used for our comparison was observed at a proxy server at TU Dortmund. It contains various bursts with very small interarrival times followed by a larger break until the next burst and therefore has high autocorrelations. As one can see from Figs. 5 and 6 the trace was difficult to fit for all algorithms. Again we used the MAPs resulting from AC and JM fitting as initial solutions for the EM algorithm. The *MAP*(4) resulting from AC fitting using a PH distribution obtained from Gfit showed to be unsuitable for this task, since the structure of the MAP caused a very poor runtime performance of the EM algorithm. Hence, we only used the MAPs that resulted from moment matching and subsequent AC or JM fitting as initial solutions.

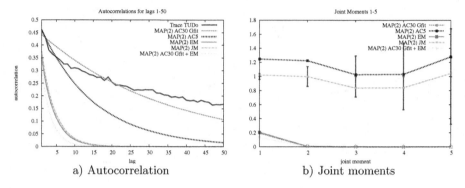

a) Autocorrelation   b) Joint moments

Fig. 5. Fitting results for MAPs of order 2 for the trace *TUDo*

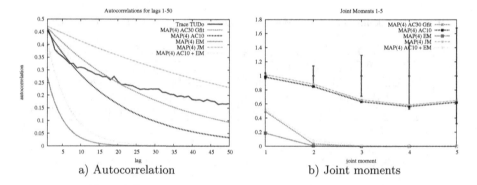

a) Autocorrelation   b) Joint moments

Fig. 6. Fitting results for MAPs of order 4 for the trace *TUDo*

4.2   Comparison of Queueing Behavior

Table 4 shows the queueing results for the different traces. The original traces and the fitted MAPs are used as arrival processes, for the service process we used an exponential distribution with different rates between $\mu = 0.6$ and $\mu = 1.2$. We use a single server system with capacity 10. The system was simulated for each of the traces until all of the interarrival times from the trace have been used. After that we simulated the model with the fitted MAPs for the same amounts of time. Table 4 contains the mean queue length and the probability that the queue is completely filled for all combinations of arrival and service processes. For each trace and order of the MAPs the results that are closest to the results of the trace are emphasized. For the Trace *BC-pAug89* one can see that the MAPs resulting from the EM algorithm result in a mean queue length that is closest to the one of the trace. Regarding the probability that the queue is completely filled all the fitted MAPs provide an appropriate approximation of the results from the trace, although in almost all cases either the pure EM or the EM algorithm combined with one of the other approaches provided the

Table 4. Queueing results

Model	Mean queue length				Probability for full queue			
	$\mu = 0.6$	0.8	1.0	1.2	$\mu = 0.6$	0.8	1.0	1.2
Trace pAug89	6.688	5.530	4.333	3.282	0.347	0.234	0.150	0.094
MAP(4) AC50	7.466	6.315	4.955	3.540	0.3779	0.246	0.139	0.066
MAP(4) EM	**6.749**	**5.556**	**4.352**	**3.321**	0.328	0.219	0.140	**0.089**
MAP(4) JM Gfit	7.363	6.290	5.027	3.627	0.374	0.249	0.143	0.068
MAP(4) JM	7.316	6.156	4.909	3.626	0.367	0.243	0.145	0.072
MAP(4) JM Gfit+EM	6.752	5.645	4.521	3.428	**0.341**	**0.231**	**0.146**	0.087
MAP(6) AC100	7.462	6.298	4.941	3.532	0.383	0.251	0.143	0.068
MAP(6) EM	**6.736**	**5.617**	**4.459**	**3.392**	**0.333**	**0.226**	0.145	0.091
MAP(6) JM	7.367	6.151	4.899	3.609	0.370	0.246	**0.147**	0.075
MAP(6) AC100+EM	6.926	5.861	4.868	3.797	**0.361**	0.253	0.164	**0.093**
Trace lbl3	7.081	5.407	4.009	2.969	0.304	0.183	0.110	0.067
MAP(3) AC10	7.309	6.015	4.590	3.312	0.333	0.206	0.115	0.059
MAP(3) EM	7.467	5.641	**4.117**	**3.019**	**0.309**	0.178	0.103	0.061
MAP(3) JM	7.461	5.838	4.325	3.163	0.313	0.184	0.105	0.059
MAP(3) JM+EM	**7.302**	**5.591**	4.121	3.020	0.310	**0.183**	**0.107**	**0.064**
MAP(4) AC10	7.311	6.016	4.593	3.313	0.335	0.208	0.116	0.059
MAP(4) EM	7.376	5.580	**4.029**	**2.939**	**0.308**	0.178	0.103	0.063
MAP(4) JM	7.528	5.941	4.432	3.212	0.323	0.193	**0.108**	0.058
MAP(4) JM+EM	**7.295**	**5.565**	4.092	3.012	0.309	**0.183**	**0.108**	**0.065**
Trace TUDo	2.510	2.226	1.999	1.816	0.137	0.114	0.098	0.086
MAP(2) AC30 Gfit	1.317	1.163	1.088	1.038	0.087	0.083	0.080	**0.078**
MAP(2) AC5	4.202	4.110	3.997	3.849	0.317	0.279	0.241	0.204
MAP(2) EM	4.894	4.552	4.245	3.934	0.308	0.260	0.214	0.172
MAP(2) JM	4.383	4.254	4.116	3.945	0.322	0.283	0.244	0.204
MAP(2) AC30 Gfit+EM	**3.645**	**2.886**	**2.417**	**2.100**	**0.119**	**0.096**	**0.083**	0.074
MAP(4) AC30 Gfit	**2.118**	**2.051**	**1.999**	**1.949**	**0.156**	**0.142**	**0.129**	0.118
MAP(4) AC10	4.343	3.930	3.547	3.186	0.236	0.193	0.158	0.131
MAP(4) EM	4.283	3.949	3.688	3.457	0.267	0.232	0.200	0.169
MAP(4) JM	3.862	3.507	3.161	2.847	0.211	0.172	0.141	**0.117**
MAP(4) AC10+EM	3.541	3.214	2.951	2.732	0.215	0.185	0.162	0.144

closest approximation. For the trace *LBL-TCP-3* we obtained similar results. As already mentioned all fitting algorithms had problems with the MAP *TUDo*. This becomes also visible in Table 4. Only the MAP(4) that has been fitted with Gfit and a subsequent fitting of the autocorrelations provided a sufficient approximation of the queueing behavior.

5 Conclusions

This paper presents a comparison of different MAP fitting approaches applied to three different traces. Two of the traces have been taken from the Internet archive and have been used several times as benchmarks for MAP fitting approaches.

However, these traces are also very old. The third trace is much newer and shows different characteristics. Our results indicate that the older traces can be fitted adequately with most approaches whereas the new trace exhibits a much stronger autocorrelation and is much harder to fit. It is an interesting question whether current network traffic, which probably differs from the traffic analyzed twenty years ago, really contains higher autocorrelations or whether this is an artifact in our measurements. However, to answer this question, more measurements are necessary.

The comparison of the different fitting methods gives a mixed picture. Obviously, using a method that fits a MAP according to one quantity, like the joint moments or the autocorrelation, gives good results according to this quantity but usually results in a bad fitting according to other quantities that are not used for fitting. Thus, no approach is superior to all others according to all quantities. However, our results indicate that fitting according to the likelihood using the EM algorithm gives the best results but is, unfortunately, also the by far most costly method. Furthermore, it should be mentioned that the fitting quality and the effort of the EM algorithm depends on the initial MAP and might be poor for badly chosen initial MAPs.

References

1. The internet traffic archive, http://ita.ee.lbl.gov/
2. Asmussen, S., Nerman, O., Olsson, M.: Fitting phase-type distributions via the EM-algorithm. Scand. J. Stat. 23(4), 419–441 (1996)
3. Bodrog, L., Heindl, A., Horváth, G., Telek, M.: A Markovian canonical form of second-order matrix-exponential processes. European Journal of Operational Research 190(2), 459–477 (2008)
4. Breuer, L.: An EM algorithm for batch Markovian arrival processes and its comparison to a simpler estimation procedure. Annals of Operations Research 112, 123–138 (2002)
5. Buchholz, P.: An EM-algorithm for MAP fitting from real traffic data. In: Kemper, P., Sanders, W.H. (eds.) TOOLS 2003. LNCS, vol. 2794, pp. 218–236. Springer, Heidelberg (2003)
6. Buchholz, P., Kriege, J.: Equivalence transformations for acyclic phase type distributions. Technical Report 827, Dep. of Informatics, TU Dortmund (2009)
7. Buchholz, P., Kriege, J.: A heuristic approach for fitting MAPs to moments and joint moments. In: Proc. of 6th International Conference on Quantitative Evaluation of SysTems (QEST 2009). IEEE, Los Alamitos (2009)
8. Buchholz, P., Panchenko, A.: A Two-Step EM Algorithm for MAP Fitting. In: Aykanat, C., Dayar, T., Körpeoğlu, İ. (eds.) ISCIS 2004. LNCS, vol. 3280, pp. 217–227. Springer, Heidelberg (2004)
9. Casale, G., Smirni, E.: MPA-AMVA: Approximate mean value analysis of bursty system. In: Proc. DSN 2009 (2009)
10. Casale, G., Zhang, E.Z., Smirni, E.: KPC-Toolbox: Simple Yet Effective Trace Fitting Using Markovian Arrival Processes. In: QEST, pp. 83–92. IEEE Computer Society, Los Alamitos (2008)

11. Horváth, A., Telek, M.: Markovian modeling of real data traffic: Heuristic phase type and MAP fitting of heavy tailed and fractal like samples. In: Calzarossa, M.C., Tucci, S. (eds.) Performance 2002. LNCS, vol. 2459, pp. 405–434. Springer, Heidelberg (2002)
12. Horváth, A., Telek, M.: PhFit: A general phase-type fitting tool. In: Field, T., Harrison, P.G., Bradley, J., Harder, U. (eds.) TOOLS 2002. LNCS, vol. 2324, pp. 82–91. Springer, Heidelberg (2002)
13. Horvath, G., Telek, M., Buchholz, P.: A MAP fitting approach with independent approximation of the inter-arrival time distribution and the lag-correlation. In: Proc. of 2nd Int. Conf. on the Quantitative Analysis of Systems. IEEE CS Press, Los Alamitos (2005)
14. Klemm, A., Lindemann, C., Lohmann, M.: Modeling IP traffic using the batch markovian arrival process. Perform. Eval. 54(2), 149–173 (2003)
15. Lawson, C.L., Hanson, B.J.: Solving Least Squares Problems. Prentice-Hall, Englewood Cliffs (1974)
16. Nelder, J.A., Mead, R.: A simplex method for function minimization. Computer Journal 7, 308–313 (1965)
17. Neuts, M.F.: A versatile Markovian point process. Journal of Applied Probability 16, 764–779 (1979)
18. Neuts, M.F.: Matrix-geometric solutions in stochastic models. Johns Hopkins University Press (1981)
19. O'Cinneide, C.A.: Characterization of phase-type distributions. Stochastic Models 6, 1–57 (1990)
20. Paxson, V., Floyd, S.: Wide-area traffic: The failure of Poisson modeling. IEEE/ACM Transactions in Networking 3, 226–244 (1995)
21. Press, W.H., Teukolsky, S.A., Vetterling, W.T., Flannery, B.P.: Numerical Recipes in C - The Art of Scientific Computing, 2nd edn. Cambridge University Press, Cambridge (1993)
22. Ryden, T.: An EM algorithm for estimation in Markov-modulated Poisson processes. Comput. Statist. Data Anal. 21(4), 431–447 (1996)
23. Stewart, W.J.: Introduction to the numerical solution of Markov chains. Princeton University Press, Princeton (1994)
24. Telek, M., Horváth, G.: A minimal representation of Markov arrival processes and a moments matching method. Perform. Eval. 64(9-12), 1153–1168 (2007)
25. Thümmler, A., Buchholz, P., Telek, M.: A Novel Approach for Phase-Type Fitting with the EM Algorithm. IEEE Trans. Dependable Sec. Comput. 3(3), 245–258 (2006)

Reducing the Cost of Generating
APH-Distributed Random Numbers

Philipp Reinecke[1], Miklós Telek[2], and Katinka Wolter[1]

[1] Freie Universität Berlin
Institut für Informatik
Takustraße 9
14195 Berlin, Germany
{philipp.reinecke,katinka.wolter}@fu-berlin.de
[2] Budapest University of Technology and Economics
Department of Telecommunications
1521 Budapest, Hungary
telek@webspn.hit.bme.hu

Abstract. Phase-type (PH) distributions are proven to be very powerful tools in modelling and analysis of a wide range of phenomena in computer systems. The use of these distributions in simulation studies requires efficient methods for generating PH-distributed random numbers. In this work, we discuss algorithms for generating random numbers from PH distributions and propose two algorithms for reducing the cost associated with generating random numbers from Acyclic Phase-Type distributions (APH).

1 Introduction

Phase-type (PH) distributions have been widely used in modelling various phenomena such as response times, inter-arrival times and failure times in computer systems [1,2,3], and several tools that fit phase-type distributions to trace data have been developed [4,5]. The fact that there are simple and elegant solution techniques available for PH distributions has made them appealing for analytic solutions.

PH distributions can also be employed in simulation studies, where they allow the introduction of realistic response-time distributions obtained from measurements into simulations without modification of the typically Markovian simulation tool. As such simulations often require many random variates and are repeated many times, generating PH-distributed random numbers efficiently is important. In this work we investigate the efficiency of generating random numbers from continuous PH distributions. Due to the fact that the Markovian representation of PH distributions is not unique the key issue to investigate is which representation of a PH distribution is most efficient for random-number generation.

In [6] we posed the following optimisation problem: Starting from a Markovian representation of a PH distribution, find the (not necessarily minimal) Markovian representation that minimises the cost associated with generating random

B. Müller-Clostermann et al. (Eds.): MMB & DFT 2010, LNCS 5987, pp. 274–286, 2010.

numbers. In this paper we study this optimisation problem for Acyclic Phase-Type (APH) distributions. We provide a result on the optimal representation and develop two algorithms that transform a given APH representation into a representation with lower simulation cost.

The paper is structured as follows. In the next section we introduce the considered model class and the notation used throughout the paper. We then describe a number of algorithms for generating random numbers from phase-type distributions (Section 3) and derive average costs (Section 4). In Section 5 we study the problem of optimising bi-diagonal representations for random-number generation. Section 6 illustrates the application of our algorithms to several theoretic and fitted phase-type distributions. Finally, in Section 7 we conclude with an outlook on future work.

2 Definitions and Notation

Continuous phase-type (PH) distributions represent the time to absorption in a continuous-time Markov chain with one absorbing state [7]. PH distributions are commonly specified as a tuple $(\alpha, \mathbf{A})$ of the initial probability vector $\alpha = (\alpha_1, \ldots, \alpha_n)$ and the transient part $\mathbf{A} = \{a_{ij}\}, 1 \leq i, j \leq n$ of the generator matrix, also referred to as transient generator matrix. The probability density function, the cumulative distribution function, the Laplace-Stieltjes Transform (LST) of the CDF, and the kth moment, respectively, are [4,7,8]:

$$f(x) = \alpha e^{\mathbf{A}x} \mathbf{a},$$
$$F(x) = 1 - \alpha e^{\mathbf{A}x} \mathbb{1},$$
$$\tilde{F}(s) = \alpha_{n+1} + \alpha(s\mathbf{I} - \mathbf{A})^{-1}\mathbf{a}, \text{ and}$$
$$E\left[X^k\right] = k!\alpha(-\mathbf{A})^{-k}\mathbb{1}.$$

where $\mathbf{a} = -\mathbf{A}\mathbb{1}$, $\mathbf{I}$ is the identity matrix, and $\mathbb{1}$ is the column vector of ones, both of appropriate size.

Phase-type distributions have rational LST. It follows that the eigenvalues of the transient generator matrix are the poles of the LST of the distribution [9].

Definition 1. *The* $(\alpha, \mathbf{A})$ *representation of a phase-type distribution is called Markovian if* $\alpha \geq 0$, $\alpha\mathbb{1} = 1$, $a_{ij} \geq 0, 1 \leq i \neq j \leq n$ *and* $\mathbf{a} = -\mathbf{A}\mathbb{1} \geq 0$. *Then, the generator matrix of the associated CTMC is*

$$\overline{\mathbf{A}} = \begin{pmatrix} \mathbf{A} \ \mathbf{a} \\ \mathbf{0} \ 0 \end{pmatrix}.$$

Definition 2. *The size of the* $(\alpha, \mathbf{A})$ *representation is the size of the vector* α, *which is equal to the size of the square matrix* $\mathbf{A}$.

The $(\alpha, \mathbf{A})$ representation is not unique. In particular, another representation of the same size can be obtained by a similarity transformation using a matrix $\mathbf{B}$:

Fig. 1. CTMC for a bi-diagonal representation

Definition 3. *When* **B** *is invertible and* $\mathbf{B}\mathbb{1} = \mathbb{1}$, *then the similarity transform*

$$(\boldsymbol{\alpha}\mathbf{B}, \mathbf{B}^{-1}\mathbf{A}\mathbf{B})$$

provides another representation of the same distribution, since its CDF is

$$1 - \boldsymbol{\alpha}\mathbf{B}e^{\mathbf{B}^{-1}\mathbf{A}\mathbf{B}x}\mathbb{1} = 1 - \boldsymbol{\alpha}\mathbf{B}\mathbf{B}^{-1}e^{\mathbf{A}x}\mathbf{B}\mathbb{1} = 1 - \boldsymbol{\alpha}e^{\mathbf{A}x}\mathbb{1}.$$

In the following we refer to a PH representation as being *bi-diagonal* (cf. Figure 1) if it meets the following requirements:

Definition 4. *A* bi-diagonal representation *of a PH distribution* $(\boldsymbol{\alpha}, \mathbf{A})$ *has* $a_{ii} < 0, a_{ii+1} = -a_{ii}$ *and* $a_{ij} = 0$ *for* $j < i$ *and* $j > i+1$. *An alternative notation is* $(\boldsymbol{\alpha}, \boldsymbol{\Lambda})$, *with* $\boldsymbol{\Lambda} = (a_1, \ldots, a_n)$ *a row vector of length* n *and* $a_i = -a_{ii}$.

Note that for a bi-diagonal representation the eigenvalues of the transient generator matrix **A**, and thus the poles of the LST of the distribution function, are given by the entries of the diagonal, a_{ii}.

In this paper we are concerned with acyclic phase-type distributions (APH):

Definition 5. *An* acyclic phase-type distribution (APH) *is a phase-type distribution that has an acyclic Markovian representation.*

We make use of the following important bi-diagonal representation:

Definition 6. *[10] The* Canonical Form 1 (CF-1 form) *is a bi-diagonal representation* $(\boldsymbol{\alpha}, \boldsymbol{\Lambda})$ *where* $\boldsymbol{\alpha}$ *is Markovian and the rates* a_i *in* $\boldsymbol{\Lambda}$ *are in increasing order:* $a_1 \leq a_2 \leq \cdots \leq a_n$.

The next theorem, which we state without proof, ensures that the distributions we consider have at least one bi-diagonal representation with a Markovian initial vector:

Theorem 1. *[10,11] Every acyclic phase-type distribution with a representation of size* n *has a unique CF-1 representation of the same size.*

We remark that smaller CF-1 representations may exist if there is redundancy in the original representation [7,12,13].

The CF-1 form for an APH given as $(\boldsymbol{\alpha}, \mathbf{A})$ can be obtained by the transformation provided in [12]. It presents a way to construct a similarity matrix **B**, which transforms **A** to a bi-diagonal matrix **G** where the entries of the diagonal are the ordered eigenvalues of the matrix **A**, i.e., $\mathbf{G} = \mathbf{B}^{-1}\mathbf{A}\mathbf{B}$. The same similarity matrix can be used to compute the initial vector $\boldsymbol{\gamma} = \boldsymbol{\alpha}\mathbf{B}$.

Example 1. Consider the phase-type distribution given by

$$\alpha = (0.3, 0.4, 0.3), \quad \mathbf{A} = \begin{pmatrix} -1 & 1 & 0 \\ 1 & -2 & 0.5 \\ 0 & 3 & -3 \end{pmatrix}.$$

The eigenvalues of $\mathbf{A}$ are -0.205168, -1.85629, and -3.93854. Let $\mathbf{G}$ be the corresponding CF-1 bi-diagonal matrix. From $\mathbf{G} = \mathbf{B}^{-1}\mathbf{A}\mathbf{B}$ we obtain the similarity transformation matrix

$$\mathbf{B} = \begin{pmatrix} 0.931611 & 0.0683893 & 0 \\ 0.740474 & 0.132575 & 0.126951 \\ 0.794832 & 0.205168 & 0 \end{pmatrix}.$$

We compute the initial probability vector as $\gamma = \alpha \mathbf{B}$ and get the CF-1 form $(\gamma, \Lambda_G) = ((0.814123, 0.135097, 0.0507803), (0.205168, 1.85629, 3.93854))$.

3 Generation of PH-Distributed Random Numbers

We now discuss two methods for generating random variates from a general PH distribution given in Markovian form. While one may apply numerical inversion of the distribution [14], we consider approaches based explicitly on the CTMC interpretation. The discussed algorithms all rely on the following elementary operation for drawing an exponentially distributed random number:

$$\mathrm{Exp}(\lambda) = -\frac{1}{\lambda} \ln(U),$$

where U denotes a $[0, 1]$ uniformly distributed pseudo-random number.

The most natural way to obtain a PH-distributed random number is to play the CTMC until absorption. By 'play' we mean to simulate the state transitions of the CTMC according to the following basic steps. Let e_i denote the row vector with 1 at position i, and 0 everywhere else.

Procedure Play:

1) clock= 0, draw an α-distributed discrete sample for the initial state,
2) the chain is in state i
   - draw an $e_i(-\mathrm{diag}\langle 1/a_{ii}, 0\rangle \overline{\mathbf{A}} + \mathbf{I})$-distributed discrete sample for the next state,
   - clock $+= \mathrm{Exp}(-a_{ii})$,
   - if the next state is the absorbing one go to 3), otherwise go to 2)
3) return the clock value

We point out that Play is suited to general PH distributions in an arbitrary form, where each phase may have several successor phases. If our simulation is such that it involves only acyclic-phase type distributions in a bi-diagonal representation (such as the CF-1 form), we can make use of the following structural restriction: For each phase, there is exactly one successor phase; consequently, there is no need to randomly choose the next state. This observation allows the following simplification of Play:

Procedure SimplePlay:

1) clock= 0, draw an $\boldsymbol{\alpha}$-distributed discrete sample for the initial state.
2) The chain is in state i.
   - clock += $\text{Exp}(-a_{ii})$,
   - i += 1,
   - if the next state is the absorbing state go to 3), otherwise go to 2).
3) Return the clock value.

In the next section we discuss costs of random-number generation using these algorithms.

4 Average Costs of Generating PH-Distributed Random Numbers

As we saw in the previous section, PH random number generation requires uniform random variates, both for state selection and for generating exponential random variates. Furthermore, for each exponential random variate a logarithm operation must be performed. Both operations are expensive in terms of computing time and can significantly increase the running-time of simulations that require many random variates. Therefore, we consider the following complexity metrics:

- #*uni*, the number of required uniform random variates, and
- #*ln*, the number of logarithms that need to be computed.

The average cost associated with drawing a random variate from a phase-type distribution depends on the average number n^* of state transitions up to absorption,

$$n^* = \boldsymbol{\alpha}(\text{diag}\langle 1/a_{ii}\rangle \mathbf{A})^{-1}\mathbb{1}.$$

For APH in bi-diagonal form this reduces to

$$n^* = \boldsymbol{\alpha}\boldsymbol{\nu}^{\mathsf{T}},$$

where $\boldsymbol{\nu} = (n, n-1, \ldots, 1)$. Thus $n^* = \sum_{i=1}^{n} \alpha_i(n-i+1)$.

Both procedures require one uniform random variate to choose the initial state. The Play procedure then needs two uniform random variates per step, because the next phase is chosen randomly. Play therefore requires #*uni* = $2n^* + 1$ uniform random variates, while SimplePlay requires only #*uni* = $n^* + 1$ uniforms. The number of logarithms required for the Play and SimplePlay procedures is #*ln* = n^*, since in each phase an exponentially distributed random variate is drawn.

We can thus conclude that for generating random numbers from an APH efficiently we should transform the distribution into a bi-diagonal representation and then apply the SimplePlay procedure.

5 Optimal Representations for APH-PRNG

As illustrated in Section 4, average costs for random-number generation depend mainly on the number of visited states, n^*. In [6] we posed the problem of finding a Markovian representation that minimises n^*.

In the following we tackle this optimisation problem for acyclic phase-type (APH) distributions $(\boldsymbol{\alpha}, \mathbf{A})$ in CF-1 form. We choose the CF-1 form as our starting point because bi-diagonal forms allow efficient random-variate generation, using the procedure `SimplePlay`, and because APHs are commonly given in CF-1 form (e.g. by the phase-type fitting tool PhFit [4]). Furthermore, Theorem 1 ensures that the results for CF-1 are applicable to the whole APH class.

In order to solve the optimisation problem, we try to find a bi-diagonal representation $(\boldsymbol{\alpha}^*, \mathbf{A}^*)$ for which the average number of traversed states,

$$n^* = \boldsymbol{\alpha}^* \boldsymbol{\nu} = \sum_{i=1}^{n} \alpha_i^* (n - i + 1). \tag{1}$$

is minimal.

From the right side of (1) it is immediately obvious that, in order to reduce n^*, probability mass must be shifted to the higher indices of the initial probability vector $\boldsymbol{\alpha}$. Formally, the new probability vector $\boldsymbol{\alpha}'$ must be stochastically larger than $\boldsymbol{\alpha}$:

Definition 7. *The stochastic ordering [15] on the set of stochastic vectors of size n is defined as follows:*

$$\boldsymbol{\alpha} \leq_{st} \boldsymbol{\alpha}' \Leftrightarrow 1 - \Pr\{\boldsymbol{\alpha} \leq k\} \leq 1 - \Pr\{\boldsymbol{\alpha}' \leq k\} \text{ for } k = 1, \ldots, n,$$

where

$$\Pr\{\boldsymbol{\alpha} \leq k\} := \sum_{i=1}^{k} \alpha_i.$$

At the same time, $(\boldsymbol{\alpha}^*, \mathbf{A}^*)$ must represent the same distribution as $(\boldsymbol{\alpha}, \mathbf{A})$, and hence the LST of its distribution function must have the same poles. This implies that the matrices $\mathbf{A}$ and $\mathbf{A}^*$ must have the same eigenvalues. In the bi-diagonal form the eigenvalues are the entries of the diagonals. Changing the order of the diagonal elements does not change the eigenvalues, hence a representation where $\mathbf{A}^*$ is obtained by re-ordering the diagonal elements is guaranteed to have the same poles as $(\boldsymbol{\alpha}, \mathbf{A})$. Consequently, we consider shifting probability mass to the right by modifying the order of the rates along the diagonals. We propose the following operator:

Definition 8. *The* `Swap`$(\boldsymbol{\alpha}, \mathbf{A}, i)$ *operator exchanges the ith rate with the $(i + 1)$th rate $(1 \leq i \leq n - 1)$ on the diagonals in a bi-diagonal representation by swapping the ith and $(i + 1)$th entry in the vector $\boldsymbol{\Lambda}$. The associated similarity transformation matrix $\mathbf{B}$ has the form*

$$\mathbf{B} = \begin{pmatrix} \ddots & 0 & 0 & 0 & 0 \\ 0 & 1 & 0 & 0 & 0 \\ 0 & b_{i+1,i} & b_{i+1,i+1} & 0 & 0 \\ 0 & 0 & 0 & 1 & 0 \\ 0 & 0 & 0 & 0 & \ddots \end{pmatrix}$$

where

$$b_{i+1,i} = \frac{a_i - a_{i+1}}{a_i}, \ and \ b_{i+1,i+1} = \frac{a_{i+1}}{a_i} \ for \ 1 \leq i \leq n-1.$$

Where appropriate, we also use the $\mathtt{Swap}(\alpha, \Lambda, i)$ notation to denote the same operator.

Remark 1. $\mathtt{Swap}(\alpha, \Lambda, i)$ only involves the ith and $(i+1)$th entries of α and Λ, which allows for the analytically tractable expressions employed in the following. Operators that produce more complex permutations in a single step do not have this property. Furthermore, the $\mathtt{Swap}$ operator is sufficiently powerful to generate all permutations of a list [16].

Let $(\alpha', \mathbf{A}')$ denote the result of applying $\mathtt{Swap}(\alpha, \mathbf{A}, i)$ on $(\alpha, \mathbf{A})$. Because $(\alpha', \mathbf{A}')$ is derived by applying a similarity transformation to $(\alpha, \mathbf{A})$, both tuples represent the same distribution. Recall from Definition 3 that

$$\alpha' = \alpha\mathbf{B}.$$

From this equation and the definition of $\mathbf{B}$ we immediately get the following properties of the result of the $\mathtt{Swap}$ operation:

$$\forall j \notin \{i, i+1\} : \alpha'_j = \alpha_j \tag{2}$$

$$\alpha'_i = \alpha_i + \alpha_{i+1}\frac{a_i - a_{i+1}}{a_i} = \alpha_i + \alpha_{i+1}(1 - \frac{a_{i+1}}{a_i}) \tag{3}$$

$$\alpha'_{i+1} = \alpha_{i+1}\frac{a_{i+1}}{a_i}. \tag{4}$$

Putting (α', A') into (1) we obtain

$$n^*(\alpha', \mathbf{A}') = n^*(\alpha, \mathbf{A}) + \alpha_{i+1}(1 - \frac{a_{i+1}}{a_i}). \tag{5}$$

Equations (2)–(5) are valid for Markovian ($\alpha \geq 0$) and non-Markovian ($\alpha \in \mathbb{R}^n$) bi-diagonal representations.

If we restrict our attention to the Markovian bi-diagonal representations then we observe the following: The $\mathtt{Swap}$ operation with adjacent rates $a_i < a_{i+1}$, results in $n^*(\alpha', A') \leq n^*(\alpha, A)$ according to (5), because in this case $1 < \frac{a_{i+1}}{a_i}$, and α_{i+1} is non-negative. Consequently, by repeatedly exchanging adjacent rates $a_i < a_{i+1}$ such that each resulting representation is Markovian until no such operations are possible anymore, we can obtain a representation that has minimal costs n^*.

On the other hand, we note that the Swap operator will result in a non-stochastic vector α' if $\alpha_i < \alpha_{i+1}(1 - \frac{a_{i+1}}{a_i})$, since then the resulting $\alpha_i' < 0$. In this case $(\alpha', \mathbf{A})$ is a non-Markovian representation of the original phase-type distribution. This representation is not suitable as input for the random-number generation algorithms discussed in Section 3. Furthermore, both the stochastic ordering and n^* are only defined for (sub-)stochastic α. We must therefore avoid Swap operations that will result in non-stochastic α'. Based on these observations we propose the following.

Lemma 1. *Given a Markovian representation $(\alpha, \mathbf{A})$ in CF-1 form, the representation $(\alpha^*, \mathbf{A}^*)$ that reverses the order of the rates is optimal with respect to n^* if α^* is a stochastic vector. In this case, all bi-diagonal representations constructed by the Swap operator are Markovian.*

Proof. The proof is composed by two steps. First we show that all bi-diagonal representations are Markovian if $(\alpha^*, \mathbf{A}^*)$ is Markovian. In the second step we show by contradiction that $(\alpha^*, \mathbf{A}^*)$ is optimal with respect to n^*.

According to property (3), a Swap operation applied to a Markovian representation can result in a non-Markovian representation only if a larger rate a_{i+1} is exchanged for a smaller rate a_i. Starting from $(\alpha^*, \mathbf{A}^*)$, all representations can be obtained by a series of Swap operations in which a smaller rate a_{i+1} is exchanged for a larger rate a_i. If $(\alpha^*, \mathbf{A}^*)$ is Markovian, none of these Swap operations can result in a non-Markovian representation.

To prove the first part of the lemma, assume that $(\alpha', \mathbf{A}')$ with rates

$$a_1', \ldots, a_i', a_{i+1}', \ldots, a_n'$$

ordered such that $a_i' < a_{i+1}'$ is optimal. Then from (5) it follows that by exchanging a_i', a_{i+1}' using the Swap operator we can obtain a representation $(\alpha'', \mathbf{A}'') = Swap(\alpha', \mathbf{A}', i)$ for which $n^*(\alpha'', \mathbf{A}'') < n^*(\alpha', \mathbf{A}')$. □

5.1 Heuristic Algorithms for Computing Optimal APH Representations

Lemma 1 states that if the reversed CF-1 form is Markovian, then it is optimal with respect to n^*. This optimal representation is easily computed by applying a similarity transformation, as illustrated in Example 1. In the following we develop algorithms for finding a Markovian APH representation that is close to optimal (with respect to n^*) when the reversed CF-1 form is non-Markovian.

The algorithms are best thought of as operating on the graph of all permutations of the rate vector Λ. From each permutation exactly $n - 1$ other permutations can be reached by applying the Swap operation. If the reversed CF-1 is non-Markovian, then some of the permutations have non-Markovian initial vectors.

The most obvious approach proceeds by exploring the complete graph. This is equivalent to generating all permutations of Λ and minimising n^* over the subset of permutations whose initial vector is stochastic. The approach is easily implemented, e.g. as a modification to the Steinhaus-Johnson-Trotter algorithm for enumerating permutations [16] and is guaranteed to find the optimum. Unfortunately, since this method explores all $n!$ permutations for an APH of size n, it is infeasible for larger APH.

Lemma 1 provides the basis for the two computationally less expensive algorithms presented in this section. The underlying intuition is as follows: The optimal representation with respect to n^* is somewhere on the Markovian side of the boundary between the Markovian and the non-Markovian representations. Lemma 1 implies that the Markovian optimum is along one of the paths from the CF-1 to the reversed CF-1. We thus need to find the (Markovian) point where the path between CF-1 and reversed CF-1 crosses the boundary between the Markovian and non-Markovian representations.

Starting with the CF-1 form (i.e. inside the Markovian representations), we know from (5) that each exchange of two adjacent rates such that after the exchange the larger rate is moved to the left constructs a new element of the path that has lower n^*, provided the new representation is Markovian. Properties (3) and (4) thus define the direction along which to search for the optimal Markovian representation without enumerating all permutations and without explicitly computing n^* for the new representation. Our first algorithm follows from this intuition. It is a modified version of the Bubblesort algorithm [17] that attempts to re-order the rates into the reversed CF-1 form:

```
Algorithm BubblesortOptimise(α, Λ):
For i = 1,...,n − 1 do
    For j = 1,...,n − 1 do
        If Λ[j] < Λ[j + 1] ∧ (α′, Λ′) := Swap(α, Λ, i) is Markovian then
            (α, Λ) := (α′, Λ′)
        Else
            break
    done
done
Return (α, Λ)
```

Note that the algorithm does not perform Swap operations whose result would be non-Markovian, i.e. it does not cross the boundary between both types of representations. The algorithm terminates once either the reversed CF-1 form is reached or there are no re-orderings left that would result in a Markovian representation with lower cost n^*. While this may mean that the algorithm does not find Markovian representations hidden 'behind' non-Markovian ones, it is necessary because n^* has no meaning for non-Markovian representations.

Our second algorithm starts from the reversed CF-1 form and searches for the point where the path towards the CF-1 first crosses the border to the Markovian representations. The path is constructed by swapping pairs of rates such that in the result the higher rate is to the right (which means that the result is closer to the CF-1). The algorithm stops when it encounters a Markovian representation. Termination is ensured by the fact that the CF-1 is Markovian:

```
Algorithm FindMarkovian:
Let (α', A') be the reversed CF-1 of (α, A).
```
While $\exists i \in \{1, \ldots, n-1\}: \alpha'_i < 0$
$\quad i := \text{argmin}_i \{\alpha'_i < 0\}$
$\quad i := \max(2, i)$
$\quad$ While α' is not Markovian $\wedge \, \exists k: \Lambda[k] \geq \Lambda[k+1]$
$\quad\quad k := \text{argmin}_j \{i-1 \leq j \leq n-1 \, : \, \Lambda[j] \geq \Lambda[j+1]\}$
$\quad\quad (\alpha', \Lambda') := \text{Swap}(\alpha', \Lambda', k)$
$\quad$ end
end
Return (α', Λ')

Note that `FindMarkovian` is also not guaranteed to find the optimum, since it stops when it finds the first Markovian representation.

6   Illustrative Examples

We will now illustrate our results on several APH distributions.

Example 2. Consider the generalised Erlang distribution with $\Lambda = (1, 2, 3, 4)$ and $\alpha = (1, 0, 0, 0)$. For this distribution, every order of rates in Λ has costs $n^* = 4$, since no probability mass can be shifted to the right. As expected, both `BubblesortOptimise` and `FindMarkovian` identify $((1, 0, 0, 0), (4, 3, 2, 1))$ as the optimal representation.

Example 3. Let $\Lambda = (1, 2, 3, 4)$, as before, and the initial probability vector $\alpha = (0.7, 0.15, 0.09, 0.06)$. Then, the average number of visited states is

$$n^*(\alpha, \Lambda) = 3.49.$$

Application of `BubblesortOptimise` results in the reversed CF-1 form with $\Lambda' = (4, 3, 2, 1)$, $\alpha' = (0.46, 0.12, 0.18, 0.24)$ and costs

$$n^*(\alpha', \Lambda') = 2.8.$$

Since the reversed CF-1 is Markovian, `FindMarkovian` gives the same result. We observe that probability mass in the initial probability vector has been shifted towards higher indices.

Example 4. We study (α, Λ) with $\alpha = (0.5, 0.4, 0.05, 0.05)$ and again $\Lambda = (1, 2, 3, 4)$. This representation has costs

$$n^*(\alpha, \Lambda) = 3.35.$$

The initial vector for the reversed CF-1 is $(-0.6, 1.4, 0, 0.2)$, and hence the reversed CF-1 form is non-Markovian. Applying the `BubblesortOptimise` algorithm to the CF-1 form provides us with a representation (α', Λ') with $\Lambda' = (2, 4, 3, 1)$ and $\alpha' = (0.1, 0.7, 0, 0.2)$, for which

$$n^*(\alpha', \Lambda') = 2.7.$$

`FindMarkovian` starts on the non-Markovian reversed CF-1 representation and generates the Markovian representation $\Lambda'' = (2, 3, 4, 1)$ and $\alpha'' = (0.1, 0.7, 0, 0.2)$, which has the same costs of 2.7. A complete enumeration of all permutations shows that both orderings are optimal with respect to n^*.

Example 5. As the last example, we fit an APH(8) to the `loss1-50-opc-1` dataset from [3] using the PhFit tool [4]. This data set contains response-time measurements from a SOA system under high load and with network packet loss. The resulting APH has initial probability vector $\alpha = (0.019, 0.006, 0.069, 0.104, 0.164, 0.371, 0.216, 0.051)$ and rate vector

$$\Lambda = (7.181 \cdot 10^{-05}, 2.4280 \cdot 10^{-04}, 5.854 \cdot 10^{-04}, 5.863 \cdot 10^{-04},$$
$$5.956 \cdot 10^{-04}, 5.965 \cdot 10^{-04}, 6.178 \cdot 10^{-04}, 6.332 \cdot 10^{-04}).$$

For this representation,

$$n^*(\alpha, \Lambda) = 3.38.$$

Again, the reversed CF-1 for this representation has negative entries in the initial vector. Application of `BubblesortOptimise` results in (α', Λ') with initial probability vector $\alpha' = (0.0047, 0.0203, 0.0614, 0.0929, 0.1327, 0.3911, 0.2417, 0.0552)$ and

$$\Lambda' = (2.4280 \cdot 10^{-04}, 7.181 \cdot 10^{-05}, 6.332 \cdot 10^{-04}, 6.178 \cdot 10^{-04},$$
$$5.965 \cdot 10^{-04}, 5.956 \cdot 10^{-04}, 5.863 \cdot 10^{-04}, 5.854 \cdot 10^{-04}),$$

which has $n^*(\alpha', \Lambda') = 3.256$. According to a complete enumeration, this is also the Markovian optimum. `FindMarkovian` returns $\alpha'' = (0.0047, 0.0203, 0.069, 0.104, 0.164, 0.371, 0.216, 0.051)$ and

$$\Lambda'' = (2.4280 \cdot 10^{-04}, 7.181 \cdot 10^{-05}, 5.854 \cdot 10^{-04}, 5.863 \cdot 10^{-04},$$
$$5.956 \cdot 10^{-04}, 5.965 \cdot 10^{-04}, 6.178 \cdot 10^{-04}, 6.332 \cdot 10^{-04}),$$

for which $n^*(\alpha'', \Lambda'') = 3.366$.

6.1   Discussion

In general, our examples indicate that there are phase-type distributions for which re-ordering of rates results in a cost reduction. The highest reduction was observed in Example 2 (20%), while for the fitted distribution in Example 5 the reduction was 3.6%. In Monte-Carlo simulations with many simulation runs, these reductions lead to significant time-savings.

On the other hand, we also observe that the effectiveness of the algorithms depends strongly on the initial representation. Representations with (generalised) Erlang structure (Example 2) are invariant to re-ordering of rates. The same holds within blocks of subsequent phases with zero initial probability. For representations where the probability mass is already concentrated at the higher indices in the CF-1, there is also little room for improvement.

We can thus identify (generalised) Erlang structure and large probability mass at the higher indices as two properties of representations that are not susceptible to the proposed optimisation. However, so far we have not been able to find more formal criteria for when and why the optimisation procedures fail. Such criteria would not only help in improving the optimisation algorithms, but may also enable the development of specialised PH-fitting methods that give APH distributions suited for efficient random-number generation.

7 Conclusion and Future Work

In this paper we considered the complexity of generating random numbers from acyclic phase-type distributions. Our focus lay on bi-diagonal representations of APH distributions, whose structural limitations enable the `SimplePlay` procedure which is more effective than the more general `Play`. By re-ordering rates along the diagonal we undertook a first attempt at optimising the bi-diagonal representation for efficient random-number generation. We presented a limited result for the optimal ordering and proposed two algorithms to optimise the representation, given an APH in CF-1 form.

We note that the effectiveness of our approach depends on the given APH. While we can provide a number of intuitive guidelines, formal criteria for deciding when re-ordering rates may offer an advantage are still future work. Furthermore, in the near future we will extend our approach to eliminate the limitations of our result, and we will apply the approach to general phase-type distributions in Monocyclic form [18].

Acknowledgements

This work was supported by DFG grants Wo 898/2-1 and Wo 898/3-1, and OTKA grant no. K-61709.

References

1. Fallahi, A., Hossain, E.: Distributed and Energy-Aware MAC for Differentiated Services Wireless Packet Networks: A General Queuing Analytical Framework. IEEE Transactions on Mobile Computing 6(4), 381–394 (2007)
2. Reinecke, P., Wolter, K.: Phase-Type Approximations for Message Transmission Times in Web Services Reliable Messaging. In: Kounev, S., Gorton, I., Sachs, K. (eds.) SIPEW 2008. LNCS, vol. 5119, pp. 191–207. Springer, Heidelberg (2008)

3. Reinecke, P., Wittkowski, S., Wolter, K.: Response-time Measurements Using the Sun Java Adventure Builder. In: QUASOSS 2009: Proceedings of the 1st International Workshop on Quality of Service-oriented Software Systems, pp. 11–18. ACM, New York (2009)

4. Horváth, A., Telek, M.: PhFit: A General Phase-Type Fitting Tool. In: Field, T., Harrison, P.G., Bradley, J., Harder, U. (eds.) TOOLS 2002. LNCS, vol. 2324, pp. 82–91. Springer, Heidelberg (2002)

5. Thümmler, A., Buchholz, P., Telek, M.: A Novel Approach for Phase-Type Fitting with the EM Algorithm. IEEE Trans. Dependable Secur. Comput. 3(3), 245–258 (2006)

6. Reinecke, P., Wolter, K., Bodrog, L., Telek, M.: On the Cost of Generating PH-distributed Random Numbers. In: Horváth, G., Joshi, K., Heindl, A. (eds.) Proceedings of the Ninth International Workshop on Performability Modeling of Computer and Communication Systems (PMCCS-9), Eger, Hungary, September 17-18 (2009)

7. Neuts, M.F.: Matrix-Geometric Solutions in Stochastic Models. An Algorithmic Approach. Dover Publications, Inc., New York (1981)

8. Telek, M., Heindl, A.: Matching Moments for Acyclic Discrete and Continous Phase-Type Distributions of Second Order. International Journal of Simulation Systems, Science & Technology 3(3-4), 47–57 (2002)

9. O'Cinneide, C.A.: Characterization of Phase-Type Distributions. Stochastic Models 6, 1–57 (1990)

10. Cumani, A.: On the Canonical Representation of Homogeneous Markov Processes Modelling Failure-time Distributions. Microelectronics and Reliability 22, 583–602 (1982)

11. O'Cinneide, C.A.: Phase-Type Distributions and Invariant Polytopes. Advances in Applied Probability 23(3), 515–535 (1991)

12. He, Q.M., Zhang, H.: Spectral Polynomial Algorithms for Computing Bi-Diagonal Representations for Phase Type Distributions and Matrix-Exponential Distributions. Stochastic Models 22, 289–317 (2006)

13. Pulungan, R.: Reduction of Acyclic Phase-Type Representations. PhD thesis, Universität des Saarlandes, Saarbrücken, Germany (2009)

14. Brown, E., Place, J., de Liefvoort, A.V.: Generating Matrix Exponential Random Variates. Simulation 70, 224–230 (1998)

15. Szekli, R.: Stochastic Ordering and Dependence in Applied Probability. Springer, Heidelberg (1995)

16. Johnson, S.M.: Generation of Permutations by Adjacent Transposition. Mathematics of Computation 17(83), 282–285 (1963)

17. Knuth, D.E.: The Art of Computer Programming, vol. 3. Addison-Wesley, Reading (1997)

18. Mocanu, S., Commault, C.: Sparse Representations of Phase-type Distributions. Commun. Stat., Stochastic Models 15(4), 759–778 (1999)

Correctness Issues of Symbolic Bisimulation Computation for Markov Chains*

Ralf Wimmer and Bernd Becker

Chair of Computer Architecture
Albert-Ludwigs-University Freiburg im Breisgau, Germany
{wimmer,becker}@informatik.uni-freiburg.de

Abstract. Bisimulation reduction is a classical means to fight the infamous state space explosion problem, which limits the applicability of automated methods for verification like model checking. A signature-based method, originally developed by Blom and Orzan for labeled transition systems and adapted for Markov chains by Derisavi, has proved to be very efficient. It is possible to implement it symbolically using binary decision diagrams such that it is able to handle very large state spaces efficiently. We will show, however, that for Markov chains this algorithm suffers from numerical instabilities, which often result in too large quotient systems. We will present and experimentally evaluate two different approaches to avoid these problems: first the usage of rational arithmetic, and second an approach not only to represent the system structure but also the transition rates symbolically. In addition, this allows us to modify their actual values *after* the quotient computation.

1 Introduction

The state space explosion problem denotes the observation that the state space of a system grows exponentially in the number of components the system consists of. The size of realistic systems limits the applicability of formal verification techniques to large designs. To alleviate this effect, numerous techniques have been developed like the usage of symbolic methods (e. g. decision diagrams in various flavors, see [1]) and abstraction techniques (e. g. partial-order reduction and symmetry reduction). Bisimulation minimization can be considered as a kind of abstraction technique which can be performed fully automatically. The idea behind bisimulation minimization is to group the states into equivalence classes such that states are considered equivalent if and only if they exhibit the same step-wise behavior. A system with a minimal number of states which has the same behavior as the original system—this means that it satisfies the same

---

* This work was partly supported by the German Research Council (DFG) as part of the Transregional Collaborative Research Center "Automatic Verification and Analysis of Complex Systems" (SFB/TR 14 AVACS). See www.avacs.org for more information.

B. Müller-Clostermann et al. (Eds.): MMB & DFT 2010, LNCS 5987, pp. 287–301, 2010.

formulas of a temporal logic like CTL or CSL—can be obtained by replacing each equivalence class of the bisimulation with a single state.

While Fisler and Vardi [2] observed that bisimulation minimization does not speed up checking invariant properties of labeled transitions systems, the contrary is often the case for stochastic systems like discrete- and continuous-time Markov chains. There, model checking involves the solution of a linear equation system and is much more expensive than in the purely digital case. Hence, model checking can benefit a lot from minimizing the model prior to checking properties [3,4].

This has led to a revival of bisimulation techniques for stochastic systems in the last few years (cf. for example [5,6,7,8,9]). One of the most efficient approaches is based on signature-based partition refinement, originally developed by Blom and Orzan [10] for labeled transition systems (LTSs). Wimmer et al. [11] extended this approach such that a large number of different kinds of bisimulations for LTSs can be computed symbolically using OBDDs. Derisavi [7] applied it successfully to continuous-time Markov chains. The problem with this signature-based approach for Markov chains is, as we will show, that it is very sensitive to numerical problems. In many cases they lead to quotient systems with too many states, and sometimes they can even prevent termination. In this paper we will address these problems: by using rational arithmetic to avoid numerical problems. Although considered to be computationally expensive typically, we will show that this is not the case for our bisimulation algorithm. Another possibility, which we will present, is to handle the transition rates not as numbers but as pure symbols. Besides avoiding numerical problems this has the advantage that the rates can be adjusted *after* the quotient computation without redoing the minimization. We will also present experimental results for this technique.

We have structured this paper as follows: in the next section we review the foundations which consist of continuous-time Markov chains, bisimulations, and the principle of signature-based bisimulation computation. In Section 3 we present methods which yield bisimulation relations in a reliable and/or parametric manner. Section 4 provides an experimental evaluation of these methods. Finally, in Section 5, we conclude and point out directions for future research.

2   Foundations

In this section we will briefly review the basics of continuous-time Markov chains (CTMCs), bisimulations and the signature-based algorithm for computing bisimulations on CTMCs symbolically.

Definition 1. *Let AP be a finite set of atomic propositions. A continuous-time Markov chain (CTMC) is a tuple $M = (S, s_0, R, L)$ such that S is a finite, non-empty set of states; $s_0 \in S$, the initial state; $R : S \times S \rightarrow \mathbb{R}^{\geq 0}$, the matrix of transition rates; and $L : S \rightarrow 2^{AP}$, a labeling function which assigns each state a set of atomic propositions from AP.*

For a set $S' \subseteq S$ of states, we use the notation $R(s, S) = \sum_{s' \in S'} R(s, s')$. The transitions of a CTMC are governed by a negative exponential distribution, i.e. the probability to take the transition from s to s' within time t is given by

$$p(s, s', t) = \frac{R(s, s')}{R(s, S)} \cdot \left(1 - e^{-R(s, S) \cdot t}\right). \tag{1}$$

A *partition* of a set S is a set $P \subseteq 2^S \setminus \{\emptyset\}$ such that the union of all elements (called blocks) of P equals S and all blocks of P are pairwise disjoint. If P is a partition of S, we write for states $s, t \in S$: $s \equiv_P t$ iff there is a block $B \in P$ such that $\{s, t\} \subseteq B$. A partition P is a *refinement* of a partition P' (denoted $P \sqsubseteq P'$) if $\forall B \in P \; \exists B' \in P' : B \subseteq B'$.

Definition 2. *Let* $M = (S, s_0, R, L)$ *be a continuous-time Markov-Chain. A partition* P *of* S *is a* bisimulation *on* M *if for all* $s, t \in S$ *with* $s \equiv_P t$ *and for all blocks* $B \in P$ *the following conditions hold:*

$$L(s) = L(t) \quad and \quad R(s, B) = R(t, B).$$

States $s, t \in S$ *are bisimilar (written* $s \approx t$*) if there is a bisimulation* P *on* M *such that* $s \equiv_P t$.

The practically most important property of bisimilarity is that states are bisimilar if and only if they satisfy the same formulas of the temporal logic CSL [12], which is widely used for specification of requirements. This enables us to use the quotient system for checking the validity of these formulas instead of the larger original system.

The idea behind signature-based bisimulation computation is to compute for each state a kind of fingerprint, such that states can only be bisimilar if their fingerprints are identical. To obtain a refined partition, the blocks are grouped according to the signatures of their states. This is formally captured in the following definition:

Definition 3. *Let* $M = (S, s_0, R, L)$ *be a CTMC,* $P^{(0)}$ *an initial partition of* S, *and* P *a partition of* S *with* $P \sqsubseteq P^{(0)}$. *The* signature *of a state* s *with respect to* P *is then given by*

$$\mathrm{sig}(s, P) = \left\{ (B, r) \in P \times \mathbb{R}^{\geq 0} \,\middle|\, r = R(s, B) \right\}.$$

The refinement $\mathrm{sigref}(P)$ *of* P *is defined as*

$$\mathrm{sigref}(P) = \left\{ \{t \in S \mid \mathrm{sig}(s, P) = \mathrm{sig}(t, P) \wedge s \equiv_{P^{(0)}} t\} \,\middle|\, s \in S \right\}.$$

The initial partition is needed if one wants the bisimulation quotient to preserve the validity of a certain logic like CSL or if additional information like state rewards has to be taken into account. If we have to preserve CSL properties, we set $P^{(0)} = \{\{s \in S \mid L(s) = L(t)\} \mid t \in S\}$; if state rewards $r : S \to \mathbb{R}^{\geq 0}$ have to be considered, we use $P^{(0)} = \{\{s \in S \mid r(s) = r(t)\} \mid t \in S\}$; otherwise, when

---

Algorithm 2.1: SIGREFINE(CTMC M, partition $P^{(0)}$)
begin

$\quad\quad i \leftarrow 0$ $\hspace{10.5cm}$ (1)

$\quad\quad$ **repeat** $\hspace{10.2cm}$ (2)

$\quad\quad\quad\quad P^{(i+1)} \leftarrow \text{sigref}(P^{(i)})$ $\hspace{7cm}$ (3)

$\quad\quad\quad\quad i \leftarrow i + 1$ $\hspace{8.6cm}$ (4)

$\quad\quad$ **until** $P^{(i)} = P^{(i-1)}$ $\hspace{7.3cm}$ (5)

$\quad\quad$ **return** P $\hspace{9.1cm}$ (6)

end

---

there are no such requirements, we can use the trivial partition $P^{(0)} = \{S\}$, which consists of only one block containing all states.

We iteratively apply the sigref-operator until a fixed point is reached. The pseudo-code of this procedure is given in Algorithm 2.1.

Derisavi has shown in [7] that this algorithm terminates after at most $|S| - |P^{(0)}| + 1$ iterations and yields the coarsest bisimulation on M that refines $P^{(0)}$.

Now we will show how this algorithm can be implemented using (MT)BDDs such that their ability to represent large state spaces in a compact way is exploited.

Symbolic Implementation: Ordered binary decision diagrams (OBDDs) [13] are a data structure which represents boolean functions $f : \{0,1\}^n \rightarrow \{0,1\}$ as a rooted acyclic digraph. They can be considered as a compressed form of the truth table of the represented function. Each assignment of the input variables corresponds to a path in the OBDD which ends at a leaf that is labeled with the value of the function under that assignment.

Multi-terminal BDDs are an extension of OBDDs for pseudo-boolean functions $f : \{0,1\}^n \rightarrow \mathbb{R}$. The only difference to OBDDs is that leaves may be labeled with arbitrary numbers (instead of being restricted to $\{0,1\}$). Both, OBDDs and MTBDDs, are called reduced if the sub-function represented at each node, is unique.

For a BDD $\mathcal{B}(\boldsymbol{x}, \boldsymbol{y})$ over the vectors $\boldsymbol{x} = (x_{n-1}, \ldots, x_0)$ and $\boldsymbol{y} = (y_{m-1}, \ldots, y_0)$ of boolean variables and a bitvector $v \in \{0,1\}^n$, the expression $\mathcal{B}(\boldsymbol{x} \leftarrow v, \boldsymbol{y})$ denotes the cofactor of $\mathcal{B}(\boldsymbol{x}, \boldsymbol{y})$ which results from fixing the variables x_i to the values given by v.

We assume that the reader is familiar with OBDDs and MTBDDs. For more information we refer the reader to Wegener's monograph [1].

OBDDs can be used to represent sets $S \subseteq \{0,1\}^n$ of bit vectors via their characteristic function χ_S such that $s \in S \Leftrightarrow \chi_S(s) = 1$. This will be used to represent the state space of the CTMC under consideration and for partitions of its state space. Several possibilities for partition representation have been proposed in the literature (cf. [9]). For the implementation of signature refinement the following technique is suited best, since it allows to execute the refinement step in linear time in the size of the signature-MTBDD [9]: each block of the partition is assigned a unique number, which is encoded using a set of $m \geq \lceil \log_2 |P| \rceil$ new OBDD variables $\boldsymbol{k} = (k_{m-1}, \ldots, k_0)$. The partition P of S is then represented by an OBDD $\mathcal{P}(\boldsymbol{s}, \boldsymbol{k})$ such that, for a block B_i of P, $s \in B_i$ iff $\mathcal{P}(\boldsymbol{s} \leftarrow \langle s \rangle, \boldsymbol{k} \leftarrow \langle i \rangle) = 1$. Here, $\langle i \rangle$ denotes the binary encoding of i.

We will use MTBDDs to represent the transition rate matrix of the CTMC under consideration and signatures of its states. For the signatures we use an MTBDD $\sigma(\boldsymbol{s}, \boldsymbol{k})$ such that $\sigma(\boldsymbol{s} \leftarrow \langle s \rangle, \boldsymbol{k} \leftarrow \langle i \rangle) = r$ iff $(r, B_i) \in \mathrm{sig}(s, P)$. Given the transition rate matrix $\mathcal{R}(\boldsymbol{s}, \boldsymbol{t})$ and the representation $\mathcal{P}(\boldsymbol{s}, \boldsymbol{k})$ of the current partition, the MTBDD representing the signatures of all states can be computed by

$$\sigma(\boldsymbol{s}, \boldsymbol{k}) = \mathcal{Q}_t^+.\big(\mathcal{R}(\boldsymbol{s}, \boldsymbol{t}) \cdot \mathcal{P}(\boldsymbol{t}, \boldsymbol{k})\big). \tag{2}$$

Thereby $\mathcal{Q}_a^\circ : \big(\mathcal{B}(\boldsymbol{x}, \boldsymbol{a})\big) = \bigcirc_{i=0}^{2^l - 1} \mathcal{B}(\boldsymbol{x}, \boldsymbol{a} \leftarrow \langle i \rangle)$ is the quantification operator for an associative and commutative binary operator $\circ$. It is a standard operation for MTBDDs.

In order to ensure that the initial partition is taken into account, we modify the signatures in Equation (2) such that two states can only have identical signatures if they are contained in the same block of the initial partition. Let p be a new BDD variable. We modify the signatures as follows:

$$\sigma'(\boldsymbol{s}, \boldsymbol{k}, p) = \sigma(\boldsymbol{s}, \boldsymbol{k}) + p \cdot \mathcal{P}^{(0)}(\boldsymbol{s}, \boldsymbol{k}). \tag{3}$$

Once we have computed the signatures, we have to get the refined partition. For this, we can exploit the following observation: if we use a variable order for the BDDs such that the state variables precede the block number variables (and the auxiliary variable p), the encoding of a state s corresponds to a path in $\sigma'(\boldsymbol{s}, \boldsymbol{k}, p)$ which ends in the node that represents the signature of s. Furthermore, since we only use reduced BDDs, the encodings of all states with the same signature as s lead to the same node. To obtain the refined partition, we have to replace all nodes that represent signatures by new block numbers. This can be done in linear time by traversing $\sigma'(\boldsymbol{s}, \boldsymbol{k}, p)$ recursively. More details on the symbolic implementation can be found in [11,7].

3   Reliable Bisimulation Computation

Almost all of today's personal computers use floating-point arithmetic according to the IEEE standard 754 [14] for numerical computations. The problem of all fixed-length representations is that the result of arithmetical operations is often not representable but has to be rounded to the nearest representable number.

Example 1. We compute $0.5 = 3 \cdot 0.1 + 4 \cdot 0.05$ by adding three times 0.1 and four times 0.05 on a IEEE 754 compatible processor (left-associative). Depending on the order of the summands we obtain the following results (using the 64-bit representation):

- $0.05 + 0.05 + 0.05 + 0.05 + 0.1 + 0.1 + 0.1$
  Result:[1] $0.01111111110.0^{52}$
- $0.05 + 0.1 + 0.05 + 0.1 + 0.05 + 0.1 + 0.05$
  Result: $0.01111111110.0^{51}1$
- $0.1 + 0.1 + 0.05 + 0.05 + 0.05 + 0.1 + 0.05$
  Result: $0.01111111101.1^{52}$

We can observe that the result depends on the order of the operands.

For more detailed information about floating-point arithmetic and its problems we refer the reader to [15].

These rounding problems also affect arithmetical operations on MTBDDs. In our application, this is mainly the signature computation. Their effect is, in general, that too many leaves with only slightly different values are created, unnecessarily blowing up the size of MTBDD. For most applications this has no impact on the correctness, but only on the speed and memory consumption of the algorithm. To weaken this effect, most implementations apply the following strategy: if a leaf with value v is requested from the MTBDD manager, it is not only checked if a leaf with exactly the same value v already exists, but also if there is a leaf whose value is close enough to v. That means, a new leaf with value v is created if there exists no leaf with value v' such that $|v - v'| \leq \varepsilon$ for a predefined constant $\varepsilon > 0$. Otherwise the already existing leaf is returned. In general, there is no value of ε which ensures that the effect of inexact computations is compensated correctly.

The signature-based refinement algorithm, however, is very sensitive to rounding errors. If the signatures of two equivalent states differ slightly due to rounding, they are represented at two different nodes in the MTBDD of signatures. Therefore they are placed in different blocks of the refined partition.

This leads to the following effects: since equivalent states may be placed in different blocks, the resulting bisimulation is often unnecessarily fine. Rounding effects can also cause signatures of states with slightly different rates to be mapped onto the same value. Then these states are erroneously placed in the same block. The resulting partition may therefore be no correct bisimulation. As we will see in the experimental section, rounding effects can even prevent termination.

We therefore consider it important to develop techniques which avoid the problems caused by inexact computations.

3.1   Rational Arithmetic

To avoid the problems we have observed for our floating-point implementation of the bisimulation algorithm, we implemented a version which makes use of rational arithmetic. Rational numbers are represented as the quotient of two arbitrarily long integer numbers. Then all operations we need (mainly the addition of numbers) can be performed precisely.

---

[1] The dots separate the sign bit from the exponent and the exponent from the mantissa. 0^n means that the digit 0 is repeated n times.

The MTBDDs used by our implementation have been modified such that rational numbers are stored in the leaves instead of floating-point values. The operations on the MTBDDs have also been adapted to cope with rational numbers. Besides this, we have set the value of ε to 0 such that the BDD package itself does not introduce errors.

3.2   Parametric Bisimulation Computation

Another idea how numerical problems can be avoided is not to work with concrete numbers for the transition rates but with pure symbols. Since there can be several transitions with the same rate from a state into a block of the current partition, we cannot use sets to collect the transition symbols leading into a given block. Instead, we have to use *multisets*.

Multisets allow an arbitrary (finite) number of copies of each element. For a multiset $\overline{S}$, we let $\mathbf{1}_{\overline{S}}(x)$ denote the multiplicity of element x in the multiset $\overline{S}$. The element-wise union $\overline{S} \uplus \overline{T}$ is the multiset such that for all elements the equation $\mathbf{1}_{\overline{S} \uplus \overline{T}}(x) = \mathbf{1}_{\overline{S}}(x) + \mathbf{1}_{\overline{T}}(x)$ holds. The set of multisets with elements from a set S is denoted by $\mathfrak{M}(S)$.

We can now define the symbolic counterpart of a CTMC:

Definition 4. *A symbolic CTMC is a tuple* $\overline{M} = (S, s_0, V, \overline{R}, L)$ *such that S is a non-empty finite set of states, $s_0 \in S$ the initial state, and $L : S \to 2^{AP}$ a labeling function. $V = \{\mu_{n-1}, \ldots, \mu_0\}$ is a finite set of symbols. $\overline{R} : S \times S \to \mathfrak{M}(V)$ is a labeling function which labels each transition with a multiset of symbols.*

If V is a set of symbols, we call a function $I : V \to \mathbb{R}^{\geq 0}$ an *interpretation* of V. For a multiset $\overline{S} \in \mathfrak{M}(V)$, we set $I(\overline{S}) = \sum_{\mu \in \overline{S}}(\mathbf{1}_{\overline{S}}(\mu) \cdot I(\mu))$. For a symbolic CTMC $\overline{M} = (S, s_0, V, \overline{R}, L)$ an interpretation I induces an ordinary CTMC $M_I = (S, s_0, R, L)$ by setting $R(s, s') = I(\overline{R}(s, t))$.

We now modify the definition of the signature of a state as follows:

$$\overline{\mathrm{sig}}(s, P) = \left\{(\overline{r}, B) \in \mathfrak{M}(V) \times P \,\middle|\, \overline{r} = \biguplus_{t \in B} \overline{R}(s, t)\right\}$$

The refinement operator remains unchanged with the exception that it now uses the modified signature:

$$\overline{\mathrm{sigref}}(P) = \left\{\{s \in S \,|\, \overline{\mathrm{sig}}(s, P) = \overline{\mathrm{sig}}(t, P) \land s \equiv_{P^{(0)}} t\} \,\middle|\, t \in S\right\}.$$

If we use this operator for partition refinement, we obtain a partition which is a bisimulation for all possible interpretations of the symbols in V. We call such a bisimulation *interpretation-independent*. Our algorithm yields the coarsest interpretation-independent bisimulation which refines the initial partition $P^{(0)}$. The reason why not the coarsest bisimulation is computed is that under a certain interpretation I different multisets of symbols may lead to the same value, i.e. that there are $\overline{S}$ and $\overline{T}$ with $\overline{S} \neq \overline{T}$ and $I(\overline{S}) = I(\overline{T})$.

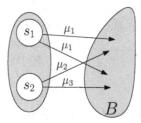

Fig. 1. Signature computation for symbolic Markov chains

If the coarsest bisimulation for a fixed interpretation is needed, it can be obtained by applying the signature refinement algorithm to the DTMC which results from applying the interpretation to the interpretation-independent quotient.

Example 2. We now consider the part of a symbolic CMTC M depicted in Figure 1 and compute the signatures of s_1 and s_2:

$$\overline{\mathrm{sig}}(s_1, P) = \left\{ (\{\!| \mu_1, \mu_1 |\!\}, B) \right\}$$
$$\overline{\mathrm{sig}}(s_2, P) = \left\{ (\{\!| \mu_2 |\!\}, B), (\{\!| \mu_3 |\!\}, B) \right\}$$

Since the states do not exhibit the same signatures, the refinement operator $\overline{\mathrm{sigref}}$ puts them in different blocks.

What are the advantages of this method? We can choose the actual transition rates, i.e., the interpretation, *after* the minimization without recomputation of the quotient. This can be beneficial if during the design phase the system structure has already been fixed, but the exact rates have to be determined experimentally. Another scenario is that the analysis shows that the error rates of some components are too high to yield the required dependability. So some components have to be replaced by more robust ones. This changes the rates of the transitions. If an interpretation-independent bisimulation quotient has been obtained, only the interpretation of its symbols has to be changed. So we can save the time for computing the quotient from scratch.

   The drawback of this approach is that not always the coarsest bisimulation quotient for the current interpretation of the rates can be computed. This has the effect that the quotient sometimes consists of more states than the one which would be returned by the version with rational arithmetic. Our experimental results (see Section 4), however, indicate that this effect does not occur for most of the models, and for the others the increase in size compared to the optimal quotient is not dramatic.

Example 3. Let us again consider the Markov chain M in Figure 1. We assume that the current interpretation is given by $I(\mu_1) = 3$, $I(\mu_2) = 1$, and $I(\mu_3) = 5$. If we compute the signatures of s_1 and s_2 for the ordinary Markov chain M_I, we obtain

$$\mathrm{sig}(s_1, P) = \mathrm{sig}(s_2, P) = \left\{ (6, B) \right\}.$$

Since both states have the same signatures, sigref places them in the same block.

Symbolic Implementation: We now show how to integrate the symbolic handling of transition rates into our BDD-based algorithm. There are mainly two possibilities: we could represent multisets as vectors in which the multiplicities of the symbols in V are stored. The leaves of the MTBDDs for the signatures would then be labeled with the representation of $\overline{R}(s, B)$ instead of with real numbers. The drawback of this option is that we have to make considerable changes in the BDD-library, since all operations and in particular the caching strategies for BDD nodes are optimized for storing integer or floating-point values.

A much simpler approach is to represent the multisets as MTBDDs in the same way as we have done for representing partitions. We pre-suppose an arbitrary, but fixed order on the symbols in V, i.e. $V = (\mu_0, \ldots, \mu_{n-1})$. We introduce $l = \lceil \log_2 n \rceil$ new BDD variables $\boldsymbol{a} = (a_{l-1}, \ldots, a_0)$ which encode the index of the symbols. A multiset $\overline{S} \in \mathfrak{M}(V)$ is then encoded by an MTBDD $\overline{S}(\boldsymbol{a})$ such that $\overline{S}(\boldsymbol{a} \leftarrow \langle i \rangle) = \mathbf{1}_{\overline{S}}(\mu_i)$ (here $\langle i \rangle$ again denotes the binary encoding of i). Instead of leaves which carries the transition rates, we have MTBDDs for the multiset encoding, resulting in an MTBDD $\mathcal{R}(\boldsymbol{s}, \boldsymbol{t}, \boldsymbol{a})$ for the transition rate matrix.

This representation integrates seamlessly into our BDD-based framework: if we use a variable order such that the variables for block numbers and multiset encoding are placed after the state variables, we do not need to modify any operations—not even the signature computation and partition refinement. Since all leaves are now labeled with multiplicities of symbolic rates, no floating-point numbers are necessary anymore. The algorithm works with integer values solely. A further advantage is that this technique allows sharing of parts of the multiset encoding.

Obtaining an ordinary CTMC from a symbolic one, given an interpretation of the symbols is efficiently possible:

If the interpretation $I : V \to \mathbb{R}^{\geq 0}$ is given by an MTBDD $\mathcal{I}(\boldsymbol{a})$ such that $\mathcal{I}(\boldsymbol{a} \leftarrow \langle i \rangle) = I(\mu_i)$, we can obtain the transition rate matrix $\mathcal{R}(\boldsymbol{s}, \boldsymbol{t})$ from $\overline{\mathcal{R}}(\boldsymbol{s}, \boldsymbol{t}, \boldsymbol{a})$ by

$$\mathcal{R}(\boldsymbol{s}, \boldsymbol{t}) = \mathcal{Q}_{\boldsymbol{a}}^+ : (\mathcal{I}(\boldsymbol{a}) \cdot \overline{\mathcal{R}}(\boldsymbol{s}, \boldsymbol{t}, \boldsymbol{a})). \tag{4}$$

4   Experiments

We have implemented the three variants of the SIGREFINE algorithm described in this paper using C++ as the programming language and the g++ compiler version 4.4.1. For the construction and manipulation of OBDDs and MTBDDs we used the CUDD library [16]. For the rational arithmetic we took the GNU Multiprecision Library (GMP) [17]. The three variants of the refinement algorithms are denoted by SIGREF$_R$ for the rational arithmetic; SIGREF$_F$, for the floating-point arithmetic; and SIGREF$_S$, for the version with symbolic representation of the transition rates. We used the default value 10^{-12} for the parameter ε, which controls the creation of new leaves in the floating-point version.

The experiments were conducted on a Dual Core AMD Opteron^{TM} 2.4 GHz CPU with 4 GB of main memory running Linux in 64-bit mode. We have stopped

Table 1. Size of the example models

Model	States	Transitions		Model	States	Transitions
cycling-2	4666	18342		robot-25	61200	325917
cycling-3	57667	305502		robot-26	68900	367397
cycling-4	431101	2742012		robot-27	77220	412253
fgf	80616	562536		robot-28	86184	460617
polling-12	73728	503808		robot-29	95816	512621
polling-13	159744	1171456		robot-30	106140	568397
polling-14	344064	2695168		p2p-4-4	65536	524289
polling-15	737280	6144000		p2p-4-5	1048576	10485761
polling-16	1572864	13893632		p2p-4-6	16777216	201326593
ftwc-2-2	15769	91232		p2p-5-4	1048576	10485761
ftwc-2-3	256932	1697760		p2p-5-5	33554432	419430401
ftwc-2-4	3803193	27771984		p2p-5-6	1073741824	16106127361
ftwc-3-1	23040	153600		p2p-6-5	1073741824	16106127361
ftwc-3-2	1889947	15302784		p2p-7-5	34359738368	601295421441
kanban-3	58400	446400		kanban-4	454475	3979850

any experiment that took more than 7200 seconds or required more than 3 GB of main memory.

We consider seven different example models from the literature to evaluate the performance of the algorithms: a fault-tolerant worstation cluster system (FTWC) [18], a peer-to-peer (P2P) protocol based on BitTorrent (studied in [19]), a cyclic server polling system [20], a robot moving through an $n \times n$ grid [21] (robot), a Kanban production system [22], and two biological models: the first one describes the Fibroblast growth factor signaling (FGF) within cells [23], and the second one is a probabilistic model of cell cycle control in eukaryotes (cycling) [24].

For the FTWC model, we converted the SAN (Stochastic Activity Network) specification to the PRISM input language. We obtained the PRISM specifications of the other six models from http://www.prismmodelchecker.org/casestudies/index.php.

All but the FGF model are parametrized. The first two models have two parameters. For FTWC, they denote the number of computers in the system and the number of memory modules in each computer, respectively. For P2P, they represent the number of clients and the number of blocks of the file to be transmitted, respectively. The remaining models have only one parameter: for the polling benchmark, the parameter denotes the number of servers; for the robot benchmark, the size of the grid; in the Kanban benchmark, the parameter denotes the number of tokens in the system, and for the cell cycle control it denotes the initial number of molecules.

For the sake of simplicity, we start with the trivial initial partition $P^{(0)} = \{S\}$. With the exception of the Kanban model, all of these Markov chains can be minimized, i. e., the quotient system is smaller than the original one. The quotient model of the Kanban system, however, has the same size as the input model. Table 1 contains the number of states and transitions of all model instances before minimization.

The results we obtained with the three program versions are shown in Table 2. For each benchmark, the table contains three lines of information; the first is for SIGREF$_R$; the second, for SIGREF$_F$; and the third line contains the results obtained using SIGREF$_S$.

If we compare the rational and the floating-point variant, the first observation is that there is a benchmark, namely fgf, for which the floating-point variant did not terminate. A more detailed look at the program output for this case shows that after eight iterations, the algorithm starts alternating between a partition consisting of 38829 blocks and one with 38833 blocks, thereby never reaching a fixed point. Numerical errors are the reason why an unnecessarily fine partition P is computed. When the signatures are computed w.r.t. P, the rounding error which had made the signatures of two blocks B, B' different, does not occur. Therefore the signatures of the states in B and B' become identical again. Therefore, B and B' are merged again. The refinement of this finer partition results in P, closing the cycle.

The second observation is that there are some benchmarks, e.g. cycling-3, cycling-4, and all ftwc-benchmarks (with the exception of ftwc-2-2) for which SIGREF$_F$ yields a finer result due to rounding errors than SIGREF$_R$. It cannot be guaranteed that this partition is a correct bisimulation at all, since rounding errors can make the signatures of states with slightly different rate equal. Furthermore, in these cases SIGREF$_F$ needs more iterations to reach the fixed point. This increases the runtime considerably.

On benchmarks for which both the variant with rational and with floating-point arithmetic yield the same result, the runtime and memory consumption of both tools are almost identical (with rational arithmetic a few hundred kilobytes more memory are required). That the runtimes are almost identical may be surprising: typically, rational arithmetic is considered much slower than floating-point arithmetic which is directly supported by the CPU. We performed a detailed profiling of SIGREF$_R$ and measured the fraction of the runtime consumed by the rational arithmetic. In no case was it more than a few percent, because the only affected function is the computation of the signatures. The runtime of this operation—like most BDD operations—is clearly dominated by cache lookups. They are needed to keep the BDD reduced (so-called UniqueTable) and to avoid unnecessary re-computations of intermediate results (ComputedTable).

Next we compare the version with rational arithmetic, SIGREF$_R$, and the version with the symbolic representation of transition rates, SIGREF$_S$. SIGREF$_R$ always returns the coarsest bisimulation for the current interpretation of the rate symbols, whereas SIGREF$_S$ yields the coarsest interpretation-independent bisimulation. The latter may be finer, but—as we can see in Table 2—for most of the models, the sizes of the quotient systems are identical. The only exceptions are the three cycling benchmarks, for which SIGREF$_S$ creates more blocks.

On the benchmarks for which both tools return the same result, SIGREF$_S$ is in most cases slightly slower than SIGREF$_R$. This is due to the additional BDD variables for encoding the rates, which make the MTBDDs larger. This is also the reason why SIGREF$_S$ requires a few Megabytes more memory. An exception

Table 2. Experimental results (first line: SIGREF$_R$, second line: SIGREF$_F$, third line: SIGREF$_S$)

Model	Iter.	Blocks	Time [s]	Mem. [MB]	Model	Iter.	Blocks	Time [s]	Mem. [MB]
cycling-2	6	3511	0.87	69.09	robot-25	49	60600	72.18	132.50
	6	3511	0.84	66.91		49	60600	72.09	130.24
	6	3997	1.14	57.17		49	60600	108.91	123.61
cycling-3	6	40659	19.55	146.18	robot-26	51	68250	87.48	134.40
	13	43742	48.29	149.07		51	68250	87.23	132.15
	6	48138	23.81	176.58		51	68250	127.78	137.68
cycling-4	6	282943	213.69	972.87	robot-27	53	76518	99.56	135.78
	13	321416	573.04	972.64		53	76518	99.51	133.53
	6	339367	311.98	1304.48		53	76518	146.66	149.06
fgf	9	38639	70.63	226.49	robot-28	55	85428	120.03	139.88
		— No termination —				55	85428	119.81	137.63
	9	38639	73.52	254.45		55	85428	162.63	163.19
polling-12	23	6144	17.20	94.79	robot-29	57	95004	140.98	145.19
	23	6144	17.11	92.55		57	95004	140.88	142.92
	23	6144	20.56	85.52		57	95004	197.68	168.32
polling-13	25	12288	52.60	121.39	robot-30	59	105270	201.14	162.48
	25	12288	52.44	119.15		59	105270	164.18	160.21
	25	12288	58.27	125.39		59	105270	228.92	181.07
polling-14	27	24576	139.42	198.44	**p2p-4-4**	3	70	0.07	39.72
	27	24576	139.44	196.19		3	70	0.06	37.46
	27	24576	166.96	200.02		2	70	0.04	37.50
polling-15	29	49152	342.98	417.63	**p2p-4-5**	3	126	0.72	65.90
	29	49152	342.37	415.39		3	126	0.69	63.61
	29	49152	429.88	377.95		2	126	0.48	63.65
polling-16	31	98304	870.61	806.26	**p2p-4-6**	3	210	12.33	122.77
	31	98304	869.71	804.01		3	210	12.27	120.64
	31	98304	1101.67	749.89		2	210	7.41	120.56
ftwc-2-2	3	703	0.31	49.20	**p2p-5-4**	3	105	0.36	45.83
	13	703	1.25	55.79		3	105	0.36	43.62
	3	703	0.27	45.43		2	105	0.23	43.62
ftwc-2-3	3	2145	1.32	75.31	**p2p-5-5**	3	196	8.00	83.20
	16	10557	56.35	139.35		3	196	7.93	80.96
	3	2145	1.24	70.59		2	196	8.77	81.11
ftwc-2-4	3	5151	6.18	90.96	**p2p-5-6**	3	336	887.49	263.14
	20	93866	919.41	854.40		3	336	885.55	261.18
	3	5151	5.08	94.14		2	336	563.10	260.90
ftwc-3-1	3	969	0.71	69.04	**p2p-6-5**	3	266	267.64	88.79
	13	2126	7.03	70.64		3	266	266.60	86.43
	3	969	0.71	66.18		2	266	137.60	85.89
ftwc-3-2	3	9139	14.73	185.31	**p2p-7-5**	3	336	2844.46	110.22
	21	24249	273.34	387.83		3	336	3780.50	107.53
	3	9139	15.61	185.93		2	336	1580.29	106.73
kanban-3	7	58400	49.40	267.68	kanban-4	8	454475	741.55	2582.63
	7	58400	52.31	248.10		8	454475	749.98	2483.12
	7	58400	52.59	284.11		8	454475	816.14	2604.74

to this trend are the p2p benchmarks. On these, SIGREF$_S$ requires one iteration less than SIGREF$_R$ to reach the fixed point. This also demonstrates the effect that $\overline{R}(s, S') \neq \overline{R}(t, S')$, but for the current Interpretation I, $I(\overline{R}(s, S')) = I(\overline{R}(t, S'))$ for some set $S' \subseteq S$. Therefore, after one refinement step, SIGREF$_R$ yields a coarser partition than SIGREF$_S$, although in the end they return the same result.

5   Conclusion

In this paper we have presented two different approaches which can be used for reliable bisimulation computation: the first one is the usage of rational arithmetic for all numerical computations. This yields an algorithm which is clearly superior to the standard variant that is based on floating-point arithmetic: using rational arithmetic, we can always obtain the coarsest bisimulation, the runtime and memory overhead is negligible, and in those cases where floating-point arithmetic creates a partition which is unnecessarily fine, rational arithmetic is even faster than floating-point arithmetic. Furthermore, termination is guaranteed if rational arithmetic is used, which is not the case for floating-point arithmetic, as one of our example benchmarks has shown.

The second approach relies on a symbolic representation of the transition rates. Using this technique we can compute the coarsest interpretation-independent bisimulation, i. e. the coarsest bisimulation which does not depend on the actual values of the transition rates. Our benchmarks have shown that we nevertheless obtain in many cases the same result as with rational arithmetic. Only for a few exceptions the algorithm returns a finer partition. This symbolic handling of the transition rates causes a little overhead due to additional BDD-variables. But its advantage is that the actual values of the rates can be chosen after quotient computation.

In summary, we can conclude that there is no reason to use floating-point arithmetic for signature-based bisimulation computation. Rational arithmetic produces reliably the coarsest bisimulation without any noticeable overhead. If the option to modify the transition rates after minimization is required, it is advantageous to use the algorithm with symbolic transition rates instead of re-computing the quotient after changing the rates.

The techniques presented here are not restricted to (strong) bisimulation for CMTCs. They can also be applied to other types of bisimulation, for instance weak and backward bisimulation for CTMCs, to strong, weak, and branching bisimulation on interactive Markov chains, and to (strong) bisimulation on discrete-time Markov chains.

Acknowledgement. We thank Holger Hermanns from the Saarland University for his helpful comments.

References

1. Wegener, I.: Branching Programs and Binary Decision Diagrams – Theory and Applications. SIAM Monographs on Discrete Mathematics and Applications, p. 408. Society for Industrial and Applied Mathematics (SIAM), Philadelphia (2000)
2. Fisler, K., Vardi, M.Y.: Bisimulation minimization and symbolic model checking. Formal Methods in System Design 21(1), 39–78 (2002)
3. Katoen, J.P., Kemna, T., Zapreev, I., Jansen, D.N.: Bisimulation minimization mostly speeds up probabilistic model checking. In: Grumberg, O., Huth, M. (eds.) TACAS 2007. LNCS, vol. 4424, pp. 87–101. Springer, Heidelberg (2007)

4. Böde, E., Herbstritt, M., Hermanns, H., Johr, S., Peikenkamp, T., Pulungan, R., Rakow, J., Wimmer, R., Becker, B.: Compositional dependability evaluation for STATEMATE. IEEE Transactions on Software Engineering 35(2), 274–292 (2009)

5. Blom, S., Haverkort, B.R., Kuntz, M., van de Pol, J.: Distributed Markovian bisimulation reduction aimed at CSL model checking. In: Černá, I., Lüttgen, G. (eds.) 7th Int'l Workshop on Parallel and Distributed Methods in Verification (PDMC). Electronic Notes in Theoretical Computer Science, vol. 220(2), pp. 35–50 (2008)

6. Derisavi, S.: A symbolic algorithm for optimal markov chain lumping. In: Grumberg, O., Huth, M. (eds.) TACAS 2007. LNCS, vol. 4424, pp. 139–154. Springer, Heidelberg (2007)

7. Derisavi, S.: Signature-based symbolic algorithm for optimal Markov chain lumping. In: 4th Int'l Conf. on Quantitative Evaluation of Systems (QEST), Edinburgh, Scotland, pp. 141–150. IEEE Computer Society Press, Los Alamitos (2007)

8. Derisavi, S., Hermanns, H., Sanders, W.H.: Optimal state-space lumping in Markov chains. Information Processing Letters 87(6), 309–315 (2003)

9. Wimmer, R., Derisavi, S., Hermanns, H.: Symbolic partition refinement with dynamic balancing of time and space. In: Rubino, G. (ed.) 5th Int'l Conf. on Quantitative Evaluation of Systems (QEST), Saint-Malo, France, pp. 65–74. IEEE Computer Society Press, Los Alamitos (2008)

10. Blom, S., Orzan, S.: Distributed state space minimization. Software Tools for Technology Transfer (STTT) 7(3), 280–291 (2005)

11. Wimmer, R., Herbstritt, M., Hermanns, H., Strampp, K., Becker, B.: Sigref – A symbolic bisimulation tool box. In: Graf, S., Zhang, W. (eds.) ATVA 2006. LNCS, vol. 4218, pp. 477–492. Springer, Heidelberg (2006)

12. Baier, C., Katoen, J.P., Hermanns, H., Wolf, V.: Comparative branching-time semantics for Markov chains. Information and Computation 200(2), 149–214 (2005)

13. Bryant, R.E.: Graph-based algorithms for Boolean function manipulation. IEEE Trans. on Computers 35(8), 677–691 (1986)

14. IEEE Computer Society Standards Committee. Working group of the Microprocessor Standards Subcommittee, American National Standards Institute: IEEE Standard for Binary Floating-Point Arithmetic. ANSI/IEEE Standard 754-1985. IEEE Computer Society Press, Silver Spring, MD 20910, USA (1985)

15. Goldberg, D.: What every computer scientist should know about floating-point arithmetic. ACM Computing Surveys 23(1), 5–48 (1991)

16. Somenzi, F.: Cudd: Cu decision diagram package, release 2.4.2 (2009)

17. GNU: GNU multiple precision arithmetic library (GMP), version 4.3.1 (2009), http://gmplib.org.

18. Sanders, W.H., Malhis, L.M.: Dependability evaluation using composed SAN-based reward models. Journal Parallel and Distributed Computing 15(3), 238–254 (1992)

19. Kwiatkowska, M., Norman, G., Parker, D.: Symmetry reduction for probabilistic model checking. In: Ball, T., Jones, R.B. (eds.) CAV 2006. LNCS, vol. 4144, pp. 234–248. Springer, Heidelberg (2006)

20. Ibe, O., Trivedi, K.: Stochastic Petri net models of polling systems. IEEE Journal on Selected Areas in Communications 8(9), 1649–1657 (1990)

21. Younes, H., Kwiatkowska, M., Norman, G., Parker, D.: Numerical vs. statistical probabilistic model checking. Software Tools for Technology Transfer (STTT) 8(3), 216–228 (2006)

22. Ciardo, G., Tilgner, M.: On the use of Kronecker operators for the solution of generalized stochastic Petri nets. ICASE Report 96–35, Institute for Computer Applications in Science and Engineering, ICASE (1996)
23. Heath, J., Kwiatkowska, M., Norman, G., Parker, D., Tymchyshyn, O.: Probabilistic model checking of complex biological pathways. Theoretical Computer Science 319(3), 239–257 (2008)
24. Lecca, P., Priami, C.: Cell cycle control in eukaryotes: A BioSpi model. Electronic Notes in Theoretical Computer Science 180(3), 51–63 (2007)

ResiLyzer: A Tool for Resilience Analysis in Packet-Switched Communication Networks*

David Hock, Michael Menth, Matthias Hartmann, Christian Schwartz,
and David Stezenbach

University of Würzburg, Institute of Computer Science
Am Hubland, D-97074 Würzburg, Germany

Abstract. We present a tool for the analysis of fault-tolerance in packet-switched communication networks. Network elements like links or routers can fail or unexpected traffic surges may occur. They lead to service disruptions and degradations. Our tool quantifies these risks and presents a comprehensive digest of the results. We explain the core idea of the analysis and illustrate the tool.

1 Resilience Analysis

In previous work [1], we developed a framework for resilience analysis of packet-switched communication networks. Before we present the tool, we give a brief insight into the theoretical concept.

To analyze the resilience of a packet-switched communication network we require a model of the network's topology and the link bandwidths. The routing is known for the failure-free case and it can be computed for all possible failure cases. Further inputs are the expected traffic matrix as well as a probabilistic model for traffic surges h. Finally, a probabilistic model for link and router failures s is needed.

A networking scenario $z = (s, h)$ is characterized by a failure pattern s and traffic pattern h. An analysis of all possible networking scenarios is prohibitive because their number increases exponentially with the network size. Therefore, the most probable networking scenarios $\mathcal{Z}$ are identified and only they are used for the analysis. The selection process is controlled by a threshold p_{min} which controls the probability of the not-considered networking scenarios and provides error bounds on the obtained results.

In case of a network element failure, traffic can be rerouted which increases the relative load on the links of the backup paths. Such an increase can also be observed due to traffic surges. To analyze this effect, we calculate the distribution of the relative load for all links in the network by analyzing the relative link load for each considered networking scenario $z \in \mathcal{Z}$ and weighting these partial results with the probability of that networking scenario. If a network is physically partitioned by the failure of network elements or if the routing algorithm cannot provide a backup path, the network may be unavailable for some ingress-egress pairs. This unavailability is also calculated.

This analysis leads to extensive results which are hard to monitor. We use a complementary cumulative distribution function (CCDF) of the relative load per link. Furthermore, we propose to condense the information of the CCDF into a single value and use

---

* This work is funded by Deutsche Forschungsgemeinschaft (DFG) under grant TR257/23-2. The authors alone are responsible for the content of the paper.

B. Müller-Clostermann et al. (Eds.): MMB & DFT 2010, LNCS 5987, pp. 302–306, 2010.

this value to color the corresponding link in the network graph. This allows to easily view the risk of overload in a network. The unavailability can be presented per ingress-egress pair, it can be aggregated per router, or it can be expressed relative to the overall traffic.

Further details and algorithms are available in [1]. In [2] we proposed additional illustrations to compare the potential overload for different routings.

2   ResiLyzer

The ResiLyzer has been developed to implement the presented concept into a software tool. An analysis with the ResiLyzer normally consists of four steps. First, the necessary input data is provided by loading existing topology, traffic matrix, and link cost files or creating new ones via the corresponding panels or menu bars. Second, the relevant networking scenarios including effective topologies and traffic matrices are configured. Third, the general analysis is invoked and the analytical results are computed. Fourth, the analytical results are interpreted by choosing one of the proposed comprehensive views or exporting the raw data for further analysis.

The ResiLyzer is implemented as an Eclipse RCP application. All elements of the tool are modular which makes them easily extensible. Figure 1 shows an overview of

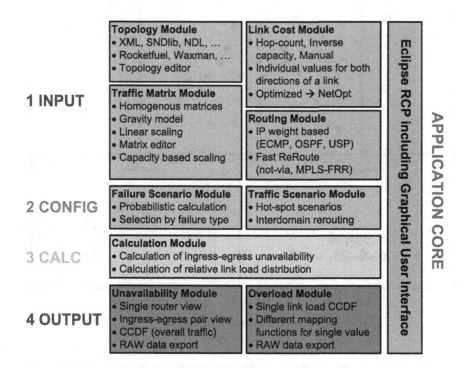

Fig. 1. Program structure of the ResiLyzer

the program structure. Each module is displayed together with its main features that are currently implemented. The application core is formed by the Eclipse RCP application and the corresponding GUI. There are currently four input modules: modules for topologies, traffic matrices, link costs, and routing. The ResiLyzer has been equipped with a large collection of precalculated example scenarios including the Rocketfuel topologies [3] and a selection of random topologies created with the Waxman model [4]. These scenarios consist of the topologies, corresponding traffic matrices created with a simple gravity model [5], and link costs optimized with our NetOpt tool [6,7]. The currently implemented routings of the ResiLyzer include ECMP, OSPF as well as Unique Shortest Path (USP) [8]. Additionally, several Fast ReRoute (FRR) mechanisms have been implemented.

The calculation of the considered networking scenarios z including failure scenarios s and traffic surges h is realized by special modules. Failure scenarios can be created either probabilistic with a threshold p_{min} or by selection of failure types, e.g., all single link and node failures. The currently supported types of traffic scenarios are hot-spot scenarios and interdomain rerouting scenarios.

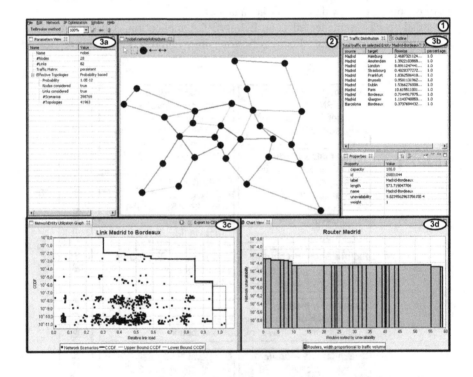

Fig. 2. Screenshot of the ResiLyzer

The interpretation and illustration of the analytical results are performed by the unavailability and the overload module. Our tool offers different views and graphs to allow for a simple monitoring of fault-tolerance. The views can be activated and deactivated separately. The user can reach a certain view intuitively by selecting the corresponding element, e.g., links or failure scenarios. For instance, selecting a failure scenario shows the unavailability and load situation in the network in this failure scenario, selecting a link shows the relative link load of this link in all failure scenarios.

Figure 2 shows a screenshot of the ResiLyzer graphical user interface. It allows the user to highly adapt one's personal view on the tool, selecting the needed menus, panels, windows, etc. In the displayed example, a possible view configured for the analysis of the resilience data is shown. The menu (1) gives access to all functionality and also allows to toggle the different views. Area (2) contains a graph of the network topology. Depending on the current mode this topology graph can be displayed differently. In this case, the links are colored indicating the potential overload due to network failures. (3a) shows a summary of the input data and the values configured for the networking scenario computation. (3b) shows the properties of the link Madrid - Bordeaux and the traffic distribution on this link. (3c) contains a conditional CCDF of the relative link load for the same link together with a lower and an upper bound for the unconditioned CCDF. (3d) contains the network unavailability perceived by all aggregates of router Madrid. Further information about these graphs can be found in [1].

3   Conclusion

We presented the ResiLyzer, a tool for resilience analysis in packet-switched communication networks. The ResiLyzer offers a clear interface to input network data and calculates disconnection probabilities per ingress-egress pair and overload probabilities per link. In addition, it provides many options for the visualization of the computed results. Our approach defines a set of networking scenarios for the analysis whose size can be controlled by parameters so that the accuracy of the results can be traded for computation time.

Acknowledgments

The authors thank Prof. Phuoc Tran-Gia for the stimulating environment which was a prerequisite for this work.

References

1. Menth, M., Duelli, M., Martin, R., Milbrandt, J.: Resilience Analysis of Packet-Switched Communication Networks. ToN 17(6), 1950–1963 (2009)
2. Hock, D., Hartmann, M., Schwartz, C., Menth, M.: Effectiveness of Link Cost Optimization for IP Rerouting and IP Fast Reroute. In: GI/ITG Conference on Measuring, Modelling and Evaluation of Computer and Communication Systems (MMB) and Dependability and Fault Tolerance (DFT), Essen, Germany (2010)
3. Spring, N., Mahajan, R., Wetherall, D., Anderson, T.: Measuring ISP Topologies with Rocketfuel. IEEE/ACM Transactions on Networking 12 (2004)
4. Zegura, E.W., Calvert, K.L., Donahoo, M.J.: A Quantitative Comparison of Graph-Based Models for Internet Topology. IEEE/ACM Transactions on Networking 5, 770–783 (1997)

5. Medina, A., Taft, N., Salamatian, K., Bhattacharyya, S., Diot, C.: Traffic Matrix Estimation: Existing Techniques and New Directions. In: ACM SIGCOMM, Pittsburgh, USA (2002)
6. Menth, M., Hartmann, M., Martin, R.: Robust IP Link Costs for Multilayer Resilience. In: IFIP-TC6 Networking Conference (Networking), Atlanta, GA, USA (2007)
7. Hartmann, M., Hock, D., Schwartz, C., Menth, M.: Objective Functions for Optimization for Resilient and Non-Resilient IP Routing. In: 7th International Workshop on Design of Reliable Communication Networks (DRCN), Washington, D.C., USA (2009)
8. Hock, D., Hartmann, M., Menth, M., Schwartz, C.: Optimizing Unique Shortest Paths for Resilient Routing and Fast Reroute in IP-Based Networks. In: IEEE Network Operations and Management Symposium (NOMS), Osaka, Japan (2010)

SyLaGen – An Extendable Tool Environment for Generating Load

Michael Striewe, Moritz Balz, and Michael Goedicke

Specification of Software Systems
Institute of Computer Science and Business Information Systems
University of Duisburg-Essen, Campus Essen, Germany
{michael.striewe,moritz.balz,michael.goedicke}@s3.uni-due.de

1 Introduction

Measuring run time behaviour of systems under load can cause the need for complex workload definitions, measurement strategies and integration of load generation techniques. In this contribution we present SyLaGen ("Synthetic Load Generator"), a load generation environment that focuses on extendability with respect to four different aspects: First, a system under test may offer different interfaces for handling external requests, thus a load generator must be able to handle different protocols randomly and in parallel. Second, load generation for a client-server system may require complex client behaviour that cannot be formulated in a simple descriptive way, but instead with non-trivial algorithms that have to be implemented programmatically. Third, more than simple atomic measurements may be required in complex environments, so that strategies applying sequences of measurements to a system should be configured. Finally, comprehensive requirements engineering may result in complex use cases that cannot be modelled as linear scripts.

The extendability of SyLaGen considering these four aspects is realized by an architecture providing a platform with load generation functionality upon which modules can be created descriptively or programmatically. They are integrated in the system by a simple provision of libraries. Thus, SyLaGen can be easily supplemented with project-specific complex functionality. SyLaGen has been in productive use with this concept since 2002.

To generate load on different independent computers, SyLaGen has a distributed architecture. The *Master* component controls the measurement process and directs *Clients* that run on different hardware nodes in a network. On each client several *Worker* threads are running that generate the actual load. Master and clients communicate by means of a socket-based protocol that can be used in a variety of programming languages. This architecture is not unusual and can be found in other load generator tools, too. However, we instrument the distribution for our purpose in special ways, as we will now describe.

2 Load Models

Load being generated is often modeled after the behaviour of human users. In many cases no linear or otherwise exactly predictable user behaviour can be

B. Müller-Clostermann et al. (Eds.): MMB & DFT 2010, LNCS 5987, pp. 307–310, 2010.
© Springer-Verlag Berlin Heidelberg 2010

assumed. In addition, a realistic scenario may require generation of moderate load during the whole measurement as well as load peeks in some rare moments. Thus the synthetic load generation faces the challenge to represent probabilistic paths being taken between singular actions. SyLaGen employs probabilistic load models which also exist as additions to other tools like JMeter [1]. Based upon this, actual workloads can be defined for different use cases measuring a system under test.

In SyLaGen workload is described in terms of *flows* which are mainly a transition system $F = \langle S, T, W \rangle$. $S = \{S_1 \ldots S_n\}$ is a set of *states* that contain load generating operations, i.e. requests to the system under test. $T = S \times S$ is a set of transitions connecting states. $W = \{W_{S_1} \ldots W_{S_n}\}$ is a set of integer weights assigned to each transition. From all weights the relative probability for each path in the transition system can be calculated. A workload may consist of several flows, again each with a weight, so different flows can be performed with different probability. Flows can also be invoked in states of other flows, providing even more flexibility. While the transition system defines possible sequences of load generating actions and their probability, expectations about the system performance are formulated in terms of *turnaround times*: SyLaGen considers the whole time needed by the system under test to respond to a request, including the complete stack of underlying platforms, e.g. the network. For each flow, two times can be defined: The *mean turnaround time* is mandatory and defines which turnaround time for the related flow is expected in the average case. The *maximum turnaround time* is optional and may define an upper bound for turnaround times that are acceptable. These time requirements are interpreted by load generation strategies (see section 4) for different purposes.

3   Adapters

Modularity with respect to different load generation technologies is realized with an *adapter* concept: SyLaGen is not limited to access a fixed set of protocols or platforms, but allows to plug in individual libraries. These libraries can be specific for different protocols, platforms, systems under test or even single use cases. Adapters for protocols exist e.g. for web services (SOAP), Java RMI, file servers (SMB), and simple web applications (HTTP). Rich Internet Applications with AJAX [2] are an example for non-trivial platforms that are supported by existing adapters. Among others, a use-case-specific adapter exists that controls a graphical user interface using macros accessing its visual components.

Although adapters are specialized, they are encapsulated by a common abstraction level allowing to address them in a consistent way in load models. The abstraction is described by *adapter methods*: Each adapter publishes the names of provided load generating operations and optionally a list of typed parameters as well as a typed result value. A global storage for return values allows to use them as parameters in other invocations, thus enabling to realize complex load scenarios and the related data flow.

During measurement, adapters are distributed in a centralized way by the Master that transfers the libraries to all participating clients. In the clients, each worker creates a dedicated instance of the adapter. Master and clients are decoupled with a simple protocol, so that libraries containing adapters can be created using different languages and platforms. So far, clients and adapters for Java and C# exist. In the case of Java, the libraries are Java Archives (JAR) including class files, other libraries and arbitrary binary resources. The Java client is run using the Java runtime environment. The same client can also be run with the IKVM virtual machine [3] allowing to integrate libraries for adapters written in C#.

4 Load Generation Strategies

Another point of extendability in SyLaGen is the support of different load generation strategies by providing an abstraction layer: On the one hand, the platform performs the measurement with given parameters like number of workers and computes the results afterwards. On the other hand, modules for load generation can be created on top of this that decide about the measurements to perform and the parameters to use. Currently, the following strategies are used:

The *single* measurement strategy performs exactly one measurement with the given workload and number of workers. The mean turnaround time defined in the workload is interpreted as user behaviour: If the system under test responds faster, SyLaGen takes random pauses before triggering the next request so that the request frequency meets the expected mean turnaround time. In contrast, the *stress* strategy does not follow any restrictions, but makes as many requests as possible to generate the maximum possible load. In both cases the results of interest are the turnaround times for the requests sent during measurement.

In the *exploration* strategy the number of workers is increased or decreased stepwise depending on the desired turnaround times. A system is considered overloaded if the mean turnaround time of all workers exceeds the desired mean turnaround time *or* the maximum turnaround time is violated by at least one adapter call. The result of this strategy is the number of workers that the system under test can serve with the given limitations regarding turnaround times.

The abstraction layer implies that load generation strategies work with a limited number of variables and describe different well-defined states in the load generation process to fulfill their purpose. They are thus candidate for modeling with state machines, but are also integrated in arbitrary program code and contain complex business logic like calculations based on measurement results. Thus their code cannot be generated from abstract model specifications. Instead, the decision was made to employ *embedded models* [4] that represent model specifications in a well-defined program code pattern. Since the approach bridges the gap between different abstraction levels, it is appropriate for modeling the load generation strategies. However, this is not mandatory since any Java component using the abstraction layer can serve as a load generation strategy.

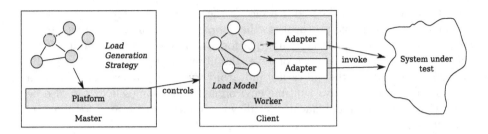

Fig. 1. Schematic view on the SyLaGen components

5   Conclusion

In this contribution we presented SYLAGEN, a load generation environment that focuses on extendability to realize complex scenarios. This concerns different interfaces of systems under test, representation of complex client activities, individual load generation strategies and non-linear client behaviour. The resulting architecture is illustrated in figure 1: The Master controlling the measurement delegates control to load generation modules. The underlying platform transfers measurement data to clients where worker threads execute probabilistic load scripts. The nodes in the scripts access adapters that provide a unified interface, but can invoke a system under test with arbitrary technologies and protocols.

Since 2002, this architecture has proven to be a dependable solution for load generation with complex use cases, unusual protocols, and problem-specific implementations of requirements. However, since SYLAGEN does mainly provide the environment and not ready solutions, simple use cases require the same effort when adapters or strategies must be created. Future work will thus focus on instrumenting the adapter concept to provide out-of-the-box solutions for different technologies and protocols.

References

1. van Hoorn, A., Rohr, M., Hasselbring, W.: Generating Probabilistic and Intensity-Varying Workload for Web-Based Software Systems. In: Kounev, S., Gorton, I., Sachs, K. (eds.) SIPEW 2008. LNCS, vol. 5119, pp. 124–143. Springer, Heidelberg (2008)
2. Paulson, L.D.: Building Rich Web Applications with Ajax. Computer 38(10), 14–17 (2005)
3. IKVM: (IKVM Website), http://www.ikvm.net/
4. Balz, M., Striewe, M., Goedicke, M.: Embedding State Machine Models in Object-Oriented Source Code. In: Proceedings of the 3rd Workshop on Models@run.time at MODELS 2008, pp. 6–15 (2008)

ProFiDo – A Toolkit for Fitting Input Models*

Falko Bause, Philipp Gerloff, and Jan Kriege

Informatik IV, TU Dortmund
D-44221 Dortmund, Germany
{falko.bause,philipp.gerloff,jan.kriege}@tu-dortmund.de

Abstract. The Processes Fitting Toolkit Dortmund (ProFiDo) provides a graphical user interface supporting the use of a variety of tools for the fitting and modelling of arrival processes. In this paper we present the first version of ProFiDo emphasising the fitting of Markovian Arrival Processes (MAPs).

1 Introduction

Very often arrival processes are specified by independent and identically distributed random variables and several tools and methods are available for fitting specific types of distributions [6,7,12]. In a variety of application areas, like computer networks, this type of specification has turned out as being insufficient (cf. [10]), since time-dependencies and correlations between arrival events are not captured. For the specification of time-dependent stationary input processes two directions are well-known: AR (Auto Regressive), ARMA (Auto Regressive Moving Average), ARIMA (Auto Regressive Integrated Moving Average) and ARTA (Auto Regressive To Anything [4]) models became prominent with the work of Box and Jenkins [2] and MAPs (Markovian Arrival Processes) whose intensive investigation started with the work of Neuts [8].

In recent years several of these input models have been incorporated into software for statistical computing, e.g. [11], or are supported by specific tools like ARTAFACTS [5], ARTAFIT [1], MAP EM [3], MAP MOEA [9]. Even though all these tools address the fitting of input models, there handling is different, since (command-line) interfaces and input/output formats differ. This makes the use and comparison of these tools and their corresponding fitting methods cumbersome.

The Processes Fitting Toolkit Dortmund (ProFiDo) described in the following section aims at reducing these deficits by providing a graphical user interface and an XML-based interchange format supporting the consistent use of tools for fitting input models.

---

* This research is supported by the Deutsche Forschungsgemeinschaft (DFG) within the project "Markovsche Ankunfts- und Bedienprozesse zur Leistungs- und Zuverlässigkeitsanalyse" (Markovian Arrival and Service Processes for Performance and Reliability Analysis).

B. Müller-Clostermann et al. (Eds.): MMB & DFT 2010, LNCS 5987, pp. 311–314, 2010.

2   The Processes Fitting Toolkit Dortmund

ProFiDo is a Java based software integrating different command-line based tools into a consistent interface allowing the user to specify a custom workflow of program execution and result propagation. To enable maximum flexibility we choose a graph based approach for displaying the workflow.

Within the graph each node, also called job in the following, represents one execution of a command-line tool. Currently a first set of jobs is supported, including fitting tools like G-FIT and MAP EM and additional utilities for input/output purposes. The latter type of jobs includes a tool Plot, which is able to visualise model characteristics, such as cumulative distribution functions and autocorrelation lags for given MAP descriptions or traces. Jobs can be placed arbitrarily on a grid-based canvas presented by the GUI's main window. Each job has its own properties window in which its parameters are defined. In order to avoid errors and to support the user, instant value checks and optional information texts for each parameter value are provided within the properties window.

The arcs of the graph represent the data flow between different jobs, with the output of a job being used as input for a subsequent job. Due to various origins and authors, most fitting tools use different input/output formats, leading to difficulties in exchanging results directly. To overcome these difficulties, we introduced an XML-based interchange format enabling a consistent data flow between different tools. In order to achieve this interchangeability we provide a set of tool specific converter scripts, which are used by the GUI to convert the input/output of each tool into the corresponding XML-description and vice versa. Since this conversion happens automatically and hidden from the user, no further consideration of different formats is needed when connecting different jobs. In this way a simple specification of workflows is possible. E.g., the output of a fitting tool can be used as input for a trace generator or a trace and the output of several fitting tools can be used as input for a plot. The GUI additionally supports the user in defining parameters for the jobs and manages default result filenames helping to avoid error-prone manual specifications. A sample workflow used to compare the fitting quality of two different tools by incorporating the above mentioned plot generator can be seen in Fig. 1. In addition to the main window's canvas the properties window of the G-FIT job is shown. The properties window allows for a check of parameters and to specify whether a parameter should be visible in the graph.

Since data flow within the graph is represented by arcs and only involves the XML-based interchange format, an additional type of node representing the conversion of external non XML-files (e. g. a trace file) into the corresponding XML-format (and accordingly vice versa) has been introduced. Those "file-nodes" (see nodes I and O in Fig. 1) can be directly connected to jobs and thus allow an easy import of data into the workflow and also enable a wide range of different outputs (Images, PS-files, etc.).

After creation of a workflow the GUI allows for the export of a folder containing all needed binaries and scripts. By analysing the data flow, the GUI

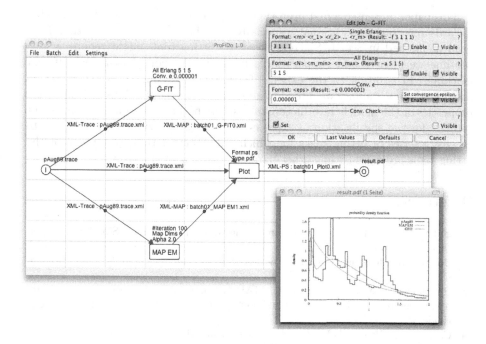

Fig. 1. Sample Workflow

is able to determine the execution order of the jobs and creates a bash script which executes the entire workflow. In order to allow a wide use of the workflow, several features for documentation purposes are implemented, including graphical export of the workflow displaying all needed information such as parameter details, result types and more.

The GUI supports the user with other helpful features like an unlimited undo history which can be saved and loaded with the graph. ProFiDo can be easily extended to incorporate other command-line based tools, since the core functionality of the GUI is specified in an XML-based configuration file which is parsed on each startup. The different job types are determined by the different tools specified in this configuration file. Therefore the GUI can be extended easily by adding a tool's description and providing corresponding converter scripts, i.e. a converter for transforming data in the XML-based interchange format into the tool's input format and a converter which transforms the tool's output into the XML-based interchange format.

3   Conclusions

We presented ProFiDo, which provides an easy to extend graphical user interface for consistent use of a variety of tools for fitting input models and uses an XML-based interchange format for model descriptions.

This paper presented a first prototype of the GUI. Future work will be directed towards integrating additional, especially "AR-based" fitting tools that have been mentioned in Sec. 1. Since some of the fitting tools might require a long runtime we plan to add support for a parallel execution of tasks on different machines. In addition to the existing feature of exporting plots of traces and fitted models as graphics we intend to add further export functions like exporting properties of the models into LaTeX tables. Furthermore, we plan to implement support for the specification of experiment series by providing a simple way to specify a series of fitting tasks for which only some of the parameters for the fitting tools are varied while other parameters are kept constant.

References

1. Biller, B., Nelson, B.L.: Fitting Time-Series Input Processes for Simulation. Oper. Res. 53(3), 549–559 (2005)
2. Box, G.E.P., Jenkins, G.M.: Time Series Analysis - forecasting and control. Holden-Day (1970)
3. Buchholz, P.: An EM-Algorithm for MAP Fitting from Real Traffic Data. In: Kemper, P., Sanders, W.H. (eds.) TOOLS 2003. LNCS, vol. 2794, pp. 218–236. Springer, Heidelberg (2003)
4. Cario, M.C., Nelson, B.L.: Autoregressive to anything: Time-series input processes for simulation. Operations Research Letters 19(2), 51–58 (1996)
5. Cario, M.C., Nelson, B.L.: Numerical Methods for Fitting and Simulating Autoregressive-To-Anything Processes. INFORMS J. on Computing 10(1), 72–81 (1998)
6. Horváth, A., Telek, M.: PhFit: A General Phase-Type Fitting Tool. In: Field, T., Harrison, P.G., Bradley, J., Harder, U. (eds.) TOOLS 2002. LNCS, vol. 2324, pp. 82–91. Springer, Heidelberg (2002)
7. Kelton, W.D., Law, A.: Simulation Modeling and Analysis. McGraw-Hill, New York (2000)
8. Neuts, M.F.: Matrix-Geometric Solutions in Stochastic Models. John Hopkins University Press (1981)
9. Panchenko, A., Buchholz, P.: A Hybrid Algorithm for Parameter Fitting of Markovian Arrival Processes. In: Proc. of 14th Int. Conf. on Analytical and Stochastic Modelling Techniques and Applications, pp. 7–12. SCS Press (2007)
10. Paxson, V., Floyd, S.: Wide-area traffic: The failure of Poisson modeling. IEEE/ACM Transactions in Networking 3, 226–244 (1995)
11. The R Project for Statistical Computing, http://www.r-project.org/
12. Thümmler, A., Buchholz, P., Telek, M.: A Novel Approach for Phase-Type Fitting with the EM Algorithm. IEEE Trans. Dependable Sec. Comput. 3(3), 245–258 (2006)

ProC/B for Networks: Integrated INET Models

Sebastian Vastag

Technische Universität Dortmund, Informatik IV,
D-44221 Dortmund, Germany
sebastian.vastag@udo.edu

Keywords: *INET*, *ProC/B*, *OMNeT++*, Process chains, DES.

1 Introduction

The *ProC/B* toolset [1] is used to model an analyze process chain models in application fields ranging from logistics systems to service oriented architectures. The language comes with an GUI supporting users with different levels of experience. Simulative analysis can be performed with *OMNeT++* [2]. A different but also *OMNeT++*-based class of models are communication networks created with the popular *INET*[1] framework. Network and process chain models have been two separate worlds. Recently we presented a hybrid approach for modeling SOA systems using *ProC/B* combined with *INET* models [3].

Our prototype offered combined models to a small group of expert users as it did not offer a user interface. Model description files had to be modified manually, a process prone to errors taking detailed knowledge of the simulation internals. To address this, a well integrated GUI was developed in [4]. The extensions to the *ProC/B*-editor shown in this paper are based on Mr. Kaufmanns [4] work.

2 Bridging Two Model Worlds

ProC/B is used to model process chains by graphic notation. The language defines two main elements: process chain elements (PCEs) and function units (FUs). PCEs are used to describe behavior in systems. They can be combined as chains to model complex activities. FUs offer services to process chains, *ProC/B* defines basic FUs like servers as waiting queues, counters for storage functions as well as composed FUs. Operators for decisions, parallelism and synchronization are available in process chains, variables assignable to model objects support them.

Model time is defined in *ProC/B* as follows: Calling a service or movement of objects along process chains is timeless. Time progress can by found at delaying process chain elements and basic function units with limited resources. Service or queueing times are located in them, several queueing strategies are choosable [1]. Synchronization of process chains also brings time consumption.

---

[1] http://inet.omnetpp.org

B. Müller-Clostermann et al. (Eds.): MMB & DFT 2010, LNCS 5987, pp. 315–318, 2010.

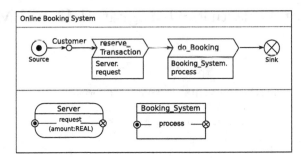

Fig. 1. *ProC/B* online booking example

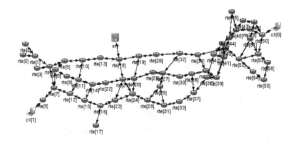

Fig. 2. INET network example

Figure 1 shows a small online booking system as an example. The process chain handles arriving customers with two PCEs: `reserve_Transaction` in will call service `Server.request` to reserve transaction time instantaneous on process arrival. The server will work for the time necessary given by `amount`. When `Server` is done the process returns immediately and continues to PCE `do_Booking`. The second PCE will call service `process` in FU `Booking_System`. Further details on *ProC/B* can be found in [1].

A tool to simulate communication networks is the *OMNeT++* discrete event simulation environment. The basic model entities called modules. Modules can either be simple or composed of other modules. Their definitions, relations and compositions are described in *OMNeT++*'s textual **.ned*-files. The modeling interface of *OMNeT++* is geared towards computer networks but does not specify any specific protocol or technology. Hence several modeling libraries have been developed for *OMNeT++*. One of the most common for TCP/IP networks is the *INET* library. It provides models of TCP/IP Stacks and predefined modes of data transmission like ethernet or wireless connections. It also offers predefined modules for common network elements like routers, switches and hosts. Figure 2 shows a typical example of an *INET* network structure with hosts connected via several routers.

As described above, both languages use *OMNeT++* as common simulator. Using the same simulation environment opens the possibilities to build hybrid simulation models with interaction between the world of process chains and information networks. In [3] we used the combined simulation approach to analyze models of SOAs. Services are described as process chains, the used communication system by *INET*.

The domains of *ProC/B* and *INET* are merged at model events when PCEs call the services of a FUs. For simulation of SOAs the process starting a call and the service provider being triggered can be located on distinct hosts, both connected with an communication network. Service calls are interpreted as data transmissions. This adds a third option of time progress to *ProC/B*: former timeless service calls in pure *ProC/B* are delayed by usage of a communication network. The delay introduced into the call is calculated with help of the *INET* model.

3   Integration of *INET* into the *ProC/B*-Editor

This requires process chain elements and function units to be related to hosts in the *INET* model. Additionally, service call packet sizes in bytes have to be specified. Our implementation used in [3] was already usable for arbitrary *ProC/B* and a wide set of *INET* models although it lacked intuitivity and user friendliness. The biggest shortfall was the required manual editing of *OMNeT++*'s *.ned files resulting from the original *ProC/B* model after automatic conversion. To activate hybrid simulation the file path to *.ned files of an existing *INET* model had to be inserted into *ProC/B* models. The network is used as an submodule. Additionally, the relations between elements of the *ProC/B* model and hosts in the *INET* world were formed by transferring valid hostnames to property fields available in *.ned-files of converted *ProC/B* models. This had to be done for every FU as there was no default host relationship. With none of the properties being able to be stored in *ProC/B* model files the complete editing had to be repeated when the original model was changed.

The editor has been improved in several ways: Now, when setting up a new *ProC/B* model, the hybrid simulation can be activated by loading the appendant *INET* model via file-chooser. The user is requested to choose a default host for every function unit. This can be done with an improved property dialog in the *ProC/B*-editor. It allows visual selection of an *INET* host that shall be allocated to a function unit. The dialog renders a representation of the *INET* model close to the known form of other *OMNeT++* tools including element positions and icons (Figure 3). When the model gets more detailed, function units can be easily assigned via the same user interface to other hosts than the default one. Choosing a host with GUI support also prevents simulation errors caused by typing errors in host names.

A technic improvement is the persistence of the relationships between hosts and FUs in *ProC/B*'s model files and incorporation in the model analysis process. The relationships and the transmission sizes are stored in comment fields in *.procb files. This format decision has two advantages: tools still unaware of the included *INET* model can read new models, thus they can interpret them in the normal way. Second, *ProC/B* models stay independent towards their *INET* part and can still be analyzed in isolation. In addition, the FU-host relationship is also transfered into the *.ned input files to the *OMNeT++* simulator.

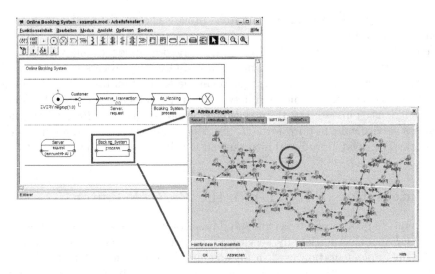

Fig. 3. Relating a host to a Function Unit in *ProC/B*-Editor

4   Conclusions

The formerly distinct model worlds of *ProC/B* and *INET* can be used in combination. Both models are simulated in a single *OMNeT++* process.

To support modellers several enhancements to the *ProC/B* editor have been made. A process chain model can be connected to one *INET* model. Function units are related to network nodes within a common user interface. A default node has to be choosen to keep the model valid. To store the relationship additional entries have been added to the original *ProC/B* file format.

References

1. Bause, F., Beilner, H., Fischer, M., Kemper, P., Völker, M.: The ProC/B toolset for modelling and analysis of process chains. In: Field, T., Harrison, P.G., Bradley, J., Harder, U. (eds.) TOOLS 2002. LNCS, vol. 2324, pp. 51–70. Springer, Heidelberg (2002)
2. Kriege, J., Vastag, S.: ProC/B goes OMNeT++: Efficient Simulation of Process Chains. In: Bause, F., Buchholz, P. (eds.) Proc. of the 14th GI/ITG Conference on Measurement, Modeling, and Evaluation of Computer and Communication Systems (MMB 2008), Dortmund. VDE Verlag (2008)
3. Bause, F., Buchholz, P., Kriege, J., Vastag, S.: A framework for simulation models of service-oriented architectures. In: Kounev, S., Gorton, I., Sachs, K. (eds.) SIPEW 2008. LNCS, vol. 5119, pp. 208–227. Springer, Heidelberg (2008)
4. Kaufmann, J.: Entwicklung und Realisierung einer Anbindung des INET-Frameworks an Prozesskettenmodelle. Master's thesis, TU Dortmund (2009)

DELTA: A Web-Based Simulation Training Environment Using JavaDEMOS

Sascha Geeren, Falk Hoppe, Axel Langhoff,
Bruno Müller-Clostermann, and Andreas Pillekeit

Institute for Computer Science and Business Information Systems
University of Duisburg-Essen, 45117 Essen, Germany
{axel.langhoff,bmc,andreas.pillekeit}@icb.uni-due.de

1 Introduction

1.1 Web-Based Simulation

Web-based simulation has its major application in teaching, education and collaborative model development. Keywords are virtual training environments (VTE), virtual classrooms, virtual labs and advanced distance learning [7, 4]. A VTE allows its participants to share editing and running of simulation models, to publish self-developed models and to collaborate in model development. The teacher (in the role of an administrator) can provide examples of good practice, templates as basis for further development and is able to supervise the participants of a simulation course.

1.2 DEMOS and JavaDEMOS

The concepts of the scenario approach of DEMOS (Discrete Event Modelling On Simula) due to Graham Birtwistle [8] have been used for purposes of teaching for nearly four decades. Many simulationists have been appreciating the concepts of building blocks like Res, Bin, CondQueue and WaitQueue, which allow the flexible and effective construction of simulation programs. These objects model resources, condition queues and other useful simulation concepts. Active elements (processes) are defined as entities that follow certain behaviour patterns [1, 5, 6].

Nowadays reimplementations of these concepts exist in Java, one of them is JavaDEMOS [3]. JavaDEMOS is a Java package that has been developed in a series of student projects at the University of Duisburg-Essen. In particular, a GUI for execution, control, and observation of JavaDEMOS simulation models has been created. JavaDEMOS is freely available for teaching and research .[3].

1.3 Motivation for the Development of DELTA

The major motivation for the development of DELTA ((Discrete Event Simulation Learn and Training Application) was to further improve and alleviate the teaching of process oriented simulation. To this end the ideas from Web- based simulation as described e.g. in [7] have been merged with the JavaDEMOS package into a virtual training environment to be used in teaching simulation courses.

B. Müller-Clostermann et al. (Eds.): MMB & DFT 2010, LNCS 5987, pp. 319–322, 2010.

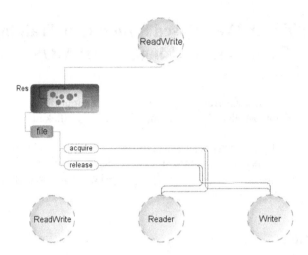

Fig. 1. Class diagram displaying acquire/release operations on a resource object

A DELTA administrator (in the role of a teacher) can provide simulation models and supervise the progress of students. Students have simple access to simulation resources, can develop and run simulation models with the help of a teacher and are able to work collaboratively in simulation projects.

2 Concepts of DELTA

The DELTA tool implements a Web service that liberates the students from installing and configuring a simulation software kit on their own. The only requirement from the user side is a Web browser. The DELTA software including JavaDEMOS is installed on the server side, where a set of simulation models is ready to be used by the students. Moreover DELTA is a platform to exchange simulation models and problem solutions among students and to let teachers provide example simulations.

Users of the DELTA environment can fully implement a JavaDEMOS-project with a Web browser. A simple development environment with syntax highlighting, line numbering, basic templates and other features is available via the Web interface. Upon completion the user can command the Web server to compile and run the simulation. After a successful run the results are accessible in various ways.

In addition to compiler messages DELTA generates class diagrams which are to support the user in identifying structural mistakes in the simulation source code. As illustrated in Fig.1, basic building blocks and associated operations are provided as a graphical representation and the correct allocation of resources can be inspected by the user.

Of course, the user generated code can be saved on the server for further refinement or presentation. A simple but effective project manager is integrated in DELTA that not only allows students to create and save simulations, but also grants administrators the right to make simulations of their choice visible to everyone.

COMPILE ERROR

```
./user_code/JackWhite/ReadWrite.java:13: ')' expected
public Reader(char symbol { this.symbol= symbol; }
             ^
1 error
```

PROJECT: READWRITE

```
JumpToLine | WhatLine | Find | FindReplace | Makro (NewSimulation) | Makro (Function) |
11  class Reader extends Entity {
12      char symbol;
13 |    public Reader(char symbol { this.symbol= symbol; }
14      public void body() {
```

Fig. 2. The editor after a compilation error. Basic editing functions and syntax and parenthesis highlighting are available. Clicking the error message placed the cursor in the according line.

Shared editing however is not possible. Simulation code can only be edited by its author and by administrators/teachers.

3 Working with DELTA

After the login an overview of the available projects is presented. These projects include globally visible example simulations as well as private simulation projects of the user. All projects can be executed, whereas editing is only allowed for private projects. Upon clicking on a simulation one enters the editing mode. The editor features syntax and parenthesis highlighting, line numbering, line jumping, text search and text replacement, the basic tools one could expect for a development environment. Macro functions further alleviate the editing process by preparing code fragments that usually reappear in JavaDEMOS simulations. Upon finishing the user can leave the editing mode by either saving or discarding the progress so far (Fig. 2).

The standard overview (Fig. 3, left) is entered that shows the code and enables the user to enter the editing mode (the pen), compile and run the simulation (the cogwheel), view a class diagram generated from the simulation code (the diagram) and view the results of the simulation run (the file). The last two options are only available after a successful compilation of the simulation. The steps of compiling and running a simulation are executed as one. If the compilation of the source code shows errors, the user is guided back to the editor. Additionally to the presented editor environment all java error messages are visible and a line throwing an error can be easily found by just clicking on the error message (Fig. 2).

After successful compilation and execution of the simulation we can view the class diagram (Fig. 1) and the simulation results by clicking the according symbols which are now coloured to indicate their availability. In the result section (Fig. 3, right) the provided JavaDEMOS reports are visible. These results are also available as spreadsheet. If histograms are part of the simulation the result page provides tabs for detailed examination of these histograms.

Fig. 3. Simulation overview (left) and results overview (right)

4 Availability, System Requirements and Future Work

The DELTA software has been developed as student work at the University of Duisburg-Essen [2] and is freely available for teaching and research. The system requirements on the server side include Unix or Linux as operating system, a Web server (typically Apache), PHP5, MySQL, the JavaJDK and of course the DELTA-software including the JavaDEMOS package. The use of a dedicated server is strongly recommended, as the security aspects of compiling and executing arbitrary code on the Web server have not been dealt with yet. On the user side only a Web browser is necessary. DELTA is expected to be in use for teaching and training. Future versions will include an improved administration of users and groups as well as improved security for the Web server.

References

1. Bratley, P., Fox, B.L., Schrage, L.E.: A guide to simulation. Springer, Heidelberg (1987)
2. Hoppe, F.: A virtual training environment for web-based simulation using the JavaDEMOS-framework. Bachelor Thesis (in German), University of Duisburg-Essen, ICB (2009)
3. JavaDEMOS User Manual. University of Duisburg-Essen, ICB (2009),
   http://sysmod.icb.uni-due.de/index.php?id=javademos
4. Kilgore, R.A., Healy, K.J., Kleindorfer, G.B.: The Future of Java-based Simulation. In: Medeiros, D.J., et al. (eds.) Proc. 1998 Winter Simulation Conference. IEEE Computer Society Press, Los Alamitos (1998)
5. Kreutzer, W.: http://www.cosc.canterbury.ac.nz/~wolfgang/, Material on simulation using DEMOS and SIMULA,
   http://www.cosc.canterbury.ac.nz/teaching/classes/cosc327/
6. Page, B., Kreutzer, W.: The Java Simulation Handbook. Shaker Verlag, Aachen (2005)
7. Rajaei, H.: A shared-edit & view web-based simulation framework. In: Proceedings of the 11th communications and networking simulation symposium, Ottawa, Canada, pp. 147–152. ACM, New York (2008)
8. Birtwistle, G.M.: DEMOS - a System for Discrete Event Modelling on Simula. Macmillan, Basingstoke (1985); also freely available as pdf-Document

Author Index